Counter-Hegemonic Teaching

A C.I.P. record for this book is available from the Library of Congress.

ISBN 978-90-8790-838-6 (paperback)
ISBN 978-90-8790-839-3 (hardback)
ISBN 978-90-8790-840-9 (e-book)

Published by: Sense Publishers,
P.O. Box 21858, 3001 AW
Rotterdam, The Netherlands
http://www.sensepublishers.com

Printed on acid-free paper

CONTENTS

PREFACE AND ACKNOWLEDGEMENT

This book was originally planned to be eight chapters which would include three of my published articles on counter-hegemonic teaching pertaining to special education inclusion, teaching bi-lingual students counter-hegemonically, and finally, teaching social studies through post-structural constructs. Because I was limited to a certain number of pages, regrettably, I was forced to cut all of these chapters. Perhaps, in the future, I will add them in another edition of *Counter-Hegemonic Teaching*. Originally, I thought the assignment would be easy, given that I managed to publish eight articles relevant to the topic. I thought: All I have to do is copy and paste some of these chapters onto a new word document, and that would be it!

Much to my chagrin, and I suppose this is poetic justice for those seeking to cut corners, I have eliminated almost all of my published chapters, leaving them just enough dignity to be quoted in several parts of the following five chapters, and relegated to a few explanatory footnotes. I suppose I also learned something about writing a book: you cannot be anything but honest to yourself and your readers. The work is hard and difficult, and coming from a former kid from the Bronx, New York, who would have thought I would be writing a book about a unique perspective on teaching and school practices as we know them today: hegemony.

On this note, I want to acknowledge all my Bronx school buddies. Having lived there almost a half a century ago, I learned what kids, growing up in a large city do and how they relate and aspire to be successful, or in some cases, just be.

As a kid, I had no idea what it would mean to be a college student. I thought I was destined, like my high school buddies, to drive a truck or a cab. That's what they became. A few others became salespeople, and still others became teachers in New York City until they received tenure and retired with a pension. I know this because I recently spoke to two of them, from two separate teen age groups I was a member of at different years of my adolescence. One friend, Eddy, was a great punch ball player in the courtyard where I lived on Walton Avenue; another, Joel, taught me how to prepare for standardized or regent exams in all subjects; and still another, Steve, was a debonair and handsome kid, who attempted to educate me about dating (which I failed). I met Joel after leaving the "Steve" and "Eddy" bunch of friends because I broke my leg playing basketball in the high school gym in my sophomore year. Other than playing ball or hanging out or simply cutting school and heading for the "D" train to take me to the village in Manhattan, and other places I enjoyed cruising, school meant very little to me.

I also had – I thought then – another alternative to pursue in my life and what few and limited dreams I had. My Dad was a partner with his brothers in a furniture retail business. His brothers had sons and daughters as well. The two stores they owned – one in Washington Heights, Manhattan, another in Astoria, Queens – provided me (in competition with my cousins) with part time work from the time I was fourteen and still in junior high school. Still, whether my duties were to "shlep" or carry boxes down into the basement after shipment, set up cribs and carriages, or sell home furnishings, I was a willing and able. I was a desirous kid who thought I could, one day, run my own business. Indeed, as it turned out through the twists and turns of my life, I did own a furniture business in Flushing, Queens, well over thirty years after I wondered about these things, and in between my two doctoral dissertation attempts.

In the aftermath of my father dying suddenly of a heart attack in 1980, my mother and I embarked on a new venture despite the fact that I was already attempting to finish my first doctoral dissertation attempt at Teachers College. After nine years of attempting this feat, I gave up and began a new furniture business during the height of Reagan's recession. At this time, I met another important and lifelong friend, David Avdul. To this day, and since the first day of classes as a full time doctoral student beginning in 1972, David remains a guiding light and confident in my life.

Anyway, it was not until 1998 that I finally finished my doctoral dissertation. A second and completely new attempt brought me to the footsteps of those red brick buildings in Morningside Heights near Harlem at the age of 52 (in 1996) to give it another try. Since then, and through ten years of teaching college education courses, I have had the luck and pleasure to meet many more people (and who did not necessarily play punch ball) and who helped me become a teacher-educator professor, writer, and eventually, a friend and scholar.

On first memory, two names come clearly to mind – my original sponsors of my first doctoral dissertation – Maxine Greene and Dwayne Heubner. Maxine was a dear friend to me, and despite the fact she was one of the country's greatest women and scholars in the field of education and the arts and humanities, I warmed to her as, I'm sure, she did to me. We recently had lunch together in her apartment in the upper east side of Manhattan – I called and she said, in her customary way: "Why don't you come over now." Huebner, as I and other students referred to him, was more stand offish. I had been to his apartment on several days, reviewing and revising my most recent draft for a dissertation proposal – a task that took me (and Heubner) at last 30 attempts over a period of six years. By the time I got to write the body of the paper, I no longer needed the proposal and all the work preceding the final draft was not necessary. Upon meeting Ira Shor at The College of Staten Island, where I worked for one year, he informed me Heubner had delayed (perhaps, not knowing it) many others from "finishing." However, despite his delaying me for over thirty years (I finally received my doctorate in 1998), I must acknowledge and thank Heubner for making me a committed scholar interested in the mysteries of language and power, making Paulo Freire's *Pedagogy of the Oppressed* available to me by listing this great book in his TY 4200 syllabus, along with getting me to look at myself and the many dimensions of justice and ethics when it came to clarifying what I'm about, and what schools and our world was and is still about.

Upon re-entry into Teachers College in 1996, for my second attempt to complete the doctorate, I needed more friends. David Avdul's sponsor, Gary A. Griffin consented to be my sponsor and navigate me through perilous waters which all doctorate candidates know about. It was not coincidence that my first job as an adjunct professor, upon passing my orals in 1998, was at Pace University where

David taught and was a former dean in the school of education. During my second doctoral attempt at Teachers College, I also became friends with Professor Margaret Jo Shepherd, the founder and director of the Special Education department and an integral force in guiding me to work with special education students as the field work segment of my thesis.

While teaching at six other colleges over a ten year period, I met many other professionals and friends. I also wish to acknowledge as being a guiding force to me: Professors Greg Seals, Deborah DeSimone, and Ira Shor of the College of Staten Island; Professors Mel Rosenthal, Roger Keeran, Kevin Wolff, and Tina Wagle of Empire State College of the State University of New York; Professors Peter Taubman, Karel Rose, Priya Parmer, Sherry Giles, Haroon Kharem, Luis Reyes, Wayne Reed, and Dean Deborah Shanley of Brooklyn College of the City University of New York; Professors David Arenson, Len Testor, and Michael Uttendorfer of New York Institute of Technology; Professors Cyndi Roemer, Lois Weiner, and Althea Hall at New Jersey City University; and finally, Professors Glenn M. Hudak, Margaret Jo Shepherd, Gary A, Griffin, and Kim Reid of Teachers College, Columbia University, and David Avdul and Kathryn DeLawter of Pace University.

And most importantly, those hundreds of students I met and had the pleasure and honor to teach. Many have kept in contact, and as any teacher knows the greatest reward in teaching is when a former student stops by or sends an email or phone call just to say hello and thank you. For all of you, thank you for making it possible to write this book on teaching and granting me permission to publish some of your wonderful pictures on Freire.

And I want to acknowledge and thank Jane, my best friend, partner and wife, for being there for me, but also being my toughest critic and the love of my life. Without her, this book and its many stories would not be possible and merely be but flashing images of what might have been.

And without any further ado, I wish to acknowledge my mother, Sylvia Marion Fleischer, who insists that she named me Lee Elliott because, "it would look on a book cover as the name of an author," and to my father, who always introduced me as "my son, the professor".

And last but not least, I want to acknowledge the late Joe Kincheloe for the support and encouragement he gave me to write *Counter-Hegemonic Teaching*. I give a special tribute to Joe in the first and last sections of the final chapter for his inspiration for me to examine more closely the work of Paulo Freire's *Pedagogy of the Oppressed,* and locate those "in-between spaces" between modernism and postmodernism, the subject and the object, and agency and structure – spaces he, too, often pondered about.

CHAPTER 1

CATCHING THAT HIERARCHICAL FEELING – A CHILL RUNNING UP AND DOWN MY SPINE!

In Search of the In-Between Terrain of Theorizing Hegemony

THE TIMES AND WHY WE NEED A COUNTER-HEGEMONIC THEORETICAL FRAMEWORK

In the days after 9/11, dangerous dualities co-existed side-by-side: On the one hand, there was and still is a kind of assurance that we are free to choose any course of action – that the sky is the limit – and that we are essentially free human beings living in a free democracy brought on by a free marketplace of trade and ideas. After all, mirroring this free orientation, the Bush doctrine proclaimed the right of our nation to feel free to make pre-emptive strikes against anyone who, as he asserted, presented themselves as a threat to our national security and named his new policy as protecting our freedoms from "terrorism." On the other hand, there is a sense that the economy, while labeled also as a "free market," is beyond our individual or concerted free choices. As it has long been recognized, "global" markets have produced many harmful effects, including the use of exploited and slave labor, slave labor of children, and the deterioration of the environment, all of which may have and still may produce reasons for threats of terrorism or unsatisfied cries and relations of "other" peoples and nations in America and throughout the world. While our present global economy may produce "low prices" for those of us who benefit with more variety of goods and services, others who may not want to see or care to see how these goods and services are brought to us at a price of how the world lives in poverty, starves, labors below a living wage all over the world. In the meantime, we consume goods and services without any corresponding thoughts or relational knowledge of the real costs to human lives and the seeds of resentment our economy and our materialist needs are producing.

Recent "crashes" on Wall Street, threatening to destroy people's life-savings, pensions, jobs, and homes, also have suddenly provided a rude awakening into how vulnerable the middle class and our economy are. We are asked to "bail out" the corporations and banks without knowing what this means. We are told over and over again how the "markets should take care of themselves." How, in capitalist theory, the "fittest survives," and in the places of the vanquished and weak, new competing forces will produce stronger entities than the previous ones. To intrude into this "freedom formula" would only upset the natural order of things, we are also told. However, with the recent stock market crash, our sense of security has been compromised. We are also reminded of how thin the "bubble of freedom," or the American dream, really is. We see the government, suddenly, reversing its

1

ideology of *laissez faire* capitalism to highly regulated economy. Yet, we stubbornly cling to the old ideology: we look with askew when suggestions are made to "spread the wealth around," implying socialism and helping those without. Yet, when the wealth is spread upward in the form of hundreds of billions of dollars to be loaned to banks and corporate CEO's, without any accountability or transparency, few raised suspicions as the Bush administration left office. We begin to take notice of contradictions existing side-by-side – opulence and poverty, giving money to the rich, denying money to the poor.[1] We may want to pause what we are told to believe. We may ask: why continue to believe in the free and open market place when facts to the contrary offer alternate directions, including more regulation and socialism?

In the schools, similar contradictions co-exist. Kids and their teachers meet in classrooms with the illusion of becoming educated for a free and just democratic way of life. Yet, they are presently mandated to accomplish these goals by maintaining austere and standardized forms of testing, teaching from the textbook in rote-like styles of learning. While all of this is happening, there appears to be little room or spaces for student and teacher voices and involvement. That is, real involvement in which they also are given responsibility to have power and trust to make the necessary changes of their schools as an expression and outgrowth of their powers. Instead, students and teachers are constantly told by higher ups, administrators, and politicians or those who "carry out orders," that students must become prepared to compete in the new world marketplace; that they should learn such knowledge as a necessity, reinforced by testing and classroom management, all along believing in a system which administrators are given the responsibility to implement scripted curricula and modes of learning. While not new in the last century throughout America, students know they must excel on these tests in order to get a piece of the American dream as well as compete against other students in foreign markets. We have produced a highly competitive, individualistic, and kill-or-be-killed cadre of students who as future adults are not so much becoming prepared to be good citizens as they are becoming prepared to become future competitive wage earners, avid consumers, and solider-patriots willing to die for a way of life which is presently approaching an ideological and identity crisis.

In the meanwhile, teachers are also being informed by another "crash," by those higher-ups who choose not to hear from them. Their administrator superiors and the state through national legislation are claiming that those of us who are "falling behind" must adapt to these circumstances in at least two ways: Students are failing to compete with comparable test scores of students in other countries; and teachers are failing to close the achievement gap here at home based on race and income differences. With the passage of No Child Left Behind, a seemingly magnanimous piece of national school legislation, with bipartisan approval in the wake of 9/11, those students who are "in need" should be given a chance to succeed in schools by "quality instruction." This need to provide quality instruction, however, is over-shadowed by the pressing need for test results. Teacher quality is thereby closely linked to student test score results.

With a sense of urgency, an inordinate amount of testing has come about by the federal government under the Bush administration, complementing local and state tests, feverishly seeking continuous and accumulative and annual progress. With this regimen of testing, however, the presence of constructive and progressive teaching is becoming more and more diminished, more so than we have seen since the days of the 1950s and earlier. A new discourse has become dominant in this process in which a majority of the time teaching and learning in schools has become more and more based on rote-learning, test-prepping, and mechanical-like responses in the classroom discussions. There is no time for other subjects, more conversational and controversial. There is no time for exposing young people to problems related to thinking critically as future citizens in a democracy. The implication is: there is nothing inherently wrong with America, except that we must catch up and compete.

WHY THE BOOK – REALLY WHY?

Here I am, completing a book dedicated to those who wish to change the hierarchical structures of school authority and administration, curriculum and teaching. These aspects of school teachings have crushed me, and teachers and students and even teacher educators, who work with me and introduce teachers to teaching. After ten years as a teacher educator, and many years before this stage of my life as a high school teacher, we couldn't do what we wanted to do as professionals in our work in schools. Many teachers and teacher-educators have had their hopes dashed or quit, others pressed on only to find themselves surrendering to the machine that characterizes schools.

I reflect on the last ten years of my teaching experience. It was no "cake walk." I have done other things with my life. In 1967, I received my master's degree in history, and wanted to be deferred from fighting in Viet-Nam. Then, without anticipating it, I entered a forty year journey which, as it turned out, led me to fight for justice and equal treatment for all in schools. Two or three impediments always got in my way. I was a person who questioned (and still question) why public schools are such alienating and compulsory places. From their role as sorters, testing everything a kid may know or should know to be loyal and unquestioning citizens and workers, to inculcating in them (and their teachers) a sense of being committed to the hierarchy, schools and the dominant institutions of our society are hardly criticized anymore, at least, not their hegemonic position which makes their practices acceptable and natural. I also wanted to understand why so much one-sided, memory-based, non-constructive testing must be mandated; and worst, how and why tests score results must be linked to teacher performance, retention, and promotion, and termination. Nowhere is there an adequate accounting for teaching students who are poor, disabled, newly arrived immigrants and who are new to speaking English as their primary language; nor is there any attention given to those students who are different and presently suffering because they are stifled due to the lack of space they need to define their own realities, albeit within some parameters of the school and teacher authority as a constructive and democratic institution, which is sorely missing in today's schools, aside from a few experiments permitted in charter schools by those few renegade or "rogue" teachers who are siphoned off or released from "normal" duties of the regular school place.

After this nation has suffered with such poor management from the Bush presidency and his administration, on down, through the economy, the schools, and other institutions (including the family, community associations, and the workplace) there are few popular mass movements demanding a democratic restructuring of its institutions in our so-called democratic state, irrespective talk of national health care, better or "reformed" educational structures, and more released time for single parents. The role of education remains compulsory, its governance structures remain hierarchical and top-down administrative, and the voices of its peoples remain muted and easy targets for manipulation, via the media, the dominant cultures and discourses, and how the masses are so easily exploited, manipulated, and divided from taking further actions in organizing themselves as a public

In this milieu, I have struggled to find a language to describe these horrendous conditions which are so hegemonic. We hardly talk about them critically anymore, or take counter-hegemonic actions, excepting those few voices and "heroes" standing up against the machine, being told to proctor a standardized exam or create a charter school whereby those who attend and teach can "do their own thing." There are signs of hope emerging. A new administration committed to "change" is taking power in Washington, and is committed to stopping the "bubble type" of standardized exam practices and connective teaching pedagogies. A moment in history may be at hand.

In the meantime, as a teacher educator, I continue to struggle on yet another front: my age. Completing my thirty year long journey and "finishing" my dissertation, I have come up against a new oppression: ageism. At 65, after teaching ten years as a professor of education, in every job interview, the same questions emerge: "Why have you been teaching in six schools for ten years? Have you recently been teaching in the public schools full time? What do you "know" of the present day problems teachers and students confront?'

These are good questions, except for the fact that they are not legitimate. I, as a teacher educator, have always been in my students classrooms (when they are teachers) or field sites (when they are taking initial foundation courses). Moreover, as Jonathan Kozol (2005) recently noted, there is emerging a new kind of educational positivism, a "presentism," as he refers to it, which, like its correlated models of positivistic empiricism, insists that "seeing is believing." Give these folks numbers, statistical formulae, multiple choice or survey questions, and rubrics to fit their data into, and they are comfortable. Talk about your story, and up emerges "red flags" warning them of "bias" or "subjective factors." What do they do with the data? They don't theorize, imagine or dream; they deduct and draw hypotheses, sometimes, more often, draw steadfast conclusions based on the assumption or claim that the scientific research "works" and is "practical," notwithstanding its wide range for error.

As a political element, *No Child Left Behind*, which mandates that research must be "non-ideological" and "neutral," there is hardly anywhere to go, notwithstanding the old stand-by of qualitative research[2] and portfolio assessment practices not encouraged or warmly received by the Bush administration for the last eight years. In addition to being a radical and 65, I have also encountered a narrow view of what scientific really means, and how schools and society can undertake new research practices. As discovered in the works of Joe Kincheloe, we can discern and account for "complex meaning systems (2003)," systems which include semiological and post-structuralist meanings and research practices, which this book, *Counter-Hegemonic Teaching*, will attempt to offer.

What I therefore want to show is how all of us, myself included, contribute to a hegemony of keeping everything quietly status quo. This is not a new feature of schools. To my knowledge, it has been happening for over forty years or longer (Becker, 1961; Callahan, 1960; Adorno, 1944; Waller, 1932). At 65 (gaining my doctorate at 55), I have suffered, like many, through the Bush years, and, sadly, through the coward-like and bureaucratic behaviors of some of us, about which, my colleagues would not like to share or comment. I also witnessed a reluctance to discuss issues that harm children and denude teachers of skill and courage, and found the fifth pillar of hegemony (which I will not discuss in this volume to the extent it deserves) of this archaic practice: tenure. School teachers and teacher educators are apt to protect themselves (CYA: Cover Your Ass) rather than join with colleagues or aid those colleagues who do speak out. Or, worse, they'll look away while one of more of their colleagues is being intimidated by one or more of the "five pillars of hegemony."[3] What I am talking about here, for the most part, are those crude practices of standardized testing in places like New York City where the Department and Board of Education will apply standardized testing to kindergarten students by the tens of thousands. I also speak of supportive classroom management techniques, and from these procedures and practices, tracking or providing questionable inclusion practices and the mistreatment of special education and ESL students. Overlapping these practices are entrenched administrative hierarchies who either turn a deaf ear to appeals complaining about such practices, or abet in frustrating teacher appeals and grievances. As a former student of mine, a thirty year teacher in Brooklyn, remarked, "Teachers can never grieve against an administrator or principal since the first step of the new grievance procedure is to get the OK from them!"

The odd thing about those who defend tenure as a way to protect their academic freedom is that it's hardly ever practiced. As I have suffered the blacklist for speaking out for civil rights of teachers and student rights since the 1970s, I have also experienced the trials and tribulations of becoming blacklisted in Long Island schools. More recently, another similar barrier has beset me: after going through dozens of applications and interviews, I have seen it in the faces of search committees, their stupefied looks upon hearing that I was over sixty and worse, not recently in a classroom. That is, as an applicant to teach or educate or become a professor of education, more concern was expressed not about my recent ten years of teacher educator experience, but about my experience full time in the classroom. How does one do both?[4]

In other years, when I had much classroom experience and lived out my life in the "trenches," as I observe today in my students' classrooms and field sites[5] very little if any "real" changes have occured. Traditional education, in the name of back to basics, austere classroom management, plus more and more testing, along with "tough love" and other such practices, it has been my position, both denies the creativity of student and teacher and continues to be the rule, overt or covert, of the school day. Despite these persistent practices, there is less and less resistance, dissent, disagreement, or questioning. There is no call for change, much less change to the hegemonic bases on which they continue to stifle practices of the school institution.[6] The only discourse one hears these days is to tighten discipline, raise student test scores and measure their results and effects on student achievement and teacher accountability. In this melee real freedom of speech, or speaking out on behalf of those who suffer under such a regime, goes unnoticed or is severely censored, suppressed and demonized. Minority students and their parents are convinced by the machine that it is the teachers who are at fault; that with better "training," teachers accompanied with scripted and packaged curricula will improve and perform their activities better. But what has happened?

As a rule, because the school system machine[7] reports results of student test scores in reading and writing and math as almost always "increasing" (usually by 1 or 2 or a fraction of one percent), they forget to add how these assessments affect school progress or the quality of life in the schools or, at what cost to human misery and harm they are achieved. What they also omit is the qualification that test score results or quantitative numbers is but one of the many criteria which can be used but, any other proposition is rarely articulated. Qualitative indicators, based on student and teacher interviews, can be accepted by stories they recount and feelings attributed to being constantly tested and "prepped" as objects of a testing regime. At the same time, students and teachers are denied submitting their own data about how they feel about their creative selves. Identities are stifled and students are denied opportunities to produce exciting discussions, and being taught in unabridged and non-compromising ways and reducing or eliminating subject-matters such as art, music, dance, social studies, and literature, has further affected by how their discussions can be informed by critical issues and formulating critical perspectives. These perspectives are removed or denied entrance into the curriculum because so much "test-prepping" must be confined to math, reading, and science – which may affect them and their school community adversely by denying them multi-cultural and global perspectives.

The concept of "discussion," or worse, "dialogue," has become a "dirty word" which inhibits kids struggling to achieve the "American dream." It has been replaced by memorizing and preparing for weekly standardized exam exercises. There are many articles recently published in newspapers how, for example, parents in New Delhi, India, will have their young children "bussed" to schools over forty miles away; or how in Korea, there are special dormitories and test prep centers established to increase student test scores so they may be accepted in the elite schools rather than ordinary colleges, thereby assuring their futures and connecting and moving them onto well-to-do professionals jobs. We, here, in the United States, also are guided by the same ideological ideas concerning success, albeit we don't call it "ruthless," "competitiveness," and "inhumane." Still, such a heavy emphasis is put on achievement through testing that success at memorization is perceived by poor and middle class families as a way to achieve the American Dream.

Such practices often serve to deny more diverse settings of learning, or as Gary Orfield (2001) and Jonathan Kozol (2005) have reported for decades, schools are becoming "re-segregated" and thereupon, the chances for minority students (people of color) to become educated with their majority peers (white people) lessens. To Orfield, de-segregated schools produce a higher degree of success in terms of those who graduate high school, go on to college, and interact better with their majority peers in real world conditions. Because there is an inordinate emphasis put on test results (made public on websites), the test averages of student test score results (along with property values) have had, perhaps, inadvertently, produced for those who want to compete with their more wealthier peers for good jobs and a better standard of living, a competiveness which has produced "push-outs." These push-out or drop outs, in turn, have, ironically, left more students behind than ahead with *No Child Left Behind*, and, at the same time, since the Reagan years after *A Nation at Risk Conference* (1983), produced a trend in which schools have become more and more re-segregated (rather than de-segregated). This means, to Orfield, re-segregated schools produce less chance for advancement if one is a member of a minority group.

Recently, as a college professor, and after reading many of the works of Jonathan Kozol[8] and Gary Orfield,[9] I asked my predominantly African-American and Caribbean students in a foundation class why integration has failed since the momentous Supreme Court decision of *Brown vs. Board of Education* (1954). I also asked them why they think this country has regressed to a condition defended by previous nineteenth century Supreme Court decision, *Plessy vs. Ferguson* (1896), whereby the courts ruled as legal racial segregation providing that the conditions of separation would be "separate but equal." My students and I realized that with the Brown decision there was sparked a national civil rights movement toward integration but because of distractions as foreign economic competiveness schools during the Reagan administration there may had been a tendency to move toward a standardized testing policy in order to compete with other countries in which their students were scoring very high in math and science compared to the results of student test scores in the United States. Ironically, as my students began to "map" the correlations between emphasis put on testing and the concomitant re-segregation of schools, they began to realize that, perhaps, emphasis on increasing test scores results, may have, inadvertently, re-segregated what were integrated schools, pushing out minority and poor test takers from the "average," and, at the same time, producing conditions (as reported by Orfield) which may have undermined minority and majority students from achieving in a better school, or racially integrated school environment in which diversity has a salutary effect on their learning and mobility.

When the class and I realized the results mandated testing had on a national level, driven harder by more recent legislation of the Bush legislation and *No Child Left Behind*, many of my students, felt duped and became angry – often at me and their classmates. They refused to believe that the present government would have lied to them; or worse, that their fellow peoples – from the same neighborhood, race, class, and ethnic groups, were destined to be channeled into dead end jobs which punctured their idealism and belief in the American Dream. Despite the *de-facto* conditions of discrimination which existed in the *Plessy case*, and how this fact was pointed out in the Warren court which overruled *Plessy* in the *Brown case*, my students insisted on re-echoing the dictates of the Supreme Court of 1896 which decided in favor of racial discrimination, provided "equal resources" would be made available. Thus, my students argued that if resources in schools in poor and racially black neighborhoods would be made available, equal to the wealthier white schools, people of color would benefit as opposed to bussing their children across town. This reaction came, despite the fact that they also read articles in which nations as India[10] and South Korea[11] practiced bussing with an end toward securing a better education for their children. Moreover, when I revealed other articles about how Japanese schools[12] and children were resisting the overemphasis on standardization of curricula, testing, and school discipline or classroom management, *koika,* as Japanese students labeled their acts of resistance, my students chose to ignore these new developments. In addition, other articles revealed how Japan as the model of an excellent educational system is souring, causing many Chinese students to decrease their visits and studies in their schools and colleges.[13]

Why such resistance to integration and bussing on the part of my students? The only thing I can conjecture was attributed to the power of ideology via hegemony and its discourses; specifically, what the American dream offers to people – particularly those who have recently immigrated here, the poor and middle classes struggling for upward mobility and seeking "success" or an identity in which one can achieve respect and wealth or have others look up to them if the promise of such a Dream was fulfilled. Was this the reason why my students resisted integrated and bussed schools? Could it be, as a white instructor, I was perceived by my students as "already made it," and by standing up to such an ideology – which poked holes into the ideology of the American dream and, inadvertently, questioning and putting into disrepute the same dream or hopes my students were pinning their hopes on? Further, talking about hegemony, even on the level of higher education in a preparatory education class for undergraduates, may have been a dangerous pursuit. Needless to say, many – not all – of my students put up an opposition which questioned my questions. Today I do not know if I will ever teach in the higher education again. That is: will I or will I not be able to talk about the hegemonic conditions of schools and society and the world we live in? Alas, then, I have come to my main reason for writing this book.

This book then was written with some degree of hesitancy and uncertainty. Actually, it was not supposed to be a book until I met three forces in my life: the necessity to survive as a professor – publish or perish; the fact that much younger professors were competing against me – even though I have attained the publication of nine chapters and articles, and finally, my meeting critical theorists as Joe Kincheloe and Shirley Steinberg who not only were responsible for publishing me (and 500 other professors) and other struggling professors and students, but further, encouraged me to write my story to the world. One of my former instructors at TC, Columbia University, Maxine Greene said to me after I sought to return to "finish" my dissertation – since my first attempt in the 1970s: "Why bother to finish…write a book." I realized, upon her saying these words that the institution was not ready for me in the 1990s, and it certainly was not ready in the 1970s – my first years attempting to "finish" my original dissertation. I recalled how I languished for almost ten years under the sponsorship of a well-known scholar who, apparently, wanted me to get it "clear." I surmised then, but no longer think about if my original title (see below) was clear or not. I now know it was clear, then and now. What was unclear was the political atmosphere of the university I attended along other factors no one would dare say or disclose to me at the time. It's like saying: "Hey, Bud, you don't question these things here, now and forever!"

APPROACHING THE DOORS OF TEACHERS COLLEGE, COLUMBIA UNIVERSITY

In 1996, as I sought to get re-admitted into the doctoral program at Teachers College to begin my second doctorate attempt, and after already spending ten years in the first doctoral attempt, and spending ten more years in my own business, I knew, approaching the doors of this institution, invested with so much time devoted to writing papers, tuition, and hard work, in a wintry day in December of 1995, that I probably would never finish. This day, however, I met one of my co-sponsors, who appeared shocked after not seeing me for fifteen years. She indicated that finishing the dissertation would be difficult. I knew I wanted to finish my original dissertation, and I anticipated it would also be critically reviewed. Given its title, "Hierarchical Structures of Authority Manipulating Classroom Discourse," I have retained fragments in this book, and when I could, disguised other elements imported into the second dissertation. I sought to keep my focus on a basic insight I never completed in my last attempted chapter in the early 1980s, which was never completed: how signification, in the form of hierarchical chains and subject-positions embedded in discourse, "positions" student and teacher toward self and joint defeating actions. I also wanted to show how, in changing these chains of positions, student and teacher may posit themselves as agents of change in creating new power relations in which they can take or negotiate hierarchical and administrative powers for the governance and leadership of their schools and teaching curricula.

Having been influenced by the writings of Paulo Freire, and specifically, *Pedagogy of the Oppressed*, along with other readings that penetrated the domain of what I would call a "post-structuralist" approach to teaching and education (Appel, 1996; Peters, 1996; Popkewitz & Brennan, 1996; Young, 1981), I knew then and as I know now that I was probably twenty years ahead of the literature in the late 1970s. I pissed people off by being connected to a neo- or post-Marxist perspective.[14] Upon my reentry into Teachers College, then, I reflected on what was becoming more and more a suffocating world of teaching and education which mostly focused on standardization of competencies in schools and teacher education programs. Goals 2000 negotiated with Democrats and Republicans (as was No Child Left Behind in 2002) became a bipartisan project mandating a new regiment of testing with little discussion regarding how schools could be framed in terms of critical concepts of oppression, suffering, or the mutual perspectives constructed by students and teachers seeking relief and redress rather than labels as "disruptive teacher" and "student discipline problem" in such conditions. Only recently, upon hearing about a few "teach-led" charter schools[15] did I begin to feel a basis for hope and relief, albeit always cautious that such "reforms" often become or serve as escape values for more fundamental changes.

I recalled how hard I worked since the early 1970s at Teachers College working on my doctoral thesis proposal. My sponsor made me revise my proposal at least thirty times, and when I submitted it for an oral defense in early 1976, I knew not one word would be used in the main body of chapters to follow! Still, my sponsor opened me to the world of a different kind of literature I had never seen before. At first the writings of Peter Berger and Thomas Luckmann (1966) revealed how social reality is constructed. Then, the writings of Jurgen Habermas and the Frankfurt School, revealed a world possible based on relations and responses of questioning and norm building in mutually consented communication and communities. And finally, after attempting to read Michel Foucault and other postmodern theorists as articulated in *Screen Magazine*, the work of Paulo Freire hit home: the feeling of being oppressed I felt always in schools since I started in elementary, middle, and high schools in Washington Heights and the Bronx in New York City. Till this day, as I write this book, this feeling continues to return to me, and I would venture a guess, to many others who have been there and know how being stuck in an alienating and cold place called schools – whether a student, teacher, or college teacher educator. I name this feeling as a hierarchical chill crawling up and down my spine. Later in this book, along with identifying the "pillars of hegemony" in Chapter 2, I will identify this feeling as a hegemonic subject-position that grips us from, as Zizek would put it, the Real, or place of the unconsciousness that shoots through the consciousness and for those who would wish and desire to change what is a compromising and suffocating place, a place called schools.

Starting in the Fall of 1972, I spent full time study and writing my thesis to the Spring of 1982, along with two full days a week of "subbing" in the New York City schools. After my fathers' sudden death due to a massive heart attack in late 1980, I decided to enter his business and continue a family tradition that none of my siblings wanted. I found it necessary, since dad's business lease had only a few months left before expiring, to start a new furniture business which, unlike my father's business, because of a shift of location, required weekly newspaper ads, and later, television advertising to attract people to come to my desolate location and offset my expenses.

THE FURNITURE STORE, THE THESIS, AND RETURNING TO TEACHERS
COLLEGE FOR A DAY

The new location of the "store" was a "dead location" or one in which few people walked by. In advertising, as in the writing of my first thesis, the notion of constructing a new language system emerged in my thinking. Indeed, by 1985, I had invented the "2 for 1 sale" that aired on mainline television commercials all over the country and weekly ads in the *Daily News*. Anyone who knows about advertising and running a business can imagine the overhead of conducting business with advertising as a single location, in which I earmarked millions of dollars each year compared to the "good" location of the "Mom and Pop" store dad and his brothers began in Washington Heights during the 1920s. Like many storeowners of small businesses they could not grasp the concept of advertising or how the media grabs one's attention and instills a need or desire to buy an item or product or service. This understanding, no doubt, was already instilled in me studying language and ideology throughout the 1970s and my abortive attempt to "finish" my first doctorate.

Still, the desire to catch the hierarchical forms and feelings of oppression returned to me. After my furniture business ended in the early 1990s, I decided to work with my brother in the window treatment business. As a result of paying a shop-at-home call on Claremont Avenue, one block west of Broadway, I noticed through the windows of a prospective customer, roofs of buildings which were green as a result of being oxidizing over the years. These were the roof tops of Columbia University. Having spent many hours with classmates after class in the Westside Bar during the 1970s and constantly perusing many bookstores on Broadway, staring outward onto the street of Columbia's green roofs, the feeling of discovering how teachers are oppressed returned to me. And then it hit me: I must return to Teachers College to complete my dissertation. A few years later, I mustered enough courage to walk into the buildings. In the halls I walked, the halls I knew too well, I caught the familiar smell of Maxine Greene's perfume, and I knew I was about to undertake a new journey, entering the doctoral program in early 1996.

On meeting Maxine Greene, however, something else happened. As she said to me earlier, "Go write a book!...You don't need a doctorate." What she really wanted to say or said between the lines, in a hoarse voice (from years of smoking), was that the political climate at Teachers College would not accept what I was about, nor what I wanted to write about. Still, with a stroke of luck, outside of Maxine's office, a professor overheard me. Afterwards, he approached me as I was about to leave disappointed, and recommended that I see a young professor on the floor above. Upon approaching his office in the old department I had majored in and made weekly visits to see my sponsor, I discovered in this young professor a light of hope. This professor was also influenced heavily by Dwayne Huebner, my first sponsor. He also knew him indirectly through his sponsor at the University of Wisconsin, the well known critical theorist, Michael Apple[16] – also a Huebner student. After a chat with him, he asked me to join his two seminars that summer and he also became my first advising professor.

Because the professor was not tenured, he could not have a major voice in my development beyond my qualification paper. Other tenured professors, as Maxine Greene, who was an adjunct at the time, insisted that "I needed a tenure professor to get me through." Once again this suggested to me I would not be able to write my dissertation. Still, by another coincidence that same summer, my original academic advisor returned to TC after almost two decades of absence, having held three deanships in colleges across the country. A surprise meeting with him produced another break. His name was Dr. Gary A. Griffin and, upon knocking on his door, hunched over unpacking his books onto shelves, he squinted his eyes and said to me after I introduced myself, without a pause, recalling what happened to me almost twenty years earlier: "I should have spoken to Dwayne. I should have. I knew. I should have."

Like Maxine Greene, Gary Griffin I knew for many years, specifically those years I was held back from finishing my dissertation because my dissertation sponsor equivocated about the "clarity" of my thesis. Thus, I was constantly told to redo and revise, it seemed, forever. Another coincidence, a former hire of Gary's in the early 1980s, whose name I shall not reveal, but was a very powerful professor in the department at the time, critiqued my original title for the dissertation I proposed in the 1970s. Not daring to resist her, I took her recommendation to change the study critical of hierarchies to a study which would gather qualitative data on special education students in New York City, stories about their lives pertaining to their desires to be included or remain in their special education tracks. The same professor almost kicked me out of class because I asked too many questions (a few, really) and she panned my qualification paper, the basis of my thesis proposal and dissertation. Gary came to the rescue with one short wave of the hand, saying, "Let me handle this." It was Gary, a co-founder of NCREST, a famous consulting network for over 800 restructuring school districts, who would help me. The other founder, Ann Lieberman, and the professor I critiqued twenty years earlier in a free speaking student newsletter (see Chapter 2 for the essence of this article) would also come to my assistance, if necessary. Strange twists do politics make.

Like myself, Gary, too, was undergoing difficult times. He returned to Teachers College after being terminated by a person whom he hired, and now sought a perch at the college. He was in his mid-sixties like myself today. And, it was through Gary that I met my friend David Avdul in 1972. Gary co-taught the course with two other professors, Dwayne Huebner and Arthur Foshay, the former became my first sponsor, while Gary became David's sponsor. I was not alone in getting help from Gary, he was very helpful in assisting many other students. Still, at a meeting with Gary and the unnamed powerful professor, it was decided that the problem of my "new" dissertation would not be a philosophical issue ("we don't do those kinds of research here anymore"). She advised that I do a qualitative study with special education students in the New York City public high schools. And so, I did.[17]

I had chosen Huebner, not Griffin (as my friend David had) as my sponsor in the 1970s, because he impressed me as a very radical person capable of helping me discover what hegemonizes students and teachers in school systems. I did not see Gary Griffin as aligned with my philosophy, albeit he was a very fine human being, nor could he be of any help, I incorrectly assumed at the time. Knowing Gary as more pragmatic than philosophical, after the grueling episode of my last full time high school job in which I got fired because I was sympathetic with student causes and discussions, in particular on civil rights and liberties and anti war sentiments, I sought to discover through philosophical research the foundations of hegemony and hierarchy. But, in my first and second tenure as a doctoral student at Teachers College the authorities let me know in many subtle and unsubtle ways, this was not to be.

In the meantime, my new attempt to present a philosophical proposal to te dissertation committee course of the Curriculum and Teaching Department was met with laughter and polite scorn. Imagine my shock upon hearing how "we don't allow philosophical duissertations to be done here anymore," in the first and largest institution for teacher professionalism and preparation in the world, in a place where John Dewey and George Counts taught for many years from the 1920s to the 1950s! Gary and others counseled me to do a study with "real" students. At this time, I was taking a course about the "Politics of Labeling in Special Education," co-taught by two professors, one whom was the chair and founder of the Special Education Department, Margaret Jo Shepherd. During the course, professor Shepherd asked me to attend a presentation by one of her teachers who brought with her many of her "special ed" students. I observed the same students the following Spring. In May of 1997 I decided some of the students of Shephard's class would be the population that would constitute my "field work," even though I have never taken a course in special educartion, nor had any interest in these kinds of students. I could not have been more wrong in my initial asessment. By deriving my material ro data from these students based on theri experiences and stories as Afrtican-American and Hispanic students in teh New York City high school system, I was able to unite my perspective with their experiences in a dissertation that was finally accepted in 1998, with distinction, and titled: "Living in Contradiction: Stories of Special Education Students.

MY EXPERIENCES AS A TEACHER: FROM THE BRONX TO LONG ISLAND AND BACK TO THE CITY

Living on Long Island with my parents throughout the 1960s, and receiving my BA and MA in history at local colleges, I never could have anticipated the world of controversy and conflict I would endure as a social studies teacher in 1967. As I reflect on my initial teaching experiences, three memories come to mind: (1) My learning experiences as student, from elementary to secondary school, (2) the experiences I had as a teacher on Long Island and as a substitute in the New York City school system, and (3) what has happened to me over the last ten years, teaching as a professor of education, a teacher-educator, in subject areas of the foundations, social studies, special education-inclusion, and critical literacy and critical theories of media and language.

As an elementary school student I was very outspoken, talkative and inquisitive. I recall saying to my kindergarten teacher: "What a big ass you have!" No doubt my ability to be more tactful managed to improve over the years at elementary school but not my talkativeness or my tendency to interrupt other students and the teachers as they talked. I always felt I had something else to contribute to the discussion and felt a burning desire to talk and say something in addition to what was being said. Having moved from Washington Heights to the Bronx in the middle of 4th grade, something happened to me without my full awareness: I became tracked in "slow" classes. Whether this tracking was done because of my test scores (I only recall a test named the Iowa test) or whether it came about because of my record as a student in grades 1 through 3, I do not know. All I know is that I was placed in classes in 4-11, 5-11, 6-12, 7-12, 8-11, and finally 9-11, one year before entering high school. This was significant because each grade had up to 13 classes per grade, 1 being the smartest or fastest, 11-13 being the slowest.

I did not understand this tracking until a special event emerged one day in fifth grade while talking to one of my classmates too much. Caught in the act, an act that was considered "disrespectful to the rights of others" on my report card, one day before a class trip to the Hayden Planetarium in New York, the teacher punished me. Instead of joining the class trip, I was to be detained in the 5th grade class across the hall. I reported to this class while my regular class enjoyed their trip. I sat in the back of the room for the entire day in class 5-1, and to my astonishment, realized I had been tracked into a slower class for many years. I listened to their kind of talk without realizing I was doing a discourse analysis. I compared the 5-1 talk I heard to what I heard routinely and realized how much more refined and eloquent these students were compared to my classmates in 5-11. Talk as a discourse also included how students carried themselves by their use of language, the way they walked and related to each other and their teacher.

Since the experience of sitting in the back of a smarter class, I realized how hierarchies worked and intruded themselves into discourse. Admittedly, I didn't realize how "slow" I was until, when playing stoop ball with some of my "Eddy buddies" in the Bronx, I said: "would you please *learn* me how to play?" Met with incredulous stares, I added: "I meant, would you please *taught* me?" This time, my request was met with laughter that insinuated I was stupid. Finally, I tried again, saying: "Oh, would you please teach me the game?" I didn't learn proper grammar that day, as much as how cruel young kids can be to each other.

The students whom I played with were very smart and placed in classes with lower numbers at a very young age. I never forgot how detrimental and harmful labeling can be. These experiences became benchmarks for guiding me to teach students once I became a teacher. Most of my published articles in special education and its inclusion speak to these concerns.[18] While there was no "special education" tracking in my schools in the 1950's, my elementary and secondary schooling experiences in the Bronx revealed a hidden track system excluding different or foreign students. I began to notice "new" students from different lands enrolling. This was a time when Puerto Rican families began to emigrate to *Nuevo York* and their children began to appear in schools. In addition, by middle school, I became aware of a gay student in my eighth grade class. Alex did not "come out" and declare this fact. I recall the subtle stares and remarks of my classmates, but nothing overtly violent or cruel – at least, I was not aware of it. Still, the difference of sexual orientation, race and ethnicity was clear to me at this time, though I was also aware of my classmates' reactions and stares. I held my judgment in reserve for the moment.

In high school I had neglected to study hard probably because I was "hanging around" with the wrong group of kids. Not accepted by the "smart kids" in my building because of grammatical deficiencies in my speech, but able to play ball better, I chose to stay with "tougher kids," the "Steve buddies," future soda truckers, who were by no means academically prone. Things changed, however, when in the 10th grade I broke my leg and received home tutoring. Upon reentry into high school I met new friends in class. They were more conscientious about study habits. Still wanting to play ball and meet girls, I did both when every Friday night I would meet with my new friends – the "Joel buddies" – to study for the regents exam via regent review books. Each study session was followed by one of their "socials," which included their younger sisters and friends.

I realized from this experience – way before reading Dewey – how meeting the social needs of students while being attuned to their cognitive abilities would and should be of equal importance. Because I came to realize too late how important academic study and course grade averages were, I attempted to get into a community college by the time I graduated high school. At this time, however, my family had decided to "buy a home" in the suburbs and I found myself, suddenly, transported to a neighborhood without hang-outs on the street corners, candy stores, and "bopping" or singing rock and roll in the echo-chambers of the subways of New York City. I recalled how often I simply refused to go to high school as I would have to walk three blocks from home and transverse the Grand Concourse to get to the school. Interceding on my way to school, I would pass the IND subway station. More times than not, I opted to "cut" school and walk through the streets of the city all day. I think much of what informs my teaching today was learned on these walking excursions in the late fifties and sixties in downtown Manhattan. I often recounted these stories to my students in urban and suburban colleges to the amazement and delight of my students.

The same students in my current education classes just as quickly changed their amazed facial expressions when they heard I graduated high school with a low 72.3 average, and did no better in college with a 2.3 GPA. Not wanting to look slow or stupid to them, I try to explain, exposing my vulnerabilities, that those special education students I worked with on my dissertation had similar problems – low averages, poor family support, being teased by fellow students. When I mention that my study was on special education students their airs of intellectual superiority soften and understanding begins to emerge. Still, I know the question that lingers in their minds is: What is this guy doing as my education professor? I believe, however, by the second week their perception changes as we get down to deep analytical exchanges. I will review and analyze in subsequent chapters of this book how college students and I go about first with exchanges of critical dialogue, and then, further breaching the limits of critical dialogue, delve into counter-hegemonic teaching and theorizing.

In much the same way, as I reflect on my teaching experiences as a social studies high school teacher in the late sixties and seventies, I recall classrooms filled with excitement, controversial issue debates, colorful bulletin boards of the students' work adoring the peripheral walls of their recent projects, and classroom barriers – student and teacher roles – that were often breached by class trips into the neighborhoods. On the issue of de-facto discrimination in home sales to people of color in my all white suburban high school, I asked the students to take surveys asking real estate agents why they practiced negotiations which excluded sale to people of color.[19] Or, why the Viet-Nam War raged on despite the fact that college and high school student demonstrations swept the nation and reports leaked out revealing how the Johnson-Nixon administrations misrepresented the war's beginnings and its reasons for continuation.[20] Till this day, I wonder how these events produced in me the need to see through contradictions as forces that get between the classroom and teaching act.

After all, this was the sixties, and I perceived my role as a facilitator and participant of the most controversial and current issues of the day – including civil right marches, women rights, student rights, gay rights, and anti-war demonstrations. I often refer to these times as "social studies heaven," despite the massive polarizations dividing the country. In my first high school I also became an activist, chairing a student club referred to as S.O.C. (Students Organized for Change).

Helping my professional development in these years, I was lucky enough to meet the head of my department as well as my mentor and evaluator, Ray Sobel. He was very pro-Union (UFT as opposed to NEA), pro-civil rights, pro-New Social Studies Curricula, and anti-war. More importantly, he had just completed a book with a professor from Queens College/CUNY about providing materials for teaching controversial issues entitled: *From Left to Right.*[21] This book contained several case studies and issues which ran along a right to left political spectrum. I was delighted to be chosen by him to present a lesson on "Inductive and Critical Thinking Approach to Teaching," which he had observed me doing in my class. I was only in my second year of teaching and twenty fours years old. The presentation dealt with optical illusions and the existence of the fact, and I got social studies teachers in attendance from both the junior high schools and the high school in the school district to partake in a few simulated teaching activities. Little did I know what a hornet's nest of trouble this act would stir up by the older, more conservative and tenured faculty.

Nevertheless, I knew in this environment I would grow professionally, supplemented by taking a few courses at TC between 1967–1969. Unanticipated troubles began in my third and forth years of teaching, however. I was "traded" away to another school because of a cut-back and re-districting of my high school's community lines, and was interviewed and received in my second social studies position in a high school known for more conservative leanings on Long Island. I had read articles in *Newsday* about how the Klu Klux Klan and the National Renaissance Party was active in local politics, along with their pressing for, and granting of, the dismissal of a library employee because she was Hispanic! Their adherents were calling for the termination of public school employees who happen to be "liberal" or "left leaning." The community also had a very active American Legion who staunchly supported the war in Viet Nam.

I took note of this fact because some of these students were not like those at the previous job. The students in my first school were mostly "A" or academic students – students destined to become "white collar" managers and professionals. In my second high school, the students appeared as vocational students, destined to become blue collar workers like their parents – auto mechanics and electricians for the boys; cosmeticians and secretaries for the girls. These high school students were tracked on the "G" line or general education. Despite the tracking in this high school, a high school which boasted over 6000 students at the time, the largest in Long Island, I was given the assignment to teach students – A and G students –

integrated into a 12th year social studies government course which emphasized a comparison between the United States and the Soviet Union.

As with all my classes, this class enjoyed a high degree of participation. In the high school newspaper (*The Paper Lion*, 1970), students wrote: "Fleischer Teaches Government by Games." By organizing the students into small groups, we began to discuss major issues comparing both societies and governments in ways which adhered to Edwin Fenton's "new curricula" emphasizing critical analysis and cross comparisons of cultures of both forms of government. I captured the students' attention and imagination by having them participate in a game called *Kohlkoz* or how a Soviet agricultural collective farm works. Some of the "G" students hooked us up from group to group and classroom to classroom with an electrical board that flashed red, yellow, and green lights. The red lights were signals that indicated it was time to stop producing so much for the collective operated for Gosplan located in Moscow, while the yellow light indicated that there would be a change in plans, a slow down, and the green light indicated resumption of production for Gosplan. Each collective signaled when they reached their Gosplan quotas, to continue to produce food for individually owned small farms located on the fringe of the collective, or *Kohlkoz* farm.

Though I and the other students did not attend seriously enough to the fact that one student always came to class wearing an all black suit with a bible in hand, I received a call one day from a school administrator who told me that the parent of this student was very upset about my government teaching. The parent claimed I put too much positive light on USA-USSR relations. I was more than willing to talk to the parent. However, a few days later, I received a letter circulated by the teacher's union, warning that non-tenure teachers were being asked to terminate their employment, with no reasons given. The following week, I received a request from the principal, along with school psychologists, the chair of my department and others in attendance, to come and meet them.

As I walked into the conference room of the principal, I could not fathom why I was being called in with so many administrators and school psychologists present. I was immediately informed that I should submit my resignation. Having only excellent written evaluations, and looking at the administrator who wrote them, I asked why. Shocked by my act of resistance, the principal stood up and yelled at the top of his lungs: "When we hired you we wanted a fresh breath of air....Not a hurricane!" I asked for clarification, which was met with a list of items considered "inappropriate," namely, teaching USA-USSR relations as a game, talking about censorship and discussing an article written by Allen Ginzberg, an advocate for free speech.

When I responded that I learned of the simulation game as played by the State Department in cooperation from The Rand Corporation, the principal continued to name other infractions. A few months earlier, I had clipped out an article by the famous poet Allen Ginsberg. In the article there was a list of words sorted by a series of columns. Isolated themselves, the words meant nothing, but if one wanted to string them together – one word from column A, another word from column B, another word from Column C, and so forth, one could easily construct a sentence that was off color, lewd, or "dirty." After explaining to the principal this was an exercise to demonstrate how censorship was culturally defined in the "mind of the beholder," he concluded that the exercise was "dirty."

After I walked out of the hour long meeting, I intended to submit my resignation letter at the end of the day, but first I wanted to speak to the president of the teachers union. As it turned out, I was not given that opportunity. In the middle of my 8th period class, another teacher poked his head in and asked me to step out. I did, in front of all my students. The teacher, an emissary from the principal, told me to leave the building and never to return! No other teacher came forth to offer a moment of solace or guidance, whether tenured or non-tenured. I knew then as I know now that when no collectivity amongst professionals exists, individualized fear establishes itself. There is a fear of getting involved or, what I will refer to later in the book as a unified self or self-fullness. I walked down the school halls that afternoon, and through their windowed doors, many of my colleagues just turned away. This was the longest walk of my life.

I stood alone about to be blacklisted. I tried to gain employment for months on Long Island, and initially did very well. Then, suddenly, upon learning from a prospective principal, who had checked my references, that my previous boss rendered a "bad" reference. This principal advised me to give up teaching, "go get a factory job!" For the remaining thirty seven years, receiving my doctorate finally in 1998, I made it a point to collect enough references from both colleagues and administrators. Still, I did not feel free of the stigma of being blacklisted or labeled in a way that prohibited me from continuing my profession. Still, I continue to this day, to fight and become, once again, employed. And, still lingering are the thoughts: am I being denied full employment because of my age or politics or both? [22]

I appealed my case to the American Civil Liberties Union in 1971. The director at the time, William F. Kunstler (the attorney who defended the Chicago 8 of the famous anti-war demonstration of the Democratic National Convention of 1968), told me I had "no case." As a non-tenured teacher I had no rights. The following year, I went to law school for a semester, dropped out, and began the following Fall of 1972 to become a full time doctoral student at TC. Simultaneous to taking courses and subbing weekly at a local junior and high school in New York City, I struggled to write a proposal that would speak of my predicament and those of many others who, at that point in time, had not been heard from then and I dare say, since.

Teaching in New York City as a substitute teacher allowed me more freedom than my previous Long Island teaching experiences. While I was spotted for some of my unconventional practices – having kids play games as *Group Therapy*, asking them to define the group dynamics and norms in the classroom, and role play how these dynamics play out in the larger society in terms of domestic and foreign affairs and issues, I felt closer to the students and teachers of the city than those of the suburbs. Still, as my teaching experiences fed into a conceptualization of language and power, I began to think about how I could take this teaching knowledge and apply it to existing critical literature, discussion groups and seminars. Under these circumstances I re-entered TC as a full time student, and met Dwayne Huebner and Maxine Greene. Here, at TC, I tried to develop my thinking processes as I presented my first proposal to complete my doctoral dissertation, but failed to have it materialize – though I reached the last chapter – as my father suddenly died in 1980.

WHAT MUST BE DONE NOW! MY ROLE AS TEACHER-EDUCATOR

As a teacher, educator-professor for the last ten years, I teach many courses in a variety of ways. Mainly, I try to model for my pre-service and in-service teachers the magic of being creative, and at the same time controversial enough to stir students' imaginations. At a recent course I taught on social studies methods, I did something I haven't tried since the first day of high school teaching. After observing the students argue about what constitutes a "fact" versus an interpretation, I asked the students to take a piece of paper and observe. The next second I flung my desk on its side producing a loud thud. The students were taken aback and shocked as they looked at me. I answered them with a question: "Now with your pen and paper describe what I did." After reading their responses a few minutes later, with comic relief, the students realized what I was trying to do.[23] In subsequent chapters I will explain how a filter or grid is sedimented into our consciousness as many layers downward – consciousness to unconsciousness – and linked inter-subjectively, through discursive formations of intersecting chains of signal givers and subject-positions, and how we can see through the genesis of consciousness as linked to the unconsciousness and each other and the more distanced horizons of society and the world. In this regard, I also try to show how the modernist notion of consciousness is displaced as merely one sutured subject-positions (of many others) passing through discursive and unconscious formations of chains of power and identity.

As Howard Zinn (2006), the famous American historian maintains of educators, teachers and professors, reflecting on his own teaching practice: "It is fascinating to make new knowledge, but only if that fascination does not become an end in itself." Rather, he continues, "the idea is to use this new knowledge to activate people and the social and others toward emancipatory ends." In the same way, I have sought as a teacher educator for the last ten years to take insights and breakthroughs with my students to a level of social and political action. Often I have volunteered to offer my services to several causes and activate conferences, demonstrations and in one case, start up a charter school for democratic leadership. In the latter case, teachers, students and parents share in running their own school of "at risk" students. At other times, I have underwritten full day conferences, committed to justice, equality, democracy and peace, with an emphasis on fear, post 9/11, creating an opposition to fear-mongering which we are constantly bombarded with in the news media, ads and in movies. In 2004, I sponsored a conference for several parent groups to come together to fight Mayor Bloomberg's effort to leave back poor and minority students in the 3rd grade by anticipating over 15,000 students would attend summer school before they were to take a standardized test. At Brooklyn College I sponsored a website and student club referred to as *Educators Speaking Out* (www.educatorsspeakout.com), serving as a sounding board for teachers to come together throughout the tri-state area of New York in order to critique and oppose existing school practices that were regressive, hegemonic and hierarchical.

Throughout *Counter-Hegemonic Teaching*, I will illustrate how my teaching experiences from elementary student to college professor feed into my present practices as a teacher educator in a variety of contexts and subject-matters. In particular, issues related to the foundations, leadership, social studies, media literacies and language use, and special education inclusion will be articulated within short case studies. I have spent over forty years thinking about this book's content, and after its publication, will continue to think about adding more dimensions to its sequel, *Counter-Hegemonic Teaching II*.[24] I ask for your comments, questions, and responses so that I may further develop professionally, and so that we may develop democratic forms of education here and abroad. For the most part, I will be looking for new forms of oppression, as they will certainly appear in this post 9/11 age of fear, terrorism and war, as fear is constantly pumped into the public consciousness. Hopefully, we'll break out of the non-participatory malaise of subject-positions. I will never forget those who came forth to help me despite personal costs and embarrassment to themselves. I seek those of you who will come forth – not merely for me or you – but for the students and children and parents by whom we are entrusted, and to resist those many harmful dimensions and hierarchical systems of teaching and school administration. Some of these systems may not, at first glance, be noticeable, since they are accepted without question, and are what I call, "hegemonic." Others, with the use of some tools, case studies and strategies offered in *Counter-Hegemonic Teaching*, may become familiar as we become creative and develop books and organizations of our own. Either way, we can begin to mount a movement which breaks the chains of oppressive, hegemonic forces that keep a hierarchical grip on our consciousness and concerted actions.

A FEW WORDS FOR THOSE CRITICAL THEORISTS WHO SEE POST-STRUCTURALISM AS NEO-LIBERAL

Many critics of schooling are leery of postmodern and post-structural approaches and have articulated their oppositions to such analyses by referring to them as "neo-liberal." They claim that neo-liberal changes in schools and society are attending only to the surface issues as opposed to more basic problems pertaining to institutionalized racism, classism and sexism. To these critics, neo-liberal educators make it appear as if issues related to class, race and gender are over or will be over soon and all that is needed are minor repairs and reforms. For example, Michael Apple, Peter McLaren and Donaldo Macedo have expressed reservations about how some changes in schools may give the impression that the problem of authority and power, and who wields it, are to be considered equally as important as "subject-positions" or the sense of identity people attending schools may have of themselves. They argue, to the contrary, that what needs to be studied is not so much the micro aspects of schooling, as much as the macro or "wider" aspects of schools and society, and how they are occluded and severed by post-modernists, or the "postie" orientation, from their structural roots and power as class, race and gender.[25]

In these critiques, it is presumed that all post-structuralist critiques of schooling and society are neo-liberal if they originate or are premised on the use post-structuralist concepts (i.e. signifying chains, subject-positions, discursive formations), and therefore, they cannot or do not attend to the wider forces (i.e. class, race, gender) at work within society's institutions, affecting schools. Halsey and Powell (1977) and others[26] made a similar critique, but rather, urging critical theorists to use concepts which address *both* micro-macro dimensions to their advantage and keep at bay binary logics. Not all were antipathetic toward post-structrural or semiological views, however.[27] In 1983, Henry Giroux took note in his *Theory and Resistance in Education: A Pedagogy for the Opposition*, citing Louis Althusser, pointing toward advancing Althusser's notion of interpellation (and how one is called or "hailed" into a subject-position to obey authority) and how such mechanisms of reproduction and ideology can be expanded, i.e. not only interpellate but inscribe in one's subjectivity a structured sets of positions with outlets to express their resistance. Giroux cites Althusser, (1971) and reveals schools as an ideological institution which turn out workers as automatons replicating capitalist values, habits, assumptions and dispositions because they are "so quiet" during this reproduction process. Giroux, Althusser and others of the traditional Marxist ilk may not have completely attended to the potential of resistances in schools.[28] In a similar way, Giroux further criticizes such studies as Samuel Bowles and Hebert Gintis's *Schooling in Capitalist America* (1976), insisting that people and workers are not dupes; they can resist despite the odds against them, ideological, real or a combination of both. To Giroux, what is key is to find those spaces that may exist in repressive and hegemonic school conditions. In this regard, Giroux points to the need for more exploration into the spheres of signification and semiotics, or how ideological and hegemonic positions of the subject may become resisted and transformed via subject-positions and other signifying constructs.[29]

As Peter McLaren and others in *Marxism against Postmodernism in Educational Theory* (2002) clearly indicate, this "post-structural" direction is presently labeled as "neo-liberal." The present study on *Counter-Hegemonic Teaching*, however, takes issue with some of these, perhaps, premature closures of a particular Marxist position. While agreeing with their critiques of neo-liberalism, I seek to widen the critique to include people already in schools and under other oppressive and hegemonic conditions within the school system which holds out potential spaces in discourse and signifying discursive formations. In this way, the potential of finding those spaces or the existence of resistant groups and individuals in hegemony does not completely foreclose their struggles, and further, the extent to which anti-hierarchical and hegemonic chains of signification − which serve as spaces on which to inscribe resistance and counter-hegemonic discourses and organizations − lies and can be potentially useful in serving liberated teaching when school oppression and hegemony are intermixed in discourse.

Thus, the present study disagrees with McLaren, Apple, and Macedo on their recent critiques of post-structualism as neo-liberal. Supported by Ernesto Laclau and Chantel Mouffe's study of *Hegemony and Socialist Strategy: Toward A Radical Democratic Politics* (1985) in which "new social movements" are forming all the time and offer an alternative to the strict classist interpretations and applications of Marxism seeking change and revolution to the present modes of capitalist production in schooling, *Counter-Hegemonic Teaching* accepts the position that class is not the only position of power and relation – albeit a powerful structural position – to take when viewing society and schools as parts of a whole in an expressive totality. As Laclau and Mouffe argue, class can be complemented with gender, race and authority power subject-positions, relations, and their associated equivalent and differential chains of meanings and words (Laclau, 1993, 2007; Thomassen, 2005).

I argue a "critical" position is exceeded by a "counter-hegemonic" position. This means that the notion of subject-positions and signifying chains which operate to both constitute and complement traditional radical class critiques by including those already inscribed or interpellated in its oppressive school systems, which can, when complemented with an additional component such as post-structuralist constructs or tools for mapping, reverse the process by inscribing and interpolating their interpellated subject-positions along the "surfaces of inscription" articulated by Laclau (1990, 1993, 2007). When this happens (discussed in detail in Chapter 4) new agentive dimensions may be revealed offering new complexities of subject-positions and chains of signifiers, including "textured and thick" surfaces on which inscriptions are over-incribed, de-inscribed and re-inscribed (Laclau, 1990, 1993, 2007).

One may see in the work of Ann Marie Smith (1996) and her review of Ernesto Laclau and Chantel Mouffe's *Hegemony and a Socialist Democratic Strategy* (1985), how the complex interactions between power relations and identities interact to produce consistent as well as contradictory subject-positions and modes of articulation. She, like Laclau and Mouffe, (1985) examine hegemony as not necessarily embedded, not only as a sutured series of subject-positions but, further, examines the "surfaces" on which these positions are articulated and changed in discourse, how they circulate amongst signifiers and speakers, leaving marks or re-surfaced surfaces, "tendentially," (Thomassen, 2001) in the inscription process for actors to make a profound difference. Thus, surfaces of class overlaying surfaces or layers of class, which, in turn, are overlaid both by traces of gender, ethnicity, age, and sexuality make for a complex of hegemony and also spaces for change and counter-hegemony. The process becomes more complex when we see these traces and overlays of inscription as containing intersections and crossings of chains of signifiers from various discursive formations and groups, representing subject-positions as constituted by metonymic chains of signifiers – fleeting glimpses – linking parts to the whole of the realities in which speakers and people make up in complex configurations of discourse, articulated to and through each other.

Smith, Laclau, and Thomassen, then, take a different position from the above critics as do McLaren, Apple, and Macedo. To Smith, one lives out their life in subject-positions linked to structural positions which are more or less "thrown into." One's perception of the world (the real) is already colored by the imaginary and the symbolic. To Smith, and her predecessors, Michel Pecheux (1982), and his mentor Jacques Lacan, (1977) the notion of Althusser's interpellation has already been revised as a series of complex modes of inscription on surfaces of subject-positions and their constituting (and interacting and intersecting) chains of signifiers; once inscribed into a subject-position, one already has an arsenal of tools widening the dimension of being ideologized in language. Acting as a signifying sieve, as they sense both oppressive and counter-oppressive subject-positions along differential alignments of dominant and dominated, hegemonic and counter-hegemonic discursive formations, people get linked in complex acts of signification and discourse.[30]

To Smith, there are many overlapping and intersecting dynamics and spaces occurring *between* race, class and gender which traditional Marxist "critiques" may overlook. These spaces may serve for a basis of counter-hegemonic and anti-oppressive states of identifications, symbolizations and discourses. Further, Smith sees race, gender and class as power relations and differentials, not as segmented or isolated from one another, serving as "reflections" or epiphenomena above an economic base. She sees through her concept of subject-positions, a more complex and nuanced picture of how power and language interact, affecting the lives of those in oppressive and hegemonic conditions of institutional society and schools.

It is from Smith and others, as will be discussed in Chapter 4, that a different position is offered to examine and re-visit Freire in a way that does not marginalize post-structural analyses. Indeed, one way to explore Freire again may be through a post-structuralist extension of his main concepts: reflection, action, dialogue, problem-posing, critical praxis, etc.

I believe this re-visit needs to be done because Freire and his contemporaries needs to extend, specifically, his major work, *Pedagogy of the Oppressed*, in order to continue to serve the cause of countering hegemony[31] and to ignite liberating, democratic causes of pedagogy and schooling in this country and other so-called 'advanced" industrialized nations in postmodern times. By utilizing a post-structural framework, one that is most appropriate for analyzing hegemony today, as Laclau (1985, 1993, 2007) and others have argued, an emphasis on how language and power interconnect on the level of signification or by signifiers and their corresponding chains and links, can be constructed representing chains of race, gender, class, and most importantly and often omitted, *chains of administrative school authority and hierarchy* which encompass school practices such as testing, classroom management, administrative and hierarchical practices, and how these procedures and policies continue to divide or diffuse potential student and teacher solidarity for control of their schools governance by democratic means.

Thus, this book will probe deeper into the notion of how subjects are positioned, and how in this probe, there may exist spaces within which counter-hegemonic critiques of complex arrangements of power, language and subjectivity can be acted on by students and teachers who, in their present antagonistic relations may see through their oppression, and see how they oppress each other and see each other as oppressors. Breaking out of these hegemonic states, creating a more critical dialogue and questioning is not only necessary for the use of language and identity categories; it also "maps out" how such complex power differentials in schools intersect and interact with each other, short circuiting broader coalitions and solidarities from forming into mass movements for democracy in schools and throughout society. Igniting in themselves new subject-positions of agency, identity and solidarity in their present power relationships, students and teachers may discover how hierarchical relations of power are constituted by hierarchical chains of signifiers and subject-positions, and thereby provide all involved with a more complex reading as to why they themselves continue to miss the reason they should maintain such hegemonic relationships, as they unwittingly do.

I seek to explore more dimensions of school oppressions, to "catch those hierarchical feelings of oppression that slide up and down my spine" and which keeps us silent and complicit in our talk. If you feel the same, *Counter-Hegemonic Teaching* is an open invitation to join the beginnings of a new teacher-student-parent mass-based movement or to link up with other movements. For example, a Freire blog-network held at McGill University under the sponsorship of Joe Kincheloe and Shirley Steinberg is yet another place to begin. Until that day comes, I can be reached at lfleis3960@aol.com

WHY DO I WRITE THIS BOOK AS A PROFESSIONAL TEACHER EDUCATOR AND TEACHER?

As a critic of schools and their lack of democratic rules, procedures, and processes over some forty years, I continue to have faith in higher education and the public schools, subject to many changes, specifically, those that make schools a more democratic, creative, autonomous, professional, loving, and awe inspiring places to be. Through these years, I have had to compromise, negotiate, and fight for a better future, and I have experienced many setbacks. Nevertheless, I've been inspired by many of my students (who are teacher-ed students and teachers), as well as fellow instructors in teacher education courses. The courageous stories and struggles they often shared with me have repeatedly renewed my belief that a better world and education system is, indeed, possible. Over the years, however, I've also received comments from students that were, quite frankly, alarming in their complicity and distain for schools and for students. It is comments like these that have compelled me to write this book:
- I like the new mandated testing and close administrative supervision; when they 'sweep' the floors checking to see if the students are studying for the test .... Students are so carefully supervised by administrators, that they are afraid to fail. As a result, my life is much easier now: students no longer are discipline problems. I like to see the students sweat." – Graduate education student in the middle of her second year of teaching middle school in math.
- "We will go over the con's of standardized testing, and then, I will help you be a better proctor for the exams." – Adjunct Instructor of graduate education course in a MAT program I evaluated.
- Everybody knows what your school administrator says is "bullshit" – but you need to follow what they say. Adjunct instructor of graduate education course.
- "I don't care what is happening to children all over the world – if it doesn't affect me, why bother to learn about them." – Graduate education student.
- My classes are mixed with 'inclusion kids,' but I can still pick out those who are and those who aren't." – 9th grade teacher and graduate Ed student.

- My ed professor asked about homophobia and gay rights being taught in public schools. When a student said he thought it was a sin, the professor moved on to another topic.
- I hate the tenured and older teachers. They ought to be removed for laziness and incompetence…. Of course, I want to get tenure – it will give me job security." – Graduate education student.
- I can't talk about racism or the war in the classroom, because parents will complain and I'll be called down to the principal's office the next day." – Graduate student and supervisor of social studies in an elementary school.
- "I'm afraid to show articles on sexism and sexual education. Parents and the administrator will make me a "sacrificial lamb and I will get fired!" – Graduate student and teacher of 7th grade social studies teacher.
- I tell my students who is *in charge* in the first days of the class. Even if it means slapping them in the head to wake them up!" "I learned this from the teacher I helped as an aide." – Undergraduate student and also teacher aide in elementary school.
- Kids are like sponges – just tell them what to absorb." – 9th grade teacher
- I'm always afraid to speak – I'm afraid of saying the wrong thing." – 8th grade teacher and graduate student.
- New teachers are like "fresh meat" to students – you can't trust them and smile. We need classroom management techniques, and to know how to refer them to the correct authorities – that's all you need to know." – Education student in her first undergraduate course.

In addition to the obvious problems inherent in the comments above, I have often thought that there were some overarching problems that needed to be identified to ameliorate the cynicism and bitterness so often found in the teaching experience. A practical and theoretical framework of "reading" teaching as occurring within a system not always sympathetic to critical thinking and critical literacy appears to be missing. This means identifying where changes in the system are necessary to *transform* educational experiences from hierarchical and administrative to democratic and emancipatory goals and practices; specifically, those oriented toward social justice, equality, and collective agency amongst the major participants – students and teachers (in the case of pre-secondary students, their parents or guardians).

As Joe Kincheloe (2004a, 2004b, 2004c, 2005, 2007, 2008), along with other school critics (Apple, 1979, 1982, 1983, 1996; Freire, 2002) Giroux, 1980, 1981, 1983, 1991; Shor, 1986, 1990) have insisted over decades in their many works, students and teachers must be able to "read power" and its complex relationships in the authoritarian circumstances inscribed in their schools. Schools, in turn, re-inscribe student and teacher inscriptions on overlapping and intruding influences by "outside" pressures applied community-wide, state-wide, nation-wide, and world-wide. These power inscriptions occur in often invisible or murky ways; they are usually forces which make us perform actions we would not be identified with. For example, how we are pitted against others of different races, classes, genders, abilities, ages, sexual orientations and ethnicities as different, and how we are marginalized on binary chains of identifications and associations.

In addition to these complex networks of power, there are other concerns; namely, how power works not as a force of circumstance one can see, resist and immediately be reflective of; but how power manifests itself as a force of hegemony which, at its most intense moment, gives one the impression that there are no problems to be concerned about or, more fatalistically, when one catches a glimpse of the problem, that everything is pre-destined to occur.

Between no problems, and the fleeting appearances of problems, there are intermediating forces at work in hegemony – often ignored by those who would prefer not to bother to include a post-structuralist understanding of this issue. Specifically, I posit a problem of hegemony as a problem of discourse, psychoanalysis and linguistics. Within this framework, counter-hegemony and its spaces may be located, read, mapped out and even produced.

While a more detailed discussion grounding a counter-framework will occur in Chapter 4, after case studies and this chapter framing of the problem, we can begin to offer a broader framework of "post-hegemonic" directions.[32] This framework will attempt to show, as one takes a subject-position and inscribes on its surfaces one's feelings, thoughts, writings and desires, also how one's inscriptions are mediated by dominant, sedimented inscriptions constituting the "habitus" or dispositions of school life and role assignments.[33] In this mix or space of mediation of forces, there may lie open spaces in which two or more discussants may construct and carve out a common ground, thereby allowing a basis for counter or relatively autonomous discursive communities to emerge (Laclau, 2007; Smith, 1996; Thomassen, 2005). These hegemonic forces accompany hierarchical institutions (schools, corporations, government, churches, media) and become infiltrated by schools and classrooms as *"points of antagonism"* between student and teacher in moments where they are attracted to various hierarchical cultures from within and outside schools. At the moment of "articulation," as spelled out by Laclau and Mouffe (1985) and later Laclau (1990, 2007) and his contemporaries, (Smith, 1996; Thomasssen, 2005; Critchley & O. Marchant, 2004) in speech as chained equivalence and difference in a discursive field, further segmented into ensembles of discourse or discursive formations, (i.e. race, class, gender, authority, ability, ethnicity, etc.) as inherent signifying functions inciting circulation and the crossing over of chains of signifiers and subject positions, their surfaces for inscription reveal metonymic and metaphoric chains of signifiers (Coward & Ellis, 1977; Z. Kovecses, 2006). Students and teachers are drawn into a web not only in which others "win their consent," but which allows them to fight against these forces in counter-hegemonic and (sometimes co-opted) forms of resistance.[34]

In these in-between terrains for speaking, feeling and sensing discourse and its elements,[35] both student and teacher may construct new questions penetrating these *"points of antagonism"* in their discourses and seek out *"points of connection."* Also, in these spaces, student and teacher may begin to build bridges between what separates them and their own discursive communities, which may be counter-hegemonic or may revert back to another form, a co-opted form of hegemonic discourse. Student and teacher (and teacher-educator) can penetrate these intervening spaces of mis-recognition of who they are and whom they act for, by piercing those identifications which see themselves as what they could be when connecting with likeminded people. This moment, however, may ignore those intervening forces which may invade, distort or create illusions that they are alone, free to choose, or otherwise omnipotent, as if living alone on a deserted island, far from those threatening forces – those hierarchical and administrative chains existing in schools and penetrating classroom relationships. One only has to recall what happens when an administrator, without fore notice, suddenly enters a classroom. Almost instantly, student and teacher come to each others' aid as the administrator undermines or attempts to bolster the teacher's authority. These and other unnamed forces demand a counter-hegemonic perspective to understand the various contradictions students and teachers live through on a daily basis, as they attempt to resolve some of these pressures in creative and courageous ways while maintaining themselves as potential critics of their surroundings and relationships (Ayers, 1998).[36]

THE SENSE OF PESSIMISM IN PRE- "POST-STRUCTURALIST" THEORIZING CLASSROOMS

There is a sense of pessimism that teachers in their practice at their jobs, and students I have taught for the last ten years, taking required courses for teacher certification or school district requirements, have a feeling in which there is little or nothing they can do to resist, question, change and take power in authoritarian school environments – at least, without suffering grave consequences. Yet, as we have seen throughout history, as Foucault (1977, 1980) to Homi Bhabha (1989), and, Bhabha in Baker, Diawara, and Lindeborg (1996) call it, lying between the autocratic or monarchical power and the people is an unpredictable territory of "third spaces" in which people may galvanize enough courage to resist and break hegemonic chains of fear. Foucault defines power (1977, 1980), not only as a force to respond obsequiously, but further, as a force to seize and, by doing so, produce more power in moments of discourse through the most "tiny tissues" of hierarchical authority (Foucault, 2006).

As Kincheloe (2005)[37] partially accounts for power and discourse – the former regulating discourse in terms of deciding who has the right to talk, what they should say, and who should address or remain silent – there is also a concern pointed to by Foucault (1977) accounting for those "most insignificant spaces of the hierarchy" which are revealed in discourse as spaces in which power is never completely consolidated or made monarchical. To Foucault (1980), and later Laclau (with Mouffe,1985, 1990, 2007) there are always contingent spaces in which those under power may produce, negotiate, organize, and seize power. *Counter-Hegemonic Teaching* is therefore written with the intent that there are interstices and interventions in which student and teacher may act in individual and collective forms of agencies.[38] This is made possible by acts of courage and collectivity, from the bottom-up and side-ways, as students and teachers begin to relate differently to each other in administrative and hierarchical authority relations. This may happen, as Maxine Greene tells us (1978; in Sadovnik, Cookson, & Semel, 2006) in moments of "awakeness" one may begin to act together with others for a common cause (a collective end-in-view) over and against those assigned to administrative hierarchical positions they are constrained into.

In such acts of awakeness, students, teachers, and teacher educators may act together, in small groups in order to band together in resisting the onslaught of hegemonic scripted curricula and teaching methods and mandated national legislation of high stake testing, which makes their schools into "testing factories" and their relationships into alienated, sterile, and unprofessional and de-skilled experiences. In effect, they can de-validate top-down student-teacher relations (as called for by Freire), along with those justifications for maintaining testing and the accountability craze overtaking the country under the Bush administration and *No Child Left Behind* (2002). What they need to see, as Dewey often advised us, are alternatives, different ends-in-view, or hear contrary views.

While there have been, and continues to be a huge number of articles and research condemning "high stake" testing as punitive and harmful to young people (Woods, et al., 2004), very little attention has been paid to how students and teachers (and in some circumstances, administrators and parents) can resist such top-down legislation, mandates, and accompanied practices. Thus, practices as "teaching for the test" remain a dominant practice and norm of school curricula, making the subject-matter very narrow and flat, bereft of discussions that may otherwise enrich (rather than dumb-down) the curricula. This may change, however, with the infusion of post-structural constructs adding or complementing the critical pedagogy debate.

WHAT CAN POST-STRUCTURALISM ADD TO THE CRITICAL PEDAGOGY
DEBATE?

Since the 1980s and 90s, the full impact of Foucault and postmodernist strands of thought (Foucault, 1972, 1973, 1980; Lyotad, 1980; Young, 1980) reached the shores of critical pedagogy. Already grounded on modernist strands of thought, was the accomplishments of the Frankfurt School (Adorno, 1944, Best & Kellner, 1991; Habermas, 1970, 1972; Horkeimer, 1972) and a neo-Marxist discussion on revising the writings of Marx (Poster, 1975, Sartre, 1960). Critical pedagogy was also becoming reformulated in the writings of Apple (1979), Giroux (1980, 1981, 1983), and earlier, in the writings of the "re-conceptualists" with William Pinar, James MacDonald, Maxine Greene, Dwayne Huebner, and John Mann (1975). The significance of post- or neo-race, feminist, and colonist theories, interwoven into class (Baker, Diaware, Lindeborg, 1996; Gordon, 1996; Hall, 1985, McRobbie, 1994; Spivak, 1988), and the continuous impact of the writings of Gramsci (Boggs, 1976, Forgacs, 2000; Gramsci, 1971: Loomba, 1998) remained in a state of debate. Post-structuralism and its emphasis on language as discourse and its effects on both the Marxist problem-positing and liberating forces from the capitalist hold as its dominates work and other societal forces, including schools, continued to this day to await further theorization on all fronts (Carlson, 2004, Carspicken, 1996; Heldke & O'Connor, 2004).

The debate has intensified as some advocates of critical pedagogy from modernist strands force us to re-examine the contributions of post-structuralism *vis-a-vis* critical pedagogy. This debate also forces us to re-examine the contributions of those who offer unique perspectives critical of hegemonic holds in which, by various degrees, capitalism invades the so-called "relative autonomy" of today's public schools, responsible for the reproduction of capitalism and schooling (Althusser, 1971; Apple (1988); Aronowitz, 1974; Bowles & Gintis, 1976; Giroux, 1983).

With the earlier post-structuralist work of Jacques Lacan (1977) and Michel Pecheux (1982) and their intersections of psychoanalysis, linguistics, discourse theory and semiotics – see, for example, Macdonnell (1986), along with the post-Marxist work of Ernesto Laclau (with Chantal Mouffe, 1985; Laclau, 1993, 2007) and his emphasis on equivalent and differential chains of empty floating and master signifiers and their construction of "tendential" (Laclau, 2005; Thomassen, 2005) subject-positions weaving into and through the fabric of schools and society, critical pedagogy, and those who critique post-structuralism, cannot move forward or, worst, can stymie movement toward a "post-hegemonic" phase. The more recent post-post-structuralist work of Slovenj Zizek (1989), as complementing the recent work of Laclau (2007), reveals how signifiers and signification may penetrate unconsciousness and its discursive states in revealing the *Real* or "kernel of the real," which, somehow, bypasses the symbolic and imaginary states of consciousness. Zizek's (1989) emphasis, taken from the earlier works of Lacan (1977) and Pecheux (1982), involves forms of intra- and trans-discourses which penetrates through the symbolic and imaginary circulating signifiers, known to him as *objets petit a*, as they weave in and through words, linked to meanings fermented by other words and meanings, and which are linked to other circulating signifiers in their chains, further linked to their subject-positions and their respective discursive formations.

Zizek, as a literary and popular culture critic, weaves these fragments of signification and discourse into what he calls desires, pleasures, and fantasies, travelling through "quilting points"[39] or *sinthomes* which, to Zizek, are the "flexible joints" connecting parts of the whole to each other. In a form of metonymic experiences, we are faced with a knot of *real* and repressed subject-positions of the unconsciousness. These desires or repressed fantasies – exhibited in pleasure, joy – *jouissance* – and sometimes in horror – cross into and through linguistic and non-linguistic, the imaginary and symbolic, and into expressions of the real or what one would describe from the "gut" or the feelings of cold sweat and fear. How clarifying these experiences which penetrate subject-position surfaces when caught in contradictory roles related to race, class, gender, authority, remains a problem to be further theorized and debated into the future of both schools and society as well as formulating new bases for re-examining the debate between modernists and postmodernists and how they intersect critical pedagogues and theorizing.

Think of the bulleted quote cited earlier in this chapter, in which a young teacher expresses pleasure and relief because her students are being watched closely by administrators sweeping the halls. As she observes her students "sweating" (also see Figure 8 in Chapter 3) in preparation for tests, she appears to be grateful to what she calls a "less fearful" environment. I have observed while visiting many of my teachers, their pleasure in the misery of fellow teachers, upon hearing that they cannot control their classes or are dismissed because they are too sympathetic to the students. In one case a teacher was dismissed because she wanted to connect with students by offering them time to listen to their I-Pods.

While it is not the main concern of this book to further examine this debate and its ramifications for a *"post-hegemonic"* mode of hegemonic and counter-hegemonic teaching,[40] I seek new directions for future research and practice, calling for more case studies and collective actions amongst students, teachers, and teacher educators, the latter displacing the role of the school administrator. Recently, there have been calls for such re-considerations made by other, well-known critical pedagogues in the field (Giroux in McLaren and Kincheloe (2007); Giroux and Kincheloe, 2008; Giroux, 2007, 2008, Kincheloe, 2004, 2005, Steinberg in McLaren and Kincheloe, 2007) affecting both public schools and higher education institutions in their teacher education programs. I will also address this later in Chapter 5.

As will be argued throughout this book, however, the basis or what may ignite counter-hegemonic modes of theorizing and teaching lies in students, teachers, and teacher-educators drawing maps for illustrating how hegemony, specifically, domination, oppression, and alienation imposes itself throughout their identifies, relations, and voices or, in post-structural terms, their subject-positions, chains of signifiers, and discursive formations. These terms break with the confines of modernist theorizing, which presupposes consciousness or subjects which already have unified, essentialized, and originary states of subjectivity, and who posit actors as meaning making entities in which they move unilaterally and individually toward the object in which they infuse or inject – from the cone of light or stream of consciousness (Berger & Luckmann, 1966; Husserl, 1962; Schutz, 1970), through intentional acts, reaching out and into objects, *noema or meaning* combining with the thing-in-itself *noesis* or what Husserl and other "intender" phenomenologists refer to as linking together the thing in a *noema-noesis* nexus.

I find an irony in this modernist position of noema-noesis linkage between subject and object, which Freire, despite his adoption of consciousness based on a Husserlian reading, has, contradictorily, not noticed up to his untimely death.[41] That is, while he opposed "depositing" lecture-like pedagogies into the heads of students, he and many of his modernist contemporaries prescribed a kind of unified notion of consciousness which stands over the object world and people and, in Husserlian terms (Russell, 2007), the subject reaches towards objects of their intentional consciousness, and in so doing, infuse meaning into the world "out there." While Freire was opposed to the "banking concept" of teaching, he and his contemporaries have only recently called attention to the concept of "signifiers" (Freire, 2007). Many of us remain torn between the heterogeneous worldview of post-structuralism, which postulates a de-centered, dispersed, and divided self – a subject of lack and desire (Foucault, 1977; Lacan, 1977; Laclau, 1977, with Mouffe, 1985; Pecheux, 1982; Zizek, 1989) versus a more certain and organized world of self-dom, predictability, and modernism.

Because Freire has adopted a Husserlian perspective to consciousness in *Pedagogy of the Oppressed* (Freire, 2002, pp. 82–83), he cannot reconcile how words speak through us – in and through our unconsciousness – shooting through us, out into the open public spaces with others, often in moments of connecting with others in solidarity and agential actions. As Lacan asserts: the unconsciousness is structured like a language" – or there are dimensions in our unconsciousness which express words through us, unintentionally, and yet with full import of reflection and seriousness (i.e. unconscious thoughts). Or, as Berger and Luckmann[42] have been theorizing—albeit inadequately – how when we engage in close proximity to one another, there is an "inter-subjective closeness" which permits us to speak as we think and know the other better than our selves. These notions defy modernist, consistent, essentialized, unified, and coherent notions of subjectivity and consciousness, much less can be the basis for counter-hegemonic teaching and theorizing.

Because much attention has already been attended to the modernist contributions – i.e. The Frankfurt School – and other more recent works on critical pedagogy, for example, in the works accomplished by Joe Kincheloe (1993, 2003, 2004a, 2004b, 2004c and 2005) and others (Apple, 1983, 1990; Giroux, 2007, 2008; Carlson, 2004, Wink, 2005), further attention on critical pedagogy ought to examine the potentials of the post-structuralist dimensions (rather than marginalizing them) and how hegemony can be identified, analyzed, and named in both teaching practices and teacher education theories.

DEVELOPING A NEW LANGUAGE FOR POST-HEGEMONIC AND COUNTER-HEGEMONIC TEACHING

Another reason I felt the need to write this book was to provide an additional language for critical pedagogy or a perspective – pushing the envelope, sort of speaking – drawn from prior critical perspectives (Apple. 1979; Giroux, 1981, 1980; 1983),[43] and to place into context various struggles for hegemony, including race, gender, and class as overlaid by an additional power relation, *hierarchical and administrative authority*. I seek to identify this level because it has been for too long ignored, and at the same time, it serves as the nuclei of other levels of power and their contradictions. A counter-hegemonic level cannot be reached unless (in addition to exceeding binary relations of the classes, races, ethnicities, sexual orientations, and abilities) student and teacher have a real stake in the running of their schools, acting against administrative and hierarchical authority.

While there are a few experiments whereby teachers along with students and parents run their own schools, specifically, charter schools and alternate schools within traditional schools, these same schools have attempted to jettison rules and practices which have been normally accepted as necessary for the support of school bureaucracies by school administrators and union leaders.[44] It would be of no surprise to anyone why innovation leading toward less bureaucracy and more democracy would be met with resistance. When we apply a post-structural analysis to school organizations and expose how hierarchical norms of identity, community-making, and relations lead to more alienation than less, change must come or be sought after. How else can we prepare the next generation of citizens to be active participants in a democratic state and world to come as opposed to remaining in the current isolated, individualistic, and non-cooperative school and classroom organizational and societal environments?

To accomplish this goal and practice, school and societal norms must be changed in which, speaking post-structurally, subjects will have to inscribe, de-inscribe, and re-inscribe on the surfaces of their subject-positions[45] they find themselves addressing new commitments and values toward social justice, equality, diversity, and democracy in schools and its governing organizations. To reach the plateau of counter-hegemonic struggles also requires penetration of the authority structures which govern the work, curricula, and relationships between students and teacher and community members of their schools. We also cannot ignore the macro forces at work – the state and federal legislation, the intrusion of corporation curricula, media, technology, and other influences affecting what teaching is, and when knowledge becomes "constructed," between teachers and their students, and how teacher-educators must construct perspectives capable of confronting hegemony on a multiplicity of fronts and forces.

MAP-MAKING: START TO STRATEGIZE COUNTER-HEGEMONICALLY

Specifically, *Counter-Hegemonic Teaching* seeks to identify a force field of discourse in which student and teacher may act as cartographers or make "maps" and images as starting points toward strategizing how and what they want to learn, and the tools appropriate for such learning. In this way, while learning various subject-matters, students and teachers may relate and ground future counter-forces against those "points of antagonism" by discussing how there may lie an in-between territory or "points of connection" – no doubt suffocated by present hierarchical and administrative discursive formations and chains of signifiers and subject-positions (including but not exclusively race, class, poverty, race, gender, authority, etc.) – which undermine their relations as well as prevents them from coalescing into discursive communities of counter-hegemonic theorizers. In this context, however, "agency" or, as Kincheloe (2004a, p. 2) defines the term, a "person's ability to shape and control their own lives, freeing self from the oppression of power," come close to what we are driving at here, except for the fact that both terms, "self" and "power," remain outside of a post-structuralist frame of theorizing. That is to say, once students, teachers, and teacher educators begin to speak up without fear of administrative reprisals or racist, sexist, and classist remarks, and speak out into the world of schools, society, and the world in order to make a difference, to the extent this does not happen, is the extent things may not change.

Unfortunately, in recent years, words as "democracy," "freedom," "diversity," and even "justice" have become co-opted in perspectives or paradigms that do little to encourage students and teachers to take a stand or to speak out in meaningful and collective ways. New forms of discourse must be imagined. Many in the field of education believe there is little that can be done, whether as an individual or in small groups of individuals. They remain cynical. Refusing to accept their cynicism as a basis of their own self defeat, I write this book in the hope that it will inspire those who wait for change to come. I want to show them that another way of thinking, and a way for them to connect with others to take counter-hegemonic actions, is possible.

Recently, in teaching a course titled "Innovations of Urban Education" in a small college in New Jersey, that claimed to be "urban" and carry out "reflective" teaching practices, I realized and articulated to my graduate students that the course's title was meaningless. To insist on "innovation," we needed fundamental changes from the bottom up in the policies currently dominating schools throughout the country and its emphasis on accountability and testing. Until those changes occurred, it would be meaningless to talk about innovations. With sincerity, my students agreed, pointing to the futility of innovating an institution that was basically backward or "retro." Until a radical change occurs, allowing one to "teach" as autonomous professionals, my students remained stalwart or suspicious of talk of change. In the meantime, they confided to me: "We are lying low." I wondered, are they really "lying low" in silence, isolated from one another, *or* are they acting as accomplices to their own hegemony and domination?

"LYING LOW" AND HIERARCHICAL AND ADMINISTRATIVE AUTHORITY

This book provides a theoretical framework and suggestions for intervening strategies. In this regard, it is critical to reflect on the discursive practice of "lying low."

My history as a teacher and professional teacher educator evolved slowly in professional and collegial relationships. It has been, by and large, an uphill struggle. But, as Kincheloe (2005) often told me and many others in his forty-five plus books and even more prolific number of articles, schools may have done more harm than good given their positivistic and narrow approach to learning – "alienated cognition" – curriculum making, standardized testing, and other forces illustrative of the top-down mind-set, which flow in a linear way so that others at the bottom do not ask enough questions. Some questions, as: "Why has, what has become, become that way (2007)?" may never get asked. Perhaps this important question, setting the school enterprise into historical, political, social, economic and other contexts does not fully examine the ideological foundations of our selves, society, and schools. That is, all of us are raised in a society that indoctrinates us to believe how wonderful schools are, how free we are, and how the "American Dream" is attainable, and therefore, maintaining us in unchangeable positions.

We all have been raised on the notion of how our economy, the free marketplace, is the source of all solutions to problems despite some of the problems we are currently experiencing, i.e., the recent Wall Street crash and bailouts. We can extend this thinking to schools, in romanticizing our favorite teachers and how they made a difference in our lives, "one child at a time." Or, put another way, we can suspend our individualistic outlook and focus on how few individuals have succeeded, when we examine wealth-poverty differentials, continuation of racial segregation in education and housing, and hidden codes which discriminate against women, gays, and immigrants. We may also want to focus on why we attribute to those who fail, a lack of initiative, intelligence, and hard work. Schools, historically, have been the transmitter of a story that lends credence toward "making it," in a supposedly free and democratic society with a "free and open" market place of ideas. This narrative may become questioned (Kozol, 2005), however. We keep hearing that with good grades and credentials, we all will be able to make it and become successful. That if one does not succeed, it is of no fault of the school or society; rather, it is the fault of the individual who has not tried hard enough, or is too lazy to learn, and finally, in the case of the poor, minority, immigrant, and ESL student, does not have the right parents or supportive home environment.

Of course this is the ideology or story in which we have been positioned to believe as truth and fact. But, is this always so? There are, as this book insists, hegemonic reasons why what happens to those who mean well, and are well educated, and "play by the rules of the game," and do not "cut corners," devise creative methods to survive. This book is written with the complete knowledge that many will attack its content by virtue of exposing a system that has far exceeded its goals by the harmful effects it showers on our children and teaching staff. Rewards are offered and granted to the few token individuals. Thus, I seek a dialogue with those people who have "fell between the cracks," or if only they would stay long enough to respond to questions and analyses of their own, would otherwise condemn this book as just "another left wing radical book on education!"

START BUILDING SPACES FOE SCHOOL DEMOCRACY!

To build a place or space for critical dialogue and discussion about how school and classroom activity are linked together not only with macro forces or micro forces, but by those "in between" forces bridging both, those resisting and negotiating with the school's administrative hierarchy for more fundamental democratic changes of teacher professionalism and student and family rights. So-called necessary administrative brokers, and the brokers themselves, for the most part, act as agents of oppressive school conditions or police stifling life out of student and teacher relations. This is not to argue for anarchy; there must be someone at the helm to count milk containers and pay remittances of bills related to materials and other sundries. Rather, this argues that the very feeling of ownership must be grounded on real power by those who have skin in the game, those who have a real stake in owning the schools where they work and think. True, at present, the huge monies given openly or indirectly by the state, large corporations, and individuals may have an effect on who owns who. What can never be owned are the many informal cultures and relationships people form under the most oppressive of circumstances, in gulags or concentration camps, not withstanding that in these desperate situations, complicity also thrives.[46]

The intricate network of resistance and reproduction in overly oppressive conditions usually goes unnoticed, and many of its important links in which people are chained to others in oppression fade from sight because we do not want to imagine alternate possibilities. People simply do not want to try on a new lens or framework from which to view, describe, and eventually map out and analyze their various interactions in oppressive schools and society. The macro interactions of authority, class, gender, race, etc. and other "power relations," specifically, admin-istrative hierarchical relations, tend to cover over more intermediate spaces and immediate links between and amongst people – students, teachers, administrators, parents, aides – as they struggle for power, identity, and meaning in their school places.

Thus, the question must be asked: What is hegemony in schools and society and the world? Does hegemony take on different forms in different places or are they transcedent to these influences? Once again, I refer to Kincheloe (2004b), who defines hegemony as: "the process by which dominant groups seek to impose their belief structures on individuals for the purpose of solidifying their power over them." Thus, Kincheloe, concludes, "hegemony seeks to win the consent of the governed to their own subjugation without the use of coercion or force (p. 15)."

RE-DEFINING HEGEMONY POST-STRUCTURALLY: DIALOGUE AS DISCURSIVE MAPPING

The remaining sections of this chapter will thusly redefine hegemony as including its possible counter-hegemonic elements, including how, in post-structural terms, the *macro* and *micro* are linked together onto a terrain of *meso* or in-between chains of signifiers, subject-positions, and surfaces on which those caught in hegemony may, nevertheless, inscribe, de-inscribe, and re-inscribe on these surfaces of their subject-positions new spaces or revise old spaces in which to wage counter-hegemonic struggles in the schools, classrooms and communities.[47] This inscriptive process is accomplished by a process of articulation in discourse (Laclau, 1977, 1985, 1990, 1993, 1996, 2005, 2007) in which dialogue is just one position in vast field of other discursive positions. These discursive processes also include a notion of consciousness as a discursive construct constituted by many forms, including whole and consistent modernist states of subjectivity as well as the subject or consciousness as borne and active in language as a signifier or dispersed as many signifiers. In the discursive realm, there may also lie more spaces for other forms of consciousness as derived in discourse through processes linking the unconsciousness to consciousness via intra-, inter-, and trans discourses in acts of identification (Hennessey, 1993; Pechuex, 1982; P. Smith, 1989; Strickland, 2005; Weedon, 1997).

This process of articulation, to be further discussed in Chapter 4, occurs "tendentially" (Thomassen, 2005). Various members of a discursive formation inscribe upon their own and each other's surfaces subject-positions or inscriptions, codes, images, feelings, thoughts, texts, rituals and more what they intend, partially intend, and desire and demand. What accrues along these surfaces are diverse spaces or partial spaces and, as the dictionary defines articulation, the construction of "flexible joints" which hold the parts of the whole together in relation to each other and the whole. This means, depending how a discursive formation interacts with other discursive formations or constituent parts of its own, how when inscribing or being inscribed in their subject-positions – including interacting with past inscriptions, as well as with present inscriptions – often opposite and contradictory – they inscribe and are inscribed by the same and different discursive formations they are simultaneously members. Hence, the notion of "tendential" comes into play as a process in which there may be a mixed or sharing of various marks of opposing positions in aligning, overlapping, and differential degrees.[48]

Also, there is a need to explore how chains of signifiers, which carve out subject-positions (Coward and Ellis, 1977, pp. 3, 8) link one discursive formation to another in complex and interacting, intersecting, and overlapping chains forming the surfaces of subject-positions on which they are further inscribed and revised. It is incumbent for those seeking a post-structuralist mode of theorizing counter-hegemonic teaching to see those "flexible joints" which hold together, tighten and loosen their holds as meanings and messages, and how the surfaces of subject-positions get inscribed and over-inscribed or how communication between students, teachers, and teacher educators emerge as complex discursive formations, one overlapping and unevenly aligned and imbricated to one another. In these configurations, much will depend on how links in chains as metonymic or metaphoric, during signifier activities, produce images or senses of thought which are not merely low level or adventitious fleeting thoughts, not to be taken seriously. Rather, in the case of metonymies or metonymic signifiers whose words and images are articulated from dissatisfied and angry students, which weave their feelings in and through labels. Educators too easily dismiss such behaviors as "disruptive" or "disciplinary problems."

In these weaved knots of meanings and feelings, student and teacher may map out, upon loosening them, what their dissatisfaction is grounded on and why they, as in Freire's book (2002), the oppressed oppress themselves and each other in deference to and for the benefit of the oppressor. Mapping out the journey of hierarchical and metonymic signifiers, as they carve out subject-positions and the surfaces on which student and teacher may inscribe their problems and predicaments, exposes a network of parts replicating to the whole or contexts within contexts, chains within chains. They are linked together by a variety of hierarchical and hegemonic signifiers and subject-positions in accordance to one's class, race, gender, and authoritarian positions, to the complex ways they sort out these structural positions, by how they construct and re-construct their subject-positions and re-align these chains of signifiers or meanings which come, surprisingly, by the use of simple words, gestures, images, feelings and desires articulated.

Thus, a person or student, teacher or teacher educator who interacts with each other from a variety of power relations and discursive communities – i.e. a black women student who is gay, unemployed, and a feminist but whose family originates from the Caribbean working class, but who emigrated to America for more opportunity, may interact very differently with a person who is also a women, white, from the middle class, sympathetic towards feminism, and whose husband owns a local factory in which the first women works.[49]

This book is therefore written to reveal how the privileged and their offspring, the inheritors of a privileged future, not only get reproduced in discourses of the classroom, but further, how this is not a pure and untrammeled territory, unblemished by the struggles of those without such privileges and powers. That is, I seek to expose how and why we are stopped or frozen into positions which hegemonize us or, conversely, put us into subject-positions of ambivalence or possible hesitancy leading to new solidarities and movements. Why, for example, would some of us turn our heads away in silence, when a fellow worker was arbitrarily dismissed with no reason or due process? Or, why some of us are too afraid to speak out and up? To speak out and up in schools requires more than courage. Educators and students require a supportive framework by which to name, frame, strategize, and finally organize their resistances and negotiations in order to facilitate them to break out of the insidious and self-defeating practices of "lying low." In effect, we need a tool kit, as Gee (1993) maintains, in which hegemonic discourses and their associated chains of signifiers, subject-positions and surfaces, can be mapped out and accounted for in new qualitative strategies of research and action.

The question this book must raise, therefore, is: What is counter-hegemonic teaching? And, does this force position hegemonic forces and activities in today's schools and teaching practices? Taking a cautionary note on the subject: How do we lay out a vision and a map of counter-hegemony but, at the same time, attend to those other forces, often dominant, overbearing, and intimidating to teachers and students? How can we attempt to find spaces for articulating a counter-hegemonic perspective without being folded into the co-option of administrative discourses, codes, and systems? How can we differentiate between an appearance of democracy in word or label and what such rubrics may hide in terms of latent and real struggles and resistances? Is there a medium or middle space to understand the hegemonic processes as they occur in language as a discourse?

In an effort to reveal how "in-between" spaces in struggle may become displaced, replaced, and transformed, we must look beyond the post-structuralist dimensions of words, language and discourse. We must cross over and peer into the splits or binarisms which have characterized modernist views and which post-structrualist and post-post-structuralism seeks to revise in terms of which segments of social reality and schools become parts of the discursive, parts of the symbolic, and parts of the real dimensions of language. On these points, which I will take up in Chapter 4, I will now turn attention toward making maps to reveal how hegemony folds into counter-hegemonic teaching processes in language as a discourse emerges.

WHAT IS COUNTER-HEGEMONIC TEACHING? NEEDED A REFLECTION IN THE ACTION METHODOLOGY

When anyone asks me the question: "what is counter-hegemonic teaching," I always reply by keeping an eye on the reflection-action splits or binarisms characteristic modernist thinking. Ultimately, I come to the notion of *reflection in the action*, and I hope I have answered the question. Of course, this response is not adequate to a complex and critical post-structuralist interpretation. I then move forward, and question such a reflection as an act in itself which may occur before, during, and after actions of teaching. I point to a kind of reflection that occurs in the action or, just as I took notice earlier in this chapter, how Berger and Luckmann's understanding of construction of reality is not necessarily occurring in a linear sequence in which reflection or action come before and after each other, but on a plane they under-theorized, but nevertheless, attributed to those constructions which may be borne *in* reflection or reflection *in the action* as opposed to *before* or *after* the action.

I attempt to illustrate a few examples of everyday occurrences to make my point about reflection as occurring in the action: What are those moments, I ask, when you leave a room, and, suddenly, you know you forgot something? While you cannot yet articulate what this experience is but, somehow, you know what is happening (I left something behind) and a moment or feeling comes to you (I forgot something). What that something is, and as you question this feeling-thought, is, you cannot know for sure, but you know something is missing.

And what about those moments in which, as you are talking to another, there are those moments in which you no longer have to pause and think and then act to speak or speak to act. All you have to do is keep talking as you think and think as you are talking. Are these moments, somehow, tied to talking and thinking, a reflection linked in action as being with another? That is, in the interaction or inter-subjectivity with the other, at a point of closeness, as Berger and Luckmann (1966) argue, you sense something. I then add, at this point of closeness, chains of signifiers trigger memory (a subject-position I have arrived on), and then, when another chain of signifiers (what is this something missing?) become articulated by another chain, which suddenly intervenes, and posits me onto another subject-position, as I (or my memory) is suddenly constructed into yet another and new subject-position. Hence, I suddenly recall what I have just forgot and which broke my previous "chain of thought," a moment before. Aren't these moments in which you know you are thinking clearly and critically, and yet, do not have to pause before talking, or pause after thinking? Why and how do these processes occur?

Such questions and subsequent conversations inevitably end up into other conversations critical of teaching, curriculum, and testing practices. For instance, I recall another conversation in which whether or not one should teach evolution or creationism or both in schools? One usually mentions science in the traditional or positivist sense in which one cannot link beliefs and values to facts. The conversation may go and eventually acknowledge science (or math) as objective and religion a "softer" human or social science. At this moment, I recall sitting with friend, my old friend, David, in many seminars we took together at Teachers College over thirty five years ago. Reading many of Huebner's articles,[50] we reflected on a newspaper editorial about teaching evolution or creationism. Critiquing this dualism between natural science and the human/social sciences, and seeing the distinctness of both fields along with their accompanying rationalities and methods of research, I maintained that such scientists are not real or "true" scientists.

As Huebner would hint to us when we were students, it is not so much about taking a narrow view on methodology which counts. Much more is involved in establishing the parameters of a "real" science or math. Indeed, I have asked myself, how do we know what we are seeing or experiencing is a real or a true event? While the dominant paradigm of natural science (the one that is dominant in current educational research then and today) has a definite answer to this question in terms of applying tests to measure what can be seen as true or probable; or, what is observer-able (i.e. learning outcomes using neutral and unbiased instruments in order to make reliable and valid assessments and predictions), I question these procedures of research methods and teaching today as the only available methods of research and theorizing to educators.

Needed, I argue, are other instruments, more sensitive and able to pick up what is not completely observer-able or measureable (Bogden and Bilkin, 1992; Carspeaken, 1996; Durham & Kellner, 2006), as well as how to collect and analyze new data, grounded on not necessarily statistical analysis but post-structuralist "stories" of "mapping." This data comes about when one senses in the field of their research, through post-structuralist constructs that what is missing are those aspects or dimensions which are complex and contradictory. I also feel that other constructs as truth, validity, confidence, and trustworthiness – as well as criteria from so-called qualitative researchers may be transcended, as divides between quantitative and qualitative research methodologies – is simply not enough to account for complex, contradictory, and quasi-intentional acts.[51]

Rather than being caught by the horns of a methodological dilemma, I began to think of what is *real* and what is *imaginary* in both dimensions. And, with the help of reading Jacques Lacan,[52] I began to imagine an intervening terrain, the *symbolic,*[53] and within its borders, how power and power relations become further constituted and constructed in discursive formations of race, class, gender, and authority as a hierarchical structure. In this process, I decided to add or complement school authority as a power relation and power signifier chain, to the "holy trinity" of race, class, and gender relations specific to administrative school hierarchies because so much of what is done in schools – with its overlapping testing, classroom management, and supervision by administrators (along with ability classifications, inclusion, and threats of censorship and administrative reprisals) – occurs in and through these traditional power relations. Moreover, omitting administrative and hierarchical chains of signifiers and discursive formations (or their invasion onto student and teacher constructed chains of signifiers, subject-positions, and discursive formations), would truncate too large a piece of the puzzle in assessing and finding/producing spaces for new discursive formations relevant to establishing social justice, equality, and more democracy in schools and teaching.[54]

The above writers provide perspectives which widen views of the world and people's relations to its power structures beyond modernist divisions as designated in traditional treatments of class, race, and gender as classical Marxists tend to posit them, and adding the element of overlapping and intersecting subject-positions in which experiences are imagined, symbolized, and felt. Post-structuralists do not ignore these "mixed" power effects of power relations. Rather, they envision the complex journey through which power passes through a complex of discursive formations, linked up to each other via respective chains of signifiers, subject-positions, and surfaces of inscription as they *interpolate* one another.[55] They see themselves and the others "through" ideas posited by traditional Marxists who consider categories as class and the economy as mutually exclusive from categories as culture, ideology, history, and feelings. To post-structualists more is involved in a subject-position;[56] they are the places whereby one gets stirred, incited, and mobilized into action and the basis for people and movements to galvanize into mass movements (as opposed to waiting for the "right moment" in which the "vanguard" of the masses take charge as hierarchical leaders). Post-structualists, thereby avoid rooting the subject or consciousness as a metaphysical entity in which ideas are borne and are contained in one's heads or as epiphenomena rising above the economic base of production, segregating the base from its super-structures.

While more contemporary post-structuralists seek to find ways to complement, rather than compete with, various strands of post-Marxism, post-colonialism, feminism, popular cultures, cultural politics, media studies, literary criticism, linguistics, and psychoanalytical treatments of society and schools, they nevertheless seek to transform the hegemonic divides between traditional critical pedagogy and more recent renditions of "post-hegemonic" phases of critical pedagogy in giving impetus to those "new movements" which support counter-hegemonic movements and discourses in schools and societies, here and around the world.

This book seeks to establish a framework in which present day students and teachers can posit as problematic post-structurally, by using the seminal works of Freire which to date may, inadvertently by its modernist roots, block or discourage student-teacher-teacher educator solidarities and their potential counter-hegemonic activities. Presently, the separation and contradiction of student and teacher remain fixed in a hegemony which divides and deters collectivities between students and teachers from forming and thereby beginning to act as agents for building democratic and professionally autonomous schools of education and classroom practices.

Whether in-service courses in public schools or those courses in schools of education in charge of certifying and preparing teachers, teachers will need to discover how they can be more collectivizing with students and parents, as opposed to individualistic in formulating new concepts and strategies for counter-hegemonic teacher practices. This means tough questions must be asked. Why should administrative hierarchies continue, or classroom management practices, and the onerous regimen of testing continue and which does not, as we have been following the news, "close the achievement gap" of poor, minority, and dissenting groups of students, teachers, and teacher educators? And, as we shall see in the next chapter, testing actually encourages students to drop out or be pushed out in order for schools to maintain increased or improved test score averages, and to which principals and teachers feel necessary because their jobs depend on such increases to define their competences or "qualifications." Therefore, testing and closely linked to classroom management and administrator or supervision and surveillance, are not only unnecessary schools practices, but often, harmful in supporting discriminating practices against those whose survival depend on student test score outcomes (Meier, 1999; Ohanian, 1997) and whose tenure as a student may be ended by a few failing tests at very young ages. If you are a member of one or all of these groups, this book is intended for you as one of its primary audiences.

WHO CAN BENEFIT FROM THIS BOOK?

This book is for all who want to know more about education. Specifically, its purposes and how it is affected by huge and complex administrative systems. This book examines how education is affected by supervisory systems, world globalization practices and markets, massive innovations of technology, science and media, and world events further mediating student and teacher in a massive and complex discursive formation, and whether or not they are an intrusion or of help in the formation of student and teacher identities, relations, and knowledge-making. Moreover, this book intends to reveal how teachers and their students may form "new" social and power relations with each other when hegemonic forces seek to discourage and destroy such spaces required for respect of their definitions, actions, and powers.

This book is also for those who can deliver messages of teacher education programs, as in the case of those teacher educators and professors of education who may be silent or non-involved in maintaining or resisting regulated practices as determined by hierarchicalized administrators and deans, accreditation agencies linked to the state, tenure and exploitative labor-adjunct arrangements, and more. In the case of public schools, this book reveals how teaching may be supervised and evaluated without the pressures of the current "testing craze" as linked to student outcomes of standardized test scores without regard to student's context (poverty, disabled, immigrant ESL, etc.). It also addresses how teacher educator practices are further linked to this limited classroom management focus by websites such as www.ratemyprofessor.com which, I believe, have been devised to pit students and teachers against one another, liberals against conservatives, instead of having them join together to overcome those hierarchical and administrative systems of regulation which mutually victimize both.

Finally, this book offers those involved in schooling with an alternate view and perspective, of the existing regimen of controls in schools which hegemonize students and teachers into thinking that their school environment and its hierarchical divisions are inevitable and sufficient to conduct business as usual. That is, student and teacher can begin to ask a basic question: to what degree are schools or college education courses an extension of their creative and cooperative thinking and acting; or, conversely, to what degree are they an extension of the hierarchical forces functioning to hegemonize them? Once this question is asked, answered, and shared, those who feel dissatisfied may begin to act in concert in counter-hegemonic blocs, unions, grass-root and fusion group (Sartre, 1960) arrangements in order to expose and break apart the illusions which operate toward making them into standardized and regulated automatons and extensions of an unquestioning school administrative system and hierarchy, which, in turn, makes them extensions of an uncaring and insensitive public, state, economy, culture, and school. On this note, I ask the reader to think of how Freire's *Pedagogy of the Oppressed* addresses the above concerns, albeit written in a different time and place. This will be further discussed in Chapters 3 and 4 which are dedicated to re-examining the foundations of critical pedagogy and Freire's *Pedagogy of the Oppressed.*

OUTLINE OF REMAINING CHAPTERS

To accomplish the goals outlined above, *Counter-Hegemonic Teaching* will study and analyze hegemony, further pushing the envelope of critical pedagogy. Toward this end, Chapter 2 will set the context of administrative systems of hierarchical control and authority in schools with various case studies, student presentations, and snippets. I refer to these forms of administrative controls and systems as administrative hierarchies, classroom management techniques and procedures, testing, and an online website used by education students called www.ratemyprofessor.com as "Pillars of Hegemony."

In Chapter 3, I examine an activity I have done with education students for the last eight years. After reading Freire's *Pedagogy of the Oppressed*, the students meet in small groups, and illustrate on transparency paper with color pens, their reactions to Freire's methods, philosophy, and visions. The exercise reveals deep levels of information emanating from their expressions and, in the case of analyzing and extending Freire's *Pedagogy of the Oppressed* – in terms of his modernist presuppositions. The student's drawings provide indicators of how and what changes may be appropriate in extending *Pedagogy of the Oppressed*.[57] I will reveal some of their feelings and images, as expressed through their drawings, cross referenced with themes of the presentations and case studies discussed in Chapters 2.

Chapter 4 is intended to provide a theoretical context in which new issues and problems of hegemony may be analyzed in their advanced and complex forms and how counter-hegemonic theorizing and teaching may be achieved. This chapter will also reflect on the findings of the previous three chapters.

And, Chapter 5 will summarize the implications of doing counter-hegemonic teaching and post-structural theorizing, along with reflecting critically on the assumptions of Freire, by re-mapping the terrain of critical pedagogy and what *Counter-Hegemonic Teaching* may offer to advance the field of critical pedagogy into a "post-hegemonic state."

CHAPTER 2

PILLARS OF SCHOOL AND CLASSROOM HEGEMONY: ADMINISTRATOR HIERARCHIES, CLASSROOM MANAGEMENT, TESTING, TENURE, AND WWW.RATEMYPROCESSOR.COM

INTRODUCTION

In this chapter, we will discuss what hegemony may look like as a process from the view point of what hierarchical structures of administrative authority may look like as it intrudes into student and teacher discourses from the perspective of educating students who are already teachers and administrators, as well as prospective teachers and administrators. Four "pillars of hegemony" are outlined in this chapter to show how power enters the classroom, as negotiated by those affected, and often, unbeknown to them. These pillars are by no means exhaustive of other pillars or places in which power rears its head, hegemonizing student and teacher criticism and potential counter-hegemonic resistances. As I have written in other places, hegemony may seep into the teaching of social studies (2007), the teaching of ESL and immigrant students (2001a, 2004), and special education students (1998, 2001b, 2005).

The first pillar of hegemony – administrative hierarchies – are aligned to hierarchical structures of authority and practices, as in special education labeling, which replicates hierarchical relationships and in which one student labels the other as "slow, as well as appealing to administrators to resolve their conflicts with their teachers,. The second pillar, classroom management, intercedes into student and teacher relating by the ways teachers respond to students when they "act out" and are labeled as "disruptive" or "discipline problems" in need of classroom management techniques. A third pillar of hegemony, testing, pressures student and teacher to achieve high test score results progressively. As mandated in NCLB, students across the country must increase their overall test scores each year. While some schools already have excellent test score results, if they do not achieve a certain level of advancement in test scores, they may be targeted for "growth" or improvement in raising their low grades averages when compared to those schools which advanced more because their average test score results were so low to begin with. In addition to these test results being publicized on websites and local community newspapers, a fourth pillar of hegemony is prevalent and felt by teacher educators who, along with all other professors throughout the country, are being evaluated by their students on the website www.ratemyprofessor.com and the impending www.ratemyteacher.com. And, finally, the fifth pillar is tenure.

These discourses – "pillars of hegemony" – and their substantial "processes of hegemony" remain discursive formations within their own right and may also be located within and linked to other discursive formations – student and teacher solidarities – which may resist them; or, may become a part of dominant discursive formations while resisting them as they are caught, in post-structural terms, on intertwining chains of signifiers, subject-positions, and surfaces of inscriptions which we will be further discussed at length in Chapter 4.

THE INTER-CONNECTED PILLARS OF HEGEMONY: TESTING, ADMINISTRATIVE HIERARCHIES, TENURE, CLASSROOM MANAGEMENT, AND RATEMYPROFESSOR.COM

Consequently, within the five pillars of school and classroom hegemony – administrative hierarchies, classroom management, testing, tenure, and websites in which students evaluate their professors anonymously – students and teachers (and teacher educators) are becoming more and more watched or evaluated, and their test results are more and more being used to evaluate both them and their teachers and schools. These test scores are very linear (i.e. bubble multiple choice type) rather than being in-depth and explanatory. Scores are capped by letter grades (A, B, C, D. and F) published periodically in local community newspapers and websites. Often, real estate values and community reputations are closely aligned to these test scores results. Often, we hear about students doing well in their schools but, just as often we hear about how schools are receiving "F's" when, in the previous year, they were doing "A" work. The notion of constantly improving test scores as mandated and the extent of such progress as measured with linear, norm-referenced tests, seeking to achieve time-scheduled deadlines for annual improvement and progress is beginning to become exposed and opposed by parent and teacher groups.[58]

The notion of both evaluating students against their previous test scores as a basis that demands constant growth, and then, no matter what the previous year's score was, somehow, the same students must do better the following year, seems unreasonable. For example, if students are doing "A" work, there is little room for improvement or "growth." Or, in the case of students who, in one year did "F" work, but in the second year advanced to "C" work, now receive a "A" for their ability to out-perform growth measurements compared to those who are doing "A" work! Needless to say, these test score results and the public acceptance of these test regimens have been met by both teachers and parents with great resentment and controversy.[59] Still, questions may be raised: Is this method of assessment enough to mount a resistance against the powers-to-be other than sporadic signs? And if sporadic, how do we interpret these signs in mounting larger forms of organized resistance?

To add to these irregularities, we hear about "comparable" test scores. This happens when one school is being compared to a similar populated school of poor, people of color, and disabled. Measurements continue to be applied to these students as including students who are also classified in special education, and students who speak English as a Second Language. While only a year or two is allowed for the later group to catch up and speak English fluently, thereby mixing them and their special education students into the same pool of regular students taking standardized exams. These practices, however, become further compounded when other irregularities are reflected in usually higher test score results by locally produced tests as opposed to those test score results produced by the federal government under *No Child Left Behind*.[60]

The harm and disarray which comes about when interpreting these scores has not stopped the politicians and school administrators from firing or transferring teachers, closing down schools, and consequently re-opening the same schools under different names or labels, armed with new teachers, often less experienced or "qualified"[61] than their predecessors. Schools continue to be embattled by a "testing craze" which principals obsess on and teachers and students are pressured and unnerved by and, in so doing, produce an overly competitive environment long noted to be harmful to students is perpetuated.[62]

In addition, I have heard stories recounted by my own students in education courses on how test pressures are overflowing into more than methods of teaching or "instruction." These students contend that test pressures are limiting, if not dismissive of content they feel they ought to have the time to teach but cannot because of "test-prepping" pressures. They reveal how so much pressure to teach math, reading, and science has begun to seriously compromise or eliminate the teaching of other subjects – as social studies, literature, art, dance, music, physical education, and the "humanities."[63] In addition, there are accounts linking tensions in schools between testing to unruly and resistant students, who are more and more being referred and labeled to school authorities as "discipline problems."[64] Teachers, school districts, and schools of education are more and more responding to this crisis in retroactive ways; specifically, institutionalizing or making mandatory course requirements emphasizing classroom management techniques and skills.[65]

Hiring practices in colleges of education have also taken a retroactive response in which prospective instructors for science and math are hired under much higher wages with small class sizes, whereas those instructors who get hired to teach more general or social oriented classes, as foundation and social studies courses, get hired under lower pay rates and titles, often receiving classes of 60-70 students. This overloading and increased of class sizes tends to make these classes as taught by lecture as opposed to a discussion group formats. In an ad I noticed seeking professorial employment I took note of how a critical pedagogy position was open only to math teachers! While this does not mean math teachers cannot teach critical pedagogy, it does mean that the subject matter dealing with basically a number as a form of articulation as opposed to a form of discussion, common to the social sciences and humanities, lends itself to more positivist types of "critical rationality." In this regard, it is easy to see why literacy critics as Gerald Garaff[66] and others have called for the need to make critical pedagogy more "standardized."

RE-EMERGENCE OF MORE STANDARDIZATION IN THE CURRICULUM

Once again, linking natural science as a preferential link to critical pedagogy may threaten to incorporate the humanities and social science disciplines more and more into the positivistic mold of science over and against alternate formats. This, in turn, may also threaten to eliminate more qualitative forms of assessment – as portfolios and authentic forms of assessment – moving the field toward more numbers and test scores. No doubt, the trend of a growing need for accountability by numbers as opposed to other qualitative dimensions for learning and testing is one which remains a stalwart one, unwilling to yield further ground. This may be why pedagogy and instruction strategies have become more and more scripted (i.e. SRA and Madeline Hunter curricula), yielding only the "essentials" of school knowledge and teacher practices, as in the so-called "best practices." And, at schools on the level of leadership, school administrators are becoming more and more finding themselves in roles of becoming police officers, "sweeping the floors" of their schools for the removing of any noise or distractions, and entering classrooms with an eye on supervising teachers and their students to be "on task," so that the smooth teaching mode of "effectiveness" for test preparation can come about and be maintained in a robot-like atmosphere in today's schools.[67]

As an evaluator myself of several community college faculties, who were former and practicing school administrators serving as instructors to alternate programs of a Master's degree in education, I have also come upon how some administrators turned instructors disguise their former roles from administrators to becoming instructional leaders. As they have reported to me in post observation conferences, they maintain their mixed roles as school managers and school instructors by insisting to their students, future teachers, they must support classroom practices – as the buzz words they refer to as "dialogue," "problem-solving," "collaboration," and "inquiry." However, as I have also observed in their classrooms as well, the same instructors who ask their students to support classroom dialogue also support, without missing a beat, give fastidious allegiance to lecture and proctoring the standardized exams of their students. Little accounting is done to differentiate how classes are marked by discipline problems attributed to test preparation, however. For example, students who are in special education get frustrated in test preparation, and during the actual test taking, their frustration may lead to student misconduct or other, more systematic dysfunctional factors.[68]

When I discussed this and other issues with these same instructors, I discovered they had problems differentiating between those discourses which are child-centered and discussion formatted and those discourses that pander to classroom management and higher test scores. As one of my bullets in the previous chapter indicated, some of these instructors combine discussion formats while lecturing about correct procedures for proctoring such exams. When their education students ask questions on this issue, the instructor usually responds in one discourse or another, dialogic-student centered or test and teacher lecture centered. In their attempt to ward off further questioning on their inconsistencies on the subject, administrators who were hired as instructors respond by compartmentalizing both discourses but who give their final allegiance to traditional or top-down forms of teaching philosophy. Left in the dark, both these instructors and their students do not get to see the overlapping and intrusive dimensions of how they are hegemonically or unwittingly giving their consent to such inconsistent and contradictory practices.[69]

Hierarchies, and their administrative representatives as well as striking fear and obedience into students and teachers to take hierarchical subject-positions, affecting their relating to each other, and thereby, coercing students and teachers to take, unwittingly, subject-positions of identification along hierarchical chains of signifiers as opposed of creating their own subject-positions, have and still do, provide for a powerful (and insidious) force field of teacher and student surveillance. As I have observed with my doctorate study on special education students, there is a tendency on part of these students to displace and carry over onto others underneath them the same mistreatments they receive from their high-ups. They refer to this kind of behavior as "one-downing" each other. That is, just as one special education student ridiculed another by referring to each other as "slow." Similarly, school administrators, turned college instructors, likewise do the same thing when they call attention to the need for more classroom management, thereby marginalizing "theory" or subjects related to critical thinking and critical pedagogy. This rationale is carried over to their students, future teachers in waiting, to belittle theory over classroom management (Fleischer, 2006).

In other ways, students and teachers also are very much affected by administrative and hierarchical discursive force fields constituting their daily lives in schools, whether in schools or schools of education in higher education. Namely, the widespread pre-scripted curricula and enforcement of standardized tests – high stake testing – have and continue to produce an intense climate of competitiveness which student and teacher encounter and which overlays administrative authority so one cannot see the relational links between them and the administrators. Moreover, other classroom management techniques teachers deploy which intervene in their present interactions between themselves and their students have profound effects. For example, a few of my education students have reported to me that they "feel good" about all the administrative regulations and the surveillance of their classrooms, particularly that administrators are constantly "sweeping the floors" and "poking their heads into their classrooms unannounced." I took note of the sadistic pleasure this student felt watching her students "sweat" while she proctored them on such exams.

Further, there are those principals, and through them parents (usually middle class), who want to see classrooms not just as "test mills" but, rather, as places where their students can dialogue and learn through student-centered approaches via smaller class size and smaller groups for differential and individualized learning techniques. In these scenarios, however, I have also observed, specifically, on www.ratemyprofessor.com how middle class students decry such approaches as "the teacher never teaches," "we have to teach ourselves through small groups," "The teacher is lazy and too liberal and never teaches." Still, what remains an overarching link to both approaches is the competitive climate in which students remain at each other's "throats" and at the teachers as well. There's a fostered need to constantly compete for grades with and against each other, other classrooms, schools and school districts. This competitiveness carries over into teacher relations.

I have often seen upon visiting my students at their teaching jobs, a "gloating" of expressions on teachers' faces, when they hear that one of their colleagues is being terminated or "let go." While one may want to know why a teacher gets pleasure out of another teacher suffering or undergoing the experience of termination, generally, this experience gets covered over by glib explanations as "the survival the fittest." Rather than hearing the merits of each case as to why a teacher is being fired or why a teacher who was let go, some of my students explained to me: "she (referring to the teacher let go) allowed the students to come into class with their i-pods, as a means to make the students feel at home and comfortable against the pressures for preparing for the tests."

Further, on the college level, wedging student against instructor, a competitive device has been recently borne to pit one student against another, as well as instructors and deans, against other instructors. I have noticed how college deans and administrators[70] observe their instructors indirectly on the website www.ratemyprofessor.com and are constantly logging in to see how the students perceive their professors. Deans usually don't have to teach courses or be subject to what is often deemed as "harsh student critiques." As the president of the website, Michael Hussey, recently interviewed on the CNN's Larry King Show (July, 2008) indicated, this is a means to: "equalize unequal power relations between student and instructor." More recently, the website has provided a component in which instructors may "answer back," and therefore begin a dialogue with anonymous student complaints, though teachers are named. This fact, that teachers are named and accusers are not, makes the site more divisive rather than conciliatory in bringing together student and teacher.

One only has to login to see how slanted student comments are against the "liberal" instructors and how some students make instructors appear as too "radical," from not staying on task to "teaching them the facts." Rather than applaud instructors for encouraging students to meet in small groups to discuss and THINK, the same students that write negative comments attribute this method of teaching to instructors who are not teaching well, are lazy, and even display their incompetence by dialogical-student-centered approaches of teaching. More on the effects of this website will be discussed below.

As I have been arguing throughout these first two chapters, what is needed are not perspectives that exceed or extend notions of dialogical approaches to teaching as tantamount to critical pedagogy. Rather, what is needed is to complement such perspectives, are counter-hegemonic perspectives capable of seeing through discourses as more than a dyadic arrangement between two or more individuals. Thus, what has become dominant is dialogue grounded on highly individualistic centered notions of intentionality or a unified consciousness in which reflection and action are structured as a sequence, acts prior to agency and intervention, including ignoring how dialogue becomes bound to a notion of serving as an "escape valve" for defusing more differentiated yet sensitive blocs of solidarity and subject-position formations by taking issue with existent hierarchical power relations. One such form I discussed in my 1978 article revealed how dialogue was used as one method among others constituting a repertoire of methods for subverting or distracting critical teaching in schools.

By making distinctions of dialogue – "dialogue" which includes but does not penetrate barriers which may be opposed to hierarchical school arrangements and their discourses, there remains ignored in the critical pedagogy literature a political conversational construct. One may see how dialogue, as one moment overlaying surfaces of power, make up other layers in discursive formations, overlook the impact of constitutive chains of signifiers, subject-positions, and surfaces in which student and teacher inscribe their messages and meanings relationally as opposed to top down. They give the illusion that "talk" may be tolerated in hierarchical structures of authority, but only to a certain point – i.e. to the point that the outcome of dialogical problem posing does not disrupt or disturb the administrative and hierarchical structures of authority.

I'll never forget the expressions on the faces of my colleagues at a large suburban high school, the last school I taught at full time, a place known to be "liberal" and "progressive" as their eyes veered away from me when an administrator's emissary, a teacher, suddenly entered my classroom and asked me into the hall and escorted me out of the building in front of my class of thirty students. I left the school that day and never returned. The charges lodged against me were from one parent and student's complaint. The student constantly walked into my classroom with a bible couched against his black suit, and, through his parent, insisted that because I was teaching about a comparison of the United States and the Soviet Union (which I was assigned to teach and the textbook required to teach units from Edwin Fenton's social studies book on the subject – a leader of the "new" social studies curricula at the time), along with a unit to teach about the "Storpenberg Affair" in which high level commanders of the German army conspire to kill Adolf Hitler. The student and his father lobbied to have me removed because, they believed, I was pro-liberal or "Marxist" and held a "Jewish" view. As I walked through the halls of this gigantic school, I saw no one come out to say good bye or offer me solace, as a fellow "liberal" teacher. Instead, they simply veered their eyes away. More discussion below will ensue on how dialogue may or may not begin with counter-hegemonic teaching in Chapter 4.

TENURE: IS THIS THE PROBLEM?

While I always thought tenure would allow individuals to "speak out" on controversial and sensitive issues, I could not square this with how some teachers merely diverted their eyes from the situation at the suburban high school, and how so many others that month were persecuted and eliminated. The union memo was dilatory in informing the faculty of these "purges." While controversy has continued for over 40 years as to whether tenure should exist, since I was not a tenured teacher, such discussions at the time were irrelevant to me and other non-tenured teachers chosen as examples to "shut up." We were liberal scapegoats at a time when the War in Viet Nam under Nixon was as disquieting and Big Brotherish as the recent War in Iraq under the Bush administration.[71]

I wish to provide a context pointing to the intense climate of testing, along with classroom management techniques, and administrative hierarchical practices, as a complexity of discourses making up an overarching canvass on which other discourses and the discursive formations are etched, using excerpts from my special education study, along with my first article in 1978, which will provide some concrete background on which to further elaborate how, through post-structural constructs, counter-hegemonic teaching may be further understood.

That is to say, stitched into the above discourses,[72] the remaining elements in this chapter will show how, through the circulation of signifiers and their chains and subject-positions and surfaces for inscribing one's feeling, thoughts, and desires – often complex and contradictory – one can see through such layers of discourse as layered within administrative, classroom management, and testing student-teacher relations or discursive formations. Further intervening these layers, one may also see how emphasis on either dialogue without positing these layers as serving hierarchical school discourses as well as counter-hierarchical discourses and their respective constructs (chains of signifiers, subject-positions, and surfaces of articulation), only serves to maintain and further envelop student and teacher from piercing through such discourses, and thereby, inhibit or deny them from joining each other in constructing new discursive formations capable of counter-hegemonic teaching and learning.

While schools and teachers are pressured in struggling to attain the overly competitive school environments of testing, and how tests are linked to teacher competence and keeping their jobs, along with further monetary rewards for administrators to "watch" teacher and student production in order to "weed out" those not producing, under the present regimen of norm-referenced tests instituted by *No Child Left Behind* and its emphasis on "accumulatively progress" or yearly increased test scores, there may be changes on the horizon with the ascendancy of the Obama administration. If for no other reason, local and state governments have already began to offset poor student national test results with tests of their own, which to no one's surprise, students seem to do always better than on the national tests administered under NCLB. There remains, then, questions as to how in the near future these discrepancies can continue to operate in silence without further outcries demanding rectification.[73]

In this maelstrom of pressure and a willingness to pander to the authorities, administrative and government officials condone increased test pressures, along with responding to parent pressures – wanting to have their children be more competent to do well and be better prepared – as well as others – real estate agents and banks – seeking to keep their school and their children's test scores high because they are usually published in newspapers affecting their real estate values of their homes – there is a corresponding need for the students (and their teachers) to "dialogue" more, and therefore, break with the consistent boredom present in today's schools. However, in this test context of dialogue, as Good and Brophy (2008) indicate, this is at best a compromised and artificial position. Both authors, long time writers of the generally accepted national textbook in the United States for the last thirty years for teaching about teaching and curriculum insist that the way out of the problem is to abbreviate parts of social studies, literature, and humanities to make room for such conversations while maintaining rigid adherence to math, science, and reading skills.

Given the conservative nature of NCLB, there is also the fear of terrorism promulgated in today's schools. Even those provisions in NCLB which support social studies do so with the proviso that such teachings must be taught from "patriotic" standpoints of history – teaching the "good" or "positive" sides of American history as opposed to the "negative" sides which hold America up for critical inspection.[74] Whatever happened to truth, justice, and the American way? To keep the teaching staffs in American high schools aware of these political bends, draped by weekly and monthly visits from military recruiters on campus, clad in uniforms, questions remain as to how American youth are benefiting by legislation that insists might is right. Attempting to gain high school students as new conscripts to serve in a very unpopular war, and to police potential "trouble spots" in the world, the presence of the military, along with the limits of teaching controversial events from more "patriotic" social studies textbooks and materials, has trivialized the number of hours and validity of social studies in the American school system today.[75]

This hegemonic, bullish presence in our nation's high schools reveals how school administrators and the pablum they peddle and test on, increasingly, expose a pattern of hierarchical chains of signifiers and subject-positions, affecting not only what students and teachers may "read" and "write," but what they see and relate to, and how their identities are becoming molded by top-down, linear, and undemocratic, hierarchical school systems emphasizing conservative viewpoints dominating social studies lessons. While reducing to a large extent social studies as a vehicle for shallow forms of critical thinking (patriotism over dissent), this chapter is presented as a metonym complex consisting of administrative authority and overlaying this authority, how teacher and students are infiltrated by all five hierarchical chains of signifiers and discourses emphasizing: testing, resultant classroom management techniques, and those online spaces referred to as "discussion boards" or "dialogical" online websites. As we will show later in this chapter, with www.ratemyprofessor.com, confines discussions strictly within the frames limiting discussion to outcomes that marginalize "liberal" over "patriotic" histories, interpretations, and teaching methods.

This overall hegemonic or intimidating presence in our nation's high schools today also reveals how school administrators and the "correct" forms of how to write "correctly" (Fleischer, 2004), and what to study in various degrees of selection are more and more showing a pattern of hierarchical chains of signifiers and the subject-positions. These chains and subject-positions encouraged by such standardized and pre-scripted curricular regimens affect not only what students and teachers may "read" and "write, " but how their identities are becoming molded by top-down, linear, and undemocratic and hierarchical school systems.

In my 1978 article, it will become apparent that the popularity to experiment and "restructure" schools to become more "participatory," "constructive," and "democratic" may have done more to bring on the use of more school administrators intervening into teacher-student relations, rather than being supportive not only of their "dialogue," but further, of dialogical arrangements which may have led to more democratic and daring relations toward real power and democracy in schools whereby administrative and hierarchical arrangements are discarded or minimized in exchange for direct popular participation. Prior to my writing this article, I wrote a chapter in my first and failed doctoral attempt in 1977 on how "hierarchical structures of authority manipulate student and teacher classroom discourse." At this juncture of my life, I was partially aware of post-structural constructs of hegemony and discourse,[76] but surmised I needed a language (and so did the field of education) to further my insights, which would not become manifested until the 1990's of my second and successful doctoral dissertation attempt.[77]

ADMINISTRATORS AS SUPPORTS FOR TEACHER DIALOGUE: A NEW CONCEPT OF LEADERSHIP?

After spending years as a substitute teacher in New York City in the 1970s, along with making the effort to gain a doctorate degree (and thereby beat the blacklist against me teaching in high schools in Long Island), I became a member of an "emancipatory collective" in the late 1970s. The collective referred to themselves as students seeking a more democratic and socially just school system and society. In their third edition of their newsletter, *Left Open: A Newsletter of the Emancipatory Collective,*[78] which was disseminated throughout Teachers College, Columbia University in the Spring of 1978, I presented and contributed an article on critiquing liberal reforms to make flexible but fundamentally not changing the hierarchical systems of school administration and leadership. While critical pedagogical theorist and co-writer with Freire, Ira Shor had spoken at the collective three times (1980), I volunteered to submit and present an article of my own (with much cooperation, input, and editing from other members of the collective), and it was circulated to the faculty, administration, and student bodies of Columbia University. As my first published article, I made bold assertions about the curricula designed to be "dialogical" yet could not stand on its own. I chose a subject-matter which critiqued a senior ranking professor known for her liberal or innovative leanings, and was a co-director of a large consultant agency committed to re-structuring schools as more dialogical, humane, and democratic structured places. I critiqued the author of an article which was then published in the *Teachers College Record.* My intent was to see how the concept of dialogue, when mixed into the embrace of hierarchical administrators, was received. I also became familiar with the concept of hegemony and how it operated through language and ideology. That is, how hegemony works when educators represent schools as a social system with neutral and benevolent administrators and scientific studies presumably in support of teacher dialogue and school change.

Identifying myself as a "Marxist-humanist," I presented a framework in which the author I was critiquing[79] could be seen as an artifact of liberal-humanist language and ideology as opposed to real change and power re-alignments for anyone concerned with teacher behavior change management and improvement of systems to have schools and teacher-student relations become "really" or existentially democratic. I maintained that the author of the article expressed a viewpoint common to humanistic models of teacher supervision and school leadership, management of change, and improvement of teacher behavior. I began my critique by asking three questions:

Who gives the orders and takes them in schools?

How does humanistic talk change or at least confront these structures?

Doesn't the author of the article choose to merely re-arrange the given school environment rather than confront its administrative hierarchies?

To this day I maintain the positions in that paper. I admit the theoretical grounding of my framework was born from a kind of Marxist-humanist mixture which stressed the importance of individual control over work. I ask once again: Who controls the work in schools? I contend that "it was in the interests of administrators – whose jobs depended on it – to maintain hierarchies in which administrators control teachers, who in turn control students." I added: "(a)dministrative jobs are coveted by teachers who long to leave classrooms where teachers and students mutually victimize each other."

I also added that, in understanding schools, liberal-humanists merely wished to make schools more viable by making them appear as if some changes would make them flexible and democratic. I, however, make a distinction between those flexible changes and more fundamental changes inherent in institutionalized schools seeking to become more democratic and student-teacher participatory. I add that the author of the article failed to address or resolve deep seated tensions, as well as "overlooking oppressive realities" that are inherent in them. Having read Paulo Freire several times, along with the works of Berger and Luckman (1965), Schutz (1972), Bowles and Gintis (1976), and others, and being in the middle of my first dissertation attempt, I had knowledge – to some degree – of the politics and social elements in a school reality. Maintaining further in my critique that liberal-humanists –which could be compared to today's neo-liberals – "do not recognize that social relations in schools replicate authority structures of the larger society." I added: "because school relationships do not follow strict boss/worker lines, it has been easy to obscure the power differentials which govern educational institutions (p. 15)."

I insisted that the author's work and others like her, (1) lacked a critical component to examine their own theory of change within existing school authoritarian structures, and (2) lacked a referent in which to ground a critique that was radical enough to confront these authority structures. Contending that if these two deficiencies could be redressed, a more authentic humanism could be established in American schooling. Until then, theories and talk of humanistic (or dialogical) management models of schools would not be sufficient to bring about changes in leadership and supervision or changes in teacher relations with peers and students. That such talk of change would remain "Utopian dreams" or naïve accounts of change within public schools. I concluded that this is because schools remain "dominated by hierarchical authority structures and relationships of student-teacher subordination to administrators." All that liberals can do, I maintained, would be to apologize for these structures and relationships and therefore mislead those who work in such conditions with "false sense(s) of hope for change."

I approached the author's treatment of teacher dialogue. I focused on the notion of dialogue within yet not necessarily against hierarchical school structures of authority and how they manifest themselves in "discourse." I showed how the author's proposal of teacher dialogue as supported by a revised role for the principal, would only preserve the very same structures of authority which had to be changed if teacher shared leadership would emerge in schools. I took issue with the author's premise that the role of the principal is a "vital determinant to teacher morale, commitment, and dialogue" (p. 16). I further contended that "without further challenging or at least clarifying the structure of authority school principals operate in, principals serving as support systems to facilitate teacher dialogue would only be a sleight of hand change or an illusion of change, instead of mounting a real force for teacher autonomy and shared decision-making. The author, however, relied on corporation-university based research studies and modes of expert intervention rather than student-teacher grass-rooted collectivities.

While acknowledging the author's work as pointing to the need for teachers to come out of their classroom isolation as well as shifting attention away from merely focusing on the child (or their resulting test scores as we have today), and providing spaces for teachers to organize relationships with other teachers and administrators in "breaking down barriers of teacher-administrators," were at least promising as "liberating moments" as was the author's claims. That is to say, how teachers would take or have more "control or at least have a say in what affects their work in schools." But, I added in a cautionary note: "But any real say in what affects their work or sense of involvement must be backed by real power." I further contended that this "cannot happen in the present "hierarchical set-up of schooling as it presently stands." I concluded that the author's revision of the principal's role as a support for teacher dialogue without considering the authoritarian-hierarchical realties would be "subject to misuse and administrative manipulation of teachers and students." (pp. 16–17)

I took a moment to see what may happen when principals support teacher dialogue. I found that when teachers are exposed to research based on dialogue and facilitated by principals, teachers may become induced to talk to one another about new ideas. To the author, the key determinant in this moment is the revised role of the principal who acts as a facilitator and supporter of dialogue. Then, from a key phrase taken from the article describing this process, I cited the following phrase: "Life could be smooth sailing, then a principal would transfer and everything would drift into disarray." The author also narrated that "day-to-day relationships among school people reveal a system unlikely to respond to simple orders for compliance." I then reacted with the following:

"Perhaps so, is this writer's impression. But what drifted into disarray?

Was it that teacher dialogue fell apart the moment the old principal left the scene? And if so, is the presence of a principal a necessary support system for dialogue? Or, was it that teacher dialogue fell apart upon hearing about a new principal who was to come – and had "the reputation for running a tight ship" – on the scene? And, if so, is teacher dialogue merely a product of the idiosyncrasy of the individual principal?" (p. 17).

I further theorized: if a principal who has the reputation for "running a tight ship" comes aboard, teachers would clam-up, stop-talking, and run in and hide behind their classroom doors. In this case, the principal is not only unnecessary to teacher dialogue, but because of his or her authority, suppresses dialogue. Seen another way, this hiding behind classroom doors gives the impression that teachers don't want to communicate and dialogue and therefore hide behind their classroom doors abstracting or obscuring an additional context: the reputation of the principal who runs a tight and authoritarian ship. Seen yet another way, obscured by the author, principals may also be seen as a necessary support system for teachers to dialogue, but because the author obscures the context of the principal's reputation – tight ship executive – one is left with the thought that "teachers are incapable of talking (and dialoguing) to one another and making decisions on their own; hence, disarray."

I therefore concluded of my critique of the author's study that "teachers can be cooperative and creative *without* *t*he help of established authorities." I maintained that when: "teachers recognize that such authority may impede rather than facilitate their dialogue, they will then be in a position to confront these authorities, control their own work, and define their own working condition." (p. 17). That is to say, "teachers can self-administer and regulate their own schools collectively or, on a rotational basis, with another disenfranchised group – students and their parents. Therefore, I claimed, the author stopped short of seeing how administrators may intimidate teachers into running behind their classroom doors, and further, whether the reputation of the principal is authoritarian or liberal, may encourage dialogue, in one moment, but in another moment, change their minds, and catch teachers in a compromising and awkward position, one which while being encouraged to dialogue and share decisions, to come out from their hiding places in the classroom, and suddenly expose and strip away any negotiations of power they may have conducted with their students; or, in another moment, after administrators visit teachers (and thereby breaking apart such accords or negotiations), leave teachers to continue to "lay low" and "hide behind their classroom doors," relying on (from the administrator's perspective) students to decide not to dialogue with each other and their teachers, but rather, register their complaints to the administrators, thereby circumventing any traces of student-teacher negotiations, mutual understandings, and solidarity blocs.

I have often observed in my field observations (and was a part of my second dissertation) and from my own teaching experiences, there are fundamentally two ways student and teacher hostilities are resolved: they either accommodate and negotiate mutual understandings or "deals" with each other; or they appeal to the administrators, usually positioned above them in a hierarchical chain of authority and command. If administrators know this, they can resort to two strategies in maintaining control over both student and teacher: they can rely on the dominating or competitive nature of student and teacher in which each betrays any solidarity which may have been negotiated, and "go over each other's heads to the principal; or, conversely, they may negotiate their differences with each other, avoid administrative interventions, and thereby maintain some degree of power and autonomy in their classrooms, which I referred to as their dependent relations. This is why, upon being visited by a colleague to "evaluate" my performance in college, or be "observed" as a teacher, two things often occurred: either the students came to my rescue and made me look good by performing along the lines of dependency and citing me as a "good teacher" – i.e. students raising their hands and politely answering questions I articulated; or, they started to coil up, remain silent, and had me ask questions as if there was no one present, or made me "look bad." I theorized that the first action – dependent relations – was grounded on prior negotiations and mutual understanding between myself and the students; the second action – dominating relations – presumed a conflicting or dominating demeanor expressed by both myself and the students in which each used a part of the administrative hierarchy to protect or enhance their own powers.

These two modes of student-teacher relations left administrators in a third position in which to guide their control over both student and teacher: either they could periodically intervene and "visit" classrooms to upset or deteriorate any solidarity being formed between student and teacher; or they can step back and wait for student or teacher to report disagreements and conflicts to the administrative authorities. In this "in and out" movement of administrators, the term "dialogue" may provide the perfect foil in which to use as an excuse for administrative interventions. Namely, if dialogue is not achieved, then the onus of the blame can be placed on the teacher for not being "dialogical" enough; or, conversely, if dialogue is achieved formulating tight bonds between student and teacher, along with penetrating questions of how they are controlled in the school's hierarchy, then, administrators have an alternate strategy (rather or in addition to waiting for student and teacher appeals) they can suddenly intervene in classrooms at an increased rate, thereby breaking asunder any student-teacher blocs and solidarities.

In an unpublished chapter I completed in my first dissertation attempt, I extended my critique of the author's article when I showed how dialogue can be perceived as a medium in language, one which carried within it subject-positions of subjects acting as "stand-ins" for the authorities and administrators above them. Foucault (1977) and the new wave of postmodernism gave me the idea that subordinates may serve as "substitute supervisors,"[80] and therefore, control their work on behalf of their administrators better than being controlled directly and on site.[81] In this way, administrators could rely on mechanisms which were built into the hierarchical structures of their administrative powers as they operated within discourses, operating hegemonically, and as I further learned with the writings of Coward and Ellis (1977) and others, operated as chains of signifiers and subject-positions. Thus, placing teachers and their students in positions that made them assume they were incapable of running their own schools, at the moment, however, when a new administrator came on the scene, whatever cooperation and solidarity they formed, soon fell apart and into disarray. It was never a matter of whether or not they were capable of dialoguing with themselves and each other. Rather, the reasons why teachers could run their own schools or classrooms, or they were incapable of coming out of their closed doors and dialoguing with each other, it could be argued, was because they pragmatically saw more benefit in splitting up as an unit with their fellow teachers (and students) and go hide since a new principal was known to be an authoritarian figure – "running a tight ship" – or being cited by teachers as a "bad" principal. Recalling this work and sharing my article with my education students the week before, I invited a former student to speak of his recent assistant principal position in a school he was a member of for the last five years. He, Charlie, began his presentation by speaking about "good" and "bad" principals.

CHARLIE'S STORY: THE GOOD PRINCIPAL AND CLASSROOM MANAGEMENT

Charles, a former education student of mine eight years ago, contacted me upon hearing that I was returning as an adjunct professor to the college we first met when he was student of mine. Having taught since then in an elementary school, Charlie was promoted and is presently taking courses toward his doctorate for school leadership and administration. He has also managed to become a dean of discipline. As is customary with Charlie, he likes to lecture, but eventually and patiently listens to my students who want to ask him questions concerned with being an administrator and how to conduct classroom management procedures. The students had also heard from another student of mine, Linda,[82] in the previous week. Linda is from another local college I taught at and I decided to ask her to co-teach with me in a class dedicated to special education para-professionals. I will take up her story after Charlie's. Her story is about her teaching in New York City for thirty years special education and she speaks of her struggles with a "bad" principal.

Rather than answer questions about the administrative harassment – as what Linda has experienced and is still suffering from at her job, Charlie responded that he too "almost got fired" many times but he is still on the job for "eight years straight." Charlie remained steadfast in wanting to be promoted and is presently the dean and assistant principal of discipline of his school. Further, Charlie insisted that the onerous image of the principal – walking into the room to survey a new teacher – can be reduced to individual terms: depending if you have a school "chief" who is a "good" or a "bad" principal. To Charlie, when a principal walks into a teacher's classroom he should always find ways for the teacher to like and love him. While he is the boss of the teacher, Charlie continues to recount, if the principal "gives the teacher support and compliments in front of his or her students, a community of 'belonging' can be developed and constructed."

At this point, some of my students started to shout out: "This is not the point!" They wanted to know if school principals are there to help teachers or to threaten them under the present environment of testing? They also pointed how charter schools through articles they had received the week before to read, indicated how in some of these schools, teachers get higher salaries than principals and where "the teacher is king."[83]

Charlie, however, stood his ground. He insisted that administration should stay in place because administrators, when seen as a support of instruction and teacher dialogue (rather than a threat when they suddenly come into a classroom to evaluate a teacher), will increase teacher morale and make them "feel good." Citing theories as bad, Charlie then pivoted into explaining – using the theories of Glasser and Maslow – how administrators as school instructional leaders can work positively. He further allowed us to see how classroom management can be a matter of memorizing numbers. Bringing in a book titled PRIM (Pre-Referral Intervention Manual)[84] with a list of over 5,000 rules as to what to do when a child misbehaves and hundreds of other categories which can fill the holes of helping a teacher, new or old, to perform her duties as a classroom manager. Charlie further asserted, showing a few pages from this voluminous book how "all that an aspiring teacher needs know is to cite a rule and the page number listed, and refer the students school administrators, deans, or guidance counselors." In addition, he urged the students to have a "discipline plan," bolstered by PRIM, in which to inform themselves and for them to work collaboratively with the school principal.

While my students had also received copies of excerpts of other literature related to classroom management,[85] Charlie had us read a list of rules to apply.[86] He also emphasized to always have a "discipline plan" and show it to your principal.[87] There was no talk however about classroom management as "facilitation" or "construction" or any other social and contractual bases on which classroom management could be negotiated and decided between students and teachers as a negotiating unit. One student got a bit testy and exclaimed that Charlie's "book" on discipline was keeping the teacher in a "plantation mentality" or maintaining a system so the "good" plantation owner can continue to have slaves and change "bad" plantation managers, whenever things got out of control, and then could be changed for a "good" plantation manager rather than attacking the plantation owner and system. Still, many other students liked the idea of referring their problematic students to others or reading up which number or rule applied to their specific problem. In my course of teaching education courses for the last ten years, most students (as did most of the school administrators turned college instructors) think that classroom management is an essentialized category, above the political fray, and not a social construction to be worked out and negotiated every day between teachers and their students and administrators. Instead, as I have also pointed to, another student in her second year of teaching took pleasure in the fact that in her school administrative surveillance and administrators "sweep the floors," poking their heads constantly into her room, is a "good thing." This form of control, for this student, means that she can work in a more relaxed way and have an easier job environment because "the administrators are making sure the students are watched and kept in control so she can do her work."

Ultimately, as Charlie's presentation ended, I asked the students to re-concept-ualize classroom management in other forms – as forms of classroom facilitation – in which larger issues of power, history, race, gender, authority, and class may be drawn into their thinking. I also distributed a few recent newspaper articles showing how race, for example was interwoven with teachers labeling and citing as "discipline problems" children of color more so than white children. I also wanted to know if there were the other bases on which to theorize about classroom management tied to teacher-student power relations in terms of overcoming racial discrimination and its possible links to school administrative hierarchies.[88]

LINDA'S STORY: THE BAD PRINCIPAL: "GET STARTED AT THE BELL STORY!"

Since Linda was a former student of mine at another college, she was willing to share with my class some very sensitive information. After I heard her story about classroom management and what was going on in her school with her principal, insofar as how the school is responding to the pressures of testing and teachers being told to "stay on task" in preparing students for these exams, I decided that my present students can get an "inside" view of the problem of classroom management and how it overlaps into other contexts, namely administrative authority and racism. She recounted to me and my students a story which overlaps the testing environment of her school, as pertaining to her principal's technique of classroom management affecting her, and how the principal perceived her role as an extension of the school's classroom manager. As I have said, she wished to remain anonymous and she was fearful of losing her long tenure of thirty years and her pension. My students, in turn, were informed of her anonymity and the conditions of her classroom management as communicated to her by her principal and in which she was to use to control her students in test preparation sessions – sessions that presently dominate everything else in her school.

I received an email from Linda[89] in early Spring this year (2008), and afterwards, we had a telephone conversation about what was going on in her high school.[90] Linda had been working for the Board of Education in New York City for almost thirty years, specifically, teaching special education students. She has had many principals in her long tenure as a teacher, but since the emphasis has been placed on test score results in recent years, her principal has decided (with other principals in the district) to carefully watch how their teachers are preparing the students for the many standardized tests they will be taking this semester. There are both negative and positive pressures accounted for by student test score results: either a principal or teacher gets fired or transferred, or upon good test scores, they get promoted and receive monetary and material bonuses.

Linda's greatest fear is that she will get a "U" or unsatisfactory rating if her students fall behind or get lower test scores than their previous year's test score results. As she informed me, the rule is the students must always raise their test scores by a rigid formula. That is, if a school or classroom was doing F work, but happened to raise their scores to C-, their scores would count more than a school attaining as an average B+ or A-work, and now simply matched their previous test scores.

Linda then began to recount a recent experience with her principal to the class. She began by saying how the principal suddenly walked into her room on five occasions in one day to assess how long it took for her students to get to work and stay on task. If the students began in one class three minutes after the bell rung, then seven minutes after the bell in the second class, and so forth, the principal would tally the minutes up and deduct off her weekly salary the percentage of minutes it took to get the students on task in all five classes. So if it took 20 minutes accumulatively in her five classes, her salary for a day was deducted one-third of a hour or the equivalent of her work hour she earned for that day.

Reflecting on this procedure, Linda began to tell me how classroom/school management has broken the back of the union and that kids (by watching the way teachers are treated by administrators – who berate teachers in front of them), receive a message or signal which communicates to them that it is acceptable to manipulate their teachers or for students to threaten teachers that they will report them to the principal. As a result, and as a part of the student agenda, they relieve themselves from doing too much work, by threatening to report their teachers to the principal. The teachers usually appease the students by allowing them to do as much work they want. Hence, a vicious cycle is created in which the teacher, positioned in the middle between the principal and the students, is victimized.

Linda then indicated when new teachers arrive replacing older teachers – they cannot control their classes – because these students "smells fresh meat" and attack or misbehave. In the meantime, with the stringent controls imposed by her principal, and the way they are carried out – i.e. berating the teacher in front of the students – Linda remains very unsure if she will receive her pension upon her soon-to-be retirement or be re-hired in her present school position. In the meantime, the students opt to resist, misbehave, and do the minimum amount of work.[91]

Linda and some of my students called this form of student resistance as "street smart." Linda also alerted us to a growing "administrator culture" under the present NYC mayor and administration, which was cited as corporate, legal and hierarchical. Linda added that such a culture was bent on "breaking the backs of the teacher union." Indeed, as Linda further informed me and the class, teachers could apply for a grievance about other teachers or students, but they cannot grieve about administrators under the new, more centralized administration. As Linda pointed out, there is a loophole in the union contract which spells out teachers can't grieve against administrators since, as the first step in the contract, one must get permission from principals to appeal. Therefore, as Linda puts it, teachers are resolved to remain acquiescent to administrators, as if to say: "What do you want me to do, and I'll do it! The teacher must do what they are told!" she added.

Linda also intimated that she noticed an email on a table outside of her principal's office sent by the superintendent's office. This letter advised all principals how they can push out recalcitrant teachers in addition to using various techniques to get a teacher in trouble! All that her union representative told her under such circumstances was to "keep a record and log/record and record this!" "That's it!," added Linda.

Linda summed up her story by stating: "The principal gets what she or he wants! A principal can go around to all the individual classrooms, stand in front of teacher and students, and clock how long it takes for students to get seated. Two teachers, Linda concludes, "left teaching before Christmas with this policy! They did not transfer, they quit teaching!"

Still, in many of my classes, I invite former students to speak to my present students what is going in schools. Many of these former students have aspired and gained administrator positions or are in current disciplinary deans positions. Others are accumulating many years and have received tenure. Oddly, these teachers still feel insecure about losing their tenure and pensions if their student test scores do not dramatically rise or, worst, if they cannot control their classes or their students' misbehaviors. They know that their principals want them to conform to government mandated testing and in which the school district seeks to be eligible to additional funding. The newer teachers are even more frightened; they fear losing control of their classrooms, as some of the new teachers think of themselves as "fresh meat."

Some, however, also realize that losing control of resistant students is not sorely a local problem, but one which occurs in other countries. To familiarize my students of how global classroom management is, I distribute to them recent newspaper articles on how Japanese public schools, the model of standardized testing, regimentation and focused study habits are beginning to realize a new student movement – koika – in which students want to be less restricted, regimented, and ruled by standardized learning and test taking.[92]

In today's competitive world and schools, teacher education courses are governed by a "dirty little secret" or silent norm—every man or woman is out for themselves – I made it, so why should I worry about you! If student to student competition was not enough to exacerbate a democratic and collegial atmosphere in classrooms and schools of education, there is in place other instruments to assure that this tense and often fracturing atmosphere continues in places as education classrooms in colleges and universities throughout the nation.

A DIRTY LITTLE SECRET: CLOSING THE ACHIEVEMENT GAP BY TESTING AND RE-SEGREGATION[93]

In this last case study of the chapter, I will bring together strands and overlapping contexts of administrative authority, classroom management, testing, and a climate of teaching about controversial topics – as racial discrimination and how testing has not only not closed the "achievement gap," but further, through the existing test regimen mandated by No Child Left Behind (along with the years preceding NCLB but following a Nation at Risk Conference (1983), may have inadvertently instigated a practice of re-segregating schools.

Having had my students read parts of the story of the civil rights movement, Brown vs. Board of Education (1954), and how since the 1980's standardized testing has kept a solitary focus on foreign competition and global markets for higher test scores in math and science to compete with students abroad, while ignoring, at the same time, a parallel development of re-segregation of schools. By focusing their attention on external forces in the marketplace or keeping their "eyes off the prize" – equal opportunity by providing for integrated classrooms and schools, as intended by the Warren Court in the Brown vs. Board of Education in 1954 – my students were clueless why integration (according to the decades of evidence compiled by the Civil Rights Division of the Civil Rights Act under the research findings of Gary Orfield's [2001]work) may be correlated to student achievement and life success. That is to say, segregated schools and classrooms are "inherently unequal," as ruled by the Supreme Court in 1954, overturning the Plessy vs. Furgeson 1896 Supreme Court decision that "separate is equal." Nevertheless, as others have monitored this nation's history of legislation and court policies, school re-segregation has become progressively a regressive movement

(Kozol, 2005; Love, 2007; Orfield, 2001). This return to segregated schools has denied those students (white or people of color and minority ethnicities and different language speaking populations) from receiving a "sound and equal education" as well as promoting a more opportunity and a fuller democracy for all.

As I showed my students by having them view several films (i.e. *Keeping Your Eye on the Prize, Eyes of the Storm, Echoes of Brown, Cultural Criticism and Transformation*), or discussed current events to my social studies teachers seeking to learn more about methods of teaching controversy (i.e. Iraq, Israeli-Palestinian Relations, Terrorism, etc.), along with articles addressed how alternate views – often positing as a problem for conservative and liberal school administrators and how they maintain student-teacher-administrative relations as becoming more and more exacerbated rather than relieved. As we attend to such problems and issues, at times on discussion boards linked to the course, as well as face-to-face discussions in the classroom, it is usually during the first few weeks of the semester, when few of us know each other, when disruptions occur. I do not say this in a cavalier attitude, but rather with an attitude to find out more as to why student and teacher react the way they do when they are exposed to controversial and complex materials and relationships. That is, why they often get triggered to act out against one another – the oppressed oppressing each other, without seeing why they act this way to begin with. This usually means, questioning students as to why they appeal to administrators and deans (or www.ratemyprofessor.com in the first weeks of the course) to register their complaints rather than meet with their instructors to "talk it over." Equally and often as a "side bar" discussion, the problems I have encountered with and amongst students are usually diffused, and maintain themselves until mutual respect and communication is restored. However, in those initial stages of this encounter, student and teacher remain at the edge of their defenses.

This is not to minimize the pressures I and my students have experienced and the demands we have made of each other, as finding out what each expects of the other and how the workload intrudes into their personal commitments. What I seek to do in the first weeks of class is to make my students as comfortable as I can without setting the agenda that there is nothing to do in class. I suppose, for those students who initially who do not feel comfortable in the classes I taught – social studies methods, foundation, and curriculum courses – the reason I would like to think is that we are both caught in a large and often invisible and unconscious hegemonic web of subject-positions and chains of signifiers that can be mapped out once we give each other a chance to become reflective yet also counter-hegemonic theorizers. I have written about this phenomenon in other case studies, including one most recent one on "Teaching Social Studies through Post-Structural Constructs (2007)."

I take very seriously my job as a teacher educator and believe in the Socratic method of igniting interaction or becoming a gadfly or "devil's advocate" to discussions that may not otherwise emerge. Often, as I reflect back on these tumultuous yet exciting and educational experiences I have had in class, I feel I have done my job. As a former supervisor counseled me: "Always challenge the students." [94] To this date, I have come up against some very interesting experiences as a teacher educator. Unfortunately, at least at the beginning of a semester, students feel anxious about getting a good grade or completing the work assigned, as they already come with them predispositions of anxiety and fear, and how much they can commit to the class given their other responsibilities. Many students have full time jobs and children, along with a full load of courses. Often, in the first class when I bring with me a bunch of articles duplicated to complement or substitute the textbook, their first reactions that the course's work is that its content is "intense" or "too much." Often, as I listen to them and often make changes based on their cries, reducing the work load as they deem fit. Other times, however, they silently make known their resentments by posting, without any fore notice to me, their angry feelings on www.ratemyprofessor.com

Reviewing some of these evaluations or critical reviews requires very tough skin, as students let it all out without any qualifications. I guess, to some extent, I deserve their admonishments. But, I also take their critiques as positive advice to do better without compromising the subject-matter and what it can offer them to be good teachers. At the same time, I hope to ameliorate their over worked conditions. This does not always happen, as other professors take these criticisms defensively[95] and further try to de-bunk them. On this note, we all must recognize that students are not as lucky as we are, they cannot be on the same equal footing of authority as we are, but they can wield their powers, individually and collectively via this website – or what I refer to as a "dirty little secret" – that few us and my colleagues are willing to share with one another even though these comments are open to the public. Still, when personalities get stubborn and get in the way of de-constructing ideological beliefs, I usually take the unpopular position of devil's advocate and challenge students to re-examine for the moment their long held beliefs and values, irrespective of the sometimes awful consequences I must take when I log in to www.ratemyprofessor.com. As another supervisor, in a not so gently way advised me, "You must suck it up."

TEACHING ABOUT THE DEFEAT OF RACIAL INTEGRATION AND BLACKBOARD-WEB CT DISCUSSIONS

As one of my more recent class exchanges with new education students (a foundation course) I came across an experience I have not had in the last ten years of my college teaching career. While there have been irruptions in class about the Iraqi War, suspension of civil liberties (i.e. torture instituted on detained people who happen to be Moslem or Arabic), the most violent encounter came to my attention when I began to introduce the students to the history and present practices of teaching students of color and who are poor as well as middle class students in urban America and how some of the wealthier people of color have endorsed school re-segregation without reading or knowing the consequences this may have for their less fortunate and less wealthier counterparts. Since many of my students are black, wealthy and poor, struggling as recent immigrants from the Caribbean, I had some very interesting exchanges of getting to know their diverse groups and histories. More specifically, I wanted to know what their attitudes are in terms of a recent book published by Jonathan Kozol, *The Shame of the Nation: The Restoration of Apartheid Schooling in America* (2005) and other shorter versions distributed in class to allow them to integrate Kozol's message with a minimum amount of reading time.

After reading the short version[96] of Kozol's book, and other articles distributed by Gary Orfield (2001)[97] and Bob Lowe (2008)[98] the students were introduced to several experiences. One experience was to view Jane Elliott's *Eye of the Storm* (1968) and her relations with her students, who were all white, and by using the color of their eyes, devised a scenario simulating their being segregated. When Elliott's students role played their segregated identities, they began to become fearful and anxious and their learning became impeded. We note in her film that when the students are labeled as a group, which is hierarchically superior or inferior to the other group, their achievement or learning increases and decreases over a short period of time. Jane Elliott switches their labels. The feeling being labeled or feeling stigmatized by becoming re-labeled as the top-dog as opposed to the bottom-dog or, euphemistically, how segregation treats people of color versus students identified as members of the dominant group (white), factors into students achievement or lack of by naming and re-naming or labeling their classroom environments. I then asked my students to role play how it would feel to be bused to a white school or, conversely, if white, how would they feel about being bused to a black school. In this role play, the students accomplished several real yet improvised scenarios structured by index cards which I asked them to use to initiate conversations with one another, white and black, congregating in the halls, waiting to enter the classroom or cafeteria, and so forth.

Afterwards, in another session, I had the students draw a "time-line," after reading a short article by Gary Orfield who as a member of the Civil Rights Division researching trends of integration and segregation in American schools for the last thirty years at Harvard University. Orfield argues that children when integrated go on to graduate high schools, attend college, and become more proficient with improving their relationships with people who are of different racial backgrounds. Orfield, argues, well before Kozol's book, that the Supreme Court decision of Brown vs. The Board of Education (1954) has not been adhered to in at least the last thirty years when schools – particularly in the South – began to follow federal orders and guidelines on integration. Due to the changes of political administrations and congresses, along with changes in returning to "Plessy," the older decision of the Supreme Court in 1896 which held if a school, a black school, was given the same resources as a white school, the students would receive the same or an equal education.

The students in this class argued both ways: many refusing to acknowledge the Supreme Court decision of 1954, which presently is the law of the land, and further justifying their opposition to forced busing of students, despite that when accomplished in other states (southern states like North Carolina and Kentucky) and in mid-western states (i..e Michigan), western states (i.e. Washington), and New England states (i.e. Massachusetts) produced higher test scores and higher mobility of students of color and who were poor. Yet, when offered additional information, like that India has students bussed over forty miles each way to gain better schooling for their children, the same students remain adamant about their position, saying: "I don't care about other countries, it is here that counts. "Besides," she added, "all that people of color need are equal resources and money to get their schools in shape, we don't need white people." She noted that black schools did very well without white integration in the South, referring to an article I distributed to them earlier, as in the writings of Frederick Douglas, black literacy societies, black churches, penny schools, and the work and preaching of Malcolm X.

Yet, when we finally constructed a time line on a long horizontal piece of paper, a new pattern revealed itself. Integration had succeeded after the civil rights movement in the mid-1960s and continued through the mid-1980s. In these twenty years or so, students of color and their test scores rose. Then, somewhere around the mid-1980s, during the Reagan administration, re-segregation increased on the basis of housing patterns and income. At the same time, test scores of students of color no longer bused begin to decline. In the meantime, in 1983, a well-known school conference – *A Nation at Risk* – convenes and is sponsored by major corporations seeking to upgrade schools capable of competing with foreign schools in Europe and Asia and participating in the new global service economy. As a result of Goals 2000, which emerges from the conference, an accord is reached between Democrats and Republicans in which more emphasis is put on standardized and mandated testing and is instituted as a driving force behind school reform and getting students in America up-to-speed with their foreign counterparts. Ironically, at this time, as local courts since the mid-1970s begin to strike down federal court orders to integrate, schools throughout the country become re-segregated in the cities, suburban and rural areas. During this time, students of color who are poor begin to register low test score results and many begin to drop out of schools. (Orfield, 2001).

We learned, therefore, from the role plays, movies and mapping out on a time line that a major irony occurred in the 1980s leading up to the present policy of standardized testing, including the more strenuous regimen of "high-stake" testing since NCLB, along with parallel developments of re-segregated schools and attention focused on the global economy as opposed to the quality of life and opportunities for poor and minority peoples. Testing, as overlapping classroom management and administrative hierarchies, following a new policy to compete with foreign students, has produced more testing but with the adverse effects of producing lower test scores amongst students of color, the poor, and "drop outs," as the achievement gap between those who have and those who do not, widens.

Two developments occurred after a series of classes were conducted around the above events: the first was reflected Online in Blackboard exchanges; the second surfaced in the website www.ratemyprofessor.com

Online Responses

Some of the students agreed with the time-line drawn showing a pattern of testing and how it was shaped by attention to standardized exams brought on by competition from foreign markets and foreign students excelling over American students, and the correlated and resultant pattern of re-segregation of schools. On this development, one student posted a message to other students in her group:

As I mentioned in our last assignment, the difficulty in answering this question is that the laws implemented in Brown vs. Board has not *technically* been broken. However, with that said, there is undoubtedly an uneven distribution in racial/ economic diversity as a result of several factors affecting integration in public schools. There are *zoning laws* that keep low-income students tethered to low-income schools, government resistance, and what in my opinion is the biggest contributing factor (outside of zoning laws), the continued complacency and overall lack of willingness within communities to band together and create change within the system.

Without describing these "zoning laws," the same student further argues:

Although I do understand the benefits (of integration by bussing), I am not completely sold on the concept of forced integration. I feel that integration is only a short term remedy, to a wide-spread, long-term problem. Ultimately I feel the solution lies in improving the condition of all schools in low-income areas. The government recognizes the need for reform but has not approached the situation in a practical, realistic manner. With the emphasis on standardized tests and "No Child Left Behind" the real problem (lack of funding, lack of training, lack of appropriate facilities and supplies for students) is not being addressed. Standardized tests only see in black and white and children and schools should not be judged on a pass or fail basis. Simply stating that a school is bad as a result of poor test scores does not address the problem, it only exacerbates it.

Another student chimes in and adds:

Ongoing hidden segregation practices (zoning laws, etc.) continue to play a large role and I feel that they outweigh any benefits that integration has provided and will continue to outweigh any benefits of current integration programs available to students. It is not about the students economic or cultural background, it's about the opportunities being made available to these students, it's about the possibilities being presented to them regarding their future. I feel that if more emphasis was placed on training teachers, improving facilities, and providing adequate supplies to all students, regardless of race, gender, or economic background that all schools would inevitably become integrated because there would be no "bad" schools, there would simply be "good" schools.

My response (after checking about "zonal laws," federal and state legislation[99]) was that the intent of zonal laws is to provide incentive and controls gauged according to one's income and ability to pay rent and mortgage. The federal law explicitly states that such legislation was designed to assist low income and moderate income families based on income. The student who raised this point did not point out how moderate income families would, by their "flight" from poor neighborhoods, contribute in de-facto discriminatory ways, "tethering" others to poor neighborhood schools. By not taking advantage of zonal laws, or moving out of neighborhoods which applied these laws, middle or moderate income families may have fled from such neighborhoods producing the effect of segregated schools in which only low-income students attended, as opposed to staying or taking advantage of zonal laws, thereby producing the effect of creating a mix of low and moderate income students sitting side by side in the same classroom. She omits this point, arguing instead for better resources for schools with homogeneous (and only poor) students rather than ascribing to the theory that classrooms, when integrated, provide a better means for student opportunity, future employment and, over-all, better chances to succeed and gain opportunities (as Orfield's report argues). To this student, "zonal laws" acted as a means to keep low income students and their families in low income neighborhoods, thereby chaining them to poor schools which were segregated by de facto factors or, as she avoided: zonal laws represented a code word[100] for "only black" or "people of color" as occupants of such residences, thereby encouraging middle class (white and black) flight or acting as a detriment for middle class students to move in. After asking the student about these dimensions of federal and state zonal laws, she did not offer a response. I then responded with a posting of my own:[101]

I have just completed reading most of your postings for Assignment #5 and I still believe you need to understand the intrinsic or inherent dimensions of integration and segregation. Once again, it is not just pouring money into "urban high need" schools (and this, no doubt, is vitally necessary if only to reach the 1896 criteria set in Plessy vs. Ferguson), but more. Namely, there has to be demonstrated (beyond student test scores) an "intrinsic" or "inherent" dimension of care and competence of the student-teacher relationship.

Once again, I must echo the words of the Warren Supreme Court when it ruled that the "hearts and minds" of poor and marginalized students must be attended to and be equalized under the 14th Amendment: and that includes the perceptions and dispositions of all the parties – the students, teachers, parents, etc. – treating all people equally, racially, and by income under law in giving everyone an equal opportunity in life.

Afterwards, the students and I received an additional response from another student in class, which I think responded to the previous student's statement in a more direct way:

There are quite a few reasons why integration is being prevented in public schools. One of the main reasons is ignorance and fear. While laws may change, morals are very permanent. Cases like Brown vs. the Board of Ed., which declared separate is not equal shows that regardless of laws passed the beast in the human mind is much harder to tame. From reading Gary Orfield's article, I feel that de-facto segregation is what is preventing integration. This type of segregation (hidden) is the scariest because it is not clearly seen, it is sneaky and underhanded.

This student continues to make her case:

> This type of segregation is not only segregated by color but also by class. If a child lives in a poor neighborhood the odds of him or her getting a good education is limited while a child living in an upper class or middle class neighborhood (he or she) will get a better more sound education. The poor child will go to the school where there are mostly blacks or minorities, whereas the middle class child will go to a school with other white children like him or herself.

This student further argues, as a poor, black minority, and immigrant member:

> In order for integration to occur, we must first "fess up" that we are a segregated society and stop pulling the shades over each other's eyes. Then we need to build some courage and say "my child should be with your child and they should learn together". It is proven that children who are taught in a non-segregated environments learn better and do better in school. If we know this is proven then what the hell are we doing? We need to stop thinking about how we feel and start thinking about what better benefits our children and their futures.

No doubt, there existed two codes or discourses on which students inscribed their positions: First, those students who wished to keep hidden how their own racism or those of others who might flee from neighborhood becoming populated with families from low to moderate incomes would be sufficient for them not to live in federal or state assisted by such zonal laws neighborhoods; and second, those other students who were willing to come forth and examine how de-facto racism and discrimination operating within those who were secretive and not forthcoming about their possible and inadvertent or intentional racism and classism become apparent.

Another Dirty Little Secret: www.RateMyProfessor.com

As a result of very exciting interchanges in the class, face-to-face and our Blackboard/webct postings, I received on my RateMyProfessor.com website, the following remarks:

> Gives you tons of homework even after class is done by means of email. So, if you have no access to a computer it's tough luck to you. Also thinks he's the next MLK, it's as though he wants to start his own civil rights movement.

Two weeks later, the same student – I suppose but I'm not sure, since their postings are anonymous – was further angered and said:

> He wants to start a revolution and all of his lessons are on black and white issues.

Other students joined in and recorded on the professor evaluation website the following postings:

Fleischer was extremely helpful with my course "edu16". He was able to demonstrate the subject matter very well. Dr. Lee helped me overcome my fear of expressing myself. To the best of my knowledge, he is an intelligent, knowledgeable and an experienced teacher I have ever had. I highly recommend him to other students to benefit from his superior ability.

Another student added:

You will never fall asleep in Dr. Fleischer's class. He is not afraid to address hot controversial topics. And because of that, some very conservative people get pissed off. He is a great professor and thought his class was terrific!

Still, one tends to feel very upset upon reading some of these postings. Often I want to respond back, but for some reason I cannot clearly articulate (I suppose I do not want to draw inordinate attention to myself and skew the debate amongst students), I let the matter, unhappily, slide. Feeling a little upset, and not knowing which student posted the above remarks, I heard from other students who explained that because they are from the Caribbean area they don't share what African-American students and families deem as important. Appraising me, "We come from the British system," which, compared to the American system, is very conservative way of life. They inform me most Caribbean people do not identify with African Americans in seeking an integrated system of education. As a result of this conversation I sent to the students a few excerpts from a book by Theresa Perry, Asa Hillard, and Claude Steele, Young, *Gifted, and Black: Promising High Achievement Among African-Americans Students* (2003) in the hope of bridging any gulfs of misunderstanding I may have of their cultural and political persuasions.

As a result of reading excerpts from this short article, specifically on the differences between Caribbean and African-American peoples and also referring to Ogbu and Bourdieu works and their emphases on the differences of blacks who were forced or not forced to come to America (in slavery or as voluntary subjects), and how those who were forced or not forced reveal very different predispositions, was of some help. To Caribbean people, who identified themselves as "voluntary immigrants (as opposed to non-voluntary slaves) drew hard fast distinctions between themselves and African-Americans, who they identify as "non-voluntary slaves." From this discussion, I was able to gain more insight and connections with the students in my class, particularly those many who are Caribbean or from the "British system."

Further, as I cited another study by Mary Waters (1999) in Perry, Hillard, and Steele, 1999), Western Indian-Caribbean immigrants as a group have a history of seeking higher mobility or moving-up in society. To Waters, African-American immigrants or those who came involuntarily to America because of slavery have adopted a "low level" of "effort optimism." As a result, Caribbean people make efforts to retain their dialects and accents or displays on their cars ornaments as their native country's flag, thereby marking themselves off as different from African Americans. However, to Waters, this distinction does not always guarantee separation between the two groups. White Americans, argues Waters, because they identify both black groups by skin color, may inadvertently combine both groups. This tendency on part of white Americans to subsume Caribbean people into the same category as African Americans does not serve Caribbean people because employers tend to hire – once they know they are dealing with Caribbean people, given their dialects and voices – them more frequently than African Americans. In the same way, Waters also discovered, white Americans tend to employ Asian people at a higher rate than Caribbean people. Concluding, Waters named this phenomenon as accountable for the overrepresentation of black Caribbean immigrants among black affirmative action admittees at Ivy League and elite colleges and universities than their African American counterparts (p. 72).

Upon reading Water's short article, I was surprised to hear that amongst Caribbean people there are further differentiations based on one's nationality. For example, people of Haiti are less respected by people from Jamaica, and further, both Haitians and Jamaicans are less respected than people from the Bahamas or St. Vincent or Barbadoes, and so forth (see Figure 44 in Chapter 3). Having temporarily absorbed the intricate and overlapping allegiances and alliances between and amongst Caribbean people, I became more sensitized as how to proceed with talking about foundational issues of education, including overlapping discourses dealing class, gender, and yes, more race.

Afterwards, I received more favorable www.ratemyprofessor.com postings, as:

> True there is a lot of reading to be done in this class,
> But again you are in college …not really hard work...
> do the work, readings, post your answers and participate
> (and) this will assure you an A in this class… he is a nice person

While there are many other times I would not prefer to share with anyone in regard to student responses of my work with students – and did *feel that cool sweat going up and down my spine.* On balance, the medium of www.ratemyporofessor.com does offer one way in which to offset these imbalances between students and teachers by offering both a gun and a trigger, and a not-so-nice way to attend to problems they might not have been noticed or take more seriously by those teachers who think they have more power than their students. Yet, as a dean of a college I held a position in, indicated to me, "I do look at this website and check up on what the students are thinking of their instructors." In doing this, this school administrator enters the domain of hegemony and, as I cringed when she said these words, I thought there may be a more open and honest way to have students and teachers talk *to* each other as opposed to talking *at* and *above* or *below* each other.

CONCLUSION

By now, it should be very clear how case studies offered here may be used to show the political dimensions of struggle between student and teacher in the school's administrative hierarchies, cross-fertilized by other power relations as race, class, and gender. This should become even more clear when using post-structuralist constructs or frames of reference in how these relations of power criss-cross each other yielding very complex and intricate dimensions of why and how students and teachers must constantly clarify and negotiate with each other within planes of language as a discourse – not settling for individualistic moments of reflection or dialogue in which they may reveal the root of very antagonistic relations. Many "points of antagonism" (Laclau & Mouffe, 1985) have already been illustrated here, raising a counter-hegemonic consciousness on those discursive formations in which they can examine and may bring about "points of connections" and spaces in which they are already hegemonized, and which may guide them into subject-positions by ways of taking note of chains of signifiers and how they are sutured into student and teacher identities, and how student and teacher slide into and throughout these subject-positions and chains of signifiers. That is, intersecting and interacting with each other, students and teachers may offer to one another newer "surfaces of inscription" to name and map out their working conditions and relationships.

When such a counter-hegemonic analytic or lens can be formed and articulated, both student and teacher will then be in a better position to begin to counter those hegemonic discursive formations with their own constructed norms and surfaces for inscribing how they feel, think, know, and desire. In this way, they may enter into the maze or network of power relations which they may not have assumed or imagined before. When moment of imagination or critical consciousness happens, a counter-hegemonic moment may also appear in the next moment, reminding those who think they are reflecting in dialoguing acts of consciousness alone, that there may be additional spaces to construct from, awaken themselves to additional series of openings and actions for their interventions and solidarity as their agential actions. In determining the outcomes of schools becoming more democratic places in which one learns and is taught to live, with knowledge of the many and complex tiers of discourse, along with the diverse and complex roles students and teachers have as democratic and global citizens and educators, it will become apparent as we turn to the critique of Frerie by my education students, that critical pedagogy must be extended (Freire included) to match their circumstances of the twentieth first century, and which may they may begin to have an active hand in transforming in counter-hegemonic ways which radicalizing Freire's critical pedagogy may produce.

On this note, I conclude the above case studies of overarching "pillars of hegemony" and introduce into the next chapter, Chapter 3, how other substantive issues of school and classroom hegemony. Specifically, as we will see in Chapter 4, how my past special education students may serve as an example in which the sliding and moving dimensions of hegemony and signification may operate in and between their chains of signifiers, subject-positions, and the surfaces. This may be why these students constantly remarked in their focus groups and to me why they must "break the chains," listen to the "flying rumors," and stop "one-downing each other."

In doing this, a common counter-hegemonic basis for both student and teacher may be to construct themselves as signifiers in naming and inscribing in various counter-hegemonic communities or discursive formations their claims and demands as to how their school's governance should be formed around democratic principles of fairness, social justice, and equality. So far ignored, repressed, or hegemonized, these bases of school governance are presently curtailed as student and teacher may see, sense, or "read" such possibilities in emerging as joint decision-makers – but because school policies and dominant norms are distracting them from such problems and conclusions, this kind of reading, sensing, and seeing, is, so far, foreclosed.

On this note, the following chapter, *Freire Illustrated*, seeks to re-open what has remained hegemoncally foreclosed in the last forty years since critical pedagogy emerged in the lexicon of school discourses.

FRIERE ILLUSTRATED: EXTENDING FRIERE THROUGH STUDENT IMPRESSIONS AND PICTURES

INTRODUCTION

As we have laid out in the previous chapter, there are many "pillars of hegemony" saturating the classroom and school discourse. Some take the form of almost neutral and taken for granted entities: not to be questioned or noticed. Instead, upon reaching almost perfect hegemony, which are accepted as "facts of life" in schools and teaching. Testing, classroom management, tenure, and administrative hierarchies to enforce these somewhat innocuous practices tower over all other discourses. Within these discursive formations – their chains of signifiers, subject-positions, and spaces to inscribe their meanings – students and teachers have become so accustomed to their presence they cannot see or map out the contours of hegemony. One must wonder if there are any other spaces left to simply exist as being in schools and classrooms? Overlapping (as the bases of discursive formations), intersecting (on the basis of chains of signifiers and how words, thoughts, and images are intricately intertwined), along with how one articulates within these cross-sections of discursive forces (metonymic images flashing through us as "second thoughts"), one must further take notice if there are any spaces left to theorize against their seemingly innocuous presence.

While Heidegger has pointed to such spaces as "clearings" in his *Being and Time* (1962) or where one becomes *Dasein* or reaches a state of being there; or, in Sartre (1943), where, in a less hopeful way, sees such spaces as already dominated by the Other, the nothingness of being made *de trop*, or as an object of existence; or, as Zizek's (1989) where one suddenly refers to those sudden experiences one feels as the Real, glimpses of the *objet petit a's* which pierce through language, leaving traces of tiny spaces and revealing the "real kernels" of existence; or, as Foucault (1977) speaks of the "murmurs" of language in which one may hear coming down through the centuries, in all these cases we must step back for the moment in attempting to grasp Freire's main work, *Pedagogy of the Oppressed* and how such a work may assist students in defining and redefining their oppressive realities – i.e. the hegemonies of testing, classroom management, tenure and administrative hierarchies, along with the intrusion of technologies[102] as www.ratemyprofessor.com in which I mentioned in the previous chapter.

Still, I wondered if my education students could elaborate further, more critically, their positions on being oppressed by a cross-fire of discursive formations we have reviewed in the previous chapter. As I usually did, I had them read Paulo Freire's *Pedagogy of the Oppressed*, as a way to initiate the critical activity and to see if they could posit as problematic not only how they were being de-humanized and de-skilled by present day tests, classroom management techniques, and administrator hierarchies, but further, how far they could go with Freire's assistance. I wanted my students to pierce the veil of yet another layer of discourse laid over and on their present theorizing by the use of what I called post-structural constructs. This second discursive dimension will be further discussed in the following chapter on developing a (not "the") theory of counter-hegemonic teaching and theorizing of oppressive realities. I also wanted to use my doctoral work with special education students to show my college students how "slow" students on the high school level, not destined to go to college, managed to become counter-hegemonic theorizers (2001). Quite surprisingly, these students were able to accomplish both critical analyzing (as in Freire sense), along with the additional overlay of counter-hegemonic theorizing (in the post-structural sense).

As I will argue in the following chapter, using post-structural constructs, one may begin to map the political geography of today's school and classroom discourses and practices. I have appropriated from post-structualist literature constructs, specifically from political, linguistic, and psychoanalytical insights of Lacan (1977), Laclau (1990, 2007), Pecheux (1982), Zizek (1989), and others to get a sense or framework in which to see how students and teachers may be assisted to differentiate signification from language, discourse from dialogue, reflection and action from interpellation and interpolation in how subject-positioning occurs in signifier-chains which intervene and come in-between student and teacher feelings and thoughts as they get caught in antagonistic relations. An example of being caught in contradictory or antagonistic circumstances is portrayed in a process of inscription as shown by Laclau and Thomassen in those tendential surfaces which are articulated by subjects in their respective subject-positions. In these experiences, a subject inscribes, de-inscribes, and re-inscribes on the surfaces of their subject-positions as assigned to them by the administrative and hierarchical authorities in complex chains of empty and equivalent meanings often resisted by the construction of their own particularistic and differential and empty signifiers as well as how, in this struggle, particularistic or fragmented empty signifiers get broken off their subject-position surfaces and become "floating signifiers.," In these signifying actions, signals are emitted to others to begin anew the process of constructing new equivalent chains to start new counter-hegemonic chains of signifiers, surfaces on subject-positions and inscriptions in the discourses from within they speak and think.

As we will see in the following Chapter 4, then, one may map out how one may articulate a voice or re-arrange the alignments of how power as constructed in signifying and discursive practices, when one is caught in contradictory, antagonistic, or other distracting dilemmas, as they often are, when their discourses are caught onto either-or modernist binaries of thinking and talking – i.e. reflection and action, dialogue and discourses – or spaces in between you and me. For example, in the space of teaching, either one should teach by lecture or use dialogical formats with their students. However, this leaves too much to be patched over by the word "dialogue." Just as lecture may be caught in chains of equivalent signifiers indicating authoritarianism vs. freedom, dialogue, in less obvious ways, may obfuscate how, while in "dialogue," subjects may be precluded from seeing how their being caught on an authoritarian-lecture chain is less clear than a subject-position caught on a hegemonic continuum which serves to contain and limit their conclusions which, while they may be reached by dialogue and the cognitions they produce between students and student and student and teacher, maintain the overarching structures of hierarchy. This continuum may also preclude student and teacher from seeing how, as they become aligned or positioned on administrative bifurgated chains and signifiers, inadvertently, maintain the construction of equivalent (and essentialized) meanings and empty signifiers whereby administrators rule without being seen in hierarchies; or, in which parts of their subject-position surfaces (of students and teachers) are dominated (or hegemonized) from the production of dialogues which conceal what lies behind labels as characterizing students as "discipline and "disruptive" and teachers as "radical" and "rogue." All that one needs is to "dialogue," the rest will take care of themselves.

In order to map out how students and teachers may act in solidarity and begin to mount a counter-hegemonic offensive amongst themselves and other forces intervening their relations – i.e. students versus teachers – what was hitherto assumed to be beyond their borders of consciousness and fear, as prescribed by the modernist dilemmas and chains of signifiers and the representations they produce in their labeling arsenal, a more complex conception of the contexts available to both student and teacher (but rarely conceptualized) may come to the fore. I came to the conclusion that Freire either was missing these insights – specifically post-structural ones – or needed to be complemented and extended to see if, once my students were exposed to his work, they may be able to grasp oppression in today's complex forms and relationships of power and discourse.

FREIRE'S LANGUAGE, LEADERSHIP, AND AUTHORITY

Because of Freire's language in his first chapter (2002) was characterized by my education students as "dense," my students for the most part jumped too quickly to the more easily reading of his second chapter. Hardly any time consequently was devoted to his third and fourth chapters as a result of my spending time in unfolding his first chapter. While Freire does mention only briefly the problem of hegemony (p. 141, 162), within a political and leadership contexts – an issue that would have been of enormous value to some of my students, specifically, those contemplating becoming administrators or deans, this context also reveals how Freire thinks of "liberalist" reforms. Freire brings to task paternalistic leaders and programs preparing teachers for leadership roles. In this regard, Freire states that such programs send out a message which says: "Let us carry out reforms 'for' and before the people carry out a revolution (p. 162)." He remains in a very critical position concerned what "leadership training courses" are. Freire declares that such courses are emerging as "the parts that promotes the whole and not the whole which ...promotes the parts."

Having produced an emerging framework of leadership, Freire insists, however, that "(t)hose members of the community who show sufficient leadership capacities to be chosen (for leadership courses) do not necessarily reflect and express the aspirations of the individuals of their community." Yet, as Freire also maintains, as "soon as they complete the course and return to the community with resources they did not formerly possess, they either use these resources to control the submerged and dominated consciousness of their comrades, or they become strangers in their own communities (p. 143)." While Freire speaks of "authentic authority" as not a mere transfer of power, he is not adverse to power occurring "through delegation or in sympathetic adherence (p. 178)." While the stress between leaders and the people must always be *with* the people in "dialogue," according to Freire, there are aspects to "dialogue" which should be explored to assess the extent leaders and followers are aware of the degrees of how their actions and words may be also crossed by contradictory orders from those above or school administrators which may be endemic and facture student and teacher solidarity and their need to continue to construct relations which are just, trusting, equal, and democratic. In response to this problem, Freire's relies on a notion of "sympathetic delegation," which he considered a code word for delegation of authority (as was in the traditional and paternalistic orders of schooling) used to "get things done." In the possible gap between trusting the people and delegating authority,[103] Freire and *Pedagogy of the Oppressed* may be giving too short shrift as to how delegations of power, customarily the norm in hierarchical and corporate settings, operates in which the leader and led are – whilst supporting democracy – inadvertently justifying the existence of hierarchical authority exempt from a critique of as a hegemonic form.

Moreover, since Freire opposes as illegitimate those with the "marks" of the oppressor and to which he suspects contributes to relations not capable of going against "antagonistic" relations[104] of oppression or "unveiling" the world with others (p. 169) – between leader and led, and teacher and student. That is to say, while trust in the people is essential for a critical praxis and dialogue to unveil the world for Freire, there are limits to Freire, nevertheless. Citing his own fear of those marked by oppression, Freire maintains that "as long as the oppressor within the oppressed is stronger than they themselves...their natural fear of freedom may lead them to denounce the revolutionary leaders instead!" (p. 169).

Upon further critical examination into the in-between spaces of being an oppressor or, alternatively, being a oppressed, in the following chapter, we may raise serious questions about the either-or dilemmas of modernism as presupposed and constructed by Freire and, perhaps, his over protection of revolutionary leaders at a cost which may sacrifice willing oppressed members to fight at each other's side against their "existential dualities" as they, at first, in a moment of awkward struggle seek to break free of the image of the oppressor. But, in another moment, and this moment is what Freire is so much concerned with, the marked oppressed may slide backward, and revert to the ways of the oppressor. This antagonistic relationship between oppressor and oppressed within a person and with others, according to post-structural theorizing and teaching, however, may reveal or unveil new moments in examining the complex layers lying between conscious selves and unconscious selves in discourse, and how speakers, when equipped with lens to see these complex zones of overlapping discourses and their layers of selves sliding from one chain of equivalent subjects positions to others, may reveal how they, in the action, may counter this sliding and consequently perceive in others, in moments which may encourage them to stop their sliding into oppressor positions while, simultaneously acting together in solidarity against those subject-positions they may have already become dis-enchained by.

LIVING IN EACH OTHER'S REFLECTIONS, COGNITIONS AND COMPLEX CONSTRUCTIONS

To post-structuralists, as Laclau and Thomassen, when people (student and teacher) begin to construct their world, a part of this construction (as Freire insists) is to live in each other's constructions or cognitions (pp. 79–81). By not ruling out antagonistic and other contradictory cognitions, however, Laclau and Thomassen seek to examine further how those who live in contradiction may also inscribe on "tendential" surfaces in which they live out their lives as students and teachers. In these inscribed spaces they articulate their feelings, thoughts, and desires onto inscriptive surfaces of their subject-positions. Freire's formula of avoiding antagonism or other ambiguities he suspects, however, does not sufficiently trust those people marked by oppressors. Consequently, Freire denies further exploration into both individual, shared, and overlapping complex forms of cognition (and their affects) which may move or incite those who are oppressed but, bearing the marks of oppression, may not be as ready to risk in acts of more sustainable and deeper criticisms necessary for understanding how they are also hegemonized. By listening to those oppressed who are marked as oppressor, *Counter-Hegemonic Teaching* offers a second look at their realities and may also offer them an opportunity to re-think their roles they are forced to perform and, alternatively, offer them a way to begin to solidify with other oppressed or partially oppressed people to mount an effective counter-hegemonic attack on their already antagonistic and marked interactions and relations.

Thus, Freire and others espousing critical pedagogy would have to respond to the following questions (which will be discussed in the next and final chapters) in making distinct critical hegemonic teaching and theorizing from critical pedagogy and theorizing:
- Who or what is the subject of oppression and its hegemonic forms?
- How do post-structural constructs posit a subject whose identity is to incite themselves and others to collectivize with the oppressed and fight hegemonic forms of oppression? For example, how does hierarchical authority and acts of delegation produce "pecking orders" in which the oppressed, once promoted as leader above others who are led, become themselves oppressors?
- How does dialogue become an expression of power which merely hides hierarchical structures of authority and ignores the complex of discursive formations of which dialogue is but one formation of many? That is, how does dialogue, then, as a method of teaching, excuse rather than posit as problematic teaching as a hierarchical-lecture-banking form? For example, what role does administrative hierarchical discursive formations, and their sub-components, as hierarchical chains of signifiers and subject-positions and their surfaces, play for student and teacher when they inscribe on their surfaces a role they play in

transforming them as oppressors as opposed to uniting with fellow oppressed within parameters not to notice hierarchical dimensions of their acting?

- What then lies between the binary chains of reflection and action, acting as hierarchical equivalent chains and empty signifiers, and how these chains and signifiers may get repositioned from an entity which is unified and consistent to an entity which is strife with contradictions and complex forms of cognition? For example, why do individuals remain consistent and coherent subjects, adhesed to their beliefs, despite evidence to the contradictory as they remain glued to their hierarchical positions and identities?
- How, therefore, is dialogue, as one possible discourse and discursive formation, linked to hegemonic reflections, cognitions, and identities which may or may not contain possible counter-hegemonic and complex reflections and cognitions?
- Because such reflections, cognitions, and identities may appear as antagonistic, different, or not pure or unified forms of consciousness, is this a sufficient reason to maintain such forms as unproblematic? Or, conversely, should such forms be made problematic as to how modernistic or binary chains of cognition maintain as hegemonic and hierarchical both dialogue and reflection?
- That is, is Freire's critical pedagogy and critical pedagogy in general, as it moves in a "post-hegemonic" direction, sufficient to reach a new plateau of counter-hegemonic teaching and theorizing through post-structural constructs in exposing the "pillars of hegemony" – administrative hierarchies, classroom management, tenure, and testing which, to this day, has already contained and co-opted student and teacher reflection and action, dialogue, and their positing or naming as problematic their oppressive school and societal conditions?
- Can counter-hegemonic teaching and theorizing (as opposed or extending critical pedagogy) see those fleeting moments and glimpses of a new terrain of oppressive and liberating fragments or signifiers from which to remake and transform the world?
- Can counter-hegemonic theorizing and teaching name these processes when augmented with post-structural constructs?

Once the above questions can begin to be responded to, along with the questions my education students asked during those classroom discussions after their artwork sessions, they (in my estimation) would have been in a better position to complement Freire with their own theorizing and extend his work as it applies to their work. Specifically, if their pictures and images depicting Freire's Pedagogy would be complemented with post-structural constructs and theorizing, then, there would also be a possibility of their grasping more of what Freire and critical pedagogy may have to offer them. However, by beginning their first artwork sessions – first in small groups, then presenting their artwork to the class as a whole and opening up discussions, students in the class, upon further examining and re-examining their previous discussions and artwork, may have developed a more deeply textured and thick understanding of Freire's Pedagogy, in particular, and critical pedagogy, in general.

Resulting from these follow-up activities, one of their main concerns about Freire's *Pedagogy of the Oppressed* was: while the second chapter was very clear in terms of explaining banking pedagogy, Freire's explanation as to what dialogical problem-posing was not, except in its most rough forms. Moreover, few students were able to read the first chapter with a confident grasp. Loss in many of their questions, discussions, and often in their artwork, then, was the significance of how reflection and action was linked to dialogical acts leading to problem-posing issues and questions. Because the students had a difficult time translating the language of the first chapter, they received a very truncated view of the links between reflection, cognition, dialogue, and problem-posing. As a result, they wanted to know more about why the oppressed oppress each other and themselves in the image of the oppressor and how they may intervene in a problem-posing way (for example, see Figure 23).

Therefore, I felt it was important to clarify how reflection, dialogue, and problem-posing were linked, and more importantly, what did Freire mean when he insisted that student and teacher, in order to avoid a banking style of teaching, must live in each other's cognitions and reflections (pp. 79–80). This led to new questions by the students, as: How can living in each other's cognitions or reflections be done? They further wanted to explore links between dialogue, which presumed reflection and action and problem-posing. Does all dialogue lead to problem–posing, they further asked; or, can dialogue also mirror those oppressive conditions which limit penetrating dialogue, and even feed into or constitute oppressive relations?

Still, others wanted to know how dialogue was able to resist the incursions of some very negative contexts, as racism, sexism, and classism and merely become displaced for "nice talk?" The education students therefore were very receptive for constructing maps which guided them to make distinctions between oppressive and liberating dialogue, as well as how dialogue may lead to or not problem-posing in hegemonic and counter-hegemonic acts of teaching and theorizing. That is, they wanted to know (and some students drew amazing pictures depicting this) what elements in their talk were possibly restraining themselves from becoming "critical" and what elements were producing in them identifications with the oppressor as opposed to the oppressed and the need for solidarity and acting up[105]. They wanted to know moreover how they and their students were contained, perhaps unconsciously, in ways that they may have overlooked or could not spot in time while they were in antagonistic relations or those moments in which they became oppressors instead of fighting alongside the oppressed. Further, they wanted to know how they and their students were becoming hegemonized and how they could also locate spaces for mounting counter hegemonic forces. They therefore wanted to construct pedagogies which responded to the need for more socially just, equal, and democratic forms of teaching and schools. Thus, my students remained in a state of puzzlement as to how to do counter-hegemonic theorizing and teaching (as distinct from critical pedagogy) could come about? Moreover, they looked to Freire for some guidance, but soon realized that he may be in need of being modified and extended to accommodate their desires. This form of post-structural theorizing will be further discussed as I introduce how my special education students accomplished this task, along with my own commentaries in the following Chapter 4.

While the drawing activity and follow up discussions began with a "surprise activity" to keep at a minimum my students edited (scripted or hegemonized) thoughts, providing a platform for their "free association" and feedback on the subject of oppression, the writer proceeded to have them move toward the construction of struggling to become counter-hegemonic teachers. It was not until a follow up activity and discussion (after the artwork sessions), did more reflective discussions ensue, albeit with much confusion and asking more questions for more clarity of Freire's work and the post-structural lens I offered them to satisfy, partially, some of their demands.

To re-summarize about the initial activity or method of conducting my research, I asked the students of the class to break up into four or five groups of two to four students in each group, and upon distributing clear transparency papers with color pens to each group, asked the students to draw or depict any images or thoughts they have which may be relevant to their reading Freire (often for the first time) and how its content (Chapters 1-2) may or may not apply to their future or present teaching. The activity described above was accomplished in over thirty classes which usually housed fifteen to thirty students over a period of eight years in four universities.

LET THE PICTURES SPEAK!

Examining the mass of over 300 pictures accumulated over the last eight years taken from at least thirty education classes and a few presentations I have given in other universities, I will in this chapter let the pictures and images speak for themselves, along with the follow up of student discussions, questions, and my commentary which attempts to summarize what my students had to say after they presented their artwork to each other, in small class group and then in a larger group formations of the whole class, as well as point to a future extending of Freire through post-structural constructs which I will explain further in the following Chapter 4.

I therefore believe that the chapter title, *Freire Illustrated*, is more than appropriate to meet the challenge to extend and/or complement Freire's brilliant work in critical pedagogy. And I will further discuss in this and the next two chapters, what are the implications of this study for the extending the field of critical pedagogy in teaching, educational research, and arguing for a new role of teacher educators to become partners and liaisons with schools, teachers, students, and parents as linked to the school place and the university. I address this challenge to both levels of education: college courses in education, along with teaching in K-12 classes, as being conducted in in-service courses and teacher-student-parents workshops for ongoing professional development of teachers in schools, public, private, and parochial. In this way, new partnerships between teachers, schools, and teacher educators and colleges may come about, whether these sessions are conducted on the terrain of schools or colleges, or ignite professional consciousness and unconsciousness-raising sessions online. Thus, a sorely neglected topic and focus of critical pedagogy and its related discourses, theoretical and practical, may begin to compete with the too long dominance of corporate and positivistic empirical emphases which, today, means more and more testing, standardized curricula, and onerous and often, intrusive administrative hierarchies which further contain or deflect more progressive and democratic modes of teaching and education (see Giroux & Saltman, 2008).

WHO AND WHAT IS A SUBJECT OF OPPRESSION?

Because Freire was not informed with post-structural constructs (to be reviewed in Chapter 4), his work left my students with questions (and myself) as to who and what is an oppressed subject (student or teacher or others) in schools and how does Freire's notion of reflection and action, as well as his notion of dialogue and problem-posing, assist us in locating oppression, and how we, interested in social justice and democracy, may be assisted in dispelling modernist modes of thinking and relating in schools and society? We, the students and I, were also curious about or not clear as to how Freire's notion of reflection, taken from Husserl as a mode of cognition, which intends or intended towards objects, and presupposes an unified subject (a subject derived from the Enlightenment or modern time eras), becomes, in effect, a process which feeds off the objects of intent? That is, ironically, I and the students claimed – after Freire appropriates Husserl's notion of the subject, as adopting a banking epistemological position, which separates (as opposes to links) subject from object, I and the other, agency and structures.

That is, as a subject intending outward, reaching out and into objects, the question was raised by my education students was: Is Freire' subject the same subject irrespective of different cultures, times, and levels of income and poverty? Other students raised additional questions, as: Does Freire's subject also include an unconsciousness who, as suggested by Freud, may be split, transgressed, divided, and unintentionally contradictory? And still a few other students asked if Freire's subject was multiple, allowing for it to intend and, at the same time, to know there may be other forces penetrating its province as a meaning-maker and which we may be (intentionally) letting pass as unimportant glimpses of other realities? Still, another student commented: If Freire is so concerned with students becoming "deposited" with knowledge owned by others (the teacher, the state, authority, etc.) then why is his sense of what a subject is so determined as intending on the object as opposed to having at least a two way conversation with the object of his or her reflections, cognitions, and intentions of themselves and other selves? Another student was quick to add, how in the name of "humanism" or of a monarch or Christian subject, how the Western explorers were able to occupy, exploit, and enslave other people after their discovery of a new world? Or, why in the name of rationalism and European high culture, did Nazi concentration camps and Hiroshima occurred? They concluded: weren't these intentional acts of consciousness of a group, country or culture?

In the following pictures and images, some of the above questions begin to be responded with their pictures and images, insofar as identifying the oppressive subject:

CHAPTER 3

Figure 1

Figure 2

Figure 3

Figure 4

Figure 5

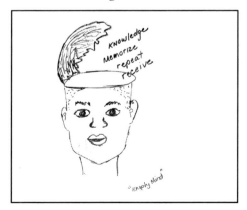

82

As the above pictures clearly illustrate, the teacher or other forces – i.e. standardized curricula based on teacher and text authority through student memorization – there is also an emphasis about not only being oppressed by top-down curricula, authority, and teaching, but further, being "de-humanized." In some cases the teacher holds the student by the ears, as if disciplining or forcing them to learn what they offer as "facts" in the "Finite Book of Knowledge."

Not veering too far from their immediate concerns, specifically how they were oppressed when they were students in schools, and now have matured into adults and teachers themselves, my students depicted why and how they are forced to take on the roles of the oppressor they previously despised and depicted as "inhumane." In a sense, this meant to many of my students how the "oppressed become oppressors" of themselves and each other. Still, they wanted to know in more detail why they perform such duties, and why and how they may feel justified, and even derive pleasure, in oppressing others. See below, Figures 6-9:

Figure 6

Figure 7

Figure 8

Figure 9

Some of the students ventured to go further to understand what "dialogue" means in terms of how one can provide a more humane and a better learning or problem-posing situation for both student and teacher. They often contrasted dialogical-problem-posing teaching to "banking" in a manner that may have maintained however binaries as lecture and dialogue, as if one would be a better choice than another.

Figure 10

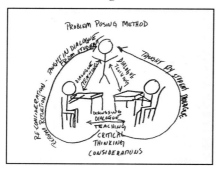

Figure 11

Figure 12

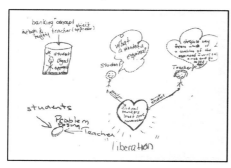

Figure 13

A few made the link between dialogue and problem-positing yet were not clear what problems would be posed by dialogical teaching. They saw dialogical problem-posing as going to heaven, dancing around a fire, or climbing up a mountain toward the sun, as follows:

Figure 14

Figure 15

Figure 16

Other students wanted their students (and themselves) to become more reflective as co-investigators in ways which moved them and their students to value social justice, equality, and democracy, see below:

Figure 17

Most of my education students wanted their students to be more reflective and act in ways that moved them to appreciate critical thinking and humanism. Only a few extended their interpretation of being humane to areas of class, gender, administrative authority, and race. See below an illustration which compares middle class teachers to how their students from the lower class relate to them:

Figure 18

Yet, when my education students are pushed to say more, they threw their hands up, and said: I cannot do things the way I want to when there are so many required standardized tests!

Figure 19

Other students felt pressured by other fears – the loss of their job, the fact they have been doing teaching one way for so long, it's hard to change, etc. They added, in trepidation, how if they do not follow this regimen of teaching top-down, lecturing as much information they could deposit into their heads of their students, they would suffer reprisals by administrators, whose jobs along with their own jobs, depended so much on high or increased student test score outcomes. Hence, they drew many pictures about the hierarchical "chain of command" of "the system" in which they were (and their teaching) incarcerated, as follows:

Figure 20   *Figure 21*

Figure 22   *Figure 23*

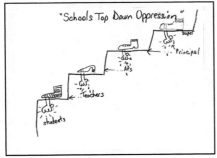

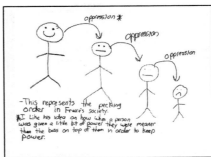

In passing, note that in Figure 23, the illustrator-student adds something new to the testing pressure. The student mentions how she likes "Freire's idea on how when a person was given a little bit of power they were meaner than the boss on top of them in order to keep (their) power." This student's picture or image led to a long and intense debate amongst the students in the class. And this debate and discussion started to probe deeper and pan outward in placing schools in a larger or macro picture of how schools replicated corporate and hierarchical structures of authority and power inimical to progressive learning and teacher autonomy, as follows:

Figure 24   *Figure 25*

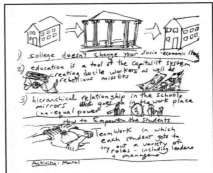

Figure 26

Figure 27

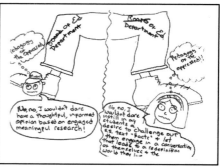

Still, the students remained connected to both macro and micro considerations of oppression. The students in the education class feared if they tried Freire's pedagogy for critical thinking and dialogue to pose as problematic oppressive classroom practices in school hierarchical settings (Figure 32), there would be reprisals by administrators which may undermine their identities as teachers. Some illustrators portrayed them-selves as split as a result of so much fear they engendered when they thought about using Freire's pedagogy in their classrooms. Others, more audacious, felt committed to act despite fears. See Figure 28-30 below:

Figure 28

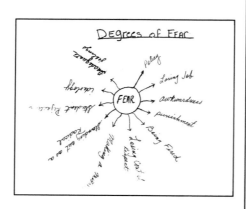

Figure 29

Other pictures portrayed a deeper sense of identity in conflict. Some argued for more dialogue – therapy-style – to transform their self-images of themselves; while others decried the "mask" they were forced to wear in schools (see Figure 31 below),

Figure 30

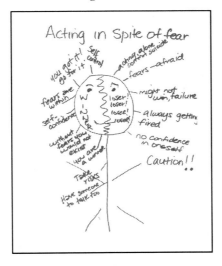

along with a split between themselves (see Figures 29, 32-33) revealing a an "intrinsic"(their necks being choked) and extrinsic faces (appearing as happy). All of these factors being brought on by "fear." One illustration, hoping Freire's pedagogy would solve such identity crises, pleaded for "dialogue" to emancipate their "inferior" self-images (see Figure 32). Another illustration, after looking at one's self in a mirror (note the stitching of the boy's head having being "deposited" by so many facts by the oppressor/teacher/school system, turns to another boy (Figures 34-35), and begins to interact with another boy, while both boys remain adhesed to their old identities (as seen reflected in the mirrors). Students, who made comments of this picture, added that they may have been moments in which both boys turned away from their individualistic reflections and moved toward each other to find out or help each other to free themselves from their oppressed circumstances.

Figure 31

Figure 32

Figure 33

Figure 34   *Figure 35*

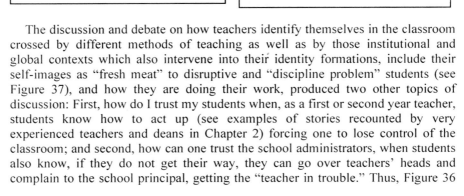

The discussion and debate on how teachers identify themselves in the classroom crossed by different methods of teaching as well as by those institutional and global contexts which also intervene into their identity formations, include their self-images as "fresh meat" to disruptive and "discipline problem" students (see Figure 37), and how they are doing their work, produced two other topics of discussion: First, how do I trust my students when, as a first or second year teacher, students know how to act up (see examples of stories recounted by very experienced teachers and deans in Chapter 2) forcing one to lose control of the classroom; and second, how can one trust the school administrators, when students also know, if they do not get their way, they can go over teachers' heads and complain to the school principal, getting the "teacher in trouble." Thus, Figure 36 reveals how a teacher confronts her administrator for correcting or challenging her in front of her students and the administrator apologizes. But, ironically enough, the prospective student who drew this image concludes of the school principal that she was "suckered" or fooled by the teacher. There were many students, who still identify themselves as students (rather than prospective teachers) so they take a position in which they see the principal as helping the student, not realizing at this point, they are to be teachers themselves! They have yet to materialize an idea for understanding how teachers, wedged between students and administrators, are placed in a very vulnerable position, in-between the cross fire of student complaints and administrator enforcement of the complaints.

Figure 36   *Figure 37*

It has been long established that teacher performance is very much dependent on student test score outcomes, much to the chagrin of those liberal or progressive educators and parents who want to see more discussion and dialogical teaching and learning formats. While the new incoming president-elect Obama has promised changes, including doing away with the "bubble-type" of questions on standardized exams, he has also sent out contradictory signs about eliminating all tests and tools of assessment and accountability. As Henry Giroux and Saltman, (2008) in a recent online article argues, corporate and top-down regulations or what has become known as the factory model of teaching and education, in which students become consumers and teacher entrepreneurs, along with their use of classroom management techniques and hierarchical administrators, who posit urban kids as criminals, remain many questions. Once again, it seems, teaching performance will be predicated on student test scores outcomes – albeit in different forms of assessment – as determining what is a "good" versus a "bad teacher.

What remained in most of my education students' minds were questions of what kind of mechanism or theory can produce for them a framework which accommodates both realities: (1) the reality that oppression, specifically, top-down administrative regulations, testing, preset curricula, and classroom management is dominant in their schools, and (2) while they want to make a difference in the lives of their students by allowing them the necessary autonomy to think and dialogue and posit as problems in their classroom instruction and content, and process. They argued they needed a map to reveal the limits of how far they can go within administrative or hierarchical structures of school authority. That is, without raising their own and each other's defences or, for that matter, those of the system and its administrators under whom they worked for.

Still, the main theme of Freire's first chapter – how the oppressed become each other's oppressor, and how their own self-image produces in themselves as oppressors, and when given a "bit of power" how they become more oppressive than their higher positioned administrators; or, in different terms, when a teacher is delegated more power from their administrator-bosses, how do they know they can take chances and innovate dialogically with their students?

The students began to theorize further, as the following last five pictures revealed. They wondered if "you should fill the bucket up or ignite a fire?" (Figure 38); teach in the traditional "waffle" way or the progressive way (spaghetti) (Figure 39). Or, as another student began to see how oppression travels in "layers" (see Figure 40), while other students saw oppression between the oppressor and the oppressed as formed in a spider-web of tentacles (Figure 41), while more subtly, one student saw the student and the teacher as separate but a part of the overlapping and intertwining process (Figure 42). See below:

Figure 38

Figure 39

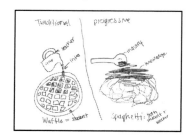

Figure 40

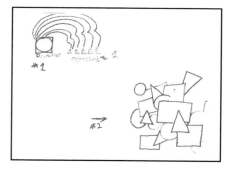

Figure 41

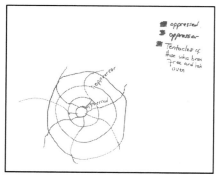

Figure 42

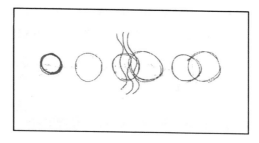

One picture drawn by a graduate student below recently came close to moving us into a post-structural mode of thinking and teaching. She drew in a circular formation a series of people, each from a different Caribbean country, developed a pecking order or how one island-nation thinks of itself as superior to another island nation. There are also lines drawn laterally across the space internal to the circle, criss-crossing each other, unnamed. As one sees the circle return to the original oppressor or labeler, they see in the horizon (in the upper right and corner) a face (which is also un-named) looking at the cycle.

Figure 43

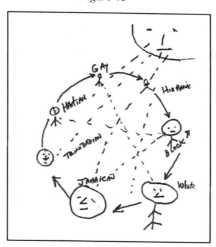

After discussion, the students named the Other as standing for several oppressive others – white people, gay people African-American people, oppression, racism, sexism, classism, etc. The face (see Figure 43) may also stand for or represent power and money interests, and more. We continued to reflect and talk about this image as I attempted to have them look at some post-structural ideas and pictures I introduced to them for consideration. These images were of chains and signifiers – some of which were named and used by my special education students for my doctoral study. Randy, one of my special education students, revealed many of his selves (see Chapter 4 for his drawn images) as he named the oppressive world of being "special" in a school seeking to reform itself and become more "inclusive," more dialogical. Randy and the other students were not "suckered" into these "new" reforms so quickly, however. They had lived in a very painful world in their school, and knew what being excluded and ignored meant, both on their identities and social relationships. They told me a story of a former classmate named Sidney. In this story, Sidney a friend of the students, was pulled out of their special track classes to be "included" in regular classes. As Zena and Lisa said to Gregory and Randy, "Sidney no longer talks to us anymore."

Still, in one of their other drawings, the notion of feeling divided in terms of how the "hierarchy" structures of authority in their schools still presented a problem, which Freire remained unclear about. In Figure 45 below, school administrators (and, perhaps, teachers) appear to yell and dictate their wishes and orders. A threaded lined wall, perhaps re[presenting a division or a porous division of many chains intervenes and intertwines between "hierarchy" and a group of people (perhaps, students, teachers, parents, administrators) interacting with "dotted" lines in between themselves. There is no explanation as to what these dotted lines represent – chains of signifiers, intermittent communications vacillating between hierarchy and liberating education. Yet, while we may interpret as a wall between hierarchy and Freire, if one looks carefully at the cover of this book, they will see (in color) how the so-called "wall" is an "intertwining string of chains," in black – connoting hierarchy, and various colors, connoting the different and diverse chains linking the various people together on the right side of the below image, and, in some instances, penetrating those of the left side, and vice-versa, as illustrated below (see front book cover):

Figure 44

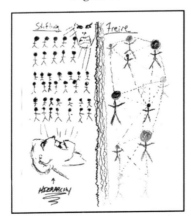

At this time, few if any of my education students saw they may further theorize about teaching as power which was oppressive, dominant, and hegemonic through post-structural constructs, as chains, signifiers, subject-positions, discursive formations, etc. By hegemonic, the writer informed the students that Freire's notion of how the oppressed become oppressors to each other and themselves was attempted to be disclosed by Freire in his last chapter. He mentioned briefly hegemony twice (2002, pp. 141 and 162), but this attempt was short and eventually became a problem as to how after a major change or revolution of the basic structures in society, what would be the roles of the leader and the led, the administrator and the administrated, teacher and student.

ENTER THE POST-STRUCTURAL MODE OF THEORIZING ABOUT FREIRE

In traditional Marxist terms, the problem of hegemony has been treated as one in which teaching and cognition are "superstructural," a mere reflection of the basic structures of society, specifically the political economy. Once the basic structures were changed or altered then, problems related to hegemony, identity, language, and cognitive constructions would change accordingly with little input from those in the structures. The notion of having my students "wait" till the broader structures and processes of the political economy would change, would mean for them to continue to live in oppressive conditions which they were now becoming aware of. It seemed hypocritical of me to challenge my students to know more, go deeper in their thoughts and experiences of teaching, and perhaps, emerge with a counter-hegemonic theory or perspective while all we could do is to wait indefinitely. I rejected this position and, following Zinn and Foucault works, asked the students not to wait or take a spectator position. This may have had an impact on my students who liked to keep their options open – most of the time "laying low" and wait. But by introducing a postmodern perspective – i.e. Foucault (1980) – in which power is not only received but seized and negotiated for when people form and organize themselves into pressure and interest groups. When my students realized that this form of power-taking is an option also, they sensed that what was possible was also attainable, and it would be more hypocritical to identify one's self as an educator, a teacher or teacher educator, committed to social justice, critical reflection, equality, and democracy, unless one has the courage to take the necessary risks in taking agential and organized actions against school and societal hierarchies and privileged elites.

Still, as I invited my students to re-examine Freire's *Pedagogy of the Oppressed*, and why some were turned off by his language in his very important first chapter, I asked them to penetrate their own limits (or the "untested feasibility") of their knowledge, by questioning Freire's and their own basic understandings of what consciousness is. We discussed how Freire, Marx, and much of critical pedagogy is a part of the Enlightenment tradition. This tradition, while valorizing the subject and the subjective, also present a subject who was a unified and solid entity. This same subject also became the humanist subject underwriting the emergence of natural science and its laws and regularities some have referred to as the positivist mode of research – much of its assumptions we follow today in assessing standardized test scores and top-down and linear thinking and school governance.[107] This modernist form of knowledge-making also posits as dualistic right from wrong, true from false, real from imaginary, and so forth. These chains of modernist thinking and logic further posit one's subjectivity or consciousness as a solid entity, which knows no wrong, no weakness, ambiguity, or doubt. This positivistic tradition of subjectivity and science is not the fluid and unstable dis-unified unity of post-structural consciousness, shot through with loose ends and doubts of thinking – namely, the presence of a unconsciousness in and through the structures of consciousness and language.

Finally, I introduced to my education students (as I did in my special education students in my doctoral study) a new framework, a post-positivist or post-modernist framework, I referred to as "post-structural theory." I also introduced them to a new language – with chains of power circulating in, through, and between us as we speak (recall Berger & Luckmann's under theorized concept in Chapter 1 in getting beyond modernist dualisms between thinking and acting), reflection and action, consciousness and unconsciousness, dialogue and discursive formations. I also revealed how in post-structural theorizing one may take multiple subject-positions but be subject to contingencies, as for example, in acts of articulation in which one or others may occupy "tendentially" or share in various degrees, surfaces of their subject-positions in which they may inscribe and get inscribed their feelings, doubts, assumptions, second-thoughts, unconscious feelings, and words articulated to each other in and through a hegemonic struggle for what is to be defined as equivalent (similar but not identical, normative but not law-like) – as opposed to be labeled as different, deviant, and demonized – in their relating to each other.

While, simultaneously, armed with this new perspective, my students began to live in a post-structural world, seeing and articulating beyond what they assumed as possible – i.e. getting beyond the myth that their beliefs were owned individualistically rather than shared and questioned as moving subject-positions formed in the intersections and interactions between equivalent and differential chains of signifiers: the former as master or sutured/anchored signifiers; the latter as empty and floating signifiers – the latter breaking off from chains of equivalence to link up with other, less powerful chains of difference or potentially counter-hegemonic chains of signifiers and subject-positions. This last consideration is very important in re-examining the foundations of Freire's main work, *Pedagogy of the Oppressed* in terms of reflection and action, dialogue and problem-posing, and finally, seeing anew how, when intersected chains of signifiers and images reveal spaces on the surfaces of subject-positions[108] which otherwise would not be seen by Freire's *Pedagogy* within "points of antagonism" as leading to "points of connection" and vice-versa between and amongst oppressors and the oppressed. More on this topic will be discussed and grounded in theoretical and historical works of Laclau (with Mouffe, 1985; 1990, 1993, 2007) in the following Chapter 4 in terms of how we live and teach in a world with young people to being sensitive, caring, and democratically committed people.

Afterwards, we began to become post-structural theorizers by looking at, very slowly, and analytically, the writings of Lacan, Laclau, Zizek, and Pecheux, and others (see Chapter 4). I wanted to them to know and, just as a possibility, so that they may – despite the abstruse language of these writers – find their own pathway toward becoming liberated and liberating others who remain hegemonized and not counter-hegemonic theorizers and teachers.

Reciting those questions made in the beginning of this chapter:
- What is the Subject as Oppressed? How does school's administrative hierarchies and testing play a role in containing and transfixing subjects as non-knowledge-makers?
- How do Post-Structural Constructs Expand this Subject to Identify and Fight Hegemonic Oppression?
- What Lies Between the Binary Chains of Reflection and Action?
- How does Dialogue Differ from Discourse and its Formations?
- How is Dialogue and Discourse linked or couched in hegemonic and hierarchical discursive formations and their signifying chains and subject positions and surfaces?

I began to organize a syllabus for my next education course using Freire's *Pedagogy of the Oppressed* as a backdrop or plane on which to bounce off with the next group of people seeking to become liberating, anti-oppressive, and counter-hegemonic educators.

Before moving onto the next and final chapter, I will delve into these "points of connection" within the context of theorizing post-structurally in extending Freire's *Pedagogy* as well as pushing the critical pedagogy field to enter, as Kincheloe and Giroux discussed on U-Tube (2008), its "post-hegemonic phase." In discussing these elements I will refer to brief allusions made about students of education I have taught and observed illustrating their immediate reactions in several aspects of their teaching under hegemony and how such forces have affected their identities, relations, and willingness to act as agents with one another for taking power against the hegemony of school administrative authority in present day school conditions under the regimen of testing and classroom management.

Further, I discuss in the last chapter what is implied for research and practice of teaching by theorizing Freire through post–structural constructs and pointing to future directions for counter-hegemonic theorizing with teachers and research committed toward teaching in non-oppressive and more democratic school conditions. Specifically, using Freire's original book, *Pedagogy of the Oppressed*, to examine more critically or counter-hegemonically how the oppressed become each other's oppressor in living out their existential dualities most of us are probably are very much familiar with but rarely articulate.

ENTER PAULO FREIRE'S PEDAGOGY OF THE OPPRESSED: A RE-EXAMINATION OF ITS FOUNDATIONS VIA POST-STRUCTURAL CONSTRUCTS

This book therefore takes very seriously critical pedagogy; particularly, those writings of Paulo Freire, and in particular, his main work, *Pedagogy of the Oppressed*. Others have described Freire as his name is equivalent to critical pedagogy and critical thinking in today's schools and universities. As Henry Giroux maintains, Freire is the "standard reference for engaging in what is often referred to as teaching for critical thinking."[109] As Joe Kincheloe (2005) noted, one cannot begin to talk about hegemony without bringing to one's attention Paulo Freire and his writings. Donaldo Macedo,[110] a protégé to Freire for many years, also recognized appropriating Freire is at best a partial experience, and at worst, one that may become distorted and chosen strictly for its emphasis on dialogue as a method of conversation and group therapy, divorced from its humane and world-changing contexts. As a college professor, I teach Freire's main work, *Pedagogy of the Oppressed,* by asking my students to draw images or thoughts that come to mind as they read his text. I have the students respond this way, without telling them in advance, but after they have read Freire's first two chapters, and after we meet in follow up class discussions, the surprise element remains.

The responses and images drawn by my students have been so revealing that I have been tempted to devote an entire chapter just to displaying and analyzing their drawings. Their artwork – over 300 pictures drawn on transparencies – for the last eight years taken from thirty classes illustrates how students perceive pedagogy of oppression and what they feel is necessary to teach against those oppressive features in our schools and society. Their reactions are often mixed and filled with questions, getting beyond the "Freire is too difficult to understand" phase. Some students take on an instrumental view, seeing Freire and his pedagogy as a means for softening up the classroom's rigid routines, transforming it into a more relaxed, almost therapeutic atmosphere of conversation. Others have recognized how oppression is a much more personal and painful experience, involving messy contexts and images of suffering, and the need for social justice. Thus, Freire becomes their sedative. Whatever may be said about their reactions, both in their artwork, images, or words, reading Freire is often a transformatory experience, introducing students to the world of liberation against the world of oppression. And, more importantly, to fight for schools having more democratic administrative and curricular structures, processes, and places to be with young and adolescent students in their struggles for justice, equality, and democracy.

The notions of dialogue and oppression are often evasive concepts. Even when Freire is implementing his pedagogy via a "dialogical method," too many educators of teachers have subverted its main message, which is to humanize the world against its oppressive structures. What these teacher educators do, however, is to subvert Freire's main message points by containing their students reading to Chapter 2 or the chapter on dialogical methods of teaching. While some may describe those processes of de-humanization as rooted in hegemony or the unconsciousness and fractured relations between teacher ad taught, and why, when they are positioned by oppression see the other, even their fellow oppressed, as the enemy or the Other, so few rarely discuss these things.

Moreover, after reading Freire, few of my students began to see how hegemony works in this context other than calling it a "false consciousness" or how fooled they become under hierarchical school conditions. What they do see (if they read the more difficult chapter 1 or more) is a more genuine look into why the oppressed become each other's oppressor and thereby fracture potential solidarities with one another. As Freire points to how in colonialized African nations amongst the natives while recently "liberated" remain nevertheless colonialized, as: "at the most slight sign (of a fellow oppressed), the other oppressed looks for his knife (p. 62)."

Referring to this phenomenon as "horizontal violence," Freire begins to open new vistas in which to see how hegemony, in part, may work. By this illustration, oppressed people do more than yield over their consent and power, they act and perceive each other as their other's Other or overseer and attack each other violently. By studying Freire on this point, my students recognize that their roles, as student and teacher, have much in common with the oppressor-oppressed relationship. In fact, my students often identified themselves, as future or current teachers as the oppressor, and conversely, they assume – whether this applies to themselves as college students or to their future students, the student is the oppressed on the oppressor-oppressed equation. So powerful are the modernist-dualistic chains of signifiers my students speak through, at this point, I try to facilitate other options of thinking about oppression and power relations. I tend to seek or show how students and teachers have more in common as they are both controlled and victimized – albeit differentially – by a system of higher ups and influences by dominant institutions throughout society.

Often, my students simply stop at the point of making a simplification of identifying students with the oppressed and teachers with the oppressors. However, based on a discussion of their artwork revealing their immediate feelings and fears as well as interpretations and images of oppression, my education students often depict in their pictures student-teacher relationships linked to images of "chains" and how student and teacher must "break the chains" of their states of oppression or de-humanization. Some students see links in the student-teacher relationships as connected also to larger institutions of society and the world. Others, on a more micro level, revealed the feelings and pain one gets when they are oppressed by chains or at the beck and call of administrators for more test drilling and other demands requiring the use of classroom management techniques and labeling. But, something stops them from perceiving larger, yet linked to smaller and more micro links and images penetrating the modernist splits between the macro and micro dimensions of oppression. At these points, in order to show that there lies an "in-between" space(s) between the macro and micro images, meso images, in which, using post-structural constructs, one can trace and map how power infiltrates both student and teacher, and at the moment of articulation, how both may see how they become a part of a negotiating process in seeing those points of connection in which – on the levels of signifiers and their chains, as well as on the surfaces of their subject-positions – how new and different identifications are possible within and against oppressive relationships; or how they may transform themselves, each other, and their school and classroom surroundings.

I have tried to point out, in the course of discussion during these artwork and follow up discussion sessions – sometimes received with shrugs of disbelief – a more basic message Freire intended to communicate, as follows: In *Pedagogy of the Oppressed,* both student and teacher act and struggle together in solidarity, in a communion of love, humility, trust, and critical thinking aimed at taking action to transform (not reform) the world, schools, and other dominant institutions. In a mutual process of problem-solving and dialogue, the oppressed and oppressor contradiction is overcome by a critical recognition of both student and teacher as they reverse their roles: student becomes a teacher, teacher becomes a student.

Pedagogy of the Oppressed, I further attempt to point out (if this isn't done by the students themselves) holds the solution to some of their problems. That is, if we feel and identify ourselves as oppressed or being denied from becoming human beings, we, in addition, also have to penetrate the hegemonic myth that portrays us as "free" individuals with a consciousness that is whole, unified, and bereft of any sudden feelings of doubt, conscious or unconscious, as we live in a society that likewise teaches all are treated equally and with justice. This state of being is referred to as the "American Dream." This dream is lived through by the existence of binary chains of existence: for those who work hard you will be rewarded and become successful, whereas those who do not work hard, are punished with unemployment and being losers in society. This binary chain allows for no interventions into contexts related to poverty and wealth, heterosexuality and homosexuality, white and people of color, ability and disability, new immigrants and old natives, and so forth.

Once a critical recognition or moment of critical consciousness is achieved of these modernist chains of signifiers, students and their teachers may grow restless. They may want to know when people bond together to overcome their oppression, how, in our technological, overly administrated, and regulated society and schools, transformation or real change is possible when those of the powers-to-be are so wealthy, privileged, and connected? My students appreciated Freire's notion of how the oppressed "house" the image of the oppressor in their head. However, his portrayal of this moment is not intervened by contrary images in which the image is displaced and transformed by other forces, ridges, sort of speak, intruding into the smooth hegemonic planes emerging from counter-hegemonic struggles and images competing with hegemonic forces. This is so, I usually respond, because Freire's work, at this point in his development, was not further informed by insights into unconscious identifications, sublimations, displacements, condensations, and projections, and other forces which have slipped away or avoided detection under modernist and binary logic and radar.

As Freud could have instructed Freire, and his post-structuralist followers as Lacan, Pecheux, and Zizek, society is not only a "structured complex whole (Althusser)," but further, one linked within a intricate set of chains and interstices which cross over one another, leaving traces of those marks of antagonism to those spaces of connection leading to new solidarities necessary for mounting emancipatory movements in and out of schools. Further, while mentioning philosophers as Gramsci and Althusser, in attempting to understand how "dominance is structured in complex whole," Freire does not pay much attention to Althusser's main construct, over-determination, in which class, for example, may spill over and dominate other forces, – but not necessarily remain fixed within them – as gender, race, authority, language, culture, etc.

Until post-structural constructs are introduced at this juncture for re-examining Freire's philosophical foundations, what continues to remain obscure is how the economy, church, culture, women, men, and gay movements, civil rights movements, and conservative corporate controls affecting our trade imbalances and unemployment rates impinge on one another at the micro level, and further for purposes of analysis, how they are carried through from the macro levels via the media onto those many conduits and passageways linking the macro to the micro levels or, how in these constructions of subject-positions of how student and teacher articulate these experiences affecting themselves and their lives, identities, and work. The students and I wanted to know more why, in attempting to fill in those yet informed or "in-between" spaces or places or "ridges" – between consciousness and unconsciousness and inter-subjective relations – how oppression and de-humanzation works.

It is not until I introduced the little known discursive theories of Michel Pecheux (1982),[111] a contemporary of Althusser, Foucault, and Zizek, and his notion of "discursive formations" that intrude in between the gaps and interstices between theory and practice, subject and object, and reflection and action, did I and the students begin to gain a better grasp and ground.[112] Instead, Freire relies to a considerable extent on the notion of consciousness as a unified entity of cognition, taken in large measure from Edmund Husserl. This means, Freire has been influenced by a notion of consciousness which is whole, unified, and moves toward and outward onto the object world, seizing or depositing in these objects an infusion of the subject's meanings whereby, in the subject, meaning originates. All is accomplished is a state of mind or moment in consciousness in which Freire's subject intends or cognizes *on* the object, as opposed *with* others and other objects which may flow in, through, and between subjects and objects.[113]

This unified or essentialized state of cognition leaves both the oppressed and oppressor in a dilemma: Should we fight against those forces that constantly divide and pit *us* against one another? And, further, who is this "us," or those who would compromise our own individual freedom, or dialogues, and subvert our desires to join together to fight against "them?" Who and what are those forces that oppress both student and teacher to manipulate each other in schools, and how do they intervene even after and while they both reflect, co-intend, sense, and share cognitions in dialogue? In other words, how does dialogue get caught in a network of discursive formations which oppress and divide student and teacher solidarity?

IF FRERIE ONLY WOULD HAVE KNOWN: MOVING TOWARD A POST-STRUCTURAL RE-EXAMINATION

Freire's text was initially addressed to under-developed countries in which peasants struggle to survive for the bare necessities, always fearful of challenging the authorities – landowners and the state – over them. They remained, for the most part, submerged in silence – in a state of adhesion or giving obedience to those who oppressed them and their labor. The only alternative open to them was a form of resistance that was from the outset subverted and to which they fragmented themselves and their potential for solidarity as one became the other's oppressor.

If Freire had lived today in an advanced industrialized and technological world,[114] how would he ask us to posit as a problem or cognize about hegemony? Would he posit as problem hegemony as a special kind of oppression acting through ideology in language that oppresses and manipulates oppressed and oppressor alike in hierarchical contexts? That is, how may one, an oppressed, gain and share power without being adhesed to being positioned structurally and hierarchically? Or, put in another way, how may one share power without necessarily elevating themselves into hierarchical power at the expense of keeping those others down and who they presumably compete against? What appears to be factual is that both students and teachers are constantly hegemonizing each other but little attention is paid by them as to how binary modes of reflecting or acting defuse their struggles by having their cognitions attached along individualistic as opposed to collective chains of meanings, signifiers, and subject-positions.

Perhaps, if Freire had known some of the post-structural constructs, as their "unconsciousness is structured like a language (Lacan, 1977), he might have expanded the definition of cognition or thinking to include unconscious experiences and their associated desires and structures along with chains of signifiers penetrating and linking up with one' identity and other external and political forces? Perhaps, he would have pointed to other contexts linked to the cognitive context in which student and teacher relations emerge in advanced industrialized, technologically-insolated, and administratively-governed societies and schools in which full cognition is already invaded or positioned through class, gender, race, and authority, and ability signifiers and their chains which, in turn, position them as subjects with surfaces for inscribing and de-inscribing both domination and resistances?

I have personally seen how college teachers cut short a more radical inter-pretation of Freire's works. This, I would contend is because they have no familiarity with post-structural constructs that posit as a problem those hierarchical, authoritarian, and even fascist subject-positions which remain existent in the daily business of teaching and being with students. The problem is not whether Freire would have posited hegemony as a problem or how his work may be re-conceptualized as a force for ideological re-structuring of subject-positions and chains of signifiers affecting students and teachers in their work, relations, and words use. The problem for a post-structural critique of Freire's work lies much deeper in the caverns and capillaries of a postmodern notion of power. In other words, how the words, gestures, stares, intonations, and other signifying experiences get trampled by authority in schools, whereas, if they could identify these spaces in which there remains possibilities between them, irrespective of the onerous impact of hierarchies and their authority structures, new forms of cognition can be imagined and be practical in grounding new forms of resistance between and over them.

Thus, as a main objective of this book, *Counter-Hegemonic Teaching* seeks an audience who wants to be stirred and will stir other teachers and students of education to take counter-hegemonic actions by re-examining critical pedagogy of Freire's *Pedagogy of the Oppressed*. Once this re-examination is made, post-structural concepts can be introduced to further or advance critical theorizing and pedagogy into a "post-hegemonic phase." If this can be done – and I support this advancement – then the problematic of how dominance (or hegemony) may deter what forces us to partake in processes of self-defeating and self and mutually inflicting dominating acts of our own and each other's actions and inactions, may finally become transformed and exceeded. As we have already seen in the previous chapters, much of this book is to show how hegemony gets reproduced and carried out in agencies of school teacher preparation programs, school curricula, and teaching practices. By offering a counter-hegemonic perspective to describe and analyze what critical pedagogy omits, yet points to, is yet another goal in the writing of *Counter-Hegemonic Teaching*, intended as an extension (not alternative) to critical pedagogy.

Counter-hegemony draws attention to how resistance can best penetrate the "system" without becoming co-opted by those counter-reactionary forces operating in school hierarchical structures and processes of signification. By critiquing the institutional foundations of administrative hierarchies, modes of classroom management, testing, and various modes of teaching which coerce teachers to take on hierarchical subject-positions, along various chains of signifiers which link them to other aspects of domination via discourses – specifically, when concept-ualized as "ridges" or those overlapping and intertwining series and layers of discursive formations constituting their signifying chains and subject-positions surfaces – a new direction may become available for critical pedagogy.[115]

CAN A *PEDAGOGY OF THE OPPRESSED* BE TRANSFORMED INTO A PEDAGOGY OF THE HEGEMONIZED?

With this book, I want to challenge students and disciples of Paulo Freire's *Pedagogy of the Oppressed* to update their insights for a pedagogy that serves to offer praxis and agency in ways which are mindful of the need (as Freire insisted) for students-to-become-teachers, and teachers-to-become-students. In our current climate of intense standardized and high stake testing, overly "managed" classrooms, and onerous administrative hierarchies who monitor and enforce both operations, and get and give rewards for test results while using these test results to evaluate or drive teachers out of the profession, needed further is an extended version of Freire's *Pedagogy* to expose new conflicts and contradictions which may act as new spaces for student-teacher interventions of solidarity and movements of change.

While this action certainly requires courage, creativity, and solidarity with likeminded people, it will also require radical actions on part of student, parent, and teacher to resist and overcome those contradictory forces with "real" teaching and "real" teacher power. The next question that must be asked, then, is: how much of the present day's teacher identity is shaped, molded, made a disposition to become counter-hierarchicalized activists and theorists? And, where can one locate those spaces to resist this molding process?

As we will see in the next two chapters, students and teachers are already in subject-positions to challenge modernist concepts of cognition and knowledge-making. There are many other chains of signifiers and subject-positions which transverse these discourses and those discourses of the "system." Turkle (1998), for example has asked us to examine the extent we are not so much what we are doing with technology and media as what technology and media are doing to us. We may want to look at both the dominating and emancipatory dimensions of technology as a discourse system operating on and through subject-positions and chains of signifiers of their own making. We may also want to look at such technology, as I-pods, the Internet, cell phones, blogger networks, and other technologically mediated discourses already circulating in and through and forming new subject-positions and surfaces, and how these devices may help or harm resistance to authorities or act as forces capable of initiating new cooperation amongst resistant counter-cultures in schools who demand more democracy and respect than blind obedience to the "powers-that-be."

POST-HEGEMONIC CRITICAL PEDAGOGY AND
COUNTER-HEGEMONIC TEACHERS

While Kincehloe (2005) correctly posits hegemonic power is a very complex phenomena – involving teaching, curriculum, assessment, and more, he also makes known that one enters the profession must be oriented to "caring skills" for counter-hegemonic teaching. Kincheloe, however, does not clarify other dimensions which may factor into this complex by offering alternate perspectives or contrary ways to critique top-down authority, curricula, and testing *while in* such conditions.[116] I compliment Kincheloe's remarks on counter-hegemonic activities, nevertheless. What is offered in this section are three dimensions not mentioned by Kincheloe, and what is the tendency on part of other critical theorists of the Freirian persuasion that may need to be extended: *First*, while understanding how students and teacher construct their worlds, ties, and relations to each other, not all power relations are equal or relative. Administrators, for example, which Kincheloe (2005, p. 11) addresses as a relatively equal category alongside students and teachers, are not necessarily innocuous categories to accept as facts of life in schools. That is, not all three – students, teachers, and administrators – have equal power, nor do they exert their powers in the same ways. How do students and teachers handle these unequal power relations under the surveillance of school administrators and principals?

Second, while recognizing that Gramsci's work is important to develop notions of hegemony and counter-hegemony, Kincheloe correctly asserts, gaining consent in complex power relations is a pedagogical act and therefore a perspective which can be taught by teachers and teacher-educators. Yet, in these teaching moments, intervened by hierarchical authority, how do students and teachers begin to build communities of discourse or discursive formations without mis-recognizing so-called neutral power relation differentials and boundaries of the school's hierarchy and administration? And further, if they see these intruding spaces, how do student and teacher negotiate and decide to act in those more or less risky spaces in which to question resist and fight back?

And, *thirdly* how do displacements and transformations as they experience them in their signifying and discursive practices act as "power-perceivers" or telescopes into the complex mass of power intertwining hierarchical and hegemonic maintaining power with more accurate and real sources of power, from both administrators and students and teachers? This area, not pointed to in Kincheloe recent work, requires more work, theoretical and practical into the future of counter-hegemonic teaching. That is, locating how in those spaces "in-between" or those intermediary spaces in which counter-hegemonic perspectives and subject-positions can be carved out from hegemonic conditions and discourses already circulating and positioning student and teacher may be "mapped out" in order to mount more effective forms of resistance against established and hegemonic authority and thereby empower student and teacher to the art or skill of mapping in which to carve out other counter-pedagogical skills, as "care skills?"

While agreeing with Kincheloe on many of the salient points he makes (2005, 2007, 2008) concerning counter-hegemonic actions and possibilities, I would also point to an analysis of those complex dimensions in the hegemonic and counter-hegemonic acts which interact with one another and name how power as a "hegemonic" accomplishes more than a moment of false resistance and/or a possible yielding over of one's consent to others located above in the school hierarchy. These acts of power produce effects which materialize themselves into subject-positions or places in which one thinks, perceives, gets incited or incites others in which student and teacher affirm or alter their assumptions in ways consistent as well as inconsistent with their intentions, and how, in these unexpected moments of contingency, they may negotiate with themselves and each other as they live and learn through their cognitions? At the same time, I would further ask Kincheloe and other critical pedagogues and theorists to probe deeper for those intermediate spaces (between subject and object, agency and structure) which may affect how and why our notions of consciousness remain essentialized and unified states of consciousness and who fail to perceive how our perceptions are led astray or mis-perceived what can also be other form of consciousness, more collective, multiple, and effective in mounting acts of counter-identifying with others within our-selves and others out there in the school and society's hierarchies of power.

Counter-identifying, to Pecheux (1982) are acts of identification in which what one assumes and perceives as beneficial in the world and its subjects and objects of identification but, in an inadvertent movement of signification (i.e. signifiers and their chains intervening each other), identifications take on or slide into other subject-positions which are not necessarily beneficial to one's interests and powers (Hennessey, 1993; P. Smith, 1988; Strickland, 2005). As Zinn has been speaking about interests and powers in the aftermath of the recent Obama victory, he extols his audiences not to get to complacent and rely on your government. He insists the interests of government, historically, have not been consistent with the interests of the people. And what is incumbent for the people to do, as Obama takes his oath of office, is to keep alive their voices by joining together in large numbers in groups which demand more pro-active actions for the welfare and interests of the people (Goodman, 2008).

For example, Kincheloe maintains that counter-hegemonic acts can be constructed as pedagogical acts (i.e. "caring skills") in order to "win the consent" of the people. He maintains that it is in these "forms of learning that engage people's conceptions of the world in such a way that transforms, not displaces them, with perspectives more compatible with various elites." (2005, p. 14). However, as *Counter-Hegemonic Teaching* will argue, what is central in reversing or resisting forms of learning which are hegemonic and "more compatible" with elites, are both acts, which occur in identification processes: displacement and transformation. That is, when student and teacher, oppressed and oppressor, seek to break loose from the hegemonic holds of their school and classroom practices, there is always those moments which signal for those disposed to act and resist hegemony to counter-identify and locate ridges or return to reactionary positions or reproduce the elitist positions they sought to break away from and transform.

CHAPTER 3

HOW DOES DISPLACEMENT AND TRANSFORMATION WORK
IN COUNTER-HEGEMONIC RESISTANCES?

In these actions of resistance, however, student and teacher resistors may become entangled and mixed into efforts at transformation through acts of displacement and, at times, acts of condensation. These actions always leave traces and excesses of the elitist and their oppressive structures of hierarchies. To see though these webs of entanglements – or how signifier chains, their links, and subject positions intersect one another, on more micro levels of their links, in which there remain traces or marks of hierarchy will remain embedded in struggles waged by students and teachers against those elite discourses and formations of oppression – administrative hierarchies, classroom management, tenure, and mandated and standardized testing. To see through these spaces will require resistant discourses and their chains and links to intertwine with the dominant discourses. That is to say, within these links may lie other interstices – links within links, chains within chains – which may provide spaces for transforming some of these links accomplished by "mapping skills" in which student and teacher further develop their "caring skills."

For example, as we will see in further analyzing Freire in the following chapter, one may grasp the contradictions of their actions in ways very different than those reported by Willis (1980) and how the Lads, a resistant group of teenagers, because their resistances reproduced elitist and hierarchical perceptions, assumptions, dispositions, and relations with their fellow students and teachers. Questions were raised how to break resistant co-opted subject-positions., That is, the Lads, by marginalizing other student groups in their school – women as "lays," immigrant groups as "Pako's," and middle class kids as "cissies" who were succeeding in their regular liberal art tracks of learning leading to middle class managerial jobs (as opposed to shop floor factory jobs of the Lads). To break with this self-defeating forms of student resistance, something else must extended in acts of resistance, particularly those acts of resistance in which, intervening chains emanating from administrative hierarchies, classroom management controls, and testing serve only to enclose and eliminate other resistances. While the special education students I worked with resisted being returned to regular education classes because they saw through a system that "fooled them" and were very wary of returning to be with regular students who constantly "teased" and belittled them.

This mechanism of returning one to an oppressed state, despite their resistances, reflections, and even dialogical actions, demands that we need to consider what in these pedagogical actions are counter-hegemonic and what continues as hegemonic or co-opted pedagogical actions. In this consideration, assisted with post-structuralist constructs, more sub-distinctions and cross-over actions may be identified and brought into play between pedagogical actions which are moments of displacement nd moments of transformation.[117] That is, there are spaces between both dimensions displacement and condensation – in which other distinctions and constructs can rendered. Displacement, however, is ruled out by Kincheloe. If we define cement as a process in language which, as a part of the process of discourse tween both "points of antagonism" and "points of connection" or those vhich may be perceived as occurring between or in intermediary spaces between hegemony and counter-hegemonic actions of resistance, then, we may penetrate more precisely what happens between the two dimensions of oppressor and the oppressed, student and teacher.

In the following chapter, the present book will examine the movement of metonymic chains of signifiers and how they skip or slide into surfaces of prior inscriptions or on the surfaces of subject-positions of other inscriptions incited by other subject-positions or how they may re-apply themselves onto the same surface of the subject-position become affected in displacements. We will also examine how and when a surface becomes filled, in which its master or empty signifiers absorb differences or resistances, there may be a setting into motion fragments of the previous subject-position surfaces or "floating signifiers."[118] Hence, we may begin to see how counter-identifying actions may produce mis-recognitions through processes of displacement in which the axes of metonymy or displacement intersect with axes of metaphor or condensation; or how the synchronic metonymic chains of signifiers of meanings become fleeting meanings of paradigmatic metaphor chains of meanings (Coward & Ellis, 1977; Kovecses, 2005), and thereby, offer a sense of displaced links toward creating new spaces and, potentially, spaces for counter-hegemonic questions.

As a process of signification in speaking communities, metonymies, as displaced and travelling traces of meanings, break away from their signfieds (or empty signifiers becoming filled) , along metonymic chains which may produce beginning points to see how displacements may emerge into transformations or, conversely, how they may break off fragments of former transformations of discourses, re-circulating into other discourses and their discursive formations (i.e. race, class, gender, authority, etc.) These chains of signifiers, depending on their own and other alignments to other discursive formations in acts of articulation may, like equivalent and empty signifiers, attempt to draw into their sphere of influence, other discursive formations as well. These gravitational-like pulls and movements, in turn, form and are formed in power struggles which may align chains of signifiers and subject-positions to get displaced and/or get condensed with other discursive formations and institutions into larger macro struggles for hegemony of a given social whole, and potentially, counter-hegemonic struggles for the micro affecting the macro.

Because post-structualists and post-Marxists as Laclau and Mouffe (1985) have been advancing new conceptions necessary to incite new social movements for democracy as a result of complex power relations and struggles – which cross over and through race, class, and gender borders – previously conceptualized on modernist terms or hierarchical chains of signifiers – new and correlated conceptualizations will be necessary to map out how these new alliances and discursive configurations can inform and further incite new agential democratic movements for schools and society (Ascroft, 2001; Ebert, 1996; Hennessey, 1992A; Ropers-Huilman, 1998; Shohat & Stam, 2003; A. M. Smith, 1996; Weedon, 1988).

These movements, in turn, may produce other spaces revealing the overlaid or imbricated layers or ridges, a "metonym complex" of previous formations of discourse and their inscriptions which leak into or "syncretize"[119] themselves onto subject-positions of both student and teacher. Students and teachers, in turn, may then re-inscribe or de-inscribe their alliances or mutual understandings or revise these understandings by positing each other from "enemy" to "friend" or, a Freire put it, as co-investigators of their common cultures and circumstances. In this way, student and teacher may not so easily fall prey to the traps of yet other hierarchical chains of signifiers, synchronized by school administrators in maintaining divisiveness between student and teacher and thereby invading their individual and joint interests. Aligned or dis-aligned or displaced discursive formations and shifts may then be brought into a more clear view allowing for the identification or emergence of new chains of signifiers to interact with both hegemonic and counter-hegemonic chains of signifiers on various intersecting and overlapping levels. These movements may produce intervening spaces in which chains of race, class, gender, authority, and a complex host of other power relations combine, get triggered and displaced into reactive states, or form new discursive formations committed to counter-hegemony of present and future articulations by student and teacher.

However, these complex hierarchical influences continue to divide student and teacher from taking joint actions as counter-hegemonic agents and advocates for each other. This aspect, exposed by post-structural constructs, is likewise missing in Kincheloe and other critical pedagogues hopeful of counter-hegemonic potentialities in today's and tomorrow's schools and society.

Therefore, as one is displaced in their hegemonic or counter-hegemonic acts in controlling others by aggrandizing themselves by their own accumulation of power or cultural capital, they are, as Kincheloe would agree, displaced from their transformatory or counter-hegemonic potential struggles. What Kincheloe misses in this mix of power relations experienced in signification and articulation, is drawing a distinction between displacement and transformation as a middle or intermediate ground to show how forces as metonymic images push to the side or center oppressor and oppressed images constructed in signifying practices. On these planes, displaced signifiers, chains, and images – as they are becoming hegemonized by dominant signifiers, chains, and images – may, nevertheless, offer intermediate planes of glimpses of alternate subject-positions on which they can inscribe and shift or swerve away from hegemonic positions, thereupon constructing new intermediate subject-positions – surfaces and spaces – on which may serve to resist reproduction, as well as serve transformatory causes. For example, when a student "answers back" to a teacher's demand for respect or discipline, there may be within these utterances components inter-mediating between both parties, in which the student answers back to the teacher: "Listen to me for a moment. I need your respect to listen and hear me out."[120] Transformation can and does occur in metonymic displacements in every student and teacher relation and utterances, in and sometimes against, the larger hierarchical structures of hegemonic authority and relationships.

While these complex configurations of discourse and their constitutive components may give one the impression of a "swirling effect" and often leads one into confusing states prior to and long after serious reflection and dialogue, they remain, however, as traces and excesses which constantly lure and provide alternate routes for critical reflection while *in* reflection and *in* dialogue. That is, they lead us back to one potent sources of identifications and mis-identifications and their correlative metonymic and displaced experiences: the unconsciousness as embedded in language as a discourse. If, while in these "in-between" spaces (between displacements and transformations) one further analyzes those deeper layers and levels of the unconsciousness – or how, as Lacan put it, the "unconsciousness is structured as a language" – then modes of pre-reflective and ongoing reflection *in* language – or, as one reflects in their acts – may posit a notion of consciousness which is not a unitary mind or entity, but rather, as minds sutured into one of many subject-positions derived and carved out by a series of aligning and dis-aligning chains of signifiers, both linked from hegemonic and hierarchical discursive formations as well as potentially new counter-hegemonic and anti-hierarchical discursive formations which, in turn, constitute spaces on subject-positions for future inscriptions and re-inscriptions, distributed in tendentially distributed ways (Thomassen, 2005). Amongst and alongside many other forms and subject-positions of consciousness, then, discursive consciousness or unconscious thoughts intertwine themselves on, in, and through each other, becoming possible sources of counter-hegemonic actions and movements.

In this way, one may see more subject-positions entangled with other subject-positions, along with their chains of signifiers and inscribed surfaces circulating and getting clotted in a variety of oppressive conditions of school and classroom life. Specifically, chains and subject-positions are intertwined by surfaces of inscription, not only by binary chains of race/racism, class/classism, and gender/sexism; but, in addition, mixed into hybrid chains and subject-positions constituting and intersected by potential anti-hierarchical and hierarchical-administrative chains of signifiers, subject-positions, and surfaces on which people inscribe and get inscribed between authority ascriptions of their roles and their own unique views.

Thus, when Kincheloe reflects on how the "power relations whirl around me" producing for him moments or lessons how his and Freire's work may be extended to better describe how hegemony and its correlative, counter-hegemony, occur in places as schools and classrooms, we may further have to start with mapping how these complex arrangements of signification are formed and re-formed.[121]

While Kincheloe's work successfully describes "power as operating to produce various representations, images, and signs, and the capacity to illustrate the complex ways that the perceptions of these images and signs affect individuals located in various race, class, and gender coordinates in the web of social reality (p. 14)," it is incumbent upon those who wish to study and advance counter-hegemonic and anti-hierarchical causes in these complex arrangements of signification how those signals and images move and migrate across a network of chains of signifiers, subject-positions, inscribed surfaces, and discursive formations of class, gender, and race.

As I have called for in this book, an important power relation and additive to race, class, and gender power relations must also include *hierarchical and administrative authority subject-positions and signifiers.* This additional element of power may allow student and teacher to inscribe onto their inter-subject chains of signifiers and surfaces other subject-positions which constrain or allow them from entering into relations which are counter-hegemonic subject-positions which (until a change can come about) mediate them as administrative and hierarchical functions as well as potential resistors. How these signifying processes of power relations become so complex with other power relations is then an activity, through mapping, which student and teacher may see and sense how what is real but not accounting for is happening to and between them, and therefore, may become the bases on which they counter-act collectively in their constructed discursive groups.

Thus, in a study[122] on special education student stories about their being included into mainstream classes, we will see how, in the following chapter, they identify themselves and their surroundings as occupying a system of displaced selves. In this situation, special education students named how each of their selves were linked to one another in a system which incarcerated them in special education. One student was able to outline his displaced parts of himself – good, bad, chilled, happy, respectful and dis-respectful selves (see Figure 45) – which became parts of a counter-hegemonic system for forming a group of respecters of fellow special education students who, like themselves would be able to identify with their peers how they were teased by regular students and teachers. The students named these selves or signifiers "flying rumors." These flying rumors circulated in chains making up a system of labels linked to teacher and administrator controls. The student began to see parts of themselves and parts of others, as a metonym complex of displaced circulating subjects and signifiers. In this process, they began to interpolate or inscribe how they would transform themselves and their schools by making their environments more free of teasing and insults, as well as more democratic and equal arrangements between themselves and the regular students, teachers, and deans. One of the group's students declared: "I don't think with my fists anymore...I think with signifiers." Thus, at this point, the students of the study began a process of minimizing their mis-recognizing of those moments they originally perceived as beneficial (getting free passes to stay out of their class which deprived them of an education) and became re-perceived as activities and relations harmful to their futures.

When the students saw a larger picture or context as to how they were a part of a set of circumstances which sought to marginalize and eliminate them from schools, they also began to recognize how they were caught in a hegemonic contradiction: unable to make distinctions between their hegemonic and counter-hegemonic actions or seeing how they, as parts of the whole, were linked to the whole, consciously and unconsciously, via metonymic chains or flashes of thought in which they began to realize that inclusion was not necessarily the solution to their problems, unless accompanied with simultaneous changes in the signifying chains and subject-positions in which the regular school population was already linked to and embroiled.

After many months of theorizing, a possible solution to their problems became apparent: the seemingly contradictory subject-positions they experienced – to be included with the regular school population or remain separated – was not a product of themselves alone, but further, how they were linked in hierarchical rather than in collective chains of signifiers and subject-positions in which they were blamed and teased as opposed to having a sense of shared blame and joint responsibility for the maintenance of signifying systems of administrative chains and labels which divided both special and regular school populations in positions of anger, fear, and blame. Any disorder or irregularity was automatically blamed –

as if on a chain – on "special" students. These labels, further, made it difficult for special and regular education students to posit as the problem, not each other, as much as the "system" which obscured for them such critical recognitions and joint interventions.

Thus, in spaces that preceded and followed transforming moments of them-selves and each other and their surroundings, the students advised one another at the end of the study to be on the "look out" for anything that displaced and condensed them and their consciousness. Thus, hegemony and hegemonic struggles became a matter of making distinctions between macro levels vying for dominance and their consent, as well as on micro levels, and how they yielded and resisted to these forms of dominance and consent. Finally, the students and researcher were able to reach a new focus which put themselves into a middle range or set of meso levels and layers in which they became a group of counter-hegemonic theorizers. In these levels or layers of discourse, the special education students of my study pierced into those metonymic moments of thoughts and feelings they had adhesed to on hegemonic chains of administrative and hierarchical selves and subject-positions. However, in their newly formed discursive formation, a counter-hegemonic community in a discursive field of power they called for new definitions and constructs to describe and analyze how power enters themselves, their language and labels, and their school of antagonisms between regular and special education.

SEGUE TO THE NEXT CHAPTER: USING POST-STRUCTURAL MAPS TO EXAMINE FREIRE'S BINARY NOTIONS OF OPPRESSION

Using post-structural constructs, one may begin to map the political geography of today's school and classroom discourses as well as Freire's embedded binary chains of oppression rooted in his modernist epistemological framework. Once these chains are noticed, Freire's work may be extended to deal with oppressive student-teacher-administrator relations. I have appropriated from post-structualist literature constructs, specifically from political, linguistic, and psychoanalytical insights of Lacan (1977), Laclau and Mouffe (1985), Laclau (1990, 1993, 2007), Pecheux (1982), Zizek (1989), Thomassen (2005), Bhabha (1989), and others to provide me with a lens or framework in which to see how students and teachers may differentiate language in its unified dimensions as having layered and signified dimensions, in which dialogue is one practice of one discursive formation of many that constitute it, and reflection and interpellation is one practice from subject-positioning and signifier-chain activities which constitute it; specifically, how empty and floating signifiers provide spaces in which both dialogue and discourses, subjects and subject-positions, signifiers and chains of signifiers interact with each other in metonymies or displaced surfaces of inscription constructed in and on subject-positions while in the act of articulation. To see how these levels and layers operate, *lying between reflection and action*, lying between dialogue and meaning-making acts of discursive formation constructions, may posit as problematic Freire's notion of oppression and questionable power relations of the oppressed or those in antagonistic relationships with each other who, unlike Freire argued, remain, to some degree fixed and unfixed in binary chains of signifiers which may or may not, to that degree, disclose other spaces for counter-hegemonic theorizing and teaching.

While Freire draws attention to many issues of oppressive and exploitative relations between workers and landowners (as they appeared in Brazil in the twentieth century, between plantation owners, managers, and workers) he missed, in my estimation, other areas which are relevant in today's postmodern and digital world of advanced industrialized and exploited and oppressed forms of labor. As evidenced by the fluctuation of the marketplace – downsizing and outsourcing – along with recent "market crashes" and "bailouts in the billions"[123]- as well as – up to recently – having less regulation and more changes toward making labor undergo neo-liberal reforms of "empowerment" and "team" work while undermining union collectivity, what is necessary today in critical pedagogy's new phase of a post-hegemonic pedagogy is to clamor for more forms of "critical thinking" and "dialogue" for children in the school place, though not underestimating the potential of such "dialogue-based" curricula to also diffuse other more incisive forms of critical curricula left to the margins.

For many years since the 1970s, there has been a growing literature focused on and critical of post-structural and "postie-style" perspectives and bodies of knowledge, across all disciplines, and in examining the extent such literature is effective in exposing both signifying and discursive dimensions of late-capitalism and hegemony (Apple, 2002; Macedo, 2002; McLaren, 2002). In order to discern how Freire missed or did not clarify some of the more subtle (yet no less oppressive) dimensions of oppression in his *Pedagogy of the Oppressed*, is more than understandable, given the time he wrote his book. However, also given the advances of the new digital and technological age, some have called for new critiques of hyper-reality of postmodernism we live in, at a time which must also raise questions that may see how power relations become enveloped by the media and its sound-byte signifier-chains[124] of reality (Fleischer, 2007; Turkle, 2004). In this context, the author seeks to extend or complement Freire in delving deeper into questions and concerns many of my education students articulated over the years when I exposed them to Freire's work. I chose to ask them to draw images as a way for them to more freely associate or allow for their unconsciousness or immediate thoughts and feelings to be released and speak though their drawings. I did this to try to get a clear idea as to where and how Freire could be complemented and extended in order to accommodate their concerns. After all, as it was asked by Kincheloe, Giroux, and others recently (2007, 2008), "Where does critical pedagogy go from here?" And, as they further ask, how can such pedagogy take on new forms for a post-hegemonic pedagogy and age?

To begin to answer these questions, we turn to the next chapter focusing on how post-structural theorizing and constructs can be made available to students who become acquainted with Freire but also want to know more in extending his work and other critical pedagogies in revealing how today's complex world of modern day electronics, hyper-reality, mass production, multi-corporations gets intertwined into their concerns and desires.

SEARCH FOR A METHOD: TOWARD LOCATING INTERMEDIATE SPACES BETWEEN HEGEMONIC AND COUNTER HEGEMONIC

Teaching by Post-Structural Theorizing

INTRODUCTION

Parts of the theoretical dimensions of this book have already been introduced throughout Chapters 1 to 3. This chapter will seek to provide a more in-depth focus on structures and processes inherent in post-structural constructs and theorizing for locating those intermediate spaces elided or omitted by Freire's *Pedagogy of the Oppressed*. My education students artwork, while pointing to these problems, exposed uncertainty as to what Freire meant by "dialogue" and its problem-posing components. Also unclear was how Freire's notion of reflection and action may provide them with a guide to what to look for, interpret, get incited by, or feel when they were oppressed, and as we came to call these states and relations leading to hegemony.

Once they read Freire's Chapter 1, they located why they would oppress others while in a state of oppression without completely knowing it. In addition, referring back to our discussions on administrative hierarchies, classroom management, tenure, and testing, my students wanted to know how, setting the problem of oppression into a context of hierarchical authority relations, they were linked to these behaviors. I usually responded to my student's questions, as we became more acquainted with post-structural constructs, with: "we may explore subject-positions and the signifying processes that constitute and carve them out of a field of discourses, by articulating to each other how we make our oppressive work processes problematic." The articulation process has a long tradition and history of philosophizing as to how we link parts to the whole and parts of the whole to each other (Freire, 2002; Sartre, 1960). I for example, teach through an art activity in which students create many illustrations and representations (see Chapter 3), along with examining my short 1978 article on authoritarian and hierarchical school conditions. We begin searching for a method to explain how we may become more adept at locating spaces in which we could begin to name and map out hegemonic relations, while additional literature is read and furthered our discussions.

Since I relied a lot on theoretical literature, this chapter will also respond to questions of post-structural theorizing. For example: what is a signifier? What are subject-positions? How do they differ, or provide equivalent states of consciousness linked to binary chains of meanings brought about since the Renaissance and Enlightenment periods? How does postmodernism extend modernistic frameworks, seeing through their essentialized categories, "unveiling" a more detailed or precise look at hegemony and its hierarchical processes? In this dual context, how does dialogue differ from a diversity of discourses when seen as nestled as one of many discursive formations? That is, how do discursive formations, of which dialogue is one manifestation, get linked and affected by other discursive formations by its internal signifying chains? How do chains of hierarchical discourses, which may penetrate or cross-over other chains from other discursive formations like standardized curriculum, tracking ability, psychometric assessments and rubrics, and labeling practices, become manifest? Finally, how does one see or sense glimpses of those discourses or a reality in and between various discursive formations? That is, how do signifiers and their chains, equivalent/empty or differential/floating, carve out and create in articulation forms of dialogue and identity which may call speakers into positions of reproduction rather than forms of resistance, interpolate[125] rather than interpellate changes to transform, resist and fight in discursive formations already linked (but not completely foreclosed) to chains of other power relations (i.e. race, class, gender, etc.) intersecting on and in discourses of school authority structures and relations? How did my students' images capture or not capture these complexes of discursive formations, experienced in dialogue and signifying contradictory images? How, after reading Freire for the first time, did these images de-construct or de-articulate amongst a field of discourses, become constituted by and productive in a complex of circulating signifiers and their metonymic or "floating" chains and meanings? We will return to these questions later.

As Freire (pp. 79–81) pointed out in *Pedagogy of the Oppressed*, student and teacher, in order to raise a critical consciousness, must "live" and "think" in each other's reflections or cognitions? Yet, Freire failed to mention how these actions would be accomplished or how we could map them out in processes, binary vs. complex circulating chains of signifiers and subject-positions forming and re-forming on the surfaces of subject-positions, and what would hinder both student and teacher when they did "live" in each other's cognitions, reflections, and thoughts? Freire did not posit cognition as a complex formation. Instead, like his predecessors, Husserl and Sartre, consciousness and the objects around him/her were divided on binary chains of thoughts of reflection and action, agency and structure, true generosity and false generosity, etc. As Husserl explains consciousness and its processes in which one intends toward (*noesis*) and grasps or retrieves to gain meaning (*noema*), the objects around one, constituting them with meanings and essences becomes an in-out and back to "in" process; or, as Sartre pointed out, man's existence in the world is determined by his "projects," as one reaches out into the world making choices to live existentially free or authentically resisting the inauthentic existence of conforming to the group norm or becoming an object of a being-in-itself. Saussure, founder of modern day linguistics and structuralism, also became subject to the binary rule of theorizing, as he linked – as if on a one-to-one correspondence – the signifier (spoken word or image) to its signified (meaning) onto chains of words to meanings, as if listed and defined in a dictionary.

POST-SAUSSUREAN ARTICULATIONS

This understanding of linguistic theorizing came to an end, however, with the introduction of post-Saussurean linguistics or discourse theory (Laclau, 1993; Macdonnell, 1985), in which the illusion of two sets of structures and processes – signifiers and signified—was broken by the likes of Lacan and others, who explained that the signifier is in a constant state of having meanings slide under its rule and, in the process, becomes sutured or anchored as other signifieds slide by, positing as real those signifieds that get conferred (anchored) with signifier status. Hence, a priority of the signifier emerges in post-structural theory as a sliding position which finds flexible joints intermediating between those meanings which become transparent on an array of signifier chains: as one chain slides under the other, further linking signifiers to discourse, and as one discursive formation slides under another discursive formation, as parts slide under and into wholes interacting with each other in the process.

How, in re-articulating these structural processes, does one become simultaneously a signifier and a subject or, in different terms, how do the oppressed become an oppressor? That is, in all three levels – discursive formations, signifying chains, and circulating, floating or metonymic signifiers – how does one become shot through by images or fleeting glimpses allowing one to penetrate or see through the many layers of discourse (some of which may be hegemonized and hierarchical), and in which post-structural theorizing constructs and holds as a possibility the potential for counter-hegemonic bases for significations in which one may be alerted to act in counter-hierarchical/hegemonic and agential ways. We can begin to see how articulation as a process works in locating intermediate spaces between hegemonic and potential counter-hegemonic discourses, spaces for teaching post-structurally in today's schools.

Viewing the recent conversations between Joe Kincheloe and Henry Giroux on U-Tube (2008), both writers argue for a "post-hegemonic" phase to critical pedagogy.[126] In the U-Tube conversation, Kincheloe was persistent in hinting in his conversation with Giroux, how finding those intermediate or "in between spaces" (between subject and object, freedom and necessity, agency and structure, etc.), would be an important component in fulfilling a post-hegemonic direction of future critical pedagogy. We will save literature reviews for a future book, instead expounding on and recapping these theories discussed here in the remainder of this book.

I have had similar conversations with critical scholars since the 1970's, as Dwayne Huebner lamented in 1975 after I raised a similar concern as Kincheloe, responding with: "we are all looking for these in-between spaces."As Kincheloe commented to me in 2000, upon hearing I was a "Huebner student," giving Huebner the honor of being one of the greatest curricular theorists of the last century,[127] he too lamented about those "in-between spaces." Recently, Maxine Greene (a critical pedagogue in her own right) recommended I read Laclau and Mouffe (1985), whom she saw as one of the best sources to attack my problem of hegemony. While I had read Laclau and Mouffe years before, I gained insights from various writers who were on the cusp of using post-structural constructs in a variety of ways, not necessarily as a means to counter the hegemony of why the oppressed become each other's oppressor, as Freire's *Pedagogy of the Oppressed* pointed to with many examples of his own and other scholars (i.e. Erich Fromm, Albert Memmi, etc.).

Thus, a particular tradition of post-structruralism has and continues to guide me toward what I would refer to as a complex and critical post-structuralism in which notions of chains of signifiers, subject-positions, and discursive formations are not only included but, further, revised to embrace other post-post structural traditions. For example, Zizek (1989) and more recently, Laclau's (1993, 2007) notion (and Lacan before him) of the subject always being in a state of flux or partially fixed into positions of desire to complete what is lacking in themselves in some whole or in relation to its constituent parts. Laclau, as Smith (1996) recounted, by the 1990s, was influenced by theorists and critics like Giles Deleuze and Slovenj Zizek – who opposed binary or closed systems or totality theorists of the earlier structuralist tradition like Saussure, Barthes, Levi-Strauss, Althusser. This aspect may affect future populist movements for inciting or radicalizing people towards democratizing institutions throughout the world.

ARTICULATION AND DISCOURSES

In this chapter, however, I will focus on an overarching construct of post-structuralism – articulation – in which post-structural concepts are further refined into chains of signifiers and subject-positions referred to as equivalent chains and their empty signifiers as well as differential signifiers and their "floating signifiers," and how they interact and intertwine together, constructing, partially and tendentially, subject-positions.[128] This approach may provide a more incisive look into how hegemonic sub-components serve as a magnet to attract to their hegemonic folds, competing chains of floating signifiers on one level, and on another level, when they exhaust their capacities to attract, become themselves fragments which circulate, pulling into their gravitation other signifiers, becoming "stand-ins" for other chains moving toward their subject-positions and surfaces.[129]

Thus, I will focus even more incisively on how, in the process of articulation, the surfaces of subject-positions not only are shared (tendentially) with other chains of signifiers linked to other discursive formations of power, composing heterogeneously popular and "new" movements, but, in the struggle for and against hegemony, there may be located on subject-position surfaces additional spaces on a third level, as empty signifiers become filled or become displaced by counter-forces or new floating signifiers – from the same or different chains of signifiers and discursive formations – in which new subject-positions and their new equivalent chains and signifiers and subject-positions are constructed as interruptions which suddenly break through these surfaces – *objets petiti a,* as Zizek refers to them – manifesting themselves as "fleeting images," articulated almost beyond words. Some of these surfaces, as we shall come to see, irrupt and break through the tendential surfaces by the thrust of sudden and immediate experiences which, it seems, cannot be expressed in language but are partially felt within and through our beings. To Zizek, these irruptions of the Real are the spaces and empty forms he refers to as *objets petit a*[130] which may be, as I read Zizek, a more direct or less mediated route in which to peer into the multifarious layers of discourses shrouding the real or core of society and its power relations, as power irrupts through these layers of discourse, producing a feeling or fantasy, pleasure – *jouissance* – that is almost beyond words.[131]

RETURNING TO FREIRE

Before I link some post-structural theories and constructs, while extending Paulo Freire's *Pedagogy of the Oppressed*, specifically, his pointing to hegemonic acts but not framing them as such, as to how the oppressed oppress each other while in states of oppression and other antagonisms. I am apt to point out how these reversals of the oppressed and oppressor are important because they represent the fractured possibilities of democratizing their work conditions, the possibility for revolution of the real and the transformation of consciousness. I always try or tend to couch these lofty ideals into more concrete settings which my students and I can relate to. Once again, there are two settings I have been engaged with regarding special education students and my role as a teacher educator in which I have had my education students consider why they are so fearful of change, and sometimes, oppress themselves and each other, as Freire observed in his research of Brazilian peasants almost a half a century ago. This chapter will first introduce post-structural theorizing I accomplished with both special education students and present day discussions with my education students in vignettes drawn, roles played, diagrammed and discussed about how they feel about administrative hierarchies, classroom management, tenure, and testing (in Chapter 2) and who are aspiring to become teachers, deans, and administrators.

In seeking to find ways to counter-hegemonize our everyday work lives as teachers, we came across many constructs I provided and my students invented (after their artwork, presentations by former students, and reading of Freire's *Pedagogy of the Oppressed)*, as well as their responding to presentations and readings I assigned to them, including an abbreviated version of my doctoral work with my special education students and an article I wrote in 1978. I returned to a post-Freirian discussion, attempting to show how both students and teachers may become post-structural theorizers and how some of these constructs may interface with critical pedagogy and how they may become counter-hegemonic teachers. After laying out two case studies, special education students as counter-hegemonic theorizers and re-considering administrative hierarchies and related practices, I will return to re-examine three constructs of Freire in need of further revision and extension – dialogue, reflection, and problem-posing. Specifically, how one may continue to use these constructs albeit supplemented by dialogues and discussions for future theorizing, formulating counter-hegemonic strategies of teaching (to be discussed in the last and final Chapter). These three constructs and their sub-components will be discussed in this chapter and can be summarized as follows:

– Dialogue as derived and productive of hegemonic to counter-hegemonic discursive formations and articulations.

- Beyond consciousness as a unified entity and how consciousness and contradictions are constitutive of a complex of subject-positions, chains of signifiers, and discursive formations in the articulation process.
- Creation of spaces for new subject-positions, chains of signifiers, and discursive formations in counter-hegemonic articulations.

This chapter will show how fragments or surfaces of subject-positions are tendential (Thomassen, 2005) and irruptive or "real" (Zizek, 1989) and breakthrough, and are subject to change without fore notice, or in the process of being constantly changed by contingent forces from points unbeknownst to anyone, in a force field of discourse, in which fragments of signifiers become new signifiers, combining (metonymies) and substituting (metaphors) with each other as a result of circulating and interacting with other signifiers and discursive formations in and through acts of articulation. As articulation sutures (via *nodal points*) or quilts (via *sinthome* experiences[132]) new equivalent chains (and differential chains) in varying degrees of consensus or dissensus form, de-form, and re-form, inscribe, de-inscribe (or erase), and re-inscribe norms of a group or norms of a coalition of groups.

In addition, I will use maps and diagrams in this and the following chapter to capture these complex and often overlapping and intertwining moments in the articulation process which penetrates both dialogue and discourse. With the help of post-structural constructs, as we will see in both case studies involving special education students and my education students, consciousness is posited as de-centered, as already in discourse and its structures, and not as an originary, underlying, transcendental, distant, or essentialized state of being (Laclau & Mouffe, 1985, Laclau, 1990, 1993, 2007), and in which we may enter into a journey as consciousness becomes hybridized in and throughout chains of signifiers, subject-positions, and discursive formations.

A JOURNEY OF HEGEMONIZED AND HYBRIDIZED ARTICULATIONS

In this journey,[133] consciousness comes about as a result of fluent or circulating parts of signifiers as signification becomes sutured, sometimes at "points of antagonism," sometimes producing a triggering reaction, in which one actor attacks the other because, as Lacan (1977, p. 211) put it, "In you, I see something I love and I want to annihilate." Next, signifiers and other signifying materials interact, cross-over, and intersect each other at "points of connection" in chains which may be aligned to other chains of signifiers within and linked to other discursive formations and possible blocs of alliances. These discursive formations (each containing layers of signifying chains and subject-positions, and surfaces to inscribe upon) may also be aligned to other chains of signifiers outside their discursive formations but inside other discursive formations. As Lacan said: "A signifier which represents a subject for another signifier," as they interact with one another in the infinite yet contingent discursive fields, constructing new discourses.[134]

And further, binary chains may re-appear, precluding a more systematic and interactive view of macro or power relations and how they may be linked to the micro dimensions of power relations, which may short-circuit, silence, or worse, hegemonize student and teacher, having them further oppress each other without knowledge that both are oppressed by the same systems of school authority, preventing each other from transforming their oppressed selves into counter-hegemonic states and subject-positions of counter oppression. In this state, student and teacher remain divided, located on binary chains of oppression, further denied from re-conceptualizing how their school and its hierarchical forms of power and authority may be examined critically and attacked counter-hegemonically. In these moments, students and teachers, cannot get a glimpse of the middle or intermediate grounds, forces, and future possible horizons of discourse which may link their teaching and learning processes to subject-positions they presently occupy, and on which they may begin to articulate new counter-hegemonic discourses and discursive formations.

This and the following chapter may offer to education student, teacher, and teacher educator a kind of glossary of terms on how counter-hegemonic teaching through post-structural theorizing may construct a new reality and language in their school settings. This chapter will use a significant portion of my dissertation exposing how special education students became counter-hegemonic theorizers with the help of post-structural constructs to grasp those fleeting moments in which they "saw through" a discourse system, which denied them equal access and help in their schools and all their classroom relationships.

SPECIAL EDUCATION STUDENTS AS COUNTER-HEGEMONIC THEORIZERS: TOWARD GRASPING POST-STRUCTURAL CONSTRUCTS LOCATED SYMBOLICALLY IN AND BETWEEN THE REAL AND THE IMAGINARY

As part of my research toward my doctoral degree, I interviewed special education students.[135] In focus group settings, I listened and had my special education students examine (after I transcribed their words for subsequent sessions) their words for peer check reveiws. These sessions usually were accompanied by deep discussions as to what they meant to say and what they did say about their special education conditions at schools in transition as special education students were being integrated into "inclusive" regular track classrooms.

The special education stories, recounted over a period of one year on a weekly basis, revealed how their insights could be further facilitated by post-structuralist concepts. Rather than adhering to modernist concepts and their binary chains of special versus regular students, smart versus dumb, ability versus disability, I chose an orientation that crossed over these divides, as well as the divides between reflection versus action, dialogue versus discourse, the real versus the imaginary. In doing this I chose to exceed the problem-solving methods articulated by Freire. That is, one acts then reflects, or conversely, one reflects then acts.

The major respondent of the study, Randy, made it possible to dig deeper into why special education students felt discriminated and marginalized by "regular students, teachers, and deans," despite inclusion attempts by the school at the time. My use of post-structural concepts assisted Randy's analyses as well as those of his fellow special education students in our small group of four. When I first encountered Randy, he spoke very quickly as he wanted to include all the various parts or dimensions of his speech into a whole story. As a result, he underwent many transgressions and tangents as he was talking. He would say: "Those men, those enemies, those others," all, as I became aware of, asking Randy to stop and tell me, were emerging as layers of discourse which he experienced at certain moments, sometimes almost simultaneously. He also drew pictures of these various selves as places or subject-positions – good, cool, chill, bad selves (see below Figure 45). These selves were linked to Randy's actions, often angry and even violent, sometimes calm and rational, and were further linked together in many overlapping and intersecting chains (which carried his identities into his interactions with others). If one happened to dis-link one chain or link from another, Randy would use his fists *or* smile calmly, depending on which link and chain was displaced. Still, as he maintained, the "system" of special education, by segregating him – "tricking him" – from continuing as a regular student in the 7th grade in middle school made him this way.

Figure 45

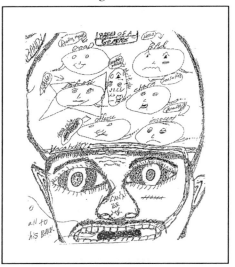

While Randy and his fellow special education students did not like being discriminated on the basis of ability from other "regular" students," they also remained distrustful of strategies which offered to include them with regular students. Randy and these other students had been "fooled" by teachers and guidance personnel by being tracked into special education at an early age, and were suspicious of returning to the place they were discriminated against as "pariahs," as "dumb" or "slow kids." As another student in our focus group, Zena, said: "How do they know we're special, do we have signs around our necks?" Another student, Lisa added, "Yeah, its that feeling I get when my special education number is called out in homeroom and all the kids would turn around and stare at me." Or, Gregory, more sympathetic to the prospect that special education kids are not slow or dumb, but just need a little help, said: "It's those who need the most help that get the least; and those who need the least help that get the most."

Figures 46, 47

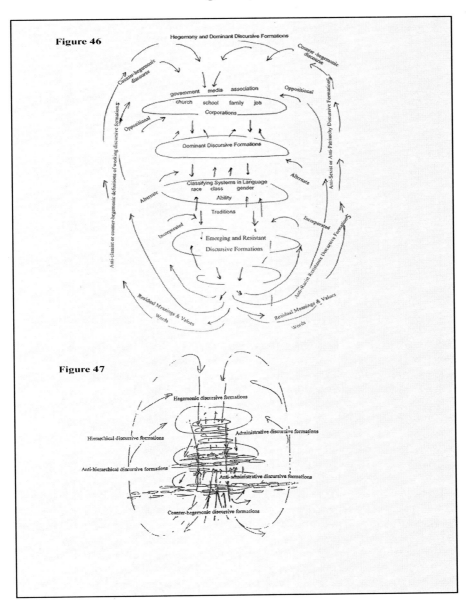

Figures 48, 49

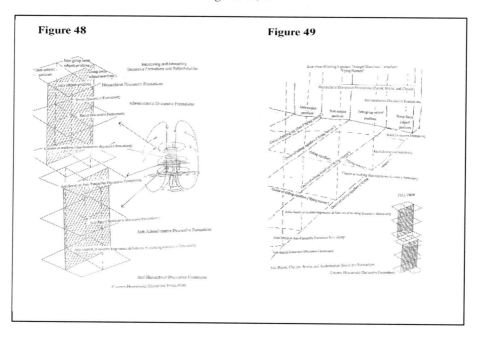

Figure 48 **Figure 49**

From these discussions the special education students wanted to construct a framework or system which would consider how they were stigmatized and marginalized by regular students. They wanted to show the regular school population (students, teachers, and administrators) that their viewpoint is of value. Their marginalized positions have experience and their "acting out" as a form of oppositional viewpoints could contribute to their regular school population as a form of critical pedagogy. Yet, in a moment of regression, Randy turned to Gregory, falling back on an old routine amongst oppressed people who oppress each other: "Hey, what are you saying, are you *slow*!" Randy further argued special education students were at a distinct disadvantage from causing a demonstration, as if to say "We can't strike or march with signs, we are special or slow and we need more help." This demonstration would only evoke more retaliation on part of regular students, teachers, and administrators as demeaning and demonizing their already low status. Less obvious was the almost ceaseless circulation of rumors, "flying rumors," as they called such a phenomenon in which everyone in the school knows who is special and who is regular. Later, after much joint theorizing with the researcher, these students were able to map or diagram how these rumors circulate in their school discourses through a notion of "flying signifiers" (see Figures 46 to 49, and 54) penetrating various discursive formations (regular, special) in the overall framework of their school's "ability" and discriminatory practices.

As the students further probed their school conditions, they were able to see how various links to chains positioning them from other formations of power (ability race, class, authority, gender) which managed to re-position them not in dialogue (didn't matter how much we talked about it) but in discursive formations (a concept the research introduced to them via maps of power in discourse. See such maps above in Figures 46-49).

Once they saw these maps introduced by the researcher, the students realized that it was not their dialogue in which their thoughts originated from themselves as isolated individuals. Rather, they began to realize that their dialogue or discussions is, in part, made up of many parts of dialogue, coming from and shooting into and through themselves from various discursive formations and institutions masking society and the world. When they spoke or articulated words or gestures or images to each other and themselves, their thoughts were already becoming linked and interacting with other thoughts, words, images, gestures, and feelings, as they spoke or *articulated* themselves, they sensed other words and meanings accompanying their speech simultaneously.

The notion of articulation meant that once speaking, they are in and are becoming a part of an intricate "system of atoms," in which one word, gesture, or image affects the way the other words, gestures, and images are laid out. Eventually, Randy and the other students were able to map out how they were stigmatized in the schools because they were labeled "special." No longer did they see each other exclusively as special, caught on a binary set of chains which communicated as black and white, slow or fast people as separated and discriminated against each other. Now, they were able to see how and where these binary chains came from and intervened as so-called contradictions they experienced between the two poles they represented later on their own images and diagrams – white and black, male and female, regular and special. Soon after drawing these diagrams (see Randy's diagrams and chains below) and images on the chalkboard, they realized that what they originally perceived as contradictory or binary may be re-perceived as emerging from a complex of discursive formations aligned and linked to hierarchical as well as to those words and images resistant to hierarchical discourses. Soon afterwards, the students also began to realize how dialogue may also be re-conceptualized. Their discussions were drawn and ignited by a complex of "discursive formations" in which their identities as ability, race, class, and gender were subject-positions which determined placement on a series of separate and interconnecting chains and words and thoughts at the same time became "signifiers." They, within this complex, also constructed their own discursive formation, as "analyzers" and "respecters," seeking to become *really included* in the regular populations of their school and society.

RANDY GOES TO THE CHALKBOARD AND POST-STRUCTURAL THEORIZING BEGINS

A moment emerged which consolidated the special education students ability to grasp or understand how their articulations and discourses operated. Randy, in the midst of a four hour theorizing session held in a large classroom at Teachers College, during a Christmas recess of 1997, suddenly went to the chalkboard. The students had already theorized "drawing diagrams"[136] as images represented their lived experiences in special education or how power enters discursive formations circulating as signifiers and their chains drawn representing different discourses and discursive formations. In one vivid example, Randy went to the chalkboard and began to illustrate chains (See Figure 50 below), one overlying the other, illustrating how several groups of chains are linked together through sliding signifiers. If one or two chains are broken, neither the whole system nor the other chains fell apart. To Randy, adhering to a binary system of signification in the first moments of this activity, the signifier "self-control" becomes stronger as it moves toward "full respect" and weaker as it slides toward "Disrespect." "Self-control," however, has a variable meaning and also acts as a "cross-over chain," keeping aligned control and respect. That is, self-control may mean behavior as defined by the dominant discursive formation or the school's administrators and teachers as a positive value. Randy showed that there were other meanings or values, however, defined by unnamed chains representing other signifiers and discursive formations, including how society's institutions, traditions, and other forces position and re-position people in self-defeating ways.

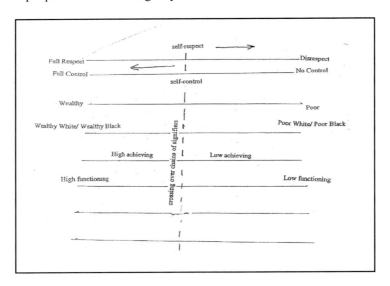

Figure 50

As we moved through the discussion, the researcher already pointed out to the students how group action and interaction occurred within a complex of discursive formations, further made up of chains, signifiers, subject-positions, and group norms. Based on this information, Randy expanded his images to include chains of wealthy and poor of all color. He theorized a correlation between one chain of positions (Full Respect – Disrespect) and other chains of positions (e.g., Wealthy – Poor, White – Black) as they slide and are aligned. This sliding is subjugated or held down by a cross-over chain of positions and signifiers. Randy thus concluded that a wealthy Black person, when aligned by a cross-over chain of positions of the dominant discursive formation (capitalism), may not feel for either a poor Black or a poor White person because the latter are connected to another chain linking "disrespect" to low achievement and low school functioning status.

After the students and the researcher added other chains of positions and signifiers (see Figure 51 below), penetrating into the deeper levels of the world of special education and its labels, a counter-hegemonic moment of theorizing occurred. This moment emerged when the researcher indicated by adding images of self with the words "I" and "We." Thus, a continuum between the "I" and "We" selves slid alongside two other chains or continuum. On one end of the continuum, selfish and individual selves were depicted. On the other end of the continuum, the unselfish and collective selves of "We" were shown (see below Figure 51).

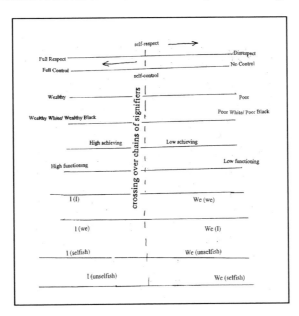

Figure 51. Introducing Randy to the Notion of Split Selves

To Randy, the signifiers "I" and "We" were not as important as "Selfish" and "Unselfish," the former aligned to "Disrespect" and the latter to "Full Respect." Then Randy, suddenly, *as if a second thought crossed his mind*, pointed out "once a Black or White person become wealthy, they never see or understand the point of view of the poor person, whether Black or White." It is at this point that Randy broke from the values he previously mapped, aligned to a dominant chain defining his individualistic need to succeed and get rich and, crossing over this discursive formation, re-aligning respect and full control not with the attainment of wealth, high achievement, and "high functioning" but, rather, fulfilling his need to be in a discursive formation of unselfish caring for others.

Collaborating with Randy, the researcher then added an additional chain of "I(I)" and "We(We)." The researcher then added another chain or continuum, this one of dis-unified entities "I(We)" and "We(I)," and further explained that these dis-unified entities or subjects or subject-positions were *split* in different degrees and slid underneath each other from one side of the continuum to the other, and could also be crossed by chains of signifiers (as we already discussed) that made possible the reversal of "I" into "We" and "We" into "I," or selfish becoming unselfish, and unselfish becoming selfish subjects or subject-positions (see Figure 52 below).

Figure 52

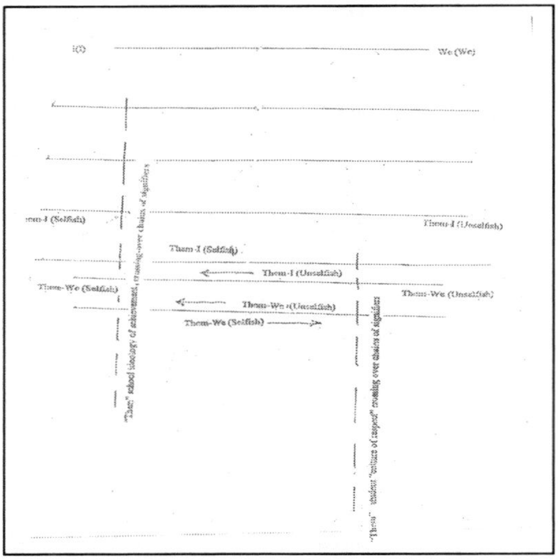

This reversal of subject-positions clarified for Randy and the other students how in a complex of discursive formations, respect and control are values that may be linked to wealth and school success while undermining the students' collective values of respect and caring. The students understood how chains of signifiers may be crossed over by other chains, producing perceived contradictions or juxtapositions of values grounded in other discursive formations, producing acts of resistance, co-option or getting manipulated,[137] and by counter-hegemonic resistance. Hence, strivings for wealth, achievement, and high functionality, originally considered by the students to be noble, were re-examined as ignoble. Losing one's sense of individualistic control (as defined in the achievement culture of the school) was considered an act of "loss," now, during and after what were becoming increasingly counter-hegemonic theorizing sessions, was revised as an act of solidarity within their own culture of respect or their counter-hegemonic discursive formation presently under construction.

Randy's diagrammatic acts then revealed his struggle between the forces of two value and belief systems, crossing into one another, as he remained in a position of contradiction yet coherence. Randy maintains a position that is constituted and crossed by both forces: the individualistic achievement orientation of the school as linked to "Full Respect" and "Full Control," and caring for others unselfishly as also linked to "Full Respect" and "Full Control."

In order to further clarify and break the limbo or crisis state Randy found himself in, the researcher then drew another chain, perpendicular to the previous chains, showing that a "unselfish We" can be crossed by a "selfish I" subject-position and, conversely, that a "unselfish I" can be crossed by a "selfish We" position. When I asked the students what occurred as the positions slid back and forth and across the poles "I(I)" and "We(We)," Randy intruded the subject-positions of "Them-I" and "Them-We" (See above Figure 52 above and Figure 53 below). Now one may see or identify themselves as either selfish or unselfish, depending on whether the "Them" is a *norm* for the school's culture or as ideology of achievement by the larger school population; or a competing norm of cariungness emerging in special student cultures yearniong for and demanding respect.

Figure 53

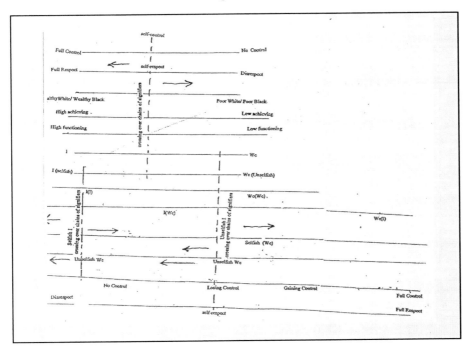

After their theorizing and diagram construction, the students came to see the significance of the "flying rumors," or floating signifiers as a central theme articulated in their stories. The constructs of "flying rumors" was seen as a positioning and repositioning mechanism affecting the students' perceptions according to two or more conflicting and overlapping value systems. "Flying rumors" also acted as expressions of the circulation of chains and signifiers constituting and crossing over one another, producing a kind of discursive or dispersed consciousness (as opposed to a unified consciousness) that maintained the students in hegemonic and potentially counter-hegemonic subject-positions.

Understanding "flying rumors" within these contexts (see Figure 53 above), then, helped Randy to clarify the meanings of the metonymic images that flashed across his mind every time he felt "disrespected." In this way, the students began to discover how "flying rumors," serving as a positioning mechanism within several discursive formations and chains of signifiers, may have accounted for their metonymic experiences as they recounted as constituting their self-defeating and divisive relations with each other and their teachers. Since they "one-downed" each other by referring to each as "slow," they named these formations as invading their "culture of respect." These invaders were administrative, hierarchical, and hegemonic discursive formations which made up the culture of the school and overlapped and intruded into their own "culture of respect."

The students began to understand their being in a state of hegemony or hegemonic subject-positions by using theoretical or post-structural constructs to integrate their themes with relevant literature, as presented by the researcher. The thrust of this literature was taken from Pecheux's (1982) notion of discursive formations, in particular, his notion of counter-identifying. In counter-identification, the oppressed and labeled subject mis-recognizes the position he or she slides into as favorable (i.e. getting a free pass to leave their classrooms and enter the cafeteria), simultaneously assuming positions that inadvertently maintain the dominant group norms. What the subject opposes as a hierarchical and discriminatory policy is what he or she, at the same time, affirms.

This reversal of positions was further examined in looking at other literature related to student resistance, in particular, the Willis (1977), McRobbie (1994), and MacLeod (1987) studies. The students wanted to know why and how the resistance of the students in these studies were short-circuited and stopped. They also wanted to know how, by questioning the system, the "Lads," the "Mods," and the "Hall-Hangers" could have taken resistant positions that were not self-defeating, counter-reactive, and reversing but, rather, pierced and penetrated the system.

As a result of these discussions, the present students were inspired to go beyond the Lads, the Mods, and the Hall-Hangers. They learned through these studies, students who only "partially penetrated" their school's ideology of individualism and achievement put themselves in positions in which their resistant selves defeated them. The special education students of the study also learned that their partial penetration into hegemonic subject-positions illustrated how the schools' overly individualistic ideology led to self-defeating and divisive subject-positions. As a result, the special education students insisted that they "could do better than the Lads, the Mods, and the Hall-Hangers." They could construct, with the researcher, a counter-hegemonic framework by which to expose the unequal practices of the special/regular education programs in their high school.

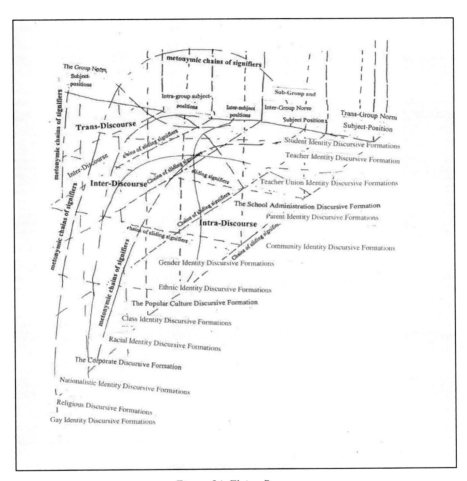

Figure 54. Flying Rumors

FLYING RUMORS AND THE ARTICULATORY PROCESS IN DISCOURSE

By applying their frameworks, the students began to understand the shifts of meaning of words that labeled them in their special education program, along with the shifting movements of signifiers and their chains within producing several aligning (overlapping) and re-aligning (intersecting) discursive formations. In these formations of discourse, the students described how "flying rumors" positioned them onto the different meanings the label "special" had for them, ranging from "slow" and "stupid," negative attributes, to "misunderstood" to "oppositional," positive attributes. By doing this, the students were able to see how the *seemingly contradictory nature* of their antagonistic and labeled experiences were, in fact, not contradictory and irreconcilable forces originating from "human nature" in something inside their heads but, rather, the *shifting of discursive formations* which aligned, dis-aligned, and re-aligned them with others located on sliding and circulating administrative and anti-administrative, hierarchical and anti-hierarchical, or hegemonic and counter-hegemonic chains of subject-positions. They further learned that this positioning was the result of a process in which words, gestures, desires, expressions, and even moments of silence become signifiers communicating subject-positions as linked to chains of positions within and crossing over them, which in turn are linked to group norms of different discursive formations – all partook in the construction and re-construction of group norms and a complex of multiple group norms. In addition, they learned that the divide between them and society is not as great as they originally assumed; but, rather, as linked by intermediate discursive formations and their chains of signifiers and subject-positions circulating in and through them in their discourses (wider and deeper than their one-to-one dialogues of two or more separate wills or individuals).[138]

In addition to my short article over thirty years ago (Fleischer, 1978) whose author posited administrators as "supports" for teacher dialogue, innovation and morale, without recognizing, at the same time, the intrusion of the school's administration into the school's regular teaching staff and student population and in which they were hegemonized to believe that by "appealing to the administrators to resolve their differences or conflicts, they would be doing themselves a service," which they were not.[139]

Hence, the word "slow," when *articulated* in the various discursive formations, constructed meanings for the students, as constructed in administrative, hierarchical, and hegemonic discursive formations, were experienced by the students along corresponding and criss-crossing chains of signifiers and subject-positions that, to them, were experienced, at first, as only "flying rumors" (see Figure 54 above) communicating only negative meanings of "slow." When the word "slow" was de-constructed and re-articulated within anti-administrative, anti-hierarchical, and counter-hegemonic discursive formations they often recounted in their stories and narratives, the changes revised or took issue with the previously held dominated meanings of the word "slow," transforming the word to mean that the special education students were uniquely "different," "misunderstood," and provided a new and marginal view opposed to what regular students and their teachers and deans could not immediately see. This transformation of their identities and constructs as a norm by the special education students permitted them to feel confident and *see through* the system that labeled them "stupid."

Further, with the frameworks constructed by the students and I, the students could begin to see how the circulation of rumors also provided a way for them to circulate "flying truths," or further the remainder of the school population: although they were different, they were of value because of their marginalized and oppositional viewpoint. Assisted by oppositional literature (Hall, 1997; Hall & Jefferson, 1975; hooks, 1984, 1997; McRobbie, 1993; Macleod, 1986; Willis, 1980), the students contended that their viewpoint, marginal of school life, was able to see through the system of hegemony and the viewpoint of the regular school population. Hence, their definition of "special" became revised from the pejorative meaning of the label and made the word a vehicle for their potential acceptance, respect, and if they chose, reconciliation with the regular school population.

BREAKING OUT OF MODERNIST CONCEPTIONS OF DIALOGUE AND CONSCIOUSNESS FOR MODES OF POST-STRUCTURAL DISCURSIVE DIALOGUE AND CONSCIOUSNESS OF THE SPECIAL EDUCATION STUDENTS.

Further, by applying an understanding of language as a discursive formation or system of circulating and containing signifiers and chains, the students also came to understand how they were triggered into self-defeating positions as they appealed to the administrators rather than themselves to resolve their differences. All of these behaviors reproduced the administrative, hierarchical, and hegemonic chains of meanings and discursive formations. Consequently, they were also able to see how power alignments played a role in positioning both regular and special education students, as well as faculty and administrators, as they were triggered into self-defeating and divisive behaviors and produced counter-reactive behaviors among "Them" – those who might be potential allies rather than enemies in acts of articulation.

By *naming* [140] or re-articulating these various discursive formations, the students were also able to show how their struggles within and against school administrative authority got hegemonized on different levels: ranging from anti-administrative action, which co-opted their resistance with the use of "free passes" to anti-hierarchical levels, which began to provide glimpses penetrating the system of school administrative and hierarchical authorities since they began to realize name calling caused racist, sexist, and classist discursive formations when mixed into counter-hegemonic levels, which provided the students with a base on which to identify themselves as their own support group, with their own criteria of "truth" and a will to fight as "analyzers."

With these insights the students re-examined why they falsely made assumpt of their own powers to "cut deals" with their teachers, and why they displaced anger by "one-downing" each other as "slow." They began to see that commu can be constructed by the use of signifiers rather than by their fists in fits and violence. One student asserted: "While I still put my alerts, I now th other as a signifier." Still another, Lisa, usually afraid to talk, broke "Now we have a system to counter stigma that allows us to speak!" M they began to realize that they could think and theorize in making th known. They also began to see how hegemony works in position sub-group of a larger group – regular students and teachers – divided from one another by the dominant group – the school those higher up than them.

In this way, the students theorized that their school, as pa of discursive formations, controlled by administrators a aligned according to hierarchical chains of positions relat ability, and authority, precluded them from seeing throu penetration, the students imagined running and governi

Special education students theorizing, as I argued over a decade ago, implies a counter-hegemonic perspective for further qualitative story research in which the subject of the story is not seen as unified but as subjects distributed across a complex of discursive formations, constructed in the chains and signifiers of language and labels. Special education student theorizing further implies an appeal for egalitarian structures of authority and shared decision making of school governance and notions of democratic leadership, which will be discussed in Chapter 5.

HOW CAN DIALOGUE BE PENETRATED AND RELEASED ONTO A FIELD OF ARTICULATION FOR COUNTER-HEGEMONIC DISCOURSES AND POWERS?

The term "dialogue" offers a multitude of interpretations when constituted in several hegemonic contexts, including those contexts in which dialogue takes on *binary* chains[141] and forms of instruction between lecture and discussion methods of teaching. Thus, there may be a quick association between lecturing as oppressive and discussion based teaching formats as liberating.[142] Indeed, most of the time, the artwork of my students tended to associate the two formats of teaching along interacting axis (or chains) of oppression, as oppressive, and discussion is liberating oppression. In the same way, after reading Freire, they tend to quickly on reversing these relations (student become teacher, and teacher becomes student). Thus, Freire did not dispel the deep seated notions of binarisms inherent in his pedagogy – or, at least, that is what my students reported to me.[143]

Today, dialogue can become an elastic concept which may serve oppressive or emancipatory purposes. While both discourses – "lecture" and "discussion" formats of teaching are presented as freeing and circulating in some classes; in other classes it may be re-interpreted as a container or escape valve in which student and teacher only feel empowered but, when contrasted to their administrative hierarchies, are not. I have observed in education classes how, after reading Chapter 1 in Freire, a new outlook may emerge. After they have read Freire, I ask the students to break into groups and on transparency paper to inscribe their immediate impressions of e and his relevancy to their work as teachers or teachers-to-be. They usually nse their understanding of Freire around one theme or image rather than a diverse themes and images. This theme is usually confined to teaching plogies and Freire's notion of "banking." Their understanding of what meant by his first chapter – how the oppressed become each other's sor and how dialogue is linked in intricate and complex ways to problem-ma problem creation are issues of discussion that are often ignored or prol Indicating how student-teacher solidarities may be linked not only to schog, but to initiating new liberating and democratic movements in scholiting as problematic traditional as well as liberal or progressive linked mentioned. Moreover, while students and teachers may also be pedaguctive knowledge-making – a progressive methodology or Even ing and learning – this notion is too vague a topic to be tackled. linked d, unless I bring it up, is how Freire's notions of dialogue is nsing in actions of reflection and relations between students and teachers, also as problems enchained in administrative hierarchies, modes of classroom management, and testing regimes.

Because most of my students are not acquainted with new paradigms of knowledge, as postmodernism and complex forms of post-structuralism, I must begin from scratch, using their immediate histories and backgrounds in the ways which may help them become educated and educate their students in schools to become more innovative and inclusive counter-hegemonic and critical ways, and posit as problematic those frameworks they have adopted over time as students, K through college. As with the special education students I worked with, my education students and I work seeking dialogue itself as a practice linked to a context of complex discursive formations and their power relations, antagonisms, and connections, reinforcing or breaking apart hegemonic and counter-hegemonic discourses. I also try to stress, again taking an insight from post-structuralist theory and literature, how, in a field of weaving networks of power, intertwined by language as in the circulating chains of signifiers and discursive formations (Lacan, 1977; Pecheux, 1982), how knowledge-making, relationships, and, in general, curriculum, teaching, and assessment are constructions which are constantly in states of change and flux, multi-layered, and how power and discourse may be articulated in ways that posit as problematic their "conventional wisdom." As a result, my students find or carve out new openings and new spaces, exposing ridges and imbricated edges, for their consideration as to how discourses articulated are constantly over-powered (over-determined but not eliminated) by administrative and hierarchical layers of discourse, which fold them into a hegemony. With such poststructural constructs, they may begin to see and map out these processes toward gaining a better understanding of them and therefore allow for united actions.

HOW TO BEGIN TO THEORIZE WITH STUDENTS POST-STRUCTURAL CONCEPTS BY RE-EXAMINING FREIRE'S *PEDAGOGY OF THE OPPRESSED* FROM A COUNTER-HEGEMONIC "DISCURSIVE" PERSPECTIVE

Usually, at the end of a long session[144] in which the education students show their artwork to each other and present their conclusions to the whole class, I intervene or add that they may extend Freire to our postmodern times. In showing how their conversation may be penetrated by hegemony or contained with modernist frameworks of theorizing, I offer to the students an additional dimension of counter-hegemonic theorizing which may penetrate Freire's notions of reflection, dialogue, and what it means to be a "conscious" subject in today's times.[145] With this explanation, I attempt to pierce the dimensions of modernist hegemony of reflection, dialogue, problem-solving, and the unified notion of subjectivity as consciousness, as pointed to but not sufficiently clarified by Freire.

Often, as happens, a student raises her hand and asks me why I asked the same question for her group and the other groups in deciphering what Freire is about? She continues: this would mean all the groups would have the same answer. I usually respond by offering an image of steps (see below Figure 55), saying: "You will see this is not always the case." I then proceed to examine with the students their images of what they think is Freire's salient concepts.

After they present their artwork on Freire, I sometimes refer to the artwork of other students from previous classes, showing how Freire and his *Pedagogy* may be interpreted and re-interpreted *ad infinitum,* all pointing to more complex dimensions of power through language. At this point I bring into the conversation the notions of post-structuralist terms, such as discourse and articulation. My first step is to draw on the chalkboard an illusion of steps:

Figure 55

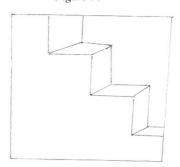

From this image I ask my students to tell me what they see. After several interpretations, – some indicating the steps are moving upward, not downward, I interject: How about neither direction? I respond further by pointing out, if one was to look down – as if from an attic looking down and seeing a room divider, they will see still another image. At this point, the student who asked me about her concern of all groups seeing the same object ceases. She perceives something else from her previous orientation which no longer applies in a post-structuralist frame of knowledge-making, interpreting, or sensing. After they have grasped this insight, I ask the students to do something else.

Forming small groups or pairs of students, I ask the students to quickly utter what they think is going on in class. I ask them further to role play as if they are reporting as journalists. Then, without their awareness, one of the pairs or an individual in a small group won't remember what they were about to say to each other. I usually intervene: "Don't worry," I enjoin, "it will come back to you, so continue." Then, as the same individual is talking, the individual who forgot what he or she was about to say suddenly regains memory and wants to talk. I usually stop this round-robin style of conversation here. I ask the person who suddenly regained memory to explain not only what he or she wanted or intended to say, but further, why did they forget in one moment, and re-gain memory in another? The person responds with a shrug and I go on to yet another activity.

In this next activity, I ask the whole class: "Have any of you had an experience whereby what you want to say suddenly gets lost? Almost all the students, no matter what their cultural identification, race, class, gender, etc., respond in the affirmative, "yes I (we) have had this experience."Also, how do you regain what you wanted or intended to say?" I ask. I may also add a few words by comparing this phenomenon of forgetting and recalling as restoring a "link" to a "chain" which disappears momentarily, and then, suddenly, re-connects to a link of another chain, as if on a track, one train car linked one after the other. I begin to use language like "chains" and "links in a chain," or "how the chain may becomes broken or re-connected." I often use the expression "losing track (or chain) of memory."

I then go on to yet another activity which seeks to address some of Freire's important work in Chapter 1 of *Pedagogy* in which he discusses how in an "existential duality" or caught on binary sets of chains or contradictions, the oppressed, once they feel free, or "get a bit of power" (See Figure 23 in Chapter 3) become attracted to the role and values of the oppressor, and thereupon, they turn on each other. Like losing and regaining one's memory, I point out that such a phenomenon is couched in many historical and cultural contexts. I show how slaves, once promoted to the position of "drivers" become more cruel to former fellow slaves than the slave owners of the plantation who promoted him or her (Genovese, 1972). I also use as an analogy how this "middle" position, wedged between slaves and owner, denies further resistance by circumventing possible forms of slave solidarity and plans to revolt. In addition, I show, in the case of Nazi concentration camps, how "capos" had the same experience as the drivers on slave plantations one hundred years earlier in a different environment. In order to extend their time to live, capos often assisted their Nazi overlords with the extermination of fellow Jewish inmates. Over and over again, this phenomenon is illustrated with literary illustrations and popular movies (i.e. *The Grey Zone, The Counterfeiter, The Reader*).[146]

Usually, at this point in our discussions, the students and I connect how the oppressed becomes oppressor and inadvertently (not intentionally) constructs a form of subjectivity they thought to be owned by "themselves," but now see as something outside yet linked to themselves. There are porous and penetrable forces at work. At this point, I put on the overhead projector a series of images in which a man, a husband, father, and dog owner, transforms himself wherein the oppressed becomes the oppressor. The cartoon (see Figure 56 below) begins with a man yelling at his child, wife, and dog. After the yelling session, he begins to get dressed (helped by his obsequious wife) and proceeds out to the street en route to his job. Upon arriving at the office, the man begins to walk up the stairs, slowly, as his shoulders become more hunched over. Upon arriving in the office, the man's boss begins to yell at the man in a very similar manner as he yelled at his wife, child, and dog.[147]

Though Freire describes oppression and de-humanization as the oppressed oppressing the oppressed in which they "adhere" an image or unified image "housed" in one's consciousness, he has not elucidated how this is done in processes of consciousness, inter-subjectivity, and the unconsciousness. Nor has Freire attended to other cognitive processes – depositing, reflection, dialogue, and positing as critical surroundings around the cognitive subject. He has not shown those links to problem-posing in which there may be complex ridges and overlaps not being spelled out in the cognitive process. Freire is being hampered by his own attempts to link reflection to problem-posing, as he is already framing his work by modernist either-or concepts related to cognition and knowledge-making, perhaps adopted, inadvertently.

Figure 56

In Freire there is no discussion contextualizing his notion of consciousness, critical and otherwise, to a historical period dating back to the Enlightenment and Descartes.[148] In this era, binary chains of existence and being, real and imaginary, I and the other, white and people of color, rich and poor, proper grammar and slang, begin their outward expansion into the fibers and tissues of modern day technology, media, and administrative systems and institutions, discourses, and power relations.[149] As Freire points out, and my students often illustrate (see Chapter 3), the need to clarify how lecture and discussion formats of teaching may have more in common than different, and may be explored further albeit with more difficulty than lecturing or the acts of "depositing" knowledge . For example, as we saw in the previous chapter and in the students' artwork, students drew images of "banking" in very clear and gruesome ways (see Chapter 3, Figures 1-4); at other times, the notion of dialogue, reflection, and problem-solving became more diffused and obscured. In some of their images there are traces of chains, intersecting and circulating within and through one another (see Figures 38-42), but these images are provisional and hesitant compared to the more explicit images of the oppressor (the teacher) depositing "information" into the heads of students. Often, in a relieved yet somewhat confused state, when I asked students what their images mean (referring to Freire's notion of dialogue), they mutter that Freire was very clear about banking as a teaching method but the reason why they chose "banking" as their first concept to draw an image was because Freire was not as clear as to what reflection and dialogue meant nor how they are linked to positing as a problem causing contradictions which may get in between student and teacher: the former they considered the oppressed, the latter, the oppressor. They had no idea how reflection and dialogue may be joined together, or in temporary moments, offer up positions for student and teacher to see those spaces in which they are constituted by a complex of subject-positions mixed into an array of possible

Therefore, we are pressed to map out how student and teacher may interact and transform each other's reflections in a process. As a way of suggesting an extension of Freire on this point, we may want to "see into" dialogue as a part of a large and overlapping systems of discourses and their formations, criss-crossing one another on a force field of power – a field dominated by modernist concepts which blind us from seeing how meanings become constituted in intricate and webbed signifying and semiotic complexes of constructs and cognitions. I would argue, upon introducing new concepts, drawn from post-structural constructs, we may see more clearly such signifying and signified processes, and images brought into relief by post-structuralist constructs; or see how chains of circulating signifiers, subject-positions and spaces or surfaces become constituted, along with the introduction of new spaces, imbricated onto the old spaces, which may inscribe, de-inscribe, and re-inscribe new articulations for de-coding or de-constructing issues of domination and oppression, as well as locating spaces for their transformation. Thus, in order to extend Freire's *Pedagogy of the Oppressed*, specifically, how the oppressed become oppressor of themselves and others, we will have to go further than Lacan, Pecheux, Laclau and Mouffe, and Zizek. We will thereby introduce some of the later works of their followers, Laclau (2007), Smith (1996), and Thomassen (2005), in furthering the meanings of articulation in and against hegemony, as will be introduced shortly.

This introduction is further important because the only images of a subject my students and their artwork could depict (see Chapter 3) was a subject, structured along solitary, individualistic, and binary terms and chains of signifiers. This binary picture however denies student and teacher a wider and deeper view as to how power and its relations (class, gender, authority, race) circulate and intersect one another, as well as how they, as subjects, may become cajoled into negative or counter-defeating relations and penetrate the various "walls" or layers of cognition and reflection which may foreclose them from seeing and feeling further. Recall, for example, in Chapter 2, how students and teachers identify the school administrator as the person to appeal to as opposed to appealing to each other as mutual decision-makers. Or, how some new teachers, out of fear, aligned themselves with the administrator against their students when they enjoyed seeing how administrative surveillance made their students sweat and suffer.

What is also missing in these intervening and intersecting spaces between student and teacher are cognizable objects of their own power potential and common goals for democratizing and empowering their relations in and resistant to hierarchical and administrative school conditions. And, further, how they may attain these subject-positions or identities through their movements in other spaces which they may carve out as signifiers (Coward and Ellis, pp. 3, 8). and became themselves circulating signifiers (partially intentional, partially intuitive) and necessary (as the special education students accomplished with their invention of "flying rumors") to open new spaces in which students and teachers may become counter-hegemonic theorizers and activists. Equipped with the support of each other, and theorizing systems of post-structural analyses, student, teacher, and teacher educator may analyze how their school relations hegemonize them to positing as problematic parts only of the whole, while ignoring the whole or goals toward which they can become empowered and trust one another enough to seize power and position by displacing or eliminating school administrators as over paid adjuncts, who must serve them, the workers and theorists, rather than the other way around.

Once student, teacher, and teacher educator take recognition of this turn of events as a future possibility (as some charter schools have already recognized), then, they will be in a better position not to become manipulated by a system which serves those at the top, rather than those at the bottom of the school's hierarchy. In this way, students, teachers, parents, and teacher educators may be able to re-frame their discourses and see what parts and dimensions of dialogue serve their interests and powers, and how these discourses emanate and are informed constantly by a wider and deeper complex of discursive formations – some hierarchical, others resistant to hierarchical school arrangements and more sympathetic to democratic arrangements. And when they further map out these discourses, more minutely and more broadly, they may see how these mixed or hybridized discourses are often linked and connected by chains of signifiers which intersect one another producing both contradictions (which may stop them from further theorizing or trigger them to take actions against one another – i.e. the oppressed becoming each other's oppressor) or initiate their own joint and agential actions as advocates and activists for each other and others in similar predicaments. They can begin this process by becoming conscious of their consciousness or how and what constitutes them to be conscious.[154]

WHAT IS CONSCIOUSNESS A LA MODERNIST AND POST-STRUCTURAL THEORISTS?

The concept of reflection as an individual experience, a concept largely taken up by the phenomenologist Edmund Husserl and adopted by Freire, has yet to be resolved, according to many critiques positing the problem of inter-subjectivity.[155] There is no discussion delving into the processes of how reflection joins together with dialogue in a problem-solving process examining cognitions critically, let alone counter-hegemonically. My students have no idea as to how these concepts, taken from modernist frameworks are linked. While the students tend to think modernistically in either/or binarisms and dilemmas, post-structuralist concepts seek to see how dialogue is set within an ensemble of discourses and discursive formations, often cutting across one another, producing sudden and (as others would claim) unconscious and interruptive "second thoughts" which seem to slide into intentional or reflective thoughts in discourses and dialogues. As Michael Apple (1979) claimed, what is needed to "analyze hegemony" are "relational concepts" or new "forms of consciousness.[156] These suggestions may provide a better context toward introducing a framework for counter-hegemonic teaching and theorizing. After a discussion on this subject of paradigms, we concluded that as much as they appreciated Freire's work as valuable, specifically, bringing to light how lecturing may be oppressive for both themselves and their students, they were at a loss of words but hesitant as to how to grasp how consciousness, dialogue, and problem-solving are connected, beyond or linked to overly simple and essentialized forms of cognition. At this point I usually introduce the writings of Laclau and others.

LACLAU AND POST-STRUCTURAL THEORIZING FOR COUNTERING HEGEMONY

Laclau (2007) and his students and followers, Smith (1996), Thomassen (2005), Chrictley and Marchant (2004) describe a process in which equivalent and differential chains of signifiers win or fail to win hegemony in competing scenarios pertaining to the struggles for getting the masses to consent to a regime or leadership. Set in the historical context of the days of the Russian Revolution and other historical periods, Laclau reveals how power is overlaid with layers of discursive power. He reveals precisely how articulations construct subjects in taking several positions in which they are overtaken or watch how their previous positions recede and become smaller, less potent spaces on the surfaces of their subject-positions. In this way, subjects may also undergo a process of constructing, co-constructing and de-constructing, or inscribing, de-inscribing, and re-inscribing their subject-positions and identities as they articulate (de-articulate and re-articulate) with their discursive surroundings. They accomplish these articulatory acts by locating points of antagonism and points of connection from which to mount their attacks and defenses against hegemony and for counter-hegemony.

As Laclau (2007, pp. 130–133) makes clear these processes, it is important to remember how relations, circulation, and contents of signifiers (empty, differential, and floating) are always in a state of flux and, *tendentially* (Thomassen. 2005) affecting the surfaces or spaces of their subject-positions, changing in degrees in which signifiers empty themselves (thereby taking on dominant position to hegemonize the content of other subject-positions) or, conversely, fill themselves with the contents of other subject-positions, thereby breaking apart those *points of caption* or anchoring points of signifiers (Lacan, 1977) or quilting points (Zizek, 1989). This means, in a different motion, how parts of signifiers may act as linchpins, flaring out (which were once intertwined fragments of chains or strands of signifiers) into other directions or anchoring points of other signifiers, other chains, and other fragments which, likewise, may be in the state of ejecting parts of themselves from filled signifiers and subject-position surfaces. This entering into or flaring outward movement produce a voyage of the signifier, their chains, and respective discursive formations and discourses in which they become circulating or floating signifiers and fragments of circulating signifiers – *objets petit a* – which may begin to coalesce with other signifiers and chains, producing equivalent and empty signifiers, capable of absorbing other fragments and hegemonizing the discursive field, on the one hand; and reversing, differential signifiers – circulating and displacing – differential or floating signifiers, capable of bringing about new and possibly new dominant chains of signifiers, subject-positions, and their surfaces to be inscribed, on the other hand.

For example, signifiers may displace or transform some of their contents thus emptying signifiers, on one alignment, allowing "room" to absorb differential signifiers or demands and desires from their own chains of signifiers and discursive formations outside of their sphere of influence. Then, in another alignment, bring together their own and other chains of signifiers and discursive formations which become mostly filled, blocking off spaces for their surfaces to be reconstituted by fragments or floating signifiers, representing differential chains of signifiers. In either alignment or direction, chains of equivalent and differential signifiers may partially satisfy demands and desires of people (but only partially in degrees of tendential-ness, never completely) which may occupy and get re-occupied and re-constituted in articulation by both types of signifiers, chains, and discursive formations, providing at times surfaces or edges of their imbricated discursive formations, one overlapping the other, linked by intertwining chains of signifiers, and as one occupies these complex surfaces in their respective subject-positions, and endures the tensions of contradictory and hybrid experiences.

When, at a certain moment, the intersection in which both chains of signifiers become articulated what may result may be a clearing for a bolder and more energized action and reaction, brought on by the circulation of fragmented or floating signifiers, ejecting or cutting loose from one discursive formation (say those people of color who want needed relief in welfare programs or natural disasters as in Katrina) and in which the fragmented or floating signifiers travels or circulates into a discursive formation (representing demands for cutting taxes and no social programs, occupied by white and black upwardly mobile and affluent people) penetrated by the circulation of these signifiers, produces counter-productive effects of – on one level – why would poor people vote for candidates against their own interests, and on another level, through the work of the fragmented or floating signifiers into another discursive formation, produce the effect: "While I am poor, I still believe in the dream that one day I will be rich."[157]

The effect of these signifying movements and how they attach to or break off from each other or intersect with other chains of signifiers, thereby "blurring" or reinforcing boundaries or frontiers they have come accustomed to believe, remains, as Thomassen (2005) argues, an open issue contingent on the unpredictable battles of hegemonic and counter-hegemonic power struggles, and, at best, only partially fix meanings, images, and subject identifications, relationships and senses and incitements of solidarity. It is this emphasis on how partial inscriptions on surfaces of subject-positions get constructed provides a basis for mapping or illustrating how articulation works when competing and traces of one discursive formation creeps into other discursive formations. As Paul Gilroy (1987) said, describing the various Caribbean cultures which compete and hegemonize one another, as a process of *syncretism* in which their power relations for dominance maintains them as distinct and different people, hierarchically superior or inferior to people coming from one island-nation to another, and from one people of color population to another, and in which pecking orders are accorded to who is from the most advanced, cultured, and educated (Figure 43 in Chapter 3).[158]

When power relations between race, class, religion, authority and gender become crossed over onto levels of discourses and discursive formations; or, on the micro levels of intersected signifying chains and subject-positions and surfaces, a map for understanding and projecting future conflicts may emerge or brought into relief how student, teacher, and teacher educator may theorize and problematize their antagonistic points as well as those points of connection which (*while* they are antagonistic to each other) may offer ways to analyze such predicaments amongst themselves. Incorporating post-structural constructs, educators may be able to discern from how, if we map out the circulating and chains of signifiers, the extent to which hegemonic discourses have intruded into potential counter-hegemonic discourses or contained discourses which may appear to be counter-hegemonic (i,e. dialogue or consciousness) but which remain contained by hegemonic forces and *vis-a-versa,* may also be abated.

MAPPING THE JOURNEY OF THE POST-STRUCTURAL EQUIVALENT
AND FLOATING SIGNIFIERS

Laclau and his protege, Lasse Thomssen have provided their readers, and I would submit, necessary for educators, illustrations or diagrams in which, taking place during the days of the Russian Revolution, various conflicting forces attempted to draw each other into their hegemonic folds, and get them to support their hegemonic interests and alliances, irrespective how some of these forces may have contained elements of being adversarial forces. Drawing a line representing a frontier (see below Diagram A) between the Tsar and other groups, representing their diverse demands and interests (in groups D1, D2, D3. D4....), Laclau and (repeated by Thomassen) reveal how, in the course of these events, one representation or demand emerges as dominant or hegemonic and is able to compete against the Tsar's demands. This dominant demand (D1), acting as a suturing point or stand in for the other demands produce an empty signifier(s) linking with other signifiers (differential and more particularistic) weaving the other demands (D2, D3, D4, D5....) into and onto (their surfaces for inscription), a chain of equivalent subject positions illustrated as a string or chain of positions by an equal (=) sign and each subject-positioned is divided by two semi-circles: the upper semi-circle representing equivalent chains of meanings as well as a place which employ signifiers travelling upon and planting their "common" demands by drawing into their gravity competing or particularistic subject-positions; the lower semi-circle represents those particularistic demands which remain dormant in each equivalent subject positions of chain of equivalence.

Diagram A

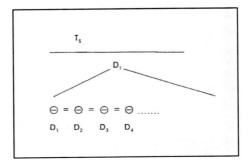

As a result of empty and floating signifiers becoming articulated with one another, determine the extent they are made to be placed on an equivalent chain. If the frontier is not as certain or clear (as indicated by the solid line between the Tsar and the populace – in Diagram A) in which the separation between the Tsar and the people pressing their demands for reforms may become competed upon each other, the solid line separating two warring camps – the Tsar and the people – becomes blurred (indicated by a dotted line – see below) in which the frontier dividing the Tsar and the populace is transgressed and something else happens when the social whole undergoes an "organic crisis," as we will see below in Diagram B.

Diagram B

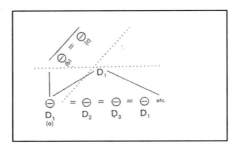

In this latter case (Diagram B), the solid line dividing the Tsar from the people is obscured by an intervening force, originating from the Tsarist camp, and in which a diagonal dotted line intersecting the hitherto solid line, produces intersecting choices of equivalent chains of signifiers and demands (replacing the dualistic division between the Tsar and the people). When this happens, the stand-in empty signifier (D1) which served to coalesce demands for reforms by the people against the Tsar, undergoes a transformation which are competed by other empty and equivalent signifiers emanating from the Tsar camp, as represented by D1 (b) and D1 (c). While the hitherto coalescing equivalent chains of signifiers (D1a) remains, when there is a counter-hegemonic complex of chains (D1 (b) and D1 (c) competing with the original counter-hegemonic set of demands (D1) emerges, and a reversal of the position of semi-circles occurs in accounting for the surfaces of their various chains of subject-positions.

As indicated before, and applied to Diagram A, the surfaces of subject-positions was represented by the upper semi-circle of the subject-positions containing spaces (tendentially included) which shared their spaces with other demands and subject-positions (D2, D3, D4, D5...). However, when an organic crisis of hegemony occurs, according to Laclau's Diagram B, or map, what was hitherto a surface for equivalent and empty signifiers and their chains, becomes occupied by a sudden and set of new chains, differential or floating signifiers, which strongly suggests, during time of organic crisis, when one side of the equation is hegemonized and counter-hegemonies the other side, manifesting the battle with a dotted line which obscures or blurs what each side (before represented clearly) now becomes a crisis in legitimation. This means that what emerges on the surfaces of subject-positions is a nettle for hegemony or equivalence through particularistic and differential signifiers or floating signifiers which, as we pointed above, may originate as fragments or "scrapings" off the surface, metaphorically speaking, of the original or cohesive and equivalent surfaces of former subject-positions, are now the fragments or traces of circulating signifiers (i.e. the "flying rumors" my special education students experienced). As Laclau (2007, p. 131) asks:

> What happens, however, if the dichotomic frontier, without disappearing, is blurred as a result of the oppressive regime is itself hegemonic – That is, trying to interrupt the equivalent chain of the popular camp (opposed to the Tsarist camp) by an alternative equivalent chain of the popular camp, in which some of the popular demands are *articulated* to entirely different links (for example...the defense of the 'small man' against power ceases to be associated to a left discourse, as in the American New Deal, and becomes linked to the 'moral majority'[a right discourse]? (Laclau, p. 133, emphasis mine)

Responding to his own question, Laclau submits: The categories of "empty" (equivalent) and floating (differential) signifiers are structurally different. The first concerns a construction of a popular identity once the presence of a stable frontier is taken for granted; the second tries conceptually to apprehend the logic of the displacements of that frontier. In practice, however, the distance between the two is not that great, argues Laclau. Both are hegemonic operations and, most importantly, largely overlap. A situation where only the category of empty signifier was relevant, with total exclusion of the floating moment is hardly imaginable. Conversely, a purely psychotic universe with only floating signifiers is not thinkable either. Thus, to Laclau, floating and empty signifiers should be conceived as partial dimensions of articulation.

Thus, Laclau concludes, shifting his original position of the upper-semicircle is constituted by only equivalent and empty signifiers is changed to a representation of demands in which the "upper semicircle is always the one that becomes autonomous in any floating (signifiers), for it is in its equivalent virtualities that the representation of the (absent) fullness of society lies (p. 132)."

What Laclau and Thomassen reveal in both diagrams A and B is a more precise location of the surfaces of subject-positions representing diverse demands of two or more conflicting parties or camps, and how, in their articulating both positions, there are shifts of position in which (on the surfaces or in the upper semi-circles of a empty signifiers) they become linked together on an equivalent and differential chains crossing over and intersecting one another. While Laclau does not clearly point out at what points empty signifiers – presumably when filled or competed on by other empty signifiers – how they become displaced or are transformed into "floating signifiers," beginning their own equivalent chains and empty signifiers in the processes of articulation (de-articulations and re-articulations), Laclau leaves these problematics for the reader to further theorize. That is, what Laclau does mention in this regard is when an equivalent chain is "interrupted" by a popular camp alternative or another equivalent chain consisting of a broad range of particularistic demands, or conversely, when the Tsar's camp offers alternatives to the popular camp and disguises these alternatives by blurring the precise line of separation between the Tsar and the people (see Diagram B), newly created alternatives become "floating signifiers" lying in the upper semicircles of subject-positions in assisting how new links of new equivalent chains may become articulated as equivalent chains of signifiers. That is, as Laclau states: "(i)t is no longer that the particularism of the demand becomes self-sufficient and independent of any equivalent articulation, but that its meaning is indeterminate *between* alternative equivalent frontiers (my emphasis, p. 131). To Laclau, then, this "in between" territory he refers to is the place whereby "floating signifiers" breaks through sutured meanings – i.e. irruptions into the equivalent chains on the surfaces of equivalent chains of signifiers and subject-position surfaces, which may reveal their particularities on a part of the same surface as equivalent subject-position surfaces (also located in the upper semicircle) and thereby suspend for us a moment of waiting to see what will come next as one differential signifier transforms itself, for the moment, into an equivalent chain or another equivalent chain representing a diversity of demands seeking hegemony and countering hegemony.

EXTENDING LACLAU FOR ANALYZING HEGEMONY IN SCHOOLS: LIVING IN CHAINS AND CONTRADICTIONS

The implication of Laclau's work for analyzing hegemony in schools is very clear: if students and teachers live in contradictory (as well as in coherent and cohesive) signifying chains and subject-positions, often some crossing over and intersecting one another, and in which through acts of articulation, these configurations are in constant flux as to the meanings and shifts of meanings of words, gestures, even pauses of silence, carrying with them the opening up of new spaces and opportunities for theorizing and mapping out how they are crossed and intersected by hegemonic and hierarchical chains penetrating their subject-positions and identities becomes apparent. That is, their teaching one another how to mount counter-hegemonic actions and movements in their classrooms, schools, and communities, if they take post-strucrural theorizing seriously, is always a clear and present danger as opposed to becoming constantly obscured and manipulated – often fatalistically and in states of fear – how they can change their school and societal circumstances. To the extent they exert pressures on their school administrative and hierarchical practices – administrative bosses hanging over their heads, along with dominant classroom management practices, and standardized exams driving a standardized and pre-scripted curriculum and evaluations of their teachers as professionals, these aspects of schooling are closely aligned to each other by these power relations penetrating and enveloping their discourses and relations.

Until student, teacher, and teacher-educator can take critical notice of these developments and everyday school realities, or, in post-structural terms of Laclua, how they are aligned to articulations which position them into relations of identities, language use, and power relations which deny them un-oppressed and un-alienated opportunities to fight these conditions through counter-hegemonic actions and activities (i.e. mapping together how student and teacher should be more conciliatory and cooperative rather than permitting themselves to be pitted against one another by the administrative regimes of authoritarian practices just mentioned), then, they (we) will have to remain quiet, lay low (contrary to my advice), and wait for a better day to act. Until that day comes we may continue to re-conceptualize how we/they are identified and put into hegemonic subject-positions as we/they often become, inadvertently, oppressors to ourselves and each other rather than counter-hegemonic allies and liberators.

ONE MORE WORD: BEGIN TO CONSTRUCT CHAINS FOR COUNTER-HEGEMONIZING

Laclau, who is very influenced by Lacan, and later by Zizek, notes how these signifier intersections (equivalent and differential chains) may be temporarily stopped or shored up by knots or suturing movements in which the flow of signifiers and their chains (some held down or sutured by *nodal points*) are stopped or lifted. He, along with Zizek (1989), also notes, on the most micro levels of signification, a pivotal point or linchpin for counter-hegemonic movements or relationships may exist in which power is determined and constituted as a trace effect or contingency of desires for wholeness and individuality within and without of structures of authority. That is, how signifiers, acting as political demands of the social, may be able to empty themselves of their differential or particular contents and relate or articulate other signifiers to partially empty and partially fill signifiers and subject-positions by acting as "stand-ins" or representing to others in their group or discursive formations, their demands for more democratic, bottom-up school authority as taking on equivalent values or differential values to perform and further to re-articulate previous articulations or articulations they may negotiate amongst themselves on the spot. Once we begin to construct a chain and articulate these values onto a chain in which we may inscribe different demands, as a compromising or mixed entity and/or in various "tendential" degrees along the surfaces of hegemonic and counter-hegemonic representations and discourses, there may lie some degree of hope or a spark to incite others to take joint actions of solidarity and agency.

When these intersections of chains of signifiers and discourses do occur, competing demands from both sides of the frontiers or borders ("us" versus "them") are overtaken, in *crossing over and positioning one in between the borders* (Giroux, 1993; Giroux & McLaren, 1994, my emphasis). While others become coalesced into hegemonic entities of their respective "sides," we can reflect on how each side seeks to hegemonize their subject-positions or empty signifiers and equivalent chains of the other. To represent what "everyone" wants and demands, attaching them onto additional sutured points along a floating influx of parti-cularistic demands and signifiers, micro differential and particularistic signifiers, and macro and empty master signifiers – i.e. the word "democracy" or "knowledge" or "excellence" — may become arenas we may act – in those in-between spaces as yet to be named – but might also serve as temporary equivalent stand-ins, and in this movement, new lines of the border or the frontier may become both "blurred," transgressed, and re-drawn.

149

In this intermediate area, we may partially make our demands known, working together by *jettisoning or loosening fragments* of reactionary demands, keeping at bay their appearance as "floating signifiers" and, once again, keep active other floating signifiers competing and offering alternatives to be further questioned, re-articulated, and re-positioned as the dominant or hegemonic sides. This circulation and mix of circulating signifiers continues to issue equivalent chains of signifiers, subject-positions, and surfaces for inscription in the struggle for hegemony of authoritarian and hierarchical school practices and policies as well as their antithetical and democratic articulatory forms of resistances.

The movement toward re-absorbing equivalent or empty signifiers or differential signifiers or floating signifiers and their corresponding demands, desires, and representations of identity of the subject, continue to circulate, intersect, and cross over one another, often breaching the borders (solid lines) representing differences, serving as signifiers which may re-cross and bridge borders in which they, a moment before, served to maintain as differential signifiers and demands. When there is a decrease in the cross-over metonymic actions of signifying chains penetrating both sides of the border (which formerly served to coalesce rather than displace and transform signifiers and demands), then the time will come for demands to become re-articulated and dis-articulated through new post-structural constructs – *object petit a's* – emerging and crossing over and into our consciousness revealing in its cross-sections series of hierarchical and anti-hierarchical, hegemonic and counter-hegemonic subject-positions and surfaces linked to and intertwining into chains of signifiers linked to all of the discursive formations we are simultaneously members of and in need of being constantly re-theorized critically and counter-hegemonically. At this moment, student, teacher and teacher educator will become counter-hegemonic theorists and have access to tools for mapping, *par excellence*.

TOWARD NAMING NEW POST-STRUCTURAL CONSTRUCTS TO THEORIZE COUNTER-HEGEMONICALLY

Probing deeper, one may locate within each discursive formation other discursive forms. Various chains of signifiers may interact and intersect each other producing glimpses of either/or dilemmas by seeing how power circulates and how subjects or speakers get de-centered as a signifier circulating in, through, and between other subjects and their subject-positions in various discursive formations. Moreover, as recent post-structuralists have proposed (Laclau, 1990), subject-positions have "surfaces" on which subjects or speakers may inscribe, de-inscribe, and re-inscribe their feelings, gestures, signals and signifiers in cognitions, intentional or un-intentional, to others in like and different discursive formations. When intervening and intersecting chains of signifiers move or shift the subject-positions of a subject-speaker by what and how he or she may interpret, or be incited to act in constructing various forms of solidarities with each other, they may inscribe on the surfaces of their subject-positions other feelings and thoughts to de-code the present day arrangement or complex of surface inscriptions which are seen and felt upon becoming subject-positioned by testing, classroom management, and administrative order routines and practices.

Student and teacher may also spot crevices or interstices in these constructed surfaces. In this way, "knowledge," "cognition," "freedom," "democracy," and "action" may be made to appear as originating or containing an omnipotent individual, looking down at the landscape of the world, observing, measuring, numbering, and defining the truth; or they may be made to be appear – in post-structural terms – as a complex of contingent, floating, and constantly shifting spaces in which one space is struggling to hegemonize another space, periodically, suturing themselves along axis of chains or "suturing" nodal points which, for the moment, makes it appear to others that such positions are eternal, natural, and normal. For the moment, however, during these periods of dominance of one discursive formation over the other, student and teacher may re-visit these same places. They may see new terrains, thick and textured (Geertz, 1973), and when framed by post-structuralist constructs, see how one subject-position cannot maintain itself forever as omnipotent; what is real is the ongoing emergence of one discursive formation intersecting another, constituting vast discursive fields of power and possible new articulations which intrude on and allow speakers to speak in often complex and unconscious-discursive-emotive-conscious ways. Thus, they may see a new terrain in which power diverse relations and possibilities are always present.

SPEAKERS BECOME SIGNIFIERS

In these de-centered subject-positions and discursive formations, speakers and subjects become signifiers (Lacan, 1977), as they may inscribe their feelings, doubts, hopes, and partial intentions (Laclau, 1990, 2007), on surfaces with other members of like or different discursive formations. As both struggle to conjoin and fight it out with others in different discursive formations and subject-positions, they may see a larger picture than the pictures they were allowed to see in modernist paradigms of thinking and knowledge-making. Subject to any contingency, new thoughts and feelings may suddenly emerge from the same or other, as well as new discursive formations of their own making, as students and teachers may transform their dialogue (as we saw with the special education students) into counter-hegemonic communities – discourses and their accompanying discursive formations – as they become supports to each other, as their words flow through each other's words (Fleischer, 1998, 2001, 2004) in a kind of mutual naming of worlds. Operating from such subject-positions, as student and teacher, as members of these various discursive formations, may contribute by revealing hegemony or those other power relations in which they are intertwined on a daily basis, and now may see beyond the modernist limits. When they do this, in another moment, they see how to penetrate through these limits and position themselves as not merely isolated and unified individuals, but as inter-subjects[159] piercing into the "multifarious layers of discourse" (Laclau & Mouffe, 1985) constructing their dialogues from hegemonic and counter-hegemonize discursive formations, linked together by chains of signifiers emanating from the surfaces of their respective subject-positions. In these moments and places, student and teacher may not only live in each other's reflections and cognitions, they may also act to construct new post-structural constructs to counter-hegemonize in their schools and classrooms. Or, at least make their joint cognitions and reflections more complex than they hitherto assumed.

MAKING COGNITIONS COMPLEX VIA POST-STRUCTURAL CONSTRUCTS

As a result of Freire not being able to see the genesis of what happens *between* people in states of oppression and their struggles to liberate themselves and each other, as locating those intermediary spaces they occupy in discourse (and dialogue); and, not referring to Lacan and others at the time of his writing of *Pedagogy of the Oppressed* (1970), in terms of explaining how those oppressed become trans-fixed, displaced, and transformed into and out of oppressive roles,[160] Freire was not able or willing to give a more complex accounting of how power infiltrates people via language as made up from discursive and signifying systems. Nor did Freire give an accounting of how student and teacher understand themselves and each other, and how they relate and speak (or do not speak) to each other, but, nevertheless, are assisted with a pedagogy which is counter-hegemonic, and which may reveal a complex field of discursive formations which are constitutive of dialogue, subject-positions, signifiers and their chains of signifiers, and those surfaces necessary for speakers to inscribe (get interpellated or interpolate[161]) themes of thought, identity, and practice.

These spaces for interpolation are already in motion and can provide entrance of the subject while they find themselves crossed by intersecting chains of signifiers, surfaces, and subject-positions. Each speaker brings with them – in their voices, dialects, gestures, songs and accents – materials to interpolate or inscribe onto the surfaces of their and other's subject-positions as linked to their multiple memberships in various discursive formations. In these interpolating moments, other signifying materials may appear, including fragments of previous subject-position surfaces which may reveal (breaking away from a binary logic) how these fragments lift off or attach to other subject-positions surfaces via "floating signifiers," which may coalesce into "empty signifiers," waiting to be filled by signifier circulation or remain, indefinitely, a loose particle of the discursive formation from whence they first appeared on their journey into the discursive and signifying fields of power. What appears, then, at first as an essentialized construction (using modernist logic), is a layering of discourses making up several discursive formation (using post-structural logic): the former in unquestioned and essential places and moments; the latter, in-between spaces, or "uneven edges," speakers or subjects may discern as a dis-alignment of prior alignments (brought on by intersecting chains of signifiers) or spaces in which their inscriptions and those of others are emerging, submerging, and dissolving. In these intersecting places and moments, dominance and resistances are expressed and appear as subject-positions and signifiers (i.e. race, class, authority, gender, etc.) mixing and being posited as a problem to be overcome by agential actions of speaker-inscriptions. Some of these inscriptions may be brief, like gestures, moments of silence, slips of the tongue, or strings of words which, somehow, re-conceptualizes what was perceived and assumed as given and unalterable a moment before. (Delpit & Dowdy, 2008; Gilroy, 1987; Smitherman, 2001)

In this complex, overlapping and intersecting discursive field of power, not accounted for by Freire's notion of consciousness (*conscientizacao*), but posited as a unitary, essentialized, and originary structure and process of cognition and reflection (a la Husserl) as opposed to a more complex mode of cognition, which incorporates the unconsciousness in language and other inter-subjective modes of relating (see Berger & Luckmann, 1965) what cannot be revealed is when two or more speakers, in a close relationship – perhaps, even communion – find themselves in subject-positions which they may sense and feel thought processes or problematic issues around and between, as shooting through them[162] as an experience not accounted for in *Pedagogy of the Oppressed*. To Freire, such experiences are characterized as "antagonistic," and thereby dismissed from further examination. During his first chapter, Freire (borrowing from Erich Fromm) describes how the oppressed undergo contradictory feelings and thoughts between the oppressed and oppressor, as they undergo "existential dualities," and become adhesed[163] to oppressor images relating to one another, there is no further description of how these actions and thoughts emerge and get submerged or can be intervened in language as an intermediate zone operating between and amongst students and teachers who may share and analyze their oppressive surroundings in more constructive ways.

ONE DOES NOT NEED EXCLUSIVELY POST STRUCTURAL CONSTRUCTS TO COUNTER-HEGEMONY

However informative post-structural insights may have a more liberating notion of the unconsciousness, on the level of inter-subjective writings, one does not have to rely exclusively on post-structuralist constructs to understand how Freire's notion of dialogue could be further extended within modernist constructs. As Berger and Luckmann, Schutz, and others have informed social phenomenology for almost a century, when a subject is in close proximity to another subject, the need to stop or pause and distance one's self from the "stream of consciousness" is not necessary. That is, the flows of their thoughts and cognitions in a "stream of consciousness" contains within them structures and processes that makes lifting one's self out of the stream as unnecessary. As these social phenomenologists argue,[164] when two or more subjects in close "inter-subjectiveness," they may *reflect-in-the-action* as each begins to see the other in themselves and the other more clearly than the other as an object of their cognition. They may pause "to reflect" in the action as they interact in close proximity to another without stepping back to reflect (Berger & Luckmann, 1965). Thus, as Berger and Luckmann argue, in the other we may know more about ourselves than of our own self-reflections in a moment of solitary reflection. Berger and Luckmann's analysis means that Freire's notion of consciousness as solitary and original entity leaves much to be desired without concomitant components of inter-subjectivity, as well as a similar component derived from the post-structural attention to the unconsciousness which asserts, in Lacan's famous words: "The unconsciousness is structured like a language."

That is, once in solidarity with each other, two or more people may not find themselves insulated, for the moment; rather they may find themselves intruded upon, intersected, and invaded by other chains of signifiers, emanating from other discursive formations, which may offer them positions but, nevertheless, not positions from which to see how these surfaces of inscription are layered on subject-positions. That is, how subject-positions get sutured (metaphorically) or, some of which are fleeting images (metonymically). Either way, they may be offered a glimpse, for a moment, of the subject-positions they occupy, and on their surfaces, in another moment, may catch a glimpse of those images as to how racism, classism, authoritarianism, and sexism are constructed, and yet in another moment, how some of these surfaces get "scrapped off," forming overlaps or imbrications or mixed complexes on which suturing and quilting points are formed along the edges, ridges, and surfaces to sense, identify, and resist such movements of power and their intersecting chains of signifiers.

While these edges or imbrications may not be seen but are felt as mixed or contradictory feelings brought onto consciousness immediately, into thought or cognitive processes, they are, nevertheless real – as Zizek (1989) always reminds us of how the residues of the real, the traces of the real kernel of existence, constantly intervenes in the everyday world. These immediate experiences may not offer actors and speakers a clear grasp of what is thoughtful about the activities they are performing, or co-habiting, but they are, nevertheless, cognitive acts (mixed in with emotions and affects) which reveal how identifying with one another, the groups we enjoin (recall Pecheux's various discourses in which subject-positions and identities are formed), may serve both hegemony or provide the spaces for alternatives to counter such discourses. With the interjection of post-structurualist constructs, however, potential counter-hegemonic resistances, which may be experienced with a modernist framework, yet collapse or get co-opted (Willis, 1980), may become resuscitated and re-examined.

What this study then seeks to do is to make even more complex how dialogue, as one of several subject-positions and discourses in several discursive formations, are constituted in crossed and hybrid ways, intermediating student and teacher discourses. This form of dialogue, set in interlocking, overlapping and complex discursive formations, may also offer student and teacher a grasp and give a glimpse of how several discursive formations lie in between their acts of reflection, cognition, action, and potential moments in which they are connected or disconnected in dialogical but contained in hegemonic forces. If we can see this, we will thereby exceed the Willis study (1980) or my own (1998) regarding special education students and students and teaching staff in general. In this way, student and teacher (and teacher educator) may posit as problematic their societal, school, and classroom surroundings in more complex and intricate ways to account for why they do things to each other that may not be to their individual and joint interests and benefits. Or, how Freire noted all too briefly, to see the oppressed oppress each other by becoming each other's oppressor. What is needed then is to extend Freire's *Pedagogy*, or map out how unconscious talk and inter-subjective modes of dialogue and discourse are surrounded and penetrated by dominant power relations in, through, and out of schools, linked to their dialogue as fragments, or "floating signifiers" or metonymic experiences felt in discursive chains and formations, including but not exhaustive of, those formed by administrative hierarchical authority, as well as race, class, gender, and other relations, which further complicate their relations by identifying them as potential critical and counter-hegemonic theorizers.

GOING FURTHER: COMPLEX COGNITIONS AS SPACES FOR CONSTRUCTING INCITEMENTS FOR AGENTIAL ACTIONS

The above analysis seeks to further cognitions for student and teacher problem-positing and dialogue, as they may desire to seek order and wholeness, they may miss themselves as crossed by more complex fields of discourse. In addition, in terms of extending Freire into forms beyond his notion of critical pedagogy – in which the subject is posited as the source of meanings – Freire may be extended into forms of counter-hegemonic teaching and theorizing. In this way, his *Pedagogy* may be used as a starting point in which students and teachers may begin to decipher, in more diffused terms, how their subjectivities are distributed along several overlapping, intertwining, and differential power axes, antagonistic and non-antagonistic, as well as contradictory relations and discursive formations. How one knows one can partake of knowledge-making as a conjoint enterprise, interpreting subject-matter assigned while experiencing images, thought in words,[165] and surrounding actions operating in and through acts of dialogue as they seek to problem-pose, meaning to find how to expand the notion of dialogue post-structurally, or how those in dialogue simultaneously take up concomitant subject-positions (double consciousness). For example, as one thinks reflectively, intruding into their thoughts or cognitions are micro cognitions or fragments of thought from other subject-positions and interconnecting discursive formations via signifying chains, providing for glimpses of metonymic signifiers flashing in and through them – perhaps, as second thoughts or other forms of hesitation – as one suddenly loses track or their train of thought, and then, just as suddenly, picks up the train or chain as one speaks or one hears another's words or gestures, and just as suddenly recalls what they intended to say to the other while talking.

Without being distracted, they, students, teachers, and teacher educators may construct complex or hybrid cognitions to be used to reflect on their reflections in dialogue as a basis on which they may *articulate* how their dialogical conditions are being limited, or not fully absorbed yet crossed in hegemony; and how, in their resistances, at this juncture of theorizing, they may begin to map out their lineages to each other over and against a variety of discursive formations, which may be hegemonic or counter-hegemonic. In these *dialogical-discursive arrangements*, there is, nevertheless, a precedence of one discourse and discursive formation over the other when a consensus cannot be reached between teacher and student. How the process of articulation operates within a complex of cognitions, subject-positions, and discursive formations, in which dialogue becomes a dimension of discourse means to locate and differentiate *points of antagonism* from *points of connection*, which we have accomplished in the previous sections pertaining to how Laclau and others have mapped their trajectories of counter-hegemonic theorizing using post-structural constructs.

ARTICULATION IN DIALOGUE: MAPPING WHAT LIES BETWEEN REFLECTION AND ACTION IN DISCOURSE

To explain what articulation is, would appear, at first notice, a simple thing to do, meaning: what we say, or attempt to say, to others in speech or in an act of writing. This is not what the term means in the context of critical post-structuralist theorizing, however. While modernist thinking assumes when one speaks, they can articulate themselves in accordance to the rules and categories offered to us in language, this is not always true. But, when re-examining articulation through a post-structural paradigm, we may use what is given in language, making necessary improvisations along the way.[166] As linguists inform us, there are more things to describe than language categories permits, including how we are hegemonized in language against our interests, powers, and relationships. Adjustments therefore have to be made. This may come about with further exploration into the notion of discourse as undergoing processes of articulation.

The uses of denotation and connotation, along with various tropes, like metaphor, metonymy, and synecdoche come into play in this adjustment process. There is much more which constitutes a discourse. James Paul Gee's (1990, p. 143) definition of a discourse as a way of using language "to think, feel, believe, value, and act as a meaningful and identifiable group or member of a social network, or to signal one is playing a role" (p. 143) are aspects of language we may sense but don't spend a lot of time theorizing about. As Gee illustrates, when we walk into a bar or tavern, we use a certain discourse in which to articulate our intended (or unintended meanings), saying: "Hey, bud, could you give me a light," as opposed to what may seem inappropriate: "Pardon me: I would be indebted if you would offer me a light to ignite my cigarette." While Gee does not offer a context of hegemony in which language acts as a discursive practice becomes an articulating process, he does point to ways, by offering speakers an "identity kit" or assemblage of tools which may be used in a variety of speaking and ideological situations.

While we may spend less time theorizing about what articulation is as a process, and even less time thinking about what links us to many features of discourse, including dialogue, we may examine the work of Laclau and Mouffe (1985), who have pointed out that there are ways in which we may combine both concepts, articulation and discourse (Laclau & Mouffe, pp. 105–114). As Laclau and Mouffe point out, discourse is a medium for language in its various formations and fields to arise from and view. The main point they make is: Language is not a function of an individual's awareness; rather, language is a part of the structures and processes in which the speaking or acting subject is already split and desires to become whole again. Thus, to Laclau and Mouffe, heavily influenced by Lacan, there is always something lacking at the moment we come into the world via words and language and, as a consequence, in which we live in spaces and subject-positions as de-centered, multiple, desirous, and striven with fragments – *objets petit a* – from other subject-positions, discourses, and discursive formations passing by and through us. In these spaces between subjects and objects and others, their reflections and actions are likewise divided along binary chains of signifiers and meanings. Speakers and actors may constitute themselves and each other on planes of circulating and chained signifiers, which, in turn, carve out new surfaces for inscription and smaller subject-positions (anchoring points which hold or suture meanings from sliding away or dissolving). When they become aware of these movements, speakers and subjects may reveal or draw a map as to how their and others' cognitions and reflections become complex as intertwined with other cognitions accounting for why subjects or speakers get caught in contradictory subject-relations and subject-positions.[167]

While modernists theorize the subject as central and unified, a founding origin of thought underlying and transcendental of constitutive arrangements of intentional meaning-making in dialogue between two or more subject speakers, positing as problematic a world accessible to their critical consciousness, counter-hegemonic theorizing and consciousness is a very different set of propositions. Informed by post-structruralist constructs, which posit the subject as circulating through a matrix or grid of power relations (i.e. class, race, gender, authority, etc.) derived and feeding into various discursive formations of a discursive field, linked together by the constant sliding of chains of signifiers, subject-positions, and their intersections, school and classroom realities are perceived as a relatively simple matter of binarisms: either you lecture or engage in dialogue, either you a "well-behaved" student or a "discipline problem," either you are an oppressor or you are oppressed. The drawings of my students tended to be encouraged – I believe – by their life experiences and reading Freire's *Pedagogy* – and his binary thought processes. That is, the students upon reading Freire for the first time, appeared to automatically identify all teachers with the role of the oppressor while all students were identified in the role of the oppressed. Without employing various theoretical paradigms, or reading further into the remaining chapters of Freire's *Pedagogy*, both student and teacher (and, some instances their system which exploits both), one can see such inclinations or traces already inscribed through the drawings of my education students in Chapter 3.

This is not to say, as modernists say, if a tree falls and there is no one around, does the sound produce a sound? The response to the question is "yes, it does make a noise." Why, because, such a question presupposes a very narrow definition of the word "sound." But how does noise manifest itself without humans around? In the terminology of a physicist, the thud of the tree would not make a noise with a sound detected on a human ear hearing decibels. Rather, the "noise" may be seen by other instruments in which, using the discourse of quantum physics, leaves a vibration of "sound waves," possibly picked up by animals, but not necessarily humans. At the same time, this is also not to say that the subject is dead, as post-structuralists since Foucault are inclined to say. Rather, that the notion of the subject must be transformed and re-conceptualized to accommodate the complex and often contradictory forces which are at work when we become positioned from simple cognitions and reflections (and dialogues positing simple problems) as opposed to dialogues caught in multiple, complex, and contradictory subject-positions, brought on by our new technological, overly administrated and media-digital surveillance systems of our society and world. If we are reading the words of this paper, we are already a part of the electronic and digital discourse or discursive formation systems which inscribe us onto subject-positions which are multiple and overlaying (signals appear in red and green alerting us to "correct" forms of grammar, punctuation, and spelling or the distraction of hyper and hotlinks) compared to the traditional and un-mediated forms of writing, as on the old typewriter without such digital chains of signifiers and their associated meanings.[168]

This brings us to a focus on the concept of articulation in discourse from a post-stucturalist perspective. Let's begin with the notion of consciousness. To post-structuralists the notion of consciousness as a "founding" consciousness, as a unitary and self-identical or individualistic source of thought, action, and cognition, is not what they have in mind when they speak of consciousness, critical, counter-hegemonic, or otherwise. What post-structualists have in mind (pardon the pun), specifically, is what Laclau and Mouffe and others have been arguing for over two decades, is that articulation is a process of speaking, signaling, and yes, mapping (Grossberg, 1992) which, as part and parcel of the unconsciousness in language (Lacan), is, like the motion of the signifier which does not reflect or derive meaning from an entity (modernist forms of consciousness) nor is a fixed or stable entity over and against the object world. Rather, articulation is a process – as with the constant sliding of the primacy of the signifier over the signified or meanings it communicates – is a product of this sliding (*glissment*) process, as linked to other contexts of sedimented signifiers, as well as those meanings which are currently being transformed – combined, substituted connected, and displaced – by the criss-crossing and intersecting of other chains of signifiers derivative from other discursive formations making up a discursive ensemble or field of power. That is to say, the subject, as a self-identical or transparent medium, experienced as consciousness in and through cognition and reflection (which is a major detriment to critical consciousness in dialogue as posing problems to Freire), is experienced as one (not the only) moment of fixation in the flux and fluidity of signification in discourse. As post-structuralists argue, the subject is more than a fixed entity. It is a de-centered array of ensemble of chains of signifiers, subject-positions, and discourses. These subject-positions are constructed in language as a discourse or, in more complex terms, constituted in a complex of discursive formations with their own surfaces lining subject-positions for identification and interpolation purposes.[169] In these discursive structures of the imaginary, symbolic, and the real (Heath, 1978; Lacan, 1977; Willeman, 1979), dimensions within which chains of signifiers in their metonymic and metaphoric forms circulate and penetrate in subjects and at which moments they may *articulate or map out* their power relations of discourse on surfaces of subject-positions, inciting both divisive as well as opportunities for egalitarian and more democratic relations (see Laclau & Mouffe, 1985, along with Laclau 1990, 1993, 2007, and Thomassen 2005). These post-structural writers offer and reveal the "textured and thick" (Geertz, 1973) overlapping layers of partially empty and partially full *vis a vis* differential and equivalent signifiers or demands they share in constituting meaning in discourses. In these ensembles, subjects carve out[170] or create spaces to name and assess the movement their subject-positions may take, and the "tendential" degree of how they may take on "dispositions"[171] in getting themselves and each other to act or get incited to identify with each other's interests as a new colleague or comrade in reflecting on their actions, including so-called reflections framed by modernist presuppositions, as Freire does. To recent critical theorists as Kincheloe, this form of combination may mean a moment in time when subjects or individuals take on subject-positions of agency. By agency,[172] Kincheloe asserts a person's ability to shape and control their own lives, freeing the self from oppression of power (2004b, p. 2). This also means that there may exist (in agential moments) moments in which people take the necessary risks to take control of their lives over and against those forces they may consider as socially oppressing and even dangerous in which they *must* take such risks or feel, intuitively, they *must for whatever reason at the time,* do so.

These spaces of agency or risk-taking (i.e. between one' structured position on the surfaces of subject-positions) do not preclude consciousness but complement or entangle thought through articulation as affective activities in discourse. As intentionality and affect come together or get relayed and displaced via chains and circulating signifiers to each other in affective assemblage, networks, or groups (Grossberg, 1993), a post-structural understanding of articulation in discourse may emerge for student and teacher to re-think and re-sense their oppressive and hegemonic societal, academic, and classroom surroundings. These activities are also constitutive of counter-hegemonic agential moments. The nexus mediating thought and action, structure and self, becomes important in assessing the degree in which *macro* power relations (i.e. race, class, gender, authority, and more) penetrate and are mediated by spaces in *micro* power relations (the feelings and subjectivities of students and teachers), and therefore, how discourse enters into subjects or individuals as communitarian spaces and relations. In these spaces, referred to as *meso* spaces for re-thinking and re-feeling prior to or anticipated acts of reflection and action, cognitions and dialogues, dispositions become powerful motivators to incite (or stop) solidarity as well as serve students, teachers, and teacher educators as a basis for forming new communitarian spaces for committed joint actions.

Hence, a bridging of the *macro* and the *micro* involves an additional or supplemental understanding of how thinking and acting, reflection and action, interact and intersect each other in terms of breaking apart one's consciousness as a unified or essentialized entity – which may be hegemonized – and also examining such entities for their potentiality to posit as problematic how hegemony penetrates subjectivity or isolated pockets of "feel good" dialogues as constituted as parts of a discursive ensemble in which circulating signifiers and chains (along with those subject-positions and discursive formations they engender) may be re-examined and re-assessed to the extent that they are either hegemonic or potentially counter-hegemonic structures, spaces, and processes.

In these "third spaces" (Bhabha in Rutherford, 1989), may lie between those *macro* and *micro* dimensions of discourse, *meso* planes in which struggles are waged and fought out as constantly shifting alignments of identity formations and changing alliances. In between macro and micro places, but on the plane of the meso, incitements produced for the formation of new subject-positions may act to provoke and overtake fear of one's acting by infusing one to struggle further. In these meso planes, there may lie additional spaces for examining the signifying and discursive mechanisms on which subjects and speakers may inscribe in their everyday interactions on the surfaces or their subject-positions, main elements constitutive of several frameworks by which to re-interpret or re-read Freire. This may be also why the students who cooperated to do artwork over the past eight years, upon reading Freire for the first time, were able, with ease, to depict the "banking concept of education" (see Figures 1-4). But, when it came to depicting Freire's notion of reflection and action as linked to dialogue and problem-posing, why the student depictions became more diffused, problematic, and blurry. See, for example, those images (Figures 4-6) depicted by the students which describe problem-solving and critical acts of reflection and dialogue as, the sun rising, dancing around a fire, and traveling to heaven – all entities which are very unified, essentialized, and homogeneous and do not allow or make it difficult to re-enter their surfaces with diverse interpretations.

According to post-structural theorists, then, lying in and circulating through students and teachers are chains of signifiers, meanings, and subject-positions in which they may "carve out" further spaces for re-inscribed subject-positions. (Coward & Ellis, 1977, pp. 3,8; Laclau, 1990) As I have observed, when the opportunity to re-inscribe is evoked, once again, in meeting with other students in groups, often a diverse pattern of responses emerges via artwork and follow up discussions. Once they realize what they are inscribing is merely their own dispositions and assumptions onto a plane of art, they begin to realize how facile but intense such activities can be as they offer more interpretations and re-interpretations to each other in groups as they underwrite new forms of resistance. Once people begin to negotiate their differences and conflicts, forming amongst themselves, self-regulating discursive bodies, they also become decision-makers and articulators of potential counter-hegemonic theorizers.[173]

And, in the case of my education students, those who have reported to me over the years, favorable and unfavorable experiences when occupying multiple surfaces of inscription, they still manage to exercise their articulatory rights, albeit in ways that may hedge and express their real, or "true" feelings of work as defined by their community and school's administrative hierarchy. As we will see, the negotiation process between student and teacher (and teacher educator as well) may evoke or suppress post-structrualist constructs in making it possible or impossible for students and teachers (and teacher educators) to become counter-hegemonic theorizers and teachers.

CONCLUSION: WHERE DO WE GO FROM HERE?

Thus, the role and process of articulation in language as a discourse, if Freire's notion of reflection and action in dialogue may be extended, means student and teacher should be made to feel less intimidated by the school's administrative hierarchy or other community "standards." This also means an arena for revealing how complex forms of cognition and unconscious desires as well as those aspects of inter-subjective relations between students and teachers as they become aligned into flexible, jointed spaces of articulation allowing for the interaction of mixed, residual, and subliminal feelings requisite for risk-taking and bold actions of agency should also be constructed so as to ignite solidarities affecting students, teachers, and teacher educators relations, and affecting the beginning movements for more democratic, diverse, and equal relations and rights in schools and their governance, curricular, and assessment practices.

While teacher-educators are being substituted for administrators in this study, there are no guarantees that such a re-alignment of school-university personnel will offer sympathy in which teachers and students may regulate their own lives in schools, in socially just, equal, and democratic ways. These "teacher educators" or professors of education, based in universities and colleges of education, however, offer some degree of geographical distance from the school's administrative hierarchies and authoritarian traditions. With a new role for teacher educators to enter into partnerships and liaison with schools, classrooms, and the university, more autonomous roles and spaces for guidance and facilitation than those spaces presently occupied by the structural positions and pulls of obedience to school administrators amongst student, parent, and teacher populations may be worth a try. In this way, teacher educators offer a less compulsory space by serving students and teachers as consultants and advisors rather than hierarchical administrative leaders in transforming leadership roles to more equal partnerships in school and classroom decision-making processes amongst students, teachers, parents and teacher educators. How this is accomplished in the real yet complex relationships cutting across power relations of schools and society is a topic to be further discussed and experimented with, as we see in a few charter schools recently (noted in Chapter 2).

In this regard, as one education student proudly diagrammed a series of images after reading and discussing my very short article written in 1978, illustrating how changes may come about in hierarchical and administrative school structures (see Diagram C below).

Diagram C

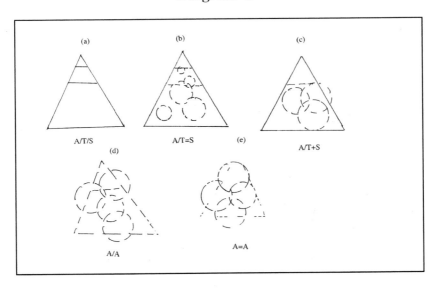

It does not take much to understand how student and teacher, when posited as opposites (A/T/S) administrators over teacher over students, teachers over students,(T/S) students over other students (S/S), may re-name their relations by using maps or diagrams to better see, incorporating some of the post-structural concepts, as chains of signifiers, subject-positions in hierarchical school arrangements of governance and their corresponding equivalent and differential chains operates and may be changed from within the system.

Thus, in figure (a) of Diagram C, this student illustrated the triplex of administrators over teachers while teachers are over students constituting the "chain of command" of school governance. Then, in Figure (b) there may also be forming informal student-teacher and student-student relations and communities within and sometimes against the formal structure of hierarchical school authority. The same student adds an additional figure (c) in which these informal communities and networks becomes closer and stronger (indicated by a more solid line rather than one that is dotted, albeit still the dominant line outlining the formal hierarchical structure of school administrative authority remains in force. Further drawing two more figures, the same student illustrates how, slowly, over time, the outside solid lines of administrative school authority becomes fractured as represented by dotted lines, when those dotted lines become more solid. The student conjectures in Figure (d) that a moment may be perceived in which students and teachers begin to see the contradiction: that while one group (teachers) has unequal power over another group (students), both groups have more in common as they are both represented as administrated workers in an overly top-down administrative system, which is represented by the equation of A/A. And, in the final figure (e), there emerges several overlapping and intersecting chains and links tying groups of students and teachers together as illustrated by the equation of A=A as the student insists power operates in and through student and teacher in counter-hegemonic, non-hierarchical, and democratic chains and their signifiers, even when they may empty or fill them in metonymical moments, combining their individualist identities with a sense of solidarity, joining together with other teachers and students to incite and name their political actions in solidarity. After viewing these images drawn and presented to the class as a whole, another student enjoined that "we" – all students and teachers – should take part in, over and against administrators in school hierarchies and their higher-ups.[174]

For example, this student further theorized, that while administrators and their higher ups may be named as "the system" and may be represented by equation of: A/T+S or how administrators rule over teachers and students, further broadening their identities and solidarities in chains of equivalence underlying them, the student felt that students ought to re-name these same people into another and re-conceptualized equation, as: A/A+T+S, since administrators above administrators may be in positions, as one goes further up the hierarchical chain, perhaps out of town or some distant place (i.e. Albany or Washington, D.C.) in which new configurations of students, teachers, and administrators may join as one force against those more distant administrators and politicians so they could build larger and more powerful coalitions of administrators, teachers, and students.

Still, as this teacher-student further acknowledged, once these chains of equivalence and differences are re-negotiated by students, teachers and administrators, it may be possible for them to perceive their roles as interchangeable parts on democratic-participatory levels: as one variant, establishing on a rotational basis for changing the administrator over the administrated equation A/A into a new equation of: A=A, when the administrator roles may become occupied, periodically, by students, parents, and teachers, who hitherto were the administrated, may, now, after realizing their commonalities, join together to remove or breach the dividing line between administrator and administrated and thereby make themselves leaders (on a rotational basis) for radicalizing and extending what Freire's original study intended.[175]

After examining the illustrations and questions of my education students in class sessions – to examining administrative and hierarchical structures of authority penetrating into classroom discourse, along with their illustrations of Freire, and how my special education students depicted the conditions of their high school which discriminated against them on the basis of being labeled "special" by the administrative authorities – we were incited to become more effective counter-hegemonic and democratic teachers, leaders, and researchers, as a result of constructing maps and articulating our desires and felt needs and commitments, that otherwise, we might not have had the courage to articulate.

In the next and final chapter the writer will draw conclusions from his experiences with special education students, education students, and fellow teachers. There will also be recommendations for future counter-hegemonic research and teaching practices. Specifically, on the use of drawing diagrams, images, and maps to articulate and ascertain where and when there may exist in spaces and surfaces on which student and teacher may incite each other to take chances and begin to take over their classrooms and schools in an effort to democratize them with their counter-hegemonic actions of agency. What makes this study so compelling is, as my students' pictures yelled out in pain: "I cannot escape images of oppression." (see Figure 32) Yet, in their pain and suffering, these same students wanted to explore and see how Freire could be further extended in addressing their fears and tensions which presently occupied their work as teachers in what they have called their "hegemonic struggle," and sometimes, as they attempted to uplift their hopeless conditions of oppression to transform them into conditions of connections and possibility.

On this note, we turn to the last chapter as to conclusions, recommendations, and implications for future research and teacher practices of *Counter-Hegemonic Teaching.*

CHAPTER 5

TOWARD REMAKING LANGUAGE OF CRITICAL PEDAGOGY FOR COUNTER HEGEMONIC TEACHING

A SPECIAL TRIBUTE TO JOE L. KINCHELOE

As I write this concluding chapter, I have just learned that Joe Kincheloe, a friend, colleague, and one of the most brilliant critical education theorists today has just passed away. Kincheloe was responsible for many of my articles and this book getting published. As with his critical theory colleagues, well known and long lasting experts in the field (Apple, Giroux, Greene, McLaren, Macedo, Steinberg, and others), Kincheloe led the field in moving all of us to explore new versions of Freire's work seeking new directions for helping and introducing school populations to the complex world of education and society. He was particularly concerned with the way race, class, gender and other power relations mix into a *bricologue* (2004c) interacting semiotically in the meaning-making process (2003) for teacher research and practice. He was particularly concerned with how macro and micro forces affect people's struggle for liberation, social justice, equality, diversity, and democracy. In this area, Joe spurred me on to write this book. His yearning to question everything influenced me and this book a great deal. Like Kincheloe, I was very interested in what happens between the macro and micro, and how people, their consciousness (and unconsciousness) interact and meet with one another on planes of language as a discourse; how they become affected in those large outer structures of authority and power, including race, class, gender, and my own contribution, in hierarchical structures of power differentials, along with the interaction of agency and structure. It's why I wrote this book.

Kincheloe called for others to join him to theorize and re-theorize, and better, to practice their crafts for transforming schools, teaching, and the world.

For this, I acknowledge him and am indebted to his courage, brilliance, perseverance, and the mountain of books and articles he produced in a relatively short period of time. Many of his publications were joint projects with well known and not so well known authors. It seemed everyone joined in with Joe, including his esteemed wife and fellow professor, Shirley Steinberg, and many others. Joe took unknown people like myself and put them on the map. Thank you, Joe. I will miss you a great deal.

ENTERING THE COMPLEX WORLD OF HEGEMONY: TWO FILMS

Because I was so impressed with Kincheloe's emphasis on the complex world of meaning-making, including his emphasis on the semiotic, I searched him out upon becoming a new professor at Brooklyn College on the recommendation of my old friend Maxine Greene. Once met, Joe responded with optimism and a love which allowed me to share his brilliant insights and enter his heart. He and his wife, Shirley, met with Paulo Freire many times, and through them, I felt also I was in the presence of Freire.

I recall, distinctly, how he and Shirley accepted to become keynote speakers at a conference I organized for several colleges in the aftermath of the United States invasion and occupation of Iraq, post- 9/11. Kincheloe, like so many radical professors to the left, opposed the Bush repressions of civil rights and liberties, the war in Iraq, and, specifically, the repression of forced standardized testing and prepping of students under the mandated provisions of *No Child Left Behind* (2002). Kincheloe was particularly opposed to standardization and the linear type of thinking which comes with "obeying orders" in school and societal hierarchies. Having taught us of the impact of "linear" and "modernist" paradigms of cognition since the Enlightenment (Kincheloe, 2004a, 2004b), Kincheloe was very critical of philosophers, like Rene Descartes and his "Cartesian" thinking which permeated much of the field of education. Kincheloe (2001) also discussed how "empiricism" and the "positivist" foundations for research and teaching continue to suffer within this narrow context. On this note, Joe Kincheloe would have enjoyed watching two recent films – *The Reader* (2008) and *Doubt* (2008).

These two films bring out points Kincheloe made and would have continued to elaborate but for his untimely death. As an admirer of the Frankfurt School, and many of its émigrés from Nazi Germany prior to the Second World War, Kincheloe knew the impact of hierarchicalization and standardization of society and schools and how they ate away at the human moral fabric. In the movie of *The Reader*, for instance, a scene shows how a former SS woman at the Seimen factory, Hannah Schmidt, is escorting women slave laborers back and forth from and to the death camps. One day, en route to escorting over three hundred women inmates to the factory, a fire broke out in the church they were staying in. All the workers or inmates were burnt alive. Despite hearing their shrieks for help and mercy as they pounded on the locked door to be released from the flames, the guards stood still, refusing to unlock the doors of the church. As she watched the church and the fire consume the inmates, others, fellow women guards, also watched and refused to intervene.

An additional function Schmidt was called upon to perform, as she testified in a court of law charging her and her fellow guards with crimes against humanity years later in West-Germany, included choosing "older women" or less productive or sick women prisoners to return to the death camps in order to make room for the younger ones. She knew when choosing that she was signing their death warrants. But, as she insisted to the court, what "else was I to do? It was my job. What would you do?" She needed to make room for the "younger ones" to produce more goods for the nation, the Reich, and she claimed, to perform her role as a loyal citizen. In addition, while testifying, the judge asked her: "But why did you do these things?" Her response was very telling as to how most Germans who worked for the Nazis and the SS linked their jobs and "following orders" with a hierarchical form of morality. That is to say, by their obedience, regardless of the awful consequences of allowing three hundred women unnecessarily burn, she felt moral and duty bound in her actions.

Following orders, according to Schmidt, can only be interpreted as "her responsibility."[176] She could not allow the prisoners to "escape" from the church. If she did, she would be contributing to acts that would have produced "chaos" and "disorder." If she opened the church doors and allowed the prisoners to escape, this act would be tantamount to disrespecting her role as being a responsible worker for the Nazis. She further claimed that when people worked for the SS, their job was to keep order, be fastidious in record-keeping, and efficient in administrating who gets returned to the death camps so new, stronger, younger incoming prisoners could serve the war effort. The question of the prisoner's life or death was not relevant in Schmidt's mind. Orderliness is what counted. Thus, to Schmidt, there was never a question in her mind whether or not she and her fellow guards should open the church doors and save the lives of the inmates. Once again, as she put it, "If I let them go free, chaos and disorder would have resulted." Once again, she repeated, "they (the prisoners) were my responsibility, and if I would have opened the doors, disorder and chaos would have resulted."

Schmidt, educated by a solemn respect for order and obeying top-down orders from her superiors, failed to see any problem with her ethics or lack thereof. She and her fellow guards allowed over three hundred prisoners to be burnt alive. To Schmidt, keeping the prisoners confined in the church was "her duty and responsibility," plain and simple. This kind of linear and hierarchical thinking, simplifying what it means to "secure" prisoners without any other compassion for their fate and welfare, did not need admit any other competing inscriptions which crossed her mind – those cries and shrieks of women yelling for mercy, pleading for their lives, asking, no, pleading to have the door opened, did not enter or affect her unified and untrammeled state of consciousness. She might have heard these cries with a counter thought, perhaps crossing into her mind, but she and her fellow guards stood still in a kind of solidarity of insulation. She could have opened the lock which separated the lives and death of the inmates she was given the responsibility to guard, but she and her fellow guards had chosen not to.

Because Schmidt was so ingrained with lessons of hierarchical authority – always respect those above and their orders from above – or as Foucault called such states of subjectivity as ones of hierarchicalized comformity; or, what is in today's schools a regimen of hierarchical systems of tests, classroom management techniques, and other mechanisms which "watch" the whereabouts of the students under the administrative gaze of school principals and teachers. In the same way, the principal's gaze in *Doubt* exposes how hierarchical and administrative authority penetrates human relations. A newcomer, a priest, is gazed upon by the principal as an expression of the new "progressive pedagogy" she assumes he represents. The principal is so traditional that she looks with disdain at the use of the newly invented ball point pens. The priest, who wants to teach and care for his students, believes in hugging and, when appropriate, touching students when they need such support.

Set within the early 1960s, in a parochial school, run by an austere principal, expresses "doubts" of the new priest's actions of using progressive methods of teaching in relating to students. These actions provokes the principal to wage a campaign seeking to terminate the priest. She suspects the priest of harming the morals of a child, and wages a campaign to dismiss him. While there is no clear evidence against the priest, other than her suspicions, the principal inscribes onto his reputation her definitions of "correct" or "appropriate" deportment for a teacher in a church school. She finally succeeds in deposing the priest.

Yet, as the priest offered in one of his sermons, "doubt may be more powerful and sustainable than any certainty." This point cuts both ways: Either doubt is more powerful than real evidence or, doubt is qualitative, and may be as powerful as fact or "certainty." In the same way, there may be those in schools – teachers, students, parents and administrators – who may doubt the validity of administrative systems supportive of constant testing as prescribed in federal law. On the other hand, the language of the law is clear: only "neutral" and "non-ideological" data can be collected via linear-like and multiple choice test questions which will serve, as the law insists, as "evidence" to assess the performance of students, and the quality of the teacher's performance.

In assessing student achievement performance to close their achievement gap between poor and wealthy, white and black, as well as gaps between other kinds of students – special education, ESL, and others – it has been extensively reported that such assessment tools may be more detrimental than of help (Good and Brophy, 2008). When this happens, a more "skewed" or "invalid" academic average or instrument is used to assess how well a school or a teacher is doing emerges and gets lost in the numbers or statistics and other empirical data reported to the press. By "helping" students, these "bubble tests," as the newly elected Obama administration has decried them, is brought to the publics' attention in sharp focus.

In both films, what emerges are undercurrent themes as to how modernist chains of equivalent thinking come to the fore in which order, authority, and respect for those above one's position is met with unquestioned obedience. There is no room for doubt and compassion in hierarchical and administrative regimens of control and testing in today's schools. As we have been hearing for many years, "tough love" is what counts, not compassion (see Kohn & Sizer, 1999; Kohn, 2004; Meier, 1998; Ohanian, 1999; Sizer, 1995). Only resolute conviction that one must carry out orders in maintaining discipline and standards amongst the inmates or students, irrespective of whether the church is on fire, or whether the priest is doing what is right, explains the hierarchal order that is top down hegemony. As Adorno and his associates (1969) offered in their famous treatise, *The Authoritarian Personality*, sponsored by the federal government during the Second World War, as respecting order, obedience, efficiency and carrying orders without question, when examining schools today, we see a similar condition for living in a modern society, whether it be a traditional school or a Nazi factory and death camp. But, as Foucault (1972) has also reminded us, such self-identifications of Schmidt and the principal illustrate how we're all vulnerable to the identifications and definitions that may be lodged as the "fascism in all of us" (Deleuze & Guatarri, 1972, p. xiii).

When an oppressed person, who may receive "a little bit of power," becomes meaner than their superiors (see student illustration in Figure 23, Chapter 3), something very ugly occurs. Therefore, one does not have to be a Nazi to be branded or marked with fascist proclivities. Those in our present day schools who believe in the solemnity of numbers of test score results as a certain and objective instrument of measurement to assess the progress of a child's learning or a sufficient means to measure teacher competencies and qualifications don't allow for circumstance (Taubman, 2009, in press). It's a 'you're for us or against us' innocuous sounding policy. But not a policy concerning terrorists or enemies, instead, one regarding the policies that dictate the education of our children. The black and white policies of the Bush administration, armed with years of head in the sand apathy have corroded our education system.

COMPLEXITY, HEGEMONY, AND GETTING A GLIMPSE OF THE COUNTER-HEGEMONIC

When examining these moments of identity through a more precise or post-structural map or mode of articulation, one may also discern, if only by a fleeting glimpse or metonymy, "floating signifiers" or fragments of signifiers and tendential surfaces of subject-positions, (Laclau, 2007; Smith, 1996; Thomassen, 2005), as we have already discussed at length in Chapter 4. When signifiers and their chains suture other signifiers and their chains, constructing as a stand-in position, in which loose ends or threads of other signifiers and their demands are brought into a larger chain of equivalence, then one can begin to recognize that consciousness or subjectivity and meaning construction is indeed a very complex business. Further, appropriating elements or constructs of post-post-structuralism like Zizek (1989), for example, we may further see how the floating signifiers may offer glimpses of metonymies which transform subjects into objects which irrupt through the symbolic, as the kernel of the Real, revealing the whole as perforated by residues of the Real.

While we have reviewed Freire's *Pedagogy of the Oppressed*, through both my education students artwork, and also using post-structural constructs to examine more specifically how hegemonic wars between equivalent chains and their empty/filled and floating signifiers emerge and get played out, how Friere's critical pedagogy and its depth of expression may be expanded to include both modernist and post-modernist inscriptions remains as work yet to be done. According to Freire, "ambiguous" behavior, or how one lives out their lives in an "existential duality" reveals that he shows little faith for a subject already marked by oppression, and their ability to cross-over from one side of the divide of oppression to the other.

That is to say, once branded as oppressor, it is more likely that a person or group of people, besides being a member of the oppressed class, will not likely resist while in a state of oppression, and while in the act of carrying out orders of their superiors, one may not "think twice" or opt to resist reproducing the oppressive structure from which they were branded or marked and labeled. Yet, as I have reported throughout this book, nothing seems to be happening. Yet, as I have also argued throughout the book, this may not be the case. That is, while one is in an oppressed state, there are always contingent moments to choose otherwise.

Still, overall, the state of inertia dominates schools and society. It, therefore, behooves us to ask: how we may further create or examine new approaches for possible resistant and counter-hegemonic actions. The same problem applies to those education students who are already teaching and are presently aspiring to become "leaders" or principals and deans. These students have reported to me that there are moments when they are able to see or sense contrary or "in-between" moments of "second thoughts" in which they manage to see their roles on competing equivalent chains of signifiers but also much, much more. For example, "either" they think "or" identify themselves as being "good" or "bad" future administrators (See Chapter 2). Or, as one education student put it, "one has to watch what they say in schools – the walls have ears."

Another education student, who is in her second year of teaching, confided to me and her classmates that she feels relief and pleasure when her students are "sweating it out" or working very hard to prepare for standardized exams and are "watched" by school administrators who are "sweeping the floors," poking their heads in her classrooms as students get "even more stiffened by their sudden presence." And yet another student felt joy and pleasure upon hearing about the termination of another teacher. This about-to-be-terminated teacher had excellent rapport with her students. She allowed her students to bring with them their I-Pods and listen to music, and as I observed, worked to gain a better rapport and understanding with the subject-matter she was teaching at the time. As my student, who invited me into her school said to me: "My principal hates I-Pods and other gadgets which students come to school with – he thinks they distract students from preparing for the many exams we give every month."

DO STUDENTS AND TEACHERS SEE CHAINS OF SIGNIFIERS PENETRATING
THEIR DISCOURSE? A POST-STRUCTURAL CONSTRUCTION OF THE
"IN-BETWEEN" DISCOURSES AND OTHER MATTERS.

As we pointed out in the two previous chapters, 3 and 4, "marks" or inscriptions of fear and oppression on some members of the oppressed (student, teacher, teacher educator) may be unwittingly adhesed to or identified with the oppressor as not the only equivalent chain and those circulating as empty signifiers hegemonizing people in their actions and roles. Taking some insights from Jacques Lacan (1977) and Slovenj Zizek (1989), who assert that what happens to a subject while in subject-position, such a position acts as an intermediary space functioning to screen or filter how one identifies themselves and the world as mediated between one's structured position (Smith, 1996) – i.e. class, race, gender – and a complex network of intertwining and intersecting subject-positions. In these in-between spaces, inscriptions or marks are "articulated" on the surfaces of a person's subject-position. These inscriptions are not conclusive; they are in constant movement and flux. Often subjected to forays of invading signifiers from other chains and discursive formations, as well as re-entering the circulation of signifiers with other signifiers, sometimes capable re-forming new chains and discursive formations and communities, students and teachers may experience a complex or mixed thoughts and feelings while in oppressed states.

And, as Laclau (2007) insists, these intersecting and intertwining chains are not only moving, but further construct links for subjects to attach themselves to other signifiers, forming sutured or anchored points of identity. These anchoring points (*nodal points*), or more complicated "quilting points" (or, as Zizek maintains, *sinthomes*) are not conclusive but always in movement. Once a series of demands or equivalent chains and their signifiers become solidified and become "stand-ins" for the other demands and signifiers, they cohere, bringing disparate demands and signifiers together; or, on the other side of the hegemonic divide, another set of equivalent chains countering with their equivalent chains and signifiers competing with each other for hegemony and counter-hegemonic movements in the larger social formation.

When there is a confrontation between both formations, there may be an organic hegemonic crisis, or a moment in which representations of two camps (i.e. friend versus enemy) become contradictory and conflicting alternatives. In these moments, different but like equivalent chains of signifiers fight over what lies on the "tendential" surfaces of subject-positions, some prevail and loosen other fragments which get scraped off and become partial surfaces of the subject-positions affected in the articulation process as they circulate in the discursive field as "floating signifiers." These floating signifiers may have the capacity to provide or position one to experience or feel sudden glimpses[177] or spaces in which one gets to see or sense as "second thoughts" or "doubts" or "sudden pleasures" (*joiussance*) when they become located at points of intersection (class interacting with race, race interacting with gender, gender interacting with class, etc). Thus, when a particular demand or cluster of signifiers become a stand-in or representative of all other competing demands and signifiers, there may be a moment when other demands become interposed amongst themselves, between subjects, and when this happens, new chains of equivalent signifiers circulating within their symbolic and discursive spheres or universes may begin to emerge.

This means that on such subject-position surfaces, there are many and various inscriptions as well as de-articulations and re-articulations including those inscriptions which may have scraped off one surface of one subject position onto another. How some signifiers which are empty and become filled signifiers, and can no longer attract other competing signifiers is a question post-structural theory has yet to answer. When a signifier begins to move onto new surfaces and create new chains in which new subject-positions are created, how the frontier of the "either-or" divides between "us" and "them" become "blurred" is, likewise, yet to be further theorized, thereby positing how new and equivalent chains and their empty signifiers in relation to the original equivalent chain and empty signifiers get formed.[178]

These marks or inscriptions constructing one's identity as "tendential" are subject to other contingent forces constantly circulating as difference in the discursive field (Laclua, 1990, 1993, 2007). Stopping or getting knotted into sutured points (nodal and quilting points) in which partial equivalent chains may become constructed, crossed through, and otherwise linked to the subject(s) onto spaces provided within links or interstices in discursive formations, providing openings of space for serving connections on which dialogue and new discourses may serve each other against traditional forms of dialogue and discourses.[179]

As I reported in my study with special education students (see Chapter 4), upon their diagramming the "chains" which pitted them against "regular students" and each other as "slow," a key signifier, the word "slow" became a code word or empty signifier which absorbs, attracts, and sometimes, leaves traces or loose ends of various other discursive formations previously occupied and grasped simultaneously. When Randy labeled Gregory as "slow," both students saw the oppressor in themselves (similar to Freire's insight, p. 44–45) "teasing" each other represented other struggles which had been waged against them constantly under the surveillance of the oppressors or, as they called them, the regular students, teachers, and administrators in their school.[180] Yet, the special education students I worked with often giggled and "played" with each other. In this process of playing, they also realized that they were making a caricature of those school conditions in which they had to live with in all of its contradictory and often hurtful experiences of being labeled "special." These students often lived simultaneously in an additional world, the world of the streets of Harlem, an all black community, as well as those other schools and communities they were members of as they were constantly transferred from more "racially mixed" schools to more segregated schools.

GLIMPSES OF FLYING RUMORS

As Randy and his special education peers got inscribed by images of the oppressor, crossing into a complex of intersecting chains of signifiers of equivalence and difference, along with their counterparts of empty and floating signifiers, they received many contradictory messages. Some may have originated from various discursive formations (i.e. streets, different communities, and sub-groups and cultural groups in and out of school), others crossed into their own discursive formations from regular students, teachers, and deans. Wherever they came from, they referred to them as "flying rumors" carrying with them subject-positions or partial surfaces on which they coalesced their thinking and perceptions onto other surfaces and messages which "seeped in" or "syncretized"[181] into their schools and classroom interactions. They were also inscribed by marks or images of the oppressor, both conforming to and resisting these images. They even became, periodically, incited to take on such inscriptions or messages in which they sought to re-form these images by images they were forming themselves as a counter-hegemonic group or discursive formation in which they desired to coalesce with other oppressed school members. They often cited how they would sit in the cafeteria with the regular Albanian and Asian kids, whereas they tried to avoid a kind of cultural war which was always going between "regular" Hispanic and "regular" African-American students.

The main point to the special education students was: While experiencing being put in subject-positions which they saw in the regular students and regular teachers, the image of the oppressor, along either-or differential chains of regular and special students, teachers, and deans, they also experienced, crossing and interlinking with and through chains of signifiers and identification as second thoughts and mixed feelings about how they felt towards themselves and the regular school population. They experienced a trapped feeling, as if held by chains as forged along parallel and intersecting chains of signifiers, in regards to one another and the regular school population. They felt resentful, for example, when Sidney, a former special education student who returned to the regular school track, found himself resistant to talk to them, because "Sidney no longer talks to us; he is not special anymore."

Living in these chains was further illustrated by Randy when he was denied entrance to the cafeteria. Normally, Randy gets a free pass to enter because none of his teachers want him to attend their classes. And one day, because the regular teacher in charge of cafeteria admission was absent, and as a result, a substitute teacher positioned outside the cafeteria did not know the "unofficial rules" that applied to Randy, confrontations broke out between Randy and the substitute teacher. It was during this confrontation, Randy recounted, which exposed how Randy thought of his place or identity in the world of being special along many layers and chains of signifiers. As he put it in rapid succession: "Those others, the man, the white man, the enemy," represented to Randy overlapping and intersecting circulating chains and signifiers and subject-positions. As Randy uttered these words, he raised his voice and eventually screamed in a rage. I began to see red tears forming in his eyes. Upon a follow up discussion of Randy's short story, he and the other special education students revealed that each of these "others" recounted by Randy represented to them a different experience or discursive formation and chain of events linking them to their and his pasts. That is, Randy kept saying that in the past, he had to deal with others who fooled and manipulated him and got him to remain in special education. Namely, the white man represented to Randy racism, his thoughts fleeting through his rapidly articulated speech pattern revealed other people – Others – who enslaved him and black people. He further recounted more others, as "The Man" who represented to Randy the "superior" or regular teachers who teased and persecuted him. And, yet still another other, "the enemy" represented to Randy the "system" of schools and society which denied him entrance into the mainstream, both in schools and in life, "them" as he referred to these others who denied him equal opportunities.

Theorizing about how he and his special education peers were being "chained" or incarcerated in the special education track, Randy drew several chains, each parallel to the other, and along their continuums, on one side spelled out "respect," on the opposite side, spelled out the word "disrespect." Paralleling these chains were other antinomies (see diagrams in Chapter 4 and below), like self-control (which was on the same side of respect), and "losing control," which was on the side of "disrespect." Together, with the facilitator (that was my role as co-theorizer), we theorized together in facilitating Randy's story-telling and problematizing his themes). Randy inscribed on a third chain, in which the notion of " I" and "We" were inscribed, along with another chain in which achievement and non-achievement went parallel with the previous three chains representing respect and non-respect.

When I asked Randy, who had chalk in hand drawing a series of chains on a chalkboard, what happens when all four chains moved in tandem, he responded by saying: "Then you have a self-respecting, achieving, individual (I). Then, I asked about the "we" side of the continuum, and Randy responded with "Well, this is a caring person that helps others." But, I further interjected, "you have the 'We' position aligned to losing control, disrespect, and loser." Randy, as a "second thought" crossed his mind, responded: "Well then you have a "Them" chain." To Randy, "them" represented those others who marginalized, teased, and persecuted him. He then added another chain, crossing over and perpendicular to the horizontal chains of signifiers, a vertical line or chain which intersected the horizontal chains which penetrated all other chains as a sliding continuum, moving across the horizontal chains. One vertical chain Randy titled "unselfish I" and yet another vertical chain "selfish we" indicated that while acting as a stand-in or sutured moment of a norm holding horizontal chains at a point, this chain may hold other chains which they crossed subservient to the over-arching vertical chains. The vertical chain is never for long in a position of hegemony, however. There are other vertical chains or overarching chains formed and forming in the process of establishing as normative that selfishness counts more than unselfishness as value in the constant give and take, back and forth struggles for hegemony of a group or a discursive field, or the various discursive formations Randy and the special education students were members of, interacting and competing with one another.

Both of these over-arching chain-producing norms served as suturing points acting as a group norm, sliding along and through the preceding chains, aligning and realigning them, according how the norm for care or carelessness switched, irrespective of horizontal chains of achievement/non-achievement, respect/disrespect, I/we, etc. may be summarized as follows below:

I then asked Randy how these new vertical chains, which crossed over the horizontal chains, may be reconciled? He declared: "Well, it's like this, one can be respectful and achieve and be a winner." He further asserted (a second thought shooting through him) "what really counts is being unselfish and caring for others, no matter how important respect is for yourself as an individual, or how respectful your actions. Because it is not so much achievement that counts, it is care for others, or whether or not you are a special or regular education student."

From this point on, the special education students re-labeled themselves as "analyzers" with "full respect" as being equal to regular students and willing to contribute to the regular school population. Because, as a marginalized group, they could see the world in a different way, in ways regular students, teachers, and deans, could not see. They concluded that their oppositional viewpoint about the regular school population would have a positive value to them in offering something new – a viewpoint from special students as opposed to the other way around. These students, armed with post-structural constructs, trust, and care, further became during our year long focus group sessions counter-hegemonic theorizers and broke away from the modernist and equivalent chains of meanings which positioned them along a hierarchical chains of subject-positions (horizontal lines) in which the regular students were always positioned over the special education students.

Summary of Diagram of Randy's Articulated Chains

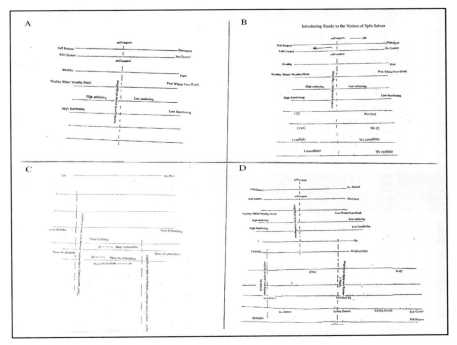

Once some of the special education students acted on behalf of the oppressor teasing one another as 'slow" or "one downing" each other, when the *oppressed become oppressors* – something inside or between them produced a doubt: they began to ask why this is so, why do they oppress each other like regular school students and teachers oppress them?[182] That is to say, Freire's categorizations of oppression, while subjects become stuck in moments of "existential dualities, may experience a set of differences in which they may sense or choose as a base on which to alter or shift their identities and relationships. Depending on contingent and unforeseeable counter and complex inscriptions on the surface of the subject-positions they occupy or hope to occupy, where they battle their ascribed or inscribed identities for hegemony (and counter-hegemony) across and into the discursive field of various discursive formations, they become more aware at intermittent, often flashing moments, who they were and what they were about to become: resistant and counter-hegemonic theorizers and teachers for one another as a group struggling to have their identities emerge. While a more precise reading would be difficult to come by – identifying exactly what moment a hierarchical-sustaining chain of subject-positions over-take or are over-taken by unselfish and collective caring chains of subject-positions with their own respective surfaces and spaces for inscription in interpolating and interpellating processes (see Chapter 4), the special education students I worked with were able to account for why they became their own oppressors as well as liberators fighting in solidarity alongside one another.

If we could penetrate the various levels of interpellation and interpolation of discursive formations containing on one level, surfaces of subject-positions, and another level chains of signifiers, and yet on a another level, links within and across them as they interact and intersect one another forging links to other discursive formations (i.e. race, class, etc.), then, perhaps we can account more systematically why the oppressed, once they are positioned, or suddenly feel they are crossed by different chains of signifiers than they suspect (i.e. race mixed in with class or sexuality chains of signifiers) may suddenly trigger them at what Freire calls "points of antagonism," but at the same time, use these points or intersections or mixed power relations as "points of connection" in which oppressed or subjugated people no longer attack each other but, rather, attack the system of oppression in which they are both embroiled. In this way, we may finally break open the problematic posed by Freire and others as to why, when, and how *the oppressed become each other's oppressor.*

Thus, in this complex and capillary world of power relations, through discourse and its formations, (including dialogue), "third space" spaces may be found and be explored (Bhabha, 1989) as a complex or hybrid conglomeration of inscriptions. In this way, we, may explore semiotic or signifying systems and how chains of signifiers cross into and intersect one another and their chains of signifiers as they re-inscribe onto and into each other, sliding along surfaces, and concomitantly, with and into other chains of signifiers suturing or loosening previously occupied subject-positions in which people experience shifts of orientations. Randy may have experienced these shifts and signifying actions in which he was crossed by and fell into various discursive formations. Randy also experienced equivalent and different interactions between race, class, gender, authority, and ability making up his diverse and often contradictory identities and worlds. Imagine, as one in the action gets triggered by another, who then triggers another, and together, suddenly realize, simultaneously, they can point to or begin to map out and speak to each other about what was just caused them to see each other as the enemy. Or, posing Freire's problematic more concisely: ask why do the oppressed become each other's oppressors?

In one of their last focus groups on theorizing about school conditions, whether they wanted to be included or remain separate in their tracks, the special education students and I came to the realization that they are not necessarily in a contradictory relationship with regular students and teachers. They were able to see how the seemingly contradictory nature of their labeled experiences were, in fact, not contradictory, irreconcilable forces but, rather, the shifting of discursive formations or man-made constructions which aligned, dis-aligned, and re-aligned them with others on administrative and anti-administrative, hierarchical or anti-hierarchical, or hegemonic or counter-hegemonic planes or chains of subject-positions, signifiers, and discursive formations. They also learned that they were from different discursive formations, linked together by crossing over and intersecting chains of signifiers and subject-positions, which they often shared with each other in their inscriptions or messages on the same surfaces. In this way the special education students theorized and articulated that they may have more in common than different with the regular school population and considered themselves, whilst from different discourse formations, parts of an intricately linked whole of their school via chains of signifiers and sudden explosive moments that, from time to time, became windows to see more through and relay stations on which they could meet and offer something of value to the regular population – their oppositional viewpoint – as well as those signifying chains acting as mirrors, they, the regular students and special education students were not positioned or permitted to see.

A MAJOR FINDING OF THE STUDY: FREIRE AS A PRECURSOR TO POST-STRUCTURAL THEORIZING? LOCATING AT WHAT MOMENTS THE OPPRESSED OPPRESS EACH OTHER AND THEMSELVES IN ARTICULATION AND DIALOGUE

As we saw several illustrations in the previous Chapter 4, as well as other students I undertook to instruct in my education classes (see Chapter 2), and to which I also facilitated student interpretations by their drawings of how they experienced (upon reading Freire for the first time in Chapter 3) oppression or de-humanization, I also wanted to know the feelings and senses the students experienced when caught in the middle of cross-sections of intersecting chains of signifiers and subject-positions. These experiences may also affect how they related to each other and their students as they engaged with each other in dialogue. To delve deeper into dialogue, I asked the students to talk about the experience and process of articulation or how, on surfaces of signifiers and their subject-positions, once they articulate a word or phrase, they may shift and re-align their perceptions of themselves and their power relations with each other and the school system, as well as the discourses which were inherent in these processes of perception and identification but linked from outside the school into their worlds.

Just as Randy was able to show how his identities and his special education peers were able to reverse their identities and attachments when they strove for achievement, I wanted to show how they may have made more complicated set of subject-positions of identity to satisfy their need to be caring and sensitive people. Randy, Zena, Lisa, and Gregory came to realize that their roles were complex and would not fit perfectly into the labels the school authorities assigned them. In the course of discussions, the special education students were able to map out the world of their identities and powers (or lack of) onto a "system" which went against stigma and labeling. The four students I worked with for over a year in a series of fifty focus group discussions, each several hours long,[183] became adept at mapping or drawing images of what they sensed were the ways power and feelings shot through them in moments of being subject-positioned by hierarchical and other kinds of circulating signifiers. I used the construct of "signifier" to show them how a theoretical construct can help further reveal their thinking and problem-positing and discussions.[184] More importantly, this experience with special education students also convinced me that students can grasp and make significant meanings of those "fleeting" and "adventitious" experiences most critical theorists and pedagogues, particularly from the modernist traditions, have marginalized.

This book is therefore about, I conclude, finding the middle ground between macro and micro forces instrumental in constructing hegemonic and counter-hegemonic theorizing and critiques against hierarchical forces which construct subject-positions as constituted from within and across hierarchical chains of signifiers on which people are placed in positions in institutions like schools or other organizations. To inscribe on their subject-position surfaces of their thoughts, images, feelings, codes, messages, desires and words, which hold them in very negative positions and relations of power, is a significant areas of study, considering that the use of force, according to critical theorists like Gramsci (1971) and Kincheloe (2004) are removed in hegemony. In its place, hegemony functions to derive the consent of the oppressed by the oppressor, who relies on or constructs a plateau for fracturing and manipulating the oppressed to become each other's oppressors, while – as my education students depicted in Chapter 3 – the oppressor looks on (Figure 43) as the oppressed fight it out amongst themselves.

The question may be answered in the affirmative when posed: Do students and their teachers know of those in-between subject-positions and chains of signifiers that constitute them?[185] The following bullets itemized in Chapter 4 may be responded in the affirmative, in the following ways:

WHAT IS THE SUBJECT OF OPPRESSION AND ITS COUNTER-HEGEMONIC FORMS OF EXPRESSION?

– How do post-structural constructs posit a subject whose identity is to incite themselves and others to collectivize the oppressed and fight hegemonic forms of oppression? For example, how does hierarchical authority and acts of delegation produce "pecking orders" in which the oppressed, once promoted, become oppressors?
– How does dialogue become an expression of power which merely hides hierarchical structures of authority and ignores how dialogue is one of many discursive formations making up a complex of discursive formations? That is, dialogue is but one formation of many, and which may excuse rather than positing one's surrounding as problematic, contradictory, and signifying in micro-meso-macro settings, and how power becomes and stays dominant and hegemonic. For example, what role do administrative hierarchical discursive formations play in constituting hierarchical chains of signifiers and subject-positions for student and teacher in which, in acts of articulation they counter each other with inscriptions on such surfaces, and which they may also play a role in transforming themselves wherein they cease to become oppressors and wage battle against old norms of hierarchicalization by construction of new norms making up new discursive and agential formations?
– What lies between the binary or modernist chains of reflection and action, which may be borne in dialogue? For example, why do individuals remain consistent, coherent, and obedient subjects, adhesed to their beliefs, despite contradictory evidence when such arrangements divide and harm their mutual interests?
– How does dialogue, as one possible discourse in a complex of discursive formations, get linked and un-linked to hegemonic reflections and cognitions,

thereupon providing sufficient spaces for limiting hegemony and allowing for counter-hegemonic discourses to surface in a complex of reflections and actions? Because Freire often slides away from these questions, revealing a distaste for the potential value of antagonistic, ambiguous and different discourses, not as pure as unified forms of consciousness, but rather those cognitions grounded in complex formations of discourse, which are struggled over on their surfaces of subject-positions and chains of signifiers, he cannot push the envelope for critical pedagogy to enter a phase Kincheloe and Giroux have recently referred to as "post-hegemonic." In order to reach this plateau for a more effective counter-hegemonic teaching and theorizing, in discerning what happens between reflection and action, between dialogue and discursive formations, between consciousness and unconsciousness, Kincheloe and Giroux would want to go the extra mile. Until critical pedagogy can posit as problematic hegemony as penetrated by these processes of signification and the discursive formations and their sub-components, the existing status of critical pedagogy may flounder or become stagnated.

In essence, the following three conditions constitute what differentiates critical pedagogy from *Counter-Hegemonic Teaching:*
— Who or what is the subject of power?
— How does dialogue differ from discourses and its complex of formations and power?
— How does a glimpse in the in-between links and connections between subject and object, dialogue and discursive formations, simple and complex cognitions create conditions for student and teacher to think and live in each other's constructions and reflections as well as provide a terrain and horizon for counter-hegemonic teaching and post-structural theorizing?

PUSHING THE ENVELOPE: WHAT DOES FINDING THE MIDDLE GROUND MEAN IN CRITICAL PEDAGOGY?

Counter-Hegemonic Teaching has attempted to push the envelope to present forms of critical pedagogy which may maintain as separate macro and micro forces of society and schools, resulting in "frivolous" wars amongst critical advocates; or which look to the "post-hegemonic" and which Giroux and Kincheloe have already pointed to. (2007, 2008)

Many famous critical pedagogues have been known to ridicule "postie" orientations as not promising, referring to them as "neo-liberal," deflecting attention away from the basic structures of capitalism, militarism, and the global world market. (Apple, 2002, Macedo, 2002, McLaren, 2002). Yet, as important as these concerns are, without simultaneous attention to the micro effects vis-a-vis the macro effects on meso or "in-between" planes of discourse, people's sense of themselves, their identities,[186] and the concomitant effects of fighting hegemony where people yield rather than resist giving consent to the powers-to-be, they'll fall short of counter-hegemony and merely legitimize hierarchical power relations and centers. Needed, then, are further examinations into relations within and in between how power and its relations are expressed in and by circulating discursive elements and signifying structures. These structures and processes may interact with one another and through subjects, as they relate and speak to one another.[187] Finding how those "in between" relations of power, derived from a complex of discursive formations, and their derived and anticipated chains of signifiers, equivalent and different, empty and floating, serve as "points of connection" (not opposed to "points of antagonism, but in them)," which theorists like Freire were wont to trust once people became "marked" with signs of the oppressor and other "ambiguous behaviors."

While Freire did have a dialectical conception of how the parts of the whole interrelate (pp. 86–87, 92–93, 96, 123), and while Freire asks educators to peel away the layers of oppressive reality, he stopped there. Until 2007, when Freire's widow, Anna Maria Araujo Freire unveils, once again, bringing to life what Giroux, twenty five years ago said, we may be on the cusp of re-examining how the power of the word as a signifier may be given more serious attention in critical pedagogy circles.[188] Here, we get a sense of, perhaps, a new beginning to Freire's "unfinished" pedagogy (Freire, 2007). Still: Can people who have been marked with oppression be mutually excluded from those who are not; or, rather, can one's act in speaking, relating, writing, performing, and articulating in words, further re-negotiate these oppressive marks, thereby allowing for new spaces or surfaces on which new norms, dispositions, and expectations may be constructed by those already oppressed, inviting them to partake in new forming, more inclusive communities of opposition and critical theorizing?

That is, while marked, but still desiring to struggle for liberation, equality, and non-oppressive and counter-hegemonic conditions, can critical pedagogy sort these mixed feelings and thoughts for the cause of liberation and emancipatory projects and movements? Can counter-hegemonic teaching and theorizing open up the way to get people to have "second thoughts," new words, and to see what we may see as routine and natural but are human or man/woman made constructions or spaces waiting for us to take power away from those who have them and who oppress and hegemonize us with these constructions?

If Freire would have lived today or Kincheloe for that matter, might they have agreed to a more subtle way of examining oppression, hegemony, and other forms of domination and injustice (in addition to a straight forward macro critique)? Without nuanced yet critical analyses, regimes of domination would only be replacing one word or label for another, thereby reproducing domination with different names, even those we call liberating, emancipating, and democratic. In this way, once we locate the middle between the subject and object, consciousness and unconsciousness, and agents and structure, we may be in a better discursive position to answer the question: How do we know we are critical counter-hegemonic theorizers?[189]

At this point, beyond the above conclusions, I wondered what other implications were inherent in our use of post-structural constructs and most important of all, for our future roles as articulators of counter-hegemonic teachers.

IMPLICATIONS FOR FUTURE RESEARCH AND PRACTICE OF COUNTER-HEGEMONIC TEACHING AND POST-STRUCTURAL THEORIZING

We learned in post-structuralist theorizing that in discourses, and between them and in their intersections with other discourses, and the formation of group norms, the notion of circulating signifiers link one discursive formation to another. These links serve to bridge several sets of chains and their sub-components of discourse into a complex which acts as a genesis making students and teachers move towards or away from, depending on how they articulate, map, and inscribe onto other discursive formations and chains, and how they construct their own counter-hegemonic discursive formations and communities. This insight was very different from the usual notion of positivism learned as the origin of the subject, the world, and other forces within empirical reach and senses. Originally, re-echoing the Husserlian notion of subject as an originator or director or intender of their own meanings and beliefs, critical educators have assumed what happened in the world had to be owned and possessed by their individual selves. As one student put it in a social studies methods class (Fleischer, 2007), "How can you change my beliefs and values, they are mine!" Otherwise, to this student, it was meaningless for him to care of such things (i.e. people starving beyond his national boundaries) since they fell outside of his individual perception. Further expanding this student's understanding by positing as real the subject as multiple or contradictory in one moment, contingently linked to others through chains of signifiers which, in turn, carve out or overlap each other in constructing new subject-positions on surfaces of inscription, in another moment, soon widened this student's view of how he could shape not merely his own self, but those of others and the world as well.

Further implied, subjects or people are not unified entities made up of one subject-position or consciousness, but rather, as a series of dispersed subjects, connected to each other on various levels and planes of discourse and in processes of their formations of identity connecting all of us to each other and reaching out to still others and, in this process, producing new an interesting chains intersecting and overlapping each other already produced by forces beyond us. They have the capability to negotiate with each other as agents of constructive actions, though. By acknowledging how subjectivity and selves are constructed in these complexes emerging or submerging in imbricated discursive formations, subject-positions and signifiers, people may inscribe, de-inscribe, and re-inscribe each other, whether within or across their surfaces of subject-positions, expanding discursive entities of the discursive field of contingency and heterogeneity indefinitely. (Thomassen, 2005; Laclau, 1990, 1993, 2007; Laclau & Mouffe, 1985)

These insights further imply what we must do as follows:

— Re-examine what dialogue is, and how, in acts of dialogical reflection and action, each party posits as problematic the world around themselves as occurring (not merely in an unified self but) in and through each dialoguer in many complicated and complex ways – through one's consciousness, unconsciousness, and discursive formations via chains of signifiers and subject-position surfaces of inscription.

— Extend Freire's study, *Pedagogy of the Oppressed* in showing how, in those moments of discourse, when the oppressed become oppressor, living in an

CHAPTER 5

existential duality, dialogue may posit such problematics, but only if accompanied with deep post-structural understanding of signification and semiotics, and how discourses occur on at least three planes – intra-discourses – between consciousness and unconsciousness; inter-discourses – between speakers and actors who attain communicative competences of gaining articulatory rights in which who speaks and who responds is grounded on the rights for anyone to freely ask the other questions in a kind of "ideal speech situation" (Bellack, 1966; Habermas, 1971, 1973; and trans-discourses – which leap across and beyond the borders of dialogue into the multifarious layers of dialogue as penetrated by multiple discursive formations). While dialogue is not an ideal entity and powerful enough for emancipatory projects, since it may become contained and hegemonized by power relations seeping into trans-discourses via racism, sexism, classism, etc., into and through intra-discourses linked to a stratum of the unconsciousness – Lacan insists in this regard, the unconsciousness is structured like a language or networks of signifiers and meanings signified as cutting spaces for signification – the notion of discourses (as opposed to language) still provides one possible discursive formation in which to negotiate and break with notions of subjectivity as formed in modernist and binary notions of reflection *and* action as opposed to seeing dialogical acts as produced and producing reflections *in* actions. This notion undermines the illusion of examining critical pedagogy as founded on, what some students believe, their "own" individualistic forms of beliefs and opinions, as if living on an isolated and barren island. This is why the work of Delueze and Guattari (1972, 1980, 1987) and others (Boorstein, 1979; Gramsci, 1971, Williams, 1975) offers a view to see how subject-positions become chained and interlocked, intersected and flow into one another in multiple directions.
  – By taking a post-structural perspective to counter hegemony, this study further implies we can see what lies between reflection and action, not only breaking from modernist or binary terms framing reality, but further, from seeing how counter-discourses, intra-inter-and trans-discourses and modes of identification, counter-identification, and de-identifications (Pecheux, 1982), can be used to further understand and articulate how discursive configurations make up discursive fields of power and knowledge-making. These fields of discourse are hetero-geneous, parts of which criss-cross each other, and in this mixed zone of discourse, subject-position formations may offer one glimpses of those "third spaces" which may unlock or break open, at least temporarily, the chains of signifiers, subjections, and subject-positions, and other limits of discourse which, likewise, demarcate critical forms of theorizing from counter-hegemonic forms of theorizing. When counter-hegemonic theorizing can extend critical theorizing, we may finally see what makes distinct modernist from postmodernist thinking, and how critical and counter-hegemonic thinking may be stitched together encountering in education-teaching preparation courses certifying teachers to become both critical and counter-hegemonic educators.
  – For those teachers contemplating becoming school leaders or administrators in school hierarchies, the present study can be useful as a supplement to those well-know studies which emphasize "constructivist" modes of leadership (Lambert & Associates, 1996; Henderson, 1999; Sergiovanni & Starrett, 1974)

and other approaches to humanize but not necessarily make democratic power sharing school leadership reality. As I wrote in 1978, from a student emancipatory journal at Teachers College, Columbia University, when administrators are called upon to support teacher dialogue, as Joe Kincheloe used to be known for saying, "I watch my wallet." Other discussions as to how authentic or real notions of offering workers "empowerment programs" or having them work in "teams" is also mentioned critically in Chapter 2.

— Also implied in this study is the need to examine what constitutes and re-shapes the surfaces of subject-positions? There is a need for more work, theoretically and qualitative ethnographic research – i.e. story-telling and autobiographical research and its discursive structures (Fleischer, 1998) to see how the surfaces of subject-positions – which incite new interpretations for people occupying their surfaces (Smith, 1996) – to constitute and create images generating desires in which to further illuminate those glimpses or metonymies of signs and signifiers we have been referring to throughout this book. This can be seen in Laclau (2007), Smith (1996) and Thomassen (2005) studies – including the example of Hannah Schmidt the Nazi guard who, despite her denials – let hundreds of prisoners be burnt alive in a church; or for those second year teachers who felt and expressed personal relief after seeing their students sweat and work hard for the standardized "high stake" exams which would raise the school's test average in fulfilling the requirements for school improvement and assessment criteria as mandated by *No Child Left Behind*; or, further, how students who hated their education professors casted their anger in derogatory remarks on a website, www.ratemyprofessor.com, seeking no response from the professor who, unlike them, could not hide in anonymity.

None of these website relations seem to point to an avenue on which student and teacher may come together in mutually supportive and caring ways, much less in dialogical communities; nor do they issue signs for solidarity, as is so sorely needed between the growing gap between student and teacher as they become more and more divided in these very conservative times.

— Further implied in this study is a need to examine how some subject-positions are formed or carved out (Coward and Ellis, 1977) and maintain a circulation of signifiers and their chains in constructing surfaces of subject-positions which are inscribed and over-inscribed and de-inscribed in ways that may serve student and teacher in mapping their conditions as hegemonized and point, at the same time, to spaces for countering hegemony. Once student and teacher begin to see beyond the fact that they are pitted against one another, they may begin to re-construct discourse, imbricated in ways in which they may see "uneven edges" of various overlapping and intersecting discourses, how illusionary student-teacher relations are merely "positioned" in conflicting and contradictory discursive formations, not as a fact of life, but as a discursive maneuver, often marginalized as a dysfunctional form of dialogue of incompatible partners. But, when dialogue is re-examined, student-teacher relations may reveal ways they may over-ride such impediments by de- and re-constructing (or inscribing) dialogue via intra- and inter- and trans-discourses and their metonymic signifiers.

- Implied in this study, then is that student and teacher may begin to locate the "tendential" surfaces produced by various signifier chains intersecting one another, each extended from their respective discursive formations constituting a uncertain and unpredictable social whole. If we look at Laclau's work (2007, pp. 130–133) on these points we may be surprised to see how the surfaces of subject-positions are very fragile and changeable. This means a society or a school system which is more responsive to individuals over those demands becoming lost in the shuffle or hegemonized by dominant or "empty" signifiers and chains which acts as a kind of vacuum cleaner or "black hole" of particular demands. These circulating or floating signifiers, may also be in the process of re-forming new subject-position surfaces or, acting as new empty signifiers or stand-ins, re-hegemonizing the field they had momentarily lost to the circulation of passing glimpses of metonymic signifiers, which pointed to the whole in relation to its parts. This loosening and re-hardening of metonymic signifiers my special education students called "flying rumors" positioning them and their regular classmate counterparts into antagonistic or – more unlikely – non-antagonistic and friendly relations.
- And further implied, we may see through the complex and capillary worlds of special education and regular education to see those microscopic and metonymic spaces which reveal those moments in which, when they slide into a subject-position aligned and linked to a chain of a particular discursive formation which displaces their intentions for more receptive spaces of feelings in seeking to identify themselves with people who are oppressed.
- Therefore further implied by post-structural theorizing (through post-structural constructs) is that we have to see how various discursive formations affect one another, as they are always affecting subject-positions and signifiers in circulation or in articulation with each other. Taking a Lacanian insight, "a signifier represents a subject for another signifier" (Lacan, 1977, p. 211), how, once these signifiers interact with each other, do some subjects take on subject-positions which mediate between their ascribed/structured societal positions and their notions of agency? In these signifying complexes, we must begin to find out to what extent do subjects assume some degree of freedom while qualifying the feelings they get in exploiting others while interacting with them within complex of chains of signifiers and various other discursive formations?
- Implied further in this study is that we must also see how in complex inter-actions – the interaction and intertwinement of race, class, gender, and ability get further mixed into authority or administrative chains of signifiers and subject-positions – as we have shown in many illustrations affecting special and regular education, along with interpretations on the various contexts of constraint exhibiting in issues related to testing and classroom management.

Adorno and associates (1969) have researched how there may be many close links to hierarchical authority and fascism. The notion that hierarchical chains of signifiers, subject-positions, and discursive formations co-exist within structurally-defined organizations common to school administrative organizations begs the question: Why haven't school people gone deeper in examining and mapping out the journey of the hierarchical signifier (and subject)? And why do we, when confronted with this question, simply resort to the nomenclature: It's just human nature?

- Implied in this study is the notion of testing, a main driver maintaining the need for further entrenching school administrative hierarchies and classroom management procedures. As Good and Brophy (2008) recently claimed, frequent and standardized testing can be accommodated with selecting parts of the required text to "cover" thereby allowing room for discussion and other constructive activities so students and teachers can "take ownership" and construct knowledge while preparing for standardized tests. While this claim is at best on flimsy grounds, "to teach as if there are no tests," the new administration coming into power appears to be taking the position that they oppose "bubble style tests" as endemic to student learning and growth. While we wait to see if such exams will be permitted, albeit not eliminating stringent systems of accountability, the basic issues of testing as a feeder of school administrative-hierarchical relations and behaviors has not been addressed yet by the Obama administration.[190]

- This action or inaction further implies that new forms of assessment or tests will be deployed in which teachers are no longer "test preppers" and in which students are no longer alienated. Without a tool to map to show how students and teachers relations are affected by the "testing craze" began with Goals 2000, what will constitute "constructive" teaching and learning (as opposed to rote learning), or how and what will be changed by a new Obama administration in Washington, may affect what the new administration does about what constitutes dialogue and discourses in the classroom.

- Implicit in this study is the need to constantly examine and re-examine to what degree such forms of dialogue take. Will real change merely reproduce the old formats while appearing to be packaged as new? As has often re-occurred, when traditional modes of instruction are replaced by so-called "innovative" modes, what happens is a change that becomes contained in the existing languages or discourses. So, we get new schools by their becoming re-labeled and re-staffed. We get charter schools which denude teacher union organizations. Is change of language enough to make a real change or difference when only seen through the lens of modernist discourses as opposed to post-modernist discourses?

- Implicit in this study is how visible is change concerned with classroom management? As we saw in the last thirty years or more, merely removing physical barriers or punishment from view are often replaced by more invisible and internalized ones. Slavin (1990) and associates, for example, have insisted when classrooms are "fun" and "enjoyable" there is no reason for students to resist and be discipline problems. Yet, as Gore (1993) has commented – qualifying that she will continue to teach by emphasizing "circle" seating arrangements in her classrooms in higher education – she notes how traditional "rows" of nailed down seats may provide a "cover" or space for students who wish and need private spaces to communicate with each other without the need of school administrative intrusions. Everhart (1983), too, seems to have put this problem in a more straightforward manner: it is the students who at times manage and control the classroom, not their teachers. This fact today is covered by language of classroom discipline and management, however (Wong & Wong, 2001). Meeting students in a space of negotiation serves more interests than attempting to covering over these relations and struggles in language.

– In the same way as not seeing what lies behind and through the label of classroom management and the like, the binary opposition between the "good" and "bad" administrators, as we have seen in Chapter 2, only serves to obscure the need for additional places for students and teachers (and perhaps, with the assistance of teacher educators from universities on a voluntary basis) to negotiate further power differentials between the two in a honest and forthright way which serves to move school organizations to become more democratic as opposed to autocratic places to learn, relate, and teach.

– And finally, while ancillary methods of leveling power relations between students and teachers, as www.ratemyprofessor.com, may prompt immediate results between both students and teachers in the short run; the notion of "equalizing" relations between student and teacher in hierarchical settings will require more sensitive discursive relations. Taking into account how such websites may do more to exacerbate student-teacher relations than re-negotiate their power differentials and feelings, I have reviewed a tiny fraction of these student postings in Chapter 2. The postings often reveal very harsh, if not very divisive ways of functioning as a mere sounding board for student vengeance rather than a two way negotiation fiat.

RECOMMENDATIONS

Counter-Hegemonic Teaching offers some suggestions to resolve, to some extent, the above implications, problems, and conclusions of the study:

– The subject is not an originary, unified, or an essentialized subject. Rather, in post-structural terms, the subject has many sides, surfaces, and subject-positions which remain in constant circulation. As the subject may be formed in acts of speech, articulation, inscription, and other signifying chains and discursive structures and processes discussed throughout the present study, there remains a need to map out as many discursive formations which constitute discursive fields of power, identity, culture, and ideology which comprise any institutionalized setting, in order to further strategize how schools may become more democratic, fair, just, and diverse rather than what we have been led to believe presently exists.

– Dialogue is a part of discourse. It is not necessarily a space for freedom or construction of knowledge-making on its own by two or more discussants. Rather, and this point seeks to extend Freire's faith in dialogue, in post-structural terms, we must begin to see how dialogue is more than a conversational moment between two individuals or dyads. Dialogue has to be placed in context which complements, penetrates, and exceeds monastic notions of two individuals with those multifarious layers of discourse constituting dialogue differentially or in layers in which discourses passes through dialogue as subject-positions, chains of signifiers, and surfaces of inscriptions. These passage ways may occur in a variety of dimensions of those involved dialogical partners. Those in dialogue must simultaneously attend to those in between spaces in which macro and micro forces come together in a *meso* plane or region of struggle, resistance, and exceeding these moments, transformation. Between those in dialogue and those forces which penetrate and contain dialogue, we must re-examine the construct of dialogue as both a modernist and post-modernist construct of signification and meaning-making. When this re-examination takes place, through post-structural constructs, dialogue becomes displaced so that those in the dialogue may see or experience those layers of discourse as linked to a constellation of discursive formations and discourses.

- Thus, dialogue is no longer viewed as an illusionary space, allowing for its individuals to be released into a space of isolated freedom. Needed, is a space in which to view how power crosses the borders of dialogue, and who makes and changes the norms and their circulation and intersection of chains of signifiers onto the surfaces of the discursive field as spaces and signifiers of power or what drives real events. As we have already seen, circulating or floating signifiers serve as metonymies or *objet petit a*, mirroring or revealing particles which trans-cross discursive formations, chains of signifiers, and subject-positions surfaces, revealing parts of the whole and parts in relation to each other. As Freire has said, this kind of probing and dialectical problem-posing is what "unveils" reality and its many layers, although he left it there.

- By imagining how existing structures of signification may offer a glimpse into the intricate and complex world of meaning-making and other constructivist teaching practices, using and re-thinking how post-structural constructs and theorizing may be used to release particles or metonymic fragments of signifiers, contingent on their aligned and dis-aligned relations of power and discourse, we may also want to think of how to provide for new surfaces and new subject-positions in which students and teachers, along with teacher educators and administrators, may ground or provide a horizon for re-conceptualizing the world of education. We may begin to re-think how chains of signifiers and discursive formations may re-constitute new spaces in which new opportunities for qualitative studies pertaining to language, power, discourse, and mapping may emerge. These signifying processes involve actions and activities which should reveal the extent school and classroom practices and practitioners are both critically reflective of their actions, and how they are also counter-hegemonic agential activists who act on their freedom with or without repressive administrative reprisals. As part of the maze one must map in the best of post-structural traditions, one may also see the contours and circulations of power affecting their images, identifications, relationships, and knowledge-making and its limits in hierarchical settings, and thereby offer those who wish to become democratic school advocates a warning zone as to how they can proceed.

    For example, imagine how chains of signifiers and subject-positions, racialized and put into class terms and discourses would become circulated, re-aligned, ricochet, displace surfaces of subject-positions, in terms of identity, relationships, and power, upon hearing that Barack Obama is the first African-American president? Imagine how inspiring this would be for minority and black kids; how liberating and freeing – from the chains of old prejudices – this would be for white kids? In a recent interview with the senior correspondent, John King of *CNN News* (January 16, 2009), Obama asserted: "Now that I will become the first African-American president, black kids will look at themselves differently, and just as important, white kids will look at black kids differently."

– Also suggested is that a call for changes in schools and scholarly research be based on critical pedagogy and counter-hegemonic teaching and theorizing, in the tradition of Joe Kincheloe and Shirley Steinberg's work (1998, 2003, 2004c) and their new founding of the Paulo and Nita Freire Institute on Critical Pedagogy at McGill University, Montreal, Canada. Members of such counter-hegemonic discursive formations must act as if they are transformatory agents or marked to perform agential actions, inviting solidarity amongst the school community while resisting the tendencies to become re-hegemonized. Freire's point on not trusting "ambiguous behavior" or those marked by the oppressor, while I have critiqued its elements, is, to some extent, appreciated and to be heeded here.

– As I was once confronted by a colleague at a college I was being interviewed for a professor position, he argued that hegemony and counter-hegemony remain dualities on modernist chains of reasoning. I countered that while they do oppose one another, not all oppositions are modernist; some as hegemony and counter-hegemony may emerge and get submerged by each other in a dialectical struggle, subject to any contingent moments and upon which a new hegemonic-counter-hegemonic relations may become stabilized or de-stabilized. Once new and unpredictable fragments or "floating signifiers" appear on the horizon which may signify the emergence or submergence of hegemony and counter-hegemony, student and teacher may take this occurrence as a sign to make distinctions between dominant chains of hierarchical signifiers, subject-positions, and discursive formations and their antimonies. In this way, students and teachers may begin to see alternatives and/or new spaces for carving out alternative signifiers and discursive formations. Conversely, they may name new tools to spot how complex words and messages are layering and intersecting constituents of chains of signifiers and subject-positions making up the thick, textured, and tendential surfaces of subject-positions and their inscriptions. In these spaces we can tear apart their porous surfaces in locating just how the oppressed identify, too quickly with the oppressed – their life styles, classes, dispositions, etc. – or how male and female, rich and poor, white and black, gay and straight, East and West dualities may be broken down further and offer complex ways into which to "journey into" their myths and modes of expressions. By doing this, we may see an alternative between do or die, black and white, and often, war and deceptive quiet lulls of peace. We may break and dis-link those modernist and equivalent chains of meanings and imaginaries so dominant in the West, and finally, those fragments circulating from these surfaces offering traces or excesses or trails – *objets petit a* – by which we all may find our way back home.

LAST REMARKS TO JOE L. KINCHELOE

As Joe Kincheloe in his recent analysis of *Critical Pedagogy* (2004) maintained, schools may be very harmful and exclusionary to *particular students* who are not served in mainstream schooling. He points to those minorities, people of color, speakers of English as a Second Language, physically disabled, and people of different sexual orientations, people who do not fit into the dominant norm. He also speaks of how the dominant class, somehow, leaves their "imprint" on those who would defy and resist the dominant norm, including the de-contextualized notions of how science has made it possible to become the dominant way to evaluate and assess students and teacher performances and what constitutes "learning" or knowledge-making, or how curricula gets designed and developed, and much more.

In *Critical Pedagogy: A Primer* and later in other books, as *Teaching: An Introduction* (2005) *and Critical Pedagogy: Where Do We Go From Here* (2007), Kincheloe calls upon educators not to ignore or hesitate or refuse to act and take an ethical stand about how bankrupt critical pedagogy may have become during the Bush years of *No Child Left Behind*. Kincheloe, in one of his most recent and last book (2007) explains whether the language used by critical theorists is too difficult to decipher by teacher educators and their teacher education students, or whether the overbearing and intimidating presence of neo-conservative and neo-liberal perspectives are simply too intimidating to respond to. This thought expressed by Kincheloe leaves us all with a feeling that we must establish a beachhead in mainstream of schooling so those who work and live in these places may feel about lodging questions, complaints, and opposition in many places and ways to articulate themselves.

Whether we keep a watchful eye on the long term effects of a positivist science constituting the existing domination of standardized tests and scripted practices; or, whether we get fractured and, as Freire mentions and is so well known for naming (but not explaining the processes) how the oppressed oppress each other, these items certainly will remain our future challenges. Kincheloe's founding and directorship of the new Nita and Paulo Freire Institute for Critical Pedagogy is one attempt to carry out the work of established as well as emerging with critical pedagogies and pedagogues. Further challenging those who mount critical forms of teaching and theorizing will be the additional push toward maintaining solidarity with like-minded people, and who are ready to mount counter-hegemonic forms of teaching and theorizing. While this book is principally targeted for those in the academy, teacher educators and their education students, I look forward to addressing those concerned with making known by their publications in *Counter-Hegemonic Teaching II,* and who live and work in schools and personify the trenches as places of fighting for their professional standings and their students' future well-being. Whatever reality we may align ourselves to we may want to recall Maxine Greene's (1978) call for attention to be focused on the daily struggles of students and teachers to reach a state of "awakeness" as opposed to a state of submersion. In *Counter-Hegemonic Teaching II,* we will call on you to come forth and join together in a new cause for liberation and justice in our schools and institutions of higher learning. Or, as Kincheloe (2004) defined the seldom used term, agency, as a "person's ability to shape and control their own lives, freeing themselves from the oppression of power (2004, p. 2), we, taking a lead from Kincheloe, and offer student and teacher not only to read about critical pedagogy, but further, take critical power and take risks and chances in the form of counter-hegemonic actions.

WHAT DID *COUNTER-HEGEMONIC TEACHING* ACCOMPLISH? – A SUMMARY

Now that we have accomplished reading through the entire length of *Counter-Hegemonic Teaching*, the shortest amount of words can respond to this question, as: (1) pushing the field of critical pedagogy to emerge into a new phase of "post-hegemonic" teaching; (2) through extending the work and assumptions of Paulo Freire's *Pedagogy of the Oppressed* examining some of the basic assumptions underlying the field of critical pedagogy, (3) adding to the ensemble of power relations and discourses as contained within the "holy trinity" of class, race, and gender, but also intruding and linked to these power relations are "administrative and hierarchical power relations," (4) these hierarchical relations were also examined on both micro and macro contexts, as well as how they interact with each other on meso levels in their engagement with hierarchical and hegemonic chains of signifiers, subject-positions and their surfaces, and act as important constitutive components constituting hierarchical and hegemonic discursive formations (and their antitheses) was also explained, (5) and finally, how, in these signifying and semiotic processes, hegemony is reproduced yet still, in these processes, reveal spaces for counter-hegemonic resistances as student and teacher take on or construct new and counter-hegemonic subject-positions, chains of signifiers, and discursive formations.

In the above accomplishments, *Counter-Hegemonic Teaching* then (6) opens the door for new advances to be made in critical pedagogy and how schools may become more egalitarian, just, and democratic places for students, teachers, their parents, and teacher educators to live. This includes raising questions about "dialogical" teaching and school governance which may or may not be genuine and effective as reforms and innovations posing to be "critical," "diverse" and/or "reflective" institutions and practices. Further, (7) dialogue as a classroom teaching method or practice also holds the keys toward more critical pedagogy but, as we also saw, this happens only to a point, unless dialogue is viewed within the context of discursive formations. When we revise our notions of dialogue and consciousness as constituted from binary to complex chains of signifiers and subject-positions, we may merely reveal one more layer to those many layers in which discursive formations align and disalign, interact and transact with each other in a discursive metonym complex. This complex arrangement is necessary so that student and teacher, through their post-structural theorizations may see how hegemony invades their spaces for real dialogue, but also, reveals those spaces in which their dialogues may open and create new spaces for counter-hegemonic agential actions

And finally (8) because post-structural constructs offer both student and teacher subject-positions in which to see how they victimize each other as oppressors instead of seeing each other as partners in the same struggle as fellows of the same oppressed or administrated class, they may now go further and stop fracturing their potential relations as dialogical partners – rather than having "nice conversations" – eventually leading to more democratic, equal, and socially just school and classroom arrangements of governance as student and teacher ascend to become leaders of their professions and participants of power in their own schools, communities, and schools of education.

NOTES

[1] In a recent debriefing of the bailouts for corporate America, appropriated in the departing Bush administration, and the lack of oversight and transparency which funded over three hundred billion dollars for "bailouts" to CEO's and banks, the newly elected President Obama remarked that some of these institutions spending taxpayer money for frivolous things, as corporate jets (50 million), commodes ($35,000, rugs ($87,000), and CEO bonuses (billions) was "shameful." Vice President Joe Biden added that this kind of behavior of corporate America can be summed up in one word: greed. See Sheryl Gay Stolberg and Stephen Labaton, "Banker Bonuses are 'Shameful,' Obama Declares: A Message to Wall Street" in *New York Times*, January 30, 2009, pp. A1, A20.

[2] A more insidious version of positivism will be discussed in subsequent chapters in the form of qualitative research which incorporates or presumes a notion of subjectivity which is unified, defined and originated. Or, as Joe Kincheloe (2003, 2004a, 2004b, 2005, 2007) has outlined, a critical pedagogical perspective of schooling as grounded on complex meaning systems, which the present study will further elaborate, expanding such perspectives within a counter-hegemonic frame grounded into post-structuralist bases defying its Enlightenment ontology and Descartian orientations.

[3] In addition to tenure, the other four pillars of hegemony which will be more thoroughly discussed in Chapter 2 are: administrative hierarchies, classroom management, testing, and www.ratemyprofessor.com.

[4] A Brooklyn College colleague, Peter Taubman, has recommended to me and the entire faculty that it would be a good idea for all full time professors to teach one class in the public schools every day simultaneously to their teaching load on the college level – an idea I fully endorsed at the time.

[5] Recently, for two years, I was given the job to observe, participate, speak in, and evaluate twenty instructors (who were part-time principals, superintendents and curriculum leaders in school districts). I wondered if I was qualified to evaluate these people given I have never been an administrator and, I further questioned: Why did the college administrators give me such a job to begin with?

[6] For years Seymour Sarason (1996) and others have called for attention for institutional and "behavioral regularities" of schools and other institutions. Yet, Sarason has not examined this problem within the context – "the more schools change, the more they remain the same" – from hegemonic or counter-hegemonic perspectives.

[7] My use of the word "machine" is both inspired by post colonial works of Gayatri Chakravorty Spivak's *Outside in the Teaching Machine* (1993), Catherine Liu, *Copying Machines: Taking Notes for the Automaton* (2000), and the post-structuralist works of Gilles Delueze and Felix Guattari, *Anti-Oedipus: Capitalism and Schizophrenia* (1972) and *A Thousand Plateaus* (1987).

[8] Jonathan Kozol, *Shame of the Nation: The Apartheid in American Schools* (New York: Crown Publishers, 2005) .

[9] Gary Orfield, Ten Years Study at The Civil Rights Division, Department of Education, 1996 segments in Gary Orfield, "Schools More Separate: Consequences of a Decade of Re-Segregation" in *Re-Thinking Schools*, Fall, 2001, Vol. 16, No. 1, pp. 14–18.

[10] "Somini Sengupta, "India's Shortage Means Glut of Parental Stress" in *New York Times*, February 6, 2008, p. A1, A6.

[11] Choe Sang-Hun, "A Taste of Failure Fuels an Appetite for Success at South Korea's Cram Schools" in *New York Times*, August 13, 2008, A6.

[12] William W. French "Educators Try to Tame Japan's Blackboard's Jungles" in New York Times, September 23, 2004, and see and compare, Brent Staples, "Why the United States Should Look to Japan for Better Schools" in *New York Times*, November 22, 2005 and the Editorial Responses, November 25, 2005, A21.

[13] Norimitsu Onishi, "Mood Sours for Japan's Other Asian Students," *New York Times*, March 24, 2004, A6.

[14] See last section of this chapter titled: "A Few Words for Those Critical Theorists Who See Post-Structuralism as Neo-Liberal."

[15] Sarah Carr, "Where Teachers Rule" in *Milwaukee Journal Sentinel*, July 18, 2005 and http://www.jsonline.com/story/index.aspx?id=341727

[16] One of the first critical theorists to write about hegemony in education is Michael Apple. See his "Analyzing Hegemony" in *Ideology and Curriculum* 3rd Edition. (New York: Routledge, 1979, 2004)

[17] Lee Fleischer, "Living in Contradiction: Stories of Special Education Students," unpublished dissertation, Teachers College, Columbia University, 1998, 317pages.

[18] See Lee Fleischer, "Living in Contradiction: Stories of Special Education Students," *unpublished dissertation*, Teachers College, Columbia University, October, 1998, 317 pages; Lee Fleischer, "Special Education Students as Counter-Hegemonic Theorizers" in Glenn M Hudak and Paul Kihn (eds.) *Labeling: Politics and Pedagogy* (New York: Routledge, 2001), pp. 115–125; Lee Fleischer, Exceptional Youth Cultures: A Framework for Instructional Strategies of Inclusive Classrooms" in *Taboo: Journal; of Culture and Education*, Vol. 9, Number 2, Fall-Winter, 2005, pp. 97–104.

[19] In my first two years of teaching social studies in a high school on Long Island there was not one student of color out of over 2000 students in attendance. Heinous, considering a nearby neighborhood contained mostly black and Hispanic students. To this day, this school remains all white in student population!

[20] The same high school just referred to was also very active with students and faculty demonstrating against the Viet Nam War. In fact, this school was the first high school to hold a counter-graduation demonstration against the war in New York State with actor, Robert Vaughn (Man From U.N.C.L.E) and my chairperson as the organizers. This occurred despite the fact that the principals' son was a West Point graduate serving in Viet Nam at the time.

[21] Raymond Sobel and Harry Robb, *From Left to Right: Teaching Controversial Issues* (New York: Benziger Publishers, 1966).

[22] This is why I recently sent out over eighty applications between 2007 and once gain in 2008, for a professor position, far exceeding my usual quota in the tri-state of New York, extending my reach nationally, armed with copies of my nine published articles and excellent student and collegiate observations and evaluations. While I received almost ten interviews in 2007, I did not land a position, even though I applied from California to Maine – and this included adjunct positions as well! I know now the reason is probably more my age than my politics.

[23] Presently, I do a similar thing when I draw on the chalkboard an illusion of steps. They appear as either steps moving downward, or conversely, as steps moving upward. I surprise everyone when I point out that they are neither. That the steps they perceived in the first two moments produces a third perception: namely, that when perceived from above, they can be seen as a room divider as one peers down from the attic. See Chapter 4 for the image I would draw on the chalkboard.

[24] In this volume I will invite professors, teachers, and students to contribute their stories of being caught in hegemony and how they perceive possibility to break out of their oppressions and the contradictory states they live in, accompanied by nuance pains, fears, and intimidations.

[25] See Donaldo Macedo's, "Introduction to the 30th Anniversary of Paulo Freire's *Pedagogy of the Oppressed*" in Paulo Freire's *Pedagogy of the Oppressed* (New York: Continuum Press, 2002), pp, 11–28; Michael Apple's "Preface: The Freirean Legacy" in Judith J. Slater, Stephen M. Fain, and Cesar A. Rossatto (eds.) *The Freirean Legacy: Educating for Social Justice* (New York: Peter Lang Publishers, 2002), pp. ix–xii; Peter McLaren and Ramin Farahmandpur, "Breaking Signifying Chains: A Marxist Position on Postmodernism" in Dave Hill, Peter McLaren, Mike Cole, and Glenn Rikowski (eds), *Marxism Against Postmodernism in Educational Theory* (New York: Lexington Books, 2002), pp. 35–66.

[26] See the critique of English and American progressive schools by Anthony Green and Rachel Sharp, *Education and Social Control: A Study in Progressive Primary Education* (Boston, MASS: Routledge & Kegan Paul, 1975) and Lisa Delpit, "Skills and Other Dilemmas of a Progressive Black Educator" in *Harvard Educational Review* (Vol. 56, No. 4, November, 1986, pp. 376–386, along with Jennifer Gore's interesting critique of progressive emphases on focusing on students' dialogue, which eliminates some of their "hiding places" for student autonomy built into traditional and hierarchical rows of chairs and desks nailed down to floor, *The Struggle for Pedagogies: Critical and Feminist Discourses as Regimes of Truth* (New York: Routledge, 1993).

[27] See, for example, Rachel Sharp's *Knowledge, Ideology, and the Politics of Schooling: Towards a Marxist Analysis of Education* (Boston, MASS: Routledge, Kegan Paul, 1980) or Madam Sarup, *Marxism and Education* (Boston, MASS: Routledge, Kegan Paul, 1978).

[28] While Apple speaks of "forms of consciousness" in his original expose of hegemony (1979), he never elaborates further how these forms are constituted in discourse or in those moments when language intersects with power at the point of articulating or inscribing such experiences.

[29] For more discussion on this point, see Henry Giroux, *Theory and Resistance in Education: A Pedagogy for the Opposition* (Westport, CONN: Bergin & Garvey Publishers, 1983), p. 113.

[30] See, for example, Pecheux's (1982) treatment of discourse as occurring on planes of intra-discourse, inter-discourse, and trans-discourse, and further how one is interpellated by means of identification, along chains of metonymic discourse in identifying, counter-identifying, and dis-identifying moments.

[31] While Freire and Macedo was in the midst of writing *Ideology Matters*, when Freire suddenly passed away, we have no way of knowing what its contents may have brought to the field of critical pedagogy or counter-hegemonic teaching and theorizing.

[32] I'm impressed with the interview and discussion between Henry Giroux and Joe Kincheloe on U-Tube (2008), in which they both agree to some kind of "post-hegemonic" framework that critical pedagogy must be addressed in the future. Both authors and critical pedagogues do not go into detail as to how such a framework(s) would look like, nor do they include, other forces already present in both schools, namely, the power differentials of those who struggle and differ under schools administrative hierarchies. More on this aspect of power, seen as hegemonic force, operating in language as a discourse system, including post-structural constructs as subject-positions and chains of hierarchical signifiers and their concomitant surfaces for inscription with their discursive formations affecting school identities and relationships, will be discussed later in this chapter and Chapter 4.

[33] Pierre Bourdieu's notion of "habitus," along with Anna Marie Smith's appropriation of his work, (1996, pp. 63–64) is an apt view of how non- or quasi intentional acts of cognition may constitute forms of reflection which, while fleeting, cross one's consciousness, may be seen as active spaces in which speakers may point out, map out and research on one of many intermediary spaces to ground their critical pedagogy, and in terms of this book, counter-hegemonic theorizing. Traditionally, Marxists have relegated such phenomena as not serious. To authors such as N.S. Volosinov, (1973) for example, these "fleeting" images or thoughts constitute merely the "lower behavioral ideology" stratum of thinking, and merely are "adventitious" constituting the "normative identity forms." Since hegemony's main function is to derive the unwitting and perhaps unconscious thoughts of peoples' power to consent or withhold their consent and cooperation, these fleeting experiences, like technology's sound-bytes, are integral to analyzing hegemony in modern day hyper-reality as schools and other places which are bombarded by media. See my article on "Teaching Social Studies through Post-Structural Constructs" in Donaldo Macedo and Shirley Steinberg (eds), *The Media Literacy* (New York, Peter Lang Publishers, 2007), pp. 626–639.

[34] A more detailed description and analysis of these hegemonic functions and forces in language as both a discursive and signifying mechanism in deriving consent and offering spaces for counter-hegemonic activities will be discussed in Chapter 4. In this regard, a more detailed look at how chains of equivalent and differential chains of signifiers, through the motion of empty signifiers and floating signifiers (which may be constituents of equivalent or differential chains) carve out spaces

(along surfaces of subject-positions tendentially) which attempt to engulf the field of competing chains of signifiers. To the extent they do, the field becomes hegemonized, whereby differences become equivalent to each other, making this struggle appear metonymic or displaced. In reality, a series of equivalent chains represent a similar image of society in which differential chains of signifiers are absorbed or co-opted. There are also moments in this process whereby such chains of equivalence or empty signifiers, after having been "filled," break off or are broken in the construction of new surfaces by differential or "floating" signifiers circulating throughout the discursive field. This movement produces new spaces or imbricates new layers of inscription upon other subject-position surfaces or a new surface of marks on the same subject-position. Whether broken off or producing enough space for circulation of differential signifiers to make their marks and spaces on the same or different surfaces of other subject-positions is discussed in Chapter 4 and clarifies the context of hegemonic struggles in articulation of the classroom discourse (Laclau & Mouffe, 1985; Thomassen, 2005; Laclau, 2007).

[35] A distinction is made here between speaking as a discourse and speaking from subject-positions presupposing a dis-unified consciousness in dialogue or the exchange of dyads with unified and binary sets of consciousness. Speaking from a discourse or dis-unified consciousness – a series of subject-positions and their surfaces of inscription are constructed in the moment of articulation by a chain of signifiers (or floating signifiers) – some overlapping; others intersecting one another – emanating from one or more discursive formations or speaking communities, producing somewhat of a dis-jointed albeit partially coherent sense of unity (i.e. equivalence) amongst diverse peoples and forces (see Note 34 above and Note 56 below). In speaking from a position of unified or equivalent constructions of consciousness and dialogue, however, two unified subjects with unified states of consciousness may become impervious to contradictory forces, or those subject-positions or interpretive frames formed in modernistic times, adhering to binary chains of signifiers and identities such as rich vs. poor, white vs. black, male vs. female, and so forth – constructed from a sutured series of subject-positions of one discursive formation or speaking community, inclusive with their signs, codes, and images representing to the subject/speaker a vantage point of a unitary consciousness which tends to marginalize differences into higher and lower hierarchical positions. More on these differences will be explained in Chapter 3 on Paulo Freire's principal work, *Pedagogy of the Oppressed* as examined through pictures drawn by my education students over the last eight years and re-examined through post-structural constructs. As such, Freire's main work will be identified as an artifact of modernist thinking or epistemology, namely for his concepts of binary consciousness: reflection and action, dialogue and monologue, and oppositional identifications between the oppressed and the oppressor in which the oppressed become oppressors to themselves and each other in hierarchialized and binary identifications.

[36] William Ayers (1993) has suggested that teachers try "creative forms of insubordination," like causing to mal-function the PA school system so student-teacher discussions won't be interrupted by announcements from the principal's office.

[37] While Kincheloe correctly posits power as a very complex phenomena involving scripted and top-down curricula, he does not clarify at least three other dimensions which may have resisted and penetrated regimens constituting testing, classroom management, and administrative hierarchies. See the snippets and case studies in Chapter 2 on the "Pillars of Hegemony."

[38] Recently, it was reported that a teacher in Seattle, Washington (2008), simply refused to administer a standardized test to his students. His actions were backed by his fellow teachers and a local parent organization. Most recently, president-elect Barack Obama said on his website www.change.org: "teachers should not be forced to spend the academic year preparing students to fill in bubbles on standardized tests." However, more recently, Giroux and Saltzman (2008) has assessed the newly elected administration in regard to their maintaining "corporatized education" more pessimistically.

[39] Quilting points or *sinthomes*, while similar to the *nodal points* popularized by Lacan, are not the same. To Zizek, in the *sinthome* experience, several strands of chains of signifiers simultaneously

intertwine themselves like a twisted rope, thereby producing experiences which release the subject in passions of pleasure, fantasy (including, I would add, horror and terror) and enjoyment.

40 More on the implications of these calls for "post-hegemonic" forms of teaching and theorizing and its relevancy toward mounting future based strategies for democratic school and classroom pedagogy, extending Freirian modes of critical pedagogy into a mode of counter-hegemonic teaching and theorizing, will be discussed later in Chapter 5.

41 While Freire has always been regarded as a critical pedagogue — indeed, the founder of critical pedagogy throughout the world – in a posthumous work recently published and edited by his daughter, he reveals to us a degreee of his sensitivity toward a post-structuralist examination of linguistics and literacy by the use of the concept of "signifiers," not a unified notion of consciousness. See Paulo Freire, *Daring to Dream: Toward A Pedagogy of the Unfinished.* Edited by Ana Maria Araujo Freire (Boulder, CO: Paradigm Publishers, 2007).

42 For a more detailed discussion on this point of intentional-unintentional forms of consciousness, see pp. 36–38 later in this chapter.

43 I have always been impressed with the pioneering work of Henry Giroux (1980, 1981, 1983, 1991), specifically, on his earlier attempts to locate how hegemony and ideology occur on the terrain of linking agency to structure, subjects to objects, in students and teachers becoming "border crossers" of school disciplinary lines and authority relations of power. While he called for a perspective for signification theories to accomplish this task (1983, p. 113), he never fully developed a theory and practice. A similar call for a complex understanding of semiotic complex meanings has more recently been made by Joe Kincheloe (2003). For more discussion, see the later sections of this chapter. Another goal of this book then is to respond to both calls Giroux and Kincheloe have articulated in developing a "post-hegemonic phase" of critical pedagogy.

44 For example, the work of Dennis Carlson, (2004) shows how various discourses of the macro – transnational capitalism – invades the micro dimensions of school discourse. When this happens, teachers seeking to do more meaningful work with their students in groups, teams or other democratic organizations, come together to run their schools with parents, removed from administrative controls, and set in "dialogical" settings. He reveals that in these local or micro settings, there is already diminished or inadequate focus on the already active circulation of wider or more dominant and powerful discourses operates not in front of but behind their backs. Because of new testing demands by the administration, teachers who wished during the first year of the experiment to be insulated from such demands, by the second year become encased in discourses demanding accountability for increasing student test scores, achievement, and more orderly classroom management styles. Eventually, what promised to be a smaller and more collegiate organization of democratic schooling lapsed into a reflection of the larger parent school, plagued by bureaucratic rules and procedures and a drain on the teachers' time.

As the smaller alternative school within the larger bureaucratic school began the second year, with many of its founders leaving to complete their doctoral studies, Carlson refrains from offering the reader glimpses of the various subject-positions in the nexus of those spaces which invade their school democratic relationships between students and teachers and their attempt to organize themselves without administrators. Carlson also fails to analyze further how chains of signifiers and the subject-positions formed circulating in everyday discourses – "We want more freedom" – once marked on their surfaces by other chains of signifiers, re-inscribing their first chains and subject-position surfaces – "Hey, this democratic thing requires a lot of time and work on administrative details" – emerged and took over or hid alternate glimpses of how contradictions are constituted when a teacher articulates the need for democracy but runs up against the need to increase administrative effort. In these momentary interstices or intersections between overlapping signifiers and their chains, and the effects they have on their subject-positions or identities and discourses, Carlson does not discuss how the trade-off for democracy at the expense of extra effort plays out, including teacher reservations and reluctances to talk further. Carlson does show other forces at work at the point of intersection with several chains, namely, in the trade-off between more democracy and bureaucracy, like how banks, international trade corporations and other forces marginalize students of color as objects to be trained as obedient workers and consumers for the future multi-national service economy.

If Carlson's analysis would have been complemented by post-structural constructs to the extent that their trade-off discourses also produced contradictions wherein certain discursive formations and their respective chains of signifiers combined with more democratic discursive formations and chains of signifiers, then a more complex subject-position would have been formed, avoiding the modernist tendency of a either/or predicament: either stay and fight for democracy or let job-training trump democracy. By mapping out how subject-positions may be constructed and overlaid by contradictory or conflicting subject-positions, student and teacher may have been in a better position to see how linking or taking up subject-positions accepting the new international relations of power (class, race, gender, authority, etc.), also requires them to arrive at different conclusions. Namely, how students and teachers experience democracy versus international capitalisms intrusion into setting their own school agenda (i.e. more testing as opposed to not having so many tests), as these outside demands and pressures cross into their discourses. Under such circumstances, student and teacher in the alternate school may have responded by stipulating demands in which they would dispute and negotiate the degree of required tests to take or not to take and get training in exchange for more power and responsibility. This negotiation or its potential spaces is not disclosed by Carlson.

[45] Anna Marie Smith (1996) defines subject-positions as an intermediary layer between the structured positions people find themselves "thrown into" by virtue of their class, gender, race privilege or non-privilege, and what mediates their so-called "free choice." To Smith, subject-positions form insulations or *lie in between* the world and individuals and groups. Smith further defines subject-positions as "interpretive frames" in which to see the world and its relationships, along with spaces in which people may be" incited" to act in agential ways.

[46] I am reminded of those relationships in which *capos* in Nazi concentrations camps, often aided their higher-ups by facilitating the movement of killing their fellow inmates in order to curry favor or live a few days longer. See Terrence De Pres, *The Survivors* (1972), or, the recent movie, *The Counterfeiters* (2008) in which solidarity amongst inmates often was fractured by fear and the need to accommodate their Nazi overseers.

[47] See my original theorizing on the macro-micro-meso nexus , in an article called: "Approaching a New Paradigm for Critical Educational Theorizing: Penetrating the Macro/Micro Divide – Reflections on Teaching a Core Course" in *Taboo: The Journal of Culture and Education* Vol. 5, Number 1, (Spring-Summer, 2001), pp. 1–16.

[48] As we will further discuss in more detail in a variety of contexts, see Chapter 4.

[49] Anna Marie Smith (196) offers a brilliant example of three women workers in a factory and how their class status as worker does not necessarily correspond to their structural positions when set in a variety of subject-positions based on other power relations, as gender, race, and sexual orientations. As post-structuralists insist, some who are of a post-Marxist persuasion, being located as a worker does not guarantee how their future actions (i.e. as voting or being supportive to and aligned to fellow workers) cannot be dismissed as a form of "false consciousness." Rather, it is a discursive form or a string of words which go back and forth as to how aligned one is to either class, gender, and race causes. This picture of power creates other images as to how structural positions are not monolithic but, because of their other locations in power in a complex of intertwining subject-positions and their reactions to a variety of scenarios, it is unpredictable as to their outcomes when interacting together. Hence, as Laclau and Mouffe (1985) have insisted, there is a need for a new perspective of hegemony for moving toward a more socialist or radical forms of democracy. Further, (Laclau, 1993) also insists that post-structualist theorizing is the best possible way to accomplish this mode of counter-hegemonic theorizing.

[50] See, for example, "Curricular Language and Classroom Meanings (1968)" and "Toward a Remaking of Curricular Language (1974)" in Dwayne Huebner, William Pinar, and Vicki Hillis (eds.), *The*

Lure of the Transcendent: The Collected Essays by Dwayne E. Huebner (Mahwah, New Jersey: Lawrence Erlbaum Publishers, 1999).

[51] See, for example, excellent reviews of how qualitative research can become "constructed" and "critical" in Bodgen and Bilken, 1992; Apple and Roman in Eisner, 1992; Lather, 1991; Carspecken, 1995; Held, 1980; Lincoln, 1992; 2000; Kincheloe, 2003. Since Halsey and Powell (1977) sought a compromise position in which the use of quantitative analysis and data collection had to account for "macro" considerations, and qualitative research had to account for the "micro" or more subjective considerations, several problems remained unresolved as to what to do about those experiences which cut across both micro and macro and transverse the meso? See, for example, Robert Merton's notion of "middle range of theorizing (1971). How in terms of life histories and autobiographical stories and narratives, one can get to see those invisible forces at work which cannot be recorded via a number system.

Starting with the work of Barthes who discloses those "semiological" dimensions of teaching and its codes, signs, and rituals, "psychoanalytical" writers in *Screen Magazine* in the late seventies (Coward & Ellis, 1977; Lacan, 1978; Willemen, 1978), in a debate between with the "culturalist" school led by Stuart Hall (Hall, 1978; Hall & Jefferson, 1976; Willis, 1977) and the "structuralist" school (Althusser, 1971; Coward & Ellis, 1977; Pecheux, 1982; Sharp, 1980) raise some very interesting (some unresolved) questions: What is between truth and interpretation, fact and opinion, objects and subjects? However, with the emergence of postmodernism in the 1980s, a new lens became available in the form of post-structuralist lenses which could better accommodate middle theorizing without having to resort to either paradigm, quantitative or qualitative, culturalist or structuralist (Hall, 1980). For more discussion, see Chapter 4 below.

[52] Jacques Lacan, *The Four Fundamental Concepts of Psycho-Analysis,* Alan Sheridan. Trans. (London, England: Hogarth Press, 1977).

[53] The readings of Louis Althusser and Antonio Gramsci began to interest me in such a problematic. However, when I read some of the secondary sources which cited both Althusser and Gramsci, as Rachel Sharp's *Knowledge, Ideology and the Politics of Schooling* (London, England: Routledge, Kegan, and Paul, 1980), along with Rosalind Coward and John Ellis, *Language and Materialism: Developments in Semiology and the Theory of the Subject* (London, England: Routledge, Kegan, and Paul, 1977), along with the earlier work of Peter Berger and Thomas Luckmann, *The Construction of Social Reality* (New York: Anchor Books, 1966), my curiosity into relations between ideology and reality as mediated by the symbol and sign became even more heightened.

[54] Since reading Lacan, I have also been influenced by other writings of the post-structural genre. These include: Michel Pecheux (1982) – his notion of discursive formation and counter-identifications (1982); Ernesto Laclau (1993, 1995, 1996, 2007 – his notion of equivalent, empty, differential, and floating signifiers constituting subject-positions); and Laclau and Chantel Mouffe (1985) – points of antagonism and points of connection (1985); Ann Marie Smith (1996) – how subject-positions become a mediating screen through which one's structural position is experienced and perceived; Lasse Thomassen (2005) – emphasis on the "tendential" degrees of subject-positions as becoming constituted by the crossing over and interacting of the inscribed – by equivalent and differential, empty and floating signifiers in constructing subject-positions in articulation; and more recently, Slovenj Zizek (1989) notion of quilting points (as opposed to anchoring points) in the *sinthome* experience of the real becoming stitched to the symbolic and imaginary experiences of the subject.

[55] Commenting on both Althusser's notion of *interpellation* in which a subject is "called" or frozen into place or a subject-position as one is "hailed" or how one freezes to attention because a person of authority calls upon one, Ashcroft (2001) perceives a different route possible; not interpellation but interpolation. He theorizes that subjects may "journey into" and alter the effects of being inter-pellated by altering the nature of subject-positions, and other structures and processes of discourse. For many illustrations I facilitated with my special education students and education students, see Chapter 4.

56 The experience of being in or taking a subject-position is akin to the fluidity of: just as one thinks they are taking a position, they are already taking another position, as a another thought intertwines itself on another chain of signifiers, crossing into their consciousness. Or, as Zizek (1989) refers of *che vuoi?*: what do you want? I mean what do you really want; what is bugging you? — releases another thread or chain of thought which penetrates, perhaps, overtakes or leaves a trace on the original thought in action.

57 Many of my undergraduate students seek to become teachers. They are already teacher aides, paraprofessionals, and substitute teachers in regular public, private, and religious schools as well as in day care centers. Some are also parents, carrying on a full load of courses, along with full-time jobs. Others are already full time teachers and administrators (if taking a course on the graduate level). While I cannot know to what extent their knowledge and life-experiences can assist in theorizing and advancing a body of critical knowledge, I am mindful of Freire's admonition that without those in the field, in the teaching trenches with their students and their parents, without trusting the people we write about and do our research on, there is no basis for positing as a problem oppression or hegemony or, for that matter, developing a theory (Freire, 2002).

While Freire used the term "hegemony" twice to signify oppression (Freire, 2002, pp. 141 and 162), after reading Freire, many of my students spoke and depicted in their artwork a notion of hegemony as "false consciousness." This effectively removed, as a starting point, the immediate spaces on which they could identify themselves as counter-hegemonic theorizers and teachers. Either they knew the "true" state consciousness or they were manipulated by those others who made them take "false" forms of consciousness. The students were ready to accept this duality as unsolvable, a part of "human nature," or too fearful of a system which would eliminate them for having the audacity to question such aspects of schools and teaching.

Many others took on a perspective which included that ideology was not merely a "false" basis of thinking, that they were fooled or duped into a "false consciousness" by the "powers-to-be." These students refused to think they could be fooled, and insisted that their notions of "belief" and their "opinions" were inherently insulated by their being essentially "free," and therefore, could not be manipulated. Divided between these two apparent extremes, I reasoned with them that irrespective of both positions, people do follow authority, either from the state, the economy, advertising media and images of the popular culture, and in the schools. Indeed, they conceded that while they think they are free, they are afraid to "say the wrong thing." As they often felt there was or would be others in the schools "spying" on them.

But, in between these two ranges of perception, I sought to introduce my students in a "third space," acting as an intermediary zone of possibility and transformation of the archaic yet dominant system we all knew and agreed was hierarchical, unjust, unequal, and oppressive.

58 See Kristen Hussey, "More Schools Miss the Mark, Raising Pressure" in *New York Times*, October 12. 2008, and Sam Dillon, "Under No Child's Law, Even Solid Schools Falter" in *New York Times*, October 13, 2008.

59 I have been personally been involved in a coalition of parent groups in New York City who resisted Mayor Bloomberg's testing program for third graders in alignment with President Bush's No Child Left Behind piece of national legislation demanding progressive improvement of test scores. This testing package was presented to parents in New York City with the punitive proviso if their children did not pass the test, they would be required to attend summer school at their 7th year of life. This assessment was partly aimed as urban populations who are multi-raced, and who, to date, are not doing as well as their suburban white counterparts. Also reported a few years earlier by the Consumer Advocate of New York City and others organizations as *Fair Testing, Time Out from Testing*, and *Classroom Size Matters*, there is growing evidence to show that the increasing regimen of testing has produced amongst poor, black, and Hispanic students a phenomena of children being "pushed out" from the student attendance rosters, or those who get lost as a statistic, producing the effect of increasing school averages in test scores. See *Pushing Out At Risk Students: Discharge*

Figures. A Report by the Public Advocate for the City of New York and Advocates for Children, Report compiled by Betsy Gutbaum, Public Advocate and Commissioner, November 21, 2002.

[60] Compare back to back test scores in New York, one school flipping from F to A grades, then, another school reversing this trend in the same locale, A to F. These tests are constructed by local school authorities, namely the New York Board of Education. See, Elissa Gootman" Low Grade For a School of Successes," *New York Times,* September 12, 2008, pp. B1, B5. Or, see Javier C. Hernandez, "A School's Grade Plummets, and the Parents are Confused" in *New York Times,* September 23, 2008, pp. B1, B6.

[61] On this subject of qualified teachers, I have had the opportunity to interview many of my students – some of whom have been practicing teachers in the New York City area for years – and asked them to come and speak to my present students who are aspiring but worried new teachers. Their stories, eye-witness accounts of what is going on in schools these days, is rather shocking. They describe a "police state" operating on teachers and their working conditions; others describe an intense competitive atmosphere in which one school competes against another, principals get bonuses and teachers get fired or transferred for not having better test results. In one case, a teacher's wages were deducted because she started her class a few minutes late in each period. Her class was observed by the principal who noted that the minutes lost accrued to 15 minutes for the entire day. Attempts were made to deduct that portion of time from her wages. For other stories on par with this story, see Jennifer Medina, "Teachers to be Measured on Student Standardized Test Scores in *New York Times,* October 2, 2008, B3. After emphasizing so many measurement criteria by complex statistical formulae, one principal in the school ended the article by stating: "I don't think anything (including test scores and their complex statistical formulas) can replace getting into the class (to really see what is happening)."

[62] See Raymond Callahan, *The Cult Efficiency* (Boston, MASS: Beacon Press,1961), Deborah Meir, *Will Standards Save Public Education?* (Boston, MASS: Beacon Press, 2000), and Susan Ohanian, *One Size Fits Few: The Folly of Educational Standards* (Portsmouth, NH: Heineman, 1999). More recently, a film revealing the harmful effects of constant and frequent standardized testing on young students is shown in Alfie Kohn and Ted Sizer's *Standardized Testing in Our Schools*, 1995. 60 minutes and *No Child Left Behind* (New York: Boondoggle Film DVD, 2004), 60 minutes.

[63] See Sam Dillon, "Schools Cut Back Subjects to Push Reading and Math" in *New York Times*, March 25, 2006, pp. 1A; Sam Dillon; "Survey Finds Teenagers Ignorant on Basic History and Literature Questions" in *New York Times*, February 27, 2008.

[64] Howard Witt, "School Discipline Tougher on African Americans" in *Chicago Tribune*, September, 25, 2007. There is an interesting set of articles indicating how, in Japan, young students are beginning to resist school regimentation as standardized testing by acting up in a mode of behavior called "yoiko." See Howard W. French, "Educators Try to Tame Japan's Blackboard's Jungles" in *New York Times*, September 21, 2004, A5. Also, other articles are referring to how special education students are being forced to take the same tests and their regular student counterparts, of often sitting in the back and crying. See Kristen Hussey, "More Schools Miss the Mark, Raising Pressure" *New York Times*, October 14, 2008,

[65] See Lee Fleischer, "Emphasizing Classroom Management at the Expense to the Detriment of Theory" in *The Academic Forum,* Journal at New Jersey City University, Vol. 14, No. 2, Spring, 2006, pp. 26–28.

[66] See Gerald Graff and Cathy Birkenstein, "A Progressive Case for Educational Standardization" Academe Online, May/.June 2008, http://www.aaup.org/AAUP/pubsres/academe/2008/MJ/Feat/graf.htm

[67] See how a teacher refused to administer a high stake exam to his students and how in some charter schools, the teacher (not the administrator) "rules." See. For example, Carl Chew, "Seattle Teacher Refuses to Administer WASL Test to Students," in Seattle Teacherctchew@earthlink.net, April20, 2008 and Sarah Carr (2005).

[68] It is for this reason, understanding student resistance, I often expose my students to a famous article on the subject. See Robert Everhart, Classroom Management and Student Resistance" in Michael Apple and Lois Weiss (eds.) *Ideology and Schooling* (Philadelphia, PA: Temple University Press, 1983), pp. 169–192 ; and, Patricia Whang's "Disrupting Discipline" in Joe Kincheloe (ed.) *Teaching: Introduction* (New York: Peter Lang Publishers, 2005), pp. 195–206.

[69] I have written on how system approaches to conceptualizing the principal as a support of teacher dialogue may, insidiously, creep into management/supervision/professional development discourses as disguising the extent students and teachers are controlled and manipulated in classroom discourse. See Lee Fleischer, "A Critique of Ann Lieberman's Article as an Expression of Liberal-Humanist Ideolog and its Concern for Teacher Behavior Change Management and Improvement" in *Left Open: A Student Newsletter and Emancipatory Collective*, published by the Teachers College Student Caucus, No. 3, May, 1978, pp. 15–18. The findings of this article will be discussed in this chapter as a case study below reflecting many of observations of instructors who have been or who are current school administrators.

[70] While I cannot reveal the source of this citing, shared in confidentiality with me from a dean of a school of education, and a dean of student discipline, who told me: "If you get a bad rating by some of your students, then get other students who like you to rate you better." I have also seen on these websites students who reacted to a "good" teacher rating and evaluation with their own curt and self-serving remarks, as "This teacher probably wrote this herself or himself." It is very doubtful whether this informal but very public vehicle will promote student-teacher solidarity, trust, care, cooperation, and critical thinking, much less aid counter-hegemonic struggles and strategies in and out of schools of education and secondary public schools, as more and more of this same vehicle is currently being extended to secondary schools throughout the nation.

[71] While I would have liked to have a discussion on the meaning of tenure – its merits and pitfalls – (along with the exploitative conditions of being an adjunct instructor, which I presently am) – and specifically, why, in the process of gaining tenure, there are few instructors and teachers who are likely to speak out; and conversely, once they have attained tenure, many still remain silenced. Since tenure was created to protect the freedom of speaking out one's mind in terms of "academic freedom" and not fearing dismissal, the irony we have here is: when one finally attains tenure, they generally remain reticent, timid and prone not to speak out. When they seek tenure, they simply shut up. One has to ask then: Why have tenure if the reasons why it was created to safeguard educators from being arbitrarily dismissed for their beliefs and statements, controversial or not, are not exercised? I would address this issue more systematically in terms of hegemony in a subsequent book, *Counter-Hegemony II*, which when published may bring teachers and professors together to join with me their perspectives on this and other critical issues of hegemonic schooling.

For recent information on the issue of tenure as potentially hegemonic, see Alan Finder, "Decline of the Tenure Track raises Concern at Colleges" in *New York Times*, November 20, 2007, pp. A12, A16; David Perlmutter, "The Joyless Quest for Tenure" in *The Chronicle of Higher Education*, November 30, 2007, pp. C1–C4; Wendy M. Williams and Stephen J. Ceci, "Does Tenure Really Work? in *The Chronicle of Higher Education*, March 9, 2007, p. B16; Patricia Chen, "On Campus, the '60s Begin to Fade as Liberal Professors Retire," in *New York Times*, July 3, 2008, pp. A1, A20; Barbara A. Lee and Judith A. Malone, "The Aging Professoriate" in *The Chronicle of High Education*," November 20, 2007, pp. B6–B7. Sam Dillon, "A School Chief Takes on Tenure, Stirring a Fight" in New York Times, November 13, 2008, pp. A1–A25.

[72] I am impressed with the use of the term "stitched" as it applies to stitching discourses together in complex ways in an institutional school setting. See Bryant Griffiths, "Stitching the Layers of Our Cultural Discourses" in Bryant Griffith, *Cultural Narration* (Rotterdam, Netherlands: Sense Publishers, 2008), pp. 81–104.

[73] For inconsistencies of test results, its links to teacher re-hiring and firings, bonuses for principals, and the validity of the tests and the meaning of their results, along with the ongoing controversies about testing kids too early of age as well as too much for any age, see Erin Einhorn, "Bad Schools Getting Shut – & Principals Getting Bonuses, *Daily News*, June 29, 2007; Carl Chew, "Seattle

Teacher Refuses to Administer WASL Test to Students," in Seattle Teacherctchew@earthlink.net, April20, 2008; Elizabeth Green, "Study Sought of Test Gains in N.Y." in *The Sun*, July 3, 2008; Winnie Hsu, "Where the Race (for Testing) Now Begins at Kindergarten" in *New York Times*, August 6, 2008; Daniel Koreta, "Interpreting Test Scores More Complicated Than You Think in *Chronicle of Higher Education*, August 15, 2008, p. A23; Susan Hobart, One Teachers Cry: Why I Hate No Child Left Behind, *The Progressive*, August, 2008; Elissa Gootman, "Mixed Results on Paying City Students to Pass Tests, *New York Times*, August 20, 2008; Jennifer Medina and Ellisa Gootman, "Plan to Give Standardized Tests to City's Youngest Pupils Stirs Criticism" in *New York Times*, August 27, 2008; Elissa Gootman, "In Brooklyn, Low Grade for a School of Successes," *New York Times*, September 12, 2008; Javier Hernandez, "A School's Grade Plummets, and Parents are Confused" in *New York Times*, September 22, 2008; Jenifer Medina, "Teachers to be Measured Based on Students' Standardized Test Scores," in *New York Times*, October 2, 2008; Kristen Hussey, "More Schools Miss the Mark, Raising Pressure," *New York Times*, October 12, 2008; Sam Dillon, "Under 'No Child' Law, Even Solid Schools Falter, New York Times, October 13, 2008; Jennifer Medina, "Making Cash a Prize for High Scores on Advanced Placement Test" in *New York Times*, October 15, 2007; Jennifer Medina and Elissa Gootman, "New York Schools Brace to be Scored, A to F" in *New York Times*, November 4, 2007 Elissa Gootman and Jennifer Medina, "50 New York Schools Fail Under New Rating System," *New York Times*, November 6, 2007.

[74] For the differences between "patriotic" and "radical" renditions of social studies, see Larry Scheikart and Michael Allen., *A Patriot History of the United States: From Columbus' Great Discovery to the War on Terrorism* (England: Sentinel Press, 2007) amd Howard Zinn's *A People's History of the United States: 1492-Present* (New York: Harpers Perrenial, 2003).

[75] See Sam Dillon, "Survey Finds Teenagers Ignorant on Basic History and Literature Questions" in *New York Times*, February 27, 2008, p. A16.

[76] My sponsor, Dwayne Heubner, in the many meetings I had with him, in late 1976, recommended to me Rosalind Coward and John Willis' *Language and Materialism: Developments in Semiology and the Theory of the Subject* (Boston, MASS: Routledge, Kegan, and Paul, 1977), along with other articles of the late-1970s related to the works of Jacques Lacan, and others.

[77] In schools of education today, classroom management has taken on a reverse position in which the students control the instructors rather than the other way around. Wedged between deans and school administrators and students, instructors are becoming more and more "sitting ducks" or targets to undergo assaults of massive pressure exerted by usually very conservative students. In addition, through pending legislation (H.R. 3077) which encourage only specific types of conversations related to social studies, and encourages students to report on their teachers to the authorities if their teachers are too radical or proselytizing. Along with websites, as www.ratemyproifessor.com, and books as David Horowitz (2006) *The Professors: The 101 Most Dangerous Academics in America*, there remains "a clear and present danger" of teacher educators becoming censored and restricting their speech in teacher education courses.

For example, a colleague of mine (name withheld), who underwent the most grueling critique and attack of her person and professionalism was cited as one of the most "dangerous" professors in the United States by David Horowitz's Professors (2006) book, along in the press for claiming that English may predispose people to be members of the oppressor class upon their use of its formal syntax in the English language. See Jacob Gershman, "'Disposition' Emerges as Issue" in the *New York Sun*, May 31, 2005. In another chapter I had published (2004) on how the formal form of English grammar may also be "hegemonic" in terms of de-politicizing students and teachers as they "write into fear."

[78] See Lee Fleischer, "A Critique of Ann Lieberman's Article as an Expression of Liberal-Humanist Ideology and its Concern for Teacher Behavior Change management and Improvement" in *Left Open: Newsletter of the Emancipatory Collective*, Vol. 1, No. 3 (May, 1978), pp. 15–18.

[79] While this article written in the 1970s cannot be lumped into other "constructivist" approaches to school leadership then and since then, the author does hold similarities with other humanistic and

"constructivist" works of the 1970s to the present. Specifically, the works of Sergiovanni and Starrett (1974), Henderson (1998), and Lambert (1995) have commonalities in which they all presuppose a unified and originary notion of a subject and limited frames of teacher dialogue and decision-making (to be discussed in detail in Chapter 4). That is, without considering those forces which limit dialogue within hierarchical and hegemonic discursive forces or force fields, my critique sought to uncover and re-frame dialogical forms of leadership by incorporating post-structural features of how language interacts with ideology. I began to do this by positing dialogue within (not outside of) discursive formations which lead to hegemonic and counter-hegemonic forms of school leadership, although I did not mention such constructs at this time. I did, however, by the late 1990s published a series of articles that do name this discursive forces and forms (Fleischer, 1998, 1999, 2000, 2001a, 2001b, 2003, 2004, 2005, 2007).

[80] Also, upon reading chapters in Clarence Karier, Joel Spring, and Paul Violas, *Roots of Crisis: New Direction of Twentieth Century Education* (Chicago, Illinois: McRandy , 1973) insofar as their notion of capitalists deploy controls by means of making workers or employees "substitute – supervisors."

[81] Foucault's notion of the panoptican (1977b) or how prisons in France were staffed by few guards positioned in a circular fashion around a cylinder of prison cells in which the inmates were given the impression that they were watched all the time.

[82] I have changed the name of this student because she feared her tenure and eligibility for a pension she had saved for the last thirty years would be endangered by the school authorities. Hence, her name for purposes of protecting her identity is called Linda.

[83] See Elissa Gootman, "At Charter School, Higher Teacher Pay in New York Times, March 7, 2008, and Sarah Carr, Where Teachers Rule" in the *Milwaukee Journal Sentinel*, July 18, 2005 and http://jsonline.com/story.aspx?id=34127

[84] Stephen B, McCarney, Pre-Referral Intervention Manual: The Most Common Problems Encountered in the Educational Environment (Columbia, MO: Hawthorne Educational Services, 1993).

[85] See Harry and Rosemary Wong, *The First Days of School: How To Be an Effective* Teacher (Mountain View, CA: Harry K. Wong Publications, 2004); Patricia Whang, "Disrupting Discipline" in Joe Kincheloe, *Classroom Teaching: An Introduction* (New York: Peter Lang, 2005), pp. 195–206; Robert Everhart, "Classroom Management, Student Opposition, and the Labor Process" in Michael Apple and Lois Weiss (eds.), *Ideology and Practice in Schooling* (Philadelphia, PA: Temple University Press, 1983), pp. 169–192.

[86] For example, under category #177, p. 377: "Allow the student to speak without being interrupted or hurried....#3; "Have the student keep a list of times and/or situations in which he/she is nervous, anxious, etc......" These lists reminded me of Connors Chart – i.e. does the student day dream, figget, stare, etc. – in which teachers and guidance counselors check off dozens of behavioral characteristics of students as a survey instrument before referring them into special education via Child Study Committees.

[87] In fairness to Charlie, he at least relies on some form of classroom management on a basis of basic cognition – reading numbers and applying which rule best fits the infraction of student behavior according to the judgment of the teacher. What is worse, as a recent interview of a young and new urban teacher recounts of her training by her principal is: one may innovate "clapping" one's hands the moment of class becomes rowdy by "snapping" one's fingers instead. The article further insists that teachers should avoid "power struggles" with students. As we shall we engage *Counter-Hegemonic Teaching*, these practices and innovations are precisely the opposite" of the perspective offered. While the article insists that teachers should avoid power struggles and politics with students, we disagree. What perspective is offered here is: by treating students as holding real power themselves, we may avoid treating as mere objects of behaviorist change. See http://www.rethinkingschools.org/archive/23_02/door232.shtml

[88] See Howard Witt, "School Discipline Tougher on African Americans" in *The Chicago Tribune*, September 25, 2007 or http:www.chicagotribune.com/news/nationworld/chi–70924discipline,1,6597576.

story?ctrack=1&cset=true. Also, I will further discuss these links of classroom management to racial discrimination in a section below as a controversial topic which raised many outspoken discussions in my education classes. As it turned out, these discussions stirred up troubles in my own classroom management style insofar as allowing as many varying points of view to be articulated.

[89] At this teacher's request, I am using a pseudonym or the name Linda to represent her real name.

[90] As former graduate student of mine in another university, Linda has also helped me co-teach a course preparing para's for special education. As a result of working closely with Linda, I know her well and trust her and that her story is real, corroborated, and legitimate.

[91] Some of my students represented Linda's story in their assignment to illustrate (after reading Freire's *Pedagogy of the Oppressed*) by picturing how the teacher is berated by the school administrator in front of students meant – See Figures in Chapter 3. Surprisingly, however, when I examined their artwork depicting Linda's predicament, they sided with both the principal and students, stating that in their Caribbean school systems, generally, very conservative systems of the "British Model," as they called it, the headmaster rules with a iron fist. More on this discussion will be cited in the following section below, insofar as re-examining student resistances and student evaluations of college teacher educators.

[92] See Howard French, "Educators Try to Tame Japan's Blackboard Jungles, *New York Times*, September 23, 2004, A5.

[93] Given the "testing craze" for last fifteen years, and more severely heightened by the legislation *of No Child Left Behind*, there has also been an emphasis on "bringing in the principals" to raise test scores and presumably, by the numbers, bridging the achievement gap. See, Diane Ravitch, "Bring In the Principals: Give Them the Power and They Will Do the Job" in *Daily News*, June 16, 2002.

However, according to Kozol (2005) and the Twenty Year Studies under the Civil Rights Division monitoring the re-segregation patterns of schools (Orfield, 2001), one may see a pattern emerging between increasing standardized testing (due to a fear Americans will fall behind their foreign student counterparts needed to compete in the new global markets) and, ironically, the widening of the achievement gap in terms of schools becoming more re-segregated.

[94] I owe this advice to my former boss at Brooklyn College and the Assistant Dean of the School of Education, and my evaluator and friend, Dr. Peter Taubman. I am also equally indebted to my former social studies high school supervisor, Chair of the Department of Social Studies at Oceanside High School, Oceanside, New York, who observed and "wrote me up" over a dozen times during my first year of teaching in the late 1960s. He also inspired me with his new book at the time, done in collaboration with Herb Robb, a history professor at Queens College of the City University of New York, entitled most fittingly, *From Left to Right: Readings of the Socio-Political Spectrum* (New York: Benziger Press, 1966). Active in leading an anti-war movement in the late 1960s, Ray Sobel, along with Congressperson Allard Lowenstein and actor Robert Vaughn – (*Man from U.N.C.L.E.*) engaged the entire high school student population in an anti-war graduation ceremony against the Viet-Nam War in 1968, the first of such activities conducted throughout the state.

[95] See, for example the very interesting article by Thomas H. Benton, "Fearing Our Students " in *The Chronicle of Higher Education*, December 14, 2007, pp. C1–C2 and David Holberg, "Student Evaluations" in the *New York Times Magazine*, July 1, 2007, p. 18. Also, the interview with Larry King and Michael Hussey, the Chief Executive Officer of www.RateMyProfessor.com CNN, July, 2008 *Turner Network News*. In this interview Mr. Hussey mistook the NEA as the chief accrediting agency of colleges rather than NCATE. He also indicated that a similar venue will be spreading to high school and middle schools.

[96] Jonathan Kozol, "Still Separate, Still Unequal: America's Educational Apartheid" in *Harper's Magazine* v. 311, no. 1864, September, 1, 2005, 35 pages.

[97] Gary Orfield, Schools More Separate: Consequences of a Decade of Re-segregation in *Re-Thinking Schools* (Volume 16, No. 1, Fall, 2001).

[98] Robert Lowe, "Backpedaling Toward Plessy, in Re-Thinking Schools (Volume 22, No. 1, Fall, 2007).

99　See the contents of zonal laws as they offer both lower and moderate income families opportunities to rent or own a house and secure a mortgage, gauged to their incomes, see Title II of the Cranston-Gonzalez Affordable Housing Act in http://hud.gov/offices/affordable housing/programs/home/index.cfm Similar legislation, programs, and entitlements exit in many states. See in New York State, http://www.cityofuntica.com/Economic Development/HOMEProgram.org

100　More on the discussion of these codes via how subject-positions may be inscribed on their surfaces in various "tendential" degrees will be discussed in Chapter 4.

101　While I have always taught about "redlining" or the practice in which real estate and bank employees "unofficially" decide who they want to show or sell a house to or offer a mortgage, this student's reference to "zoning laws" appears to overlay or mystify what she means by "zoning laws," or perhaps, inadvertently, are expressing facts which do not exist other than her prejudices or other de facto discriminatory practices she may be practicing – as, for example, blaming zoning laws for white flight when its intent was the very opposite.

102　As I have mentioned in another one of my publications (2007), technology mediating today's classroom may have the effect of students no longer looking at each other. Rather, because they are saturated with the omnipresent computer screen, they face only the computer. This tendency to look at an inanimate object as opposed to fellow student classmates, may have the effect which may breach into potential student-student and student-teacher solidarity and relationship. In addition the fact that there are so many hotlinks when reading a document to be researched, often leads students not to focus on an in-depth area of study – being distracted by so many tangents in each links which brings to the researcher student, sidestepping their original goals and journey. For more information on this subject, see Laura Lamash, "Social History, Technology, and the Building of Inclusive Classroom Communities, (2004)."

103　In fairness to Freire, as the educational minister of San Paulo, Brazil, he was able to organize de-centralized and bring about democratic forms of school governance through assemblies of students, parents, and teachers, thereby overcoming what he projected as "delegated" in theory twenty years earlier. See Paulo Freire, *Pedagogy of the City* (New York: Continuum, 1993).

104　To Freire, 'the unity of the elite (oppressor) derives (its power) from its antagonism with the people; the unity of the revolutionary leadership group grows out of communion with the (united) people. Yet, in this struggle, there is for Freire little latitude for a struggle for gaining adherents from the oppressed, already "marked" group, who are embedded or "housing" an image of the oppressor as internalized and adhesed to.

Grounding his position on modernist chains of either-or images: either you are an oppressor or you are an oppressed, denies, according to post-structural theorizing, a complex, overlaying, and intersecting images of both oppressor and oppressed in which one experiences both forces, simultaneously and intermittently, in hybrid group associations or mixed experiences. While Freire does not trust this "ambiguity," he maintains an either-or presentation: you are with us in communion or remain too vulnerable to be trusted to work with. As one who is a member of the latter group – one marked by the oppressor – there is always a chance that such a subject may undergo slippage and slide back into a regressive forms of consciousness, as penetrated by the oppressor in one's unconsciousness. Freire, once again, does not trust or relies upon such members of the oppressed group for mounting a mass-based popular movement opposed to oppression and hegemony. As we will discuss in the following chapter, and as we see with Smith (1996), Laclau (2007), and Thomassen (2005), the surfaces of subject-positions are always in states of flux and simultaneously share mixed, opposed, and even contradictory subject-positions, identities, and various forms of incitements or what makes subjects act in agential actions as they articulate, de-articulate, and re-articulate their positions of being oppressed or otherwise controlled and dominated as well as seeking spaces for new alliances in which to resist their domination, oppression, and the their general hegemonic conditions.

105　As Howard Zinn recently spoke about how America under the new Obama administration will have to act up and take power in their vocal cries, meeting in groups, and their larger organizations pressuring to be heard and get what they want. Zinn advised his audience that while they may be in the habit of assuming the interests of the government is coincidental to their interests, historically, this is not always the case. Zinn also reminded the audience, the interests of the government are not necessarily the interests of the people. See Interview with Howard Zinn and excerpts of his lecture at the State University of New York at Binghamton, November 5, 2008, in Amy Goodman's *Democracy Now*, PBS-TV, www.democracynow.org

[106] See Giroux & Saltman, 2008), http://webmail.aol.com/40627/aol/en-us/Mail/printmessage.aspx).

[107] As a movie I recently saw, called *Doubt (2008)* indicated by the priest sermonizing his congregation in the early 1960s, seeking to break through the hegemonic constraints of traditional education and traditional liturgy, said: "Doubt is just as powerful and sustaining as certainty." This young priest may have used the same sermon to teach those empirical and psychometric educators in charge with our nation's most recent reforms today in having kids tested over and over again to achieve some artificial and positivistic goals which are neither real nor true nor valid, given the popular opposition growing in the last eight years to *No Child Left Behind* and its regressive and harmful effects on children and their teachers. See works of Wood, et. al (2004), Kohn and Sizer (2002), and Meirer (1999).

[108] As Anna Marie Smith (1996) informs us, a subject-position is an intermediate position between our own self identities and those identities ascribed or assigned to us by larger corporate or school structures of authority. As such, one can see those finer points of transaction between what one assumes and expects is their work role, and how such assumptions and expectations become constructed in the intersections between structural positions and subject-positions of self as well as how these positions interact with others undergoing the same process, albeit unequally, experiencing oppression from whence they are assigned in the hierarchical organization structures of assigned positions.

More concretely, but taken from a another subject-position, imagine as you think and speak, suddenly you get an idea which passes through you or your consciousness. While the idea is passing through you, and as you are engaged with another speaker at the moment, you have already begun to think or experience another idea.

[109] See Henry Giroux, "Paulo Freire and The Politics of Post-Colonialism" in Peter McLaren and Peter Leonard, (eds.) *Paulo Freire: A Critical Encounter* (New York: Routledge, 1993), pp. 177–187.

[110] See Donaldo Macedo's "Introduction" to Paulo Freire's 30th Anniversary of *Pedagogy of the Oppressed* (New York: Continuum Press, 2002), pp. 11–28.

[111] For further clarification on Pecheux's theories of discourse and discursive formations see Hennessey, (1993); MacDonnel (1986); P. Smith (1988): and Strickland (2005). While Pecheux theorizes discourse as consisting of constituent metonymic signifiers and chains, Laclau (2007) understands discourse within equivalent and differential chains, as well as empty or master signifiers and fragmented or floating signifiers which may provide the beginning materials to construct new equivalent chains in which to dominate or hegemonize the discursive field. More to be discussed in Chapter 4.

[112] See Chapter 5, for more discussion on Pecheux (1982), Laclua (2007), and Zizek (1989) which attempts to move their theoretical insights forward in areas of research which grounds post-structuralist theory and practices of research of hegemony and counter-hegemonic – areas that are ideological and more fitting for the stand-stills of human inaction despite circumstances which warrant human activity and intervention. These areas have been pointed to by Giroux since the early 1980s (1980, 1981, 1983).

[113] See, for example, the recent work of Sherry Turkle (ed.), *Evocative Objects: Things We Think With* (Cambridge, MASS: MIT Press, 2007), and Slavoj Zizek, *The Sublime of Object of Ideology* (New York: Verso Press, 1989).

[114] As Macedo reports in his Introduction of the 2002 edition of *Pedagogy of the Oppressed*, he and Freire were collaborating on a new book, *Ideology Matters*, until Freire's untimely death. What ideology means to Freire and Macedo – a reflection of false (versus true) consciousness rather than a more post-structuralist and complex notion of hegemony in which discourses and their formations and thought processes combine to serve as a base for a less unified notion of consciousness as interacting with complex formulations of race intersected by class, class intersected by gender, race, and class intersected by authority, and so forth, remains a moot question. *Counter-Hegemonic Teaching* then also seeks to fill in some of these spaces left vacant by Freire and Macedo.

[115] Freire's *Pedagogy of the Oppressed*, for example, offers an insight in the first two chapters, but does not outline the processes of how such circumstances arise in revealing that there is a parallel development between the oppressor and the oppressed. That is, how student and teacher may break their "existential duality" or their desire to want to excel by becoming oppressors of the oppressed, or outcompete fellow students; or, in the case of teachers, gain tenure and monetary rewards for high student test scores outcomes.

While Freire does not address how one may see the binary oppositions between winners and losers – or know how to recognize contradictions not as oppositions generated by some vague reference to cognition as initiated by an intentional , unified, and solitary consciousness, there is much in the post-structural literature that urges us to take notice that how one appropriates knowledge and cognition, but still persists in acting on a course that is already recognized by one as counter and self-defeating (Zizek, 1989, 2008). We know, for example, that it is not wise to do what we do, but we do it anyway! In this gap between what we know and do, reflect and act, lies (according to post-structuralists) another form of knowledge that examines how modernist chains of signifiers maintain contradictory behaviors and reactions without further explaining why these binary chains persist. The recent work of Joe Kincheloe broaches this problem in a most elegant and historical manner when reaching back to the days of Descartes (Kincheloe, 2004a, 2004b, 2005, 2007).

The present study, however, seeks to ground critical thinking on a counter-hegemonic basis of post-structural theorizing in examining how multiple and complex processes of consciousness are linked to discourses and their discursive formations. The present study also seeks to show how these linkages are bridged together by intra-, inter-, and trans-discourses circulating between and within discursive formations in metonymic "flashes" or "fleeting" moments in chains of signifiers, linked to hierarchical and unconscious acts. These metonymic signifiers are further linked to layers of discourses constructed and intertwined into more layers of subject-positions and their surfaces. This complex arrangement of chains, links, subject-positions and their surfaces is what makes up a discursive formation to Pecheux (1982), and according to the writer, are the various discursive formations – some hierarchical-maintaining, others as countering the hegemony of hierarchies in the everyday validations and non-validations of a school system. See Chapter 4 for further documentation by Laclau as to how these complex formations operate in non-school but in historical and politically institutional contexts.

[116] In their well circulated and used textbook, *Looking into Classrooms*, 10th Edition (Pearson, Allyn & Bacon, 2008), p. 297, Thomas Good and Jere Brophy insist that much of the standardized testing operating for the last seven years may have produced more harm than help in closing the achievement gap. Both authors insist that what can be done within the crunch to always teaching-for-the-test is to abbreviate many required units so that constructive discussion may occur in one's classroom. For example, teach by abbreviating units on reading and math, so that there is time for social studies discussions in which students may take "ownership" of the subject-matter and learn by principles of constructivism. While this solution does not account for those reprisals led by hierarchical administrators and the pressures they will wield against resistant teachers, it, at least, offers one alternative, albeit not very satisfying one in today's onerous and oppressive classroom conditions dominated by top-down teaching-for- the-test regimes.

[117] Taken as an insight developed by Paul Gilroy in *There Ain't No Black in the Union Jack* (Chicago, Illinois: University of Chicago Press, 1987), notions of both displacement and condensation may be used as "syncretisms" or ways to "journey into" the complex caverns of overlaying discourses disguising or opening up new avenues for re-examining the significance of Western colonization patterns on native peoples as they were colonized and how these behaviors at present continue to persist in post-colonized times, in which counter-identifications and self-defeating actions amongst former colonized occur and which the oppressed become oppressors or how the former oppressed become each other's oppressors.

[118] The notions of "floating signifiers" or differential chains of signifiers and "empty signifiers" and equivalent chains of signifiers are further discussed in Chapter 4 when Laclau (2007) and Thomassen's (2001) analyses are brought to bear in the present study.

[119] I would rather use the terms "the journey in" as used by Said (in Ascroft, 2001); or "syncretize" as used by Gilroy (in Smith, p. 96) or "third spaces" as used by Bhahba (in Baker, Diawara, and Lindeborg 1996) or articulation as used in Smith 1996. Freire also uses the term (without explanation) " syncretize" in *Pedagogy of the Oppressed.*

John Ascroft's treatment of the concept of interpolation as opposed to interpellation describes how interstices or tiny spaces wedge between flexible joints or integuments connect parts to each other and the whole. For our purposes, we can use Ascroft's (2001) invention of "interpolation" to superimposed onto the notion of chains and how, as in metonymic relations of signifiers, the process of articulation may operate as a process of guiding or mapping inscribers of subject-position surfaces into the complex circulation of signifying chains and the subject-position layers of discourse they carve out (see Coward & Ellis, 1977; Laclau, 2007; Thomassen, 2005). According to political post-structuralist philosophers (Laclau & Mouffe, 1985), there are always contingencies or leaks and residues into which one may penetrate further and "see" into the "multifarious layers" how these tiny spaces offer themselves up as contingent powers available to trigger collective agential actions as well as counter-reactions. For more discussion see chapters in John Ascroft, "Resistances" and "Interpolation" in *Post-Colonial Transformation* (New York: Routledge, 2001), pp. 18–44, 45–56.

[120] For more extensive discussion, see Lee Fleischer, "Emphasizing Classroom Management to the Detriment of Theory" in *The Academic Forum of New Jersey City University*, Vol. 14, No. 2 (Spring, 2006), pp. 26–28.

[121] In this regard, my conversations with the special education high school students participating in my doctoral research revealed these complex components of signification. In a focus group setting, the students talked about their desire to become successful and own Mercedes cars. In the midst of these discussions, as if in a flash of consciousness or a second thought intruding into their first thought, one student noted, "poor people never look back and care for those they leave behind, when they succeed and get wealthy." Then, in another moment, another student added: "Yeah, those who need the most help get the least, and those who need the least help, get the most." Finally, another student followed with: "I guess it's the Mercedes that counts." This remark led the students to discuss and draw lines or "chains" of "me," "we," and "them" subject-positions in a succession of overlaying lines or chains. These successive lines or chains led to a transformatory discussion in which the students felt they could trace overlapping thoughts ranging from oppression or "one-downing others" – special education students labeling each other as "slow" – to establishing a community of respect and care for all.

[122] See Chapter 4 for detailed analysis of these students. Also, see, Lee Fleischer, "Living in Contradiction: Stories of Special Education Students," *unpublished dissertation,* Teachers College, Columbia University, 1998, 317 pages.

[123] See, for example, Adrianne Appel, "Where Have the Bailout Billions Gone? (December 17, 2008) in http://ipsnews.net/news.asp?idnews=45152

[124] Once again in fairness to Freire and the recent efforts by Freire and his successors, there is a new interest emerging how the various dimensions of power may be examined from a post-structural or

signifier-oriented frame of reference. See Ana Maria Araujo Freire, *Daring to Dream: Toward a Pedagogy of the Unfinished* (Boulder, CO: Paradigm Press, 2007).

[125] John Ascroft's (2001) treatment of the concept of interpolation as opposed to interpellation describes how interstices may exist and be wedged between flexible joints or integuments connecting links to each other on signifying chains, or how parts may interact with each other and the whole, and how people's voices may intrude themselves into power and their institutional arrangements. For our purposes, we can use Ascroft's (2001) invention of "interpolation" to superimpose onto the notion of chains, as in metonymic relations of signifiers, how the process of articulation may operate as a *process of guiding or mapping inscribers as if on subject-position surfaces* linked to a complex circulation of signifying chains and their overlapping, intersecting, and intertwining layers of discourse and how they carve out new spaces for the creation of new subject-positions. (see Coward & Ellis, 1977; Laclau, 2007; Thomassen, 2005) According to political post-structuralist philosophers, like Laclau and Mouffe (1985), there are always contingencies or leaks, traces, and residues into which one may penetrate further and "see" into the "multifarious layers" of reality. In these tiny spaces, they may offer themselves up as contingent powers available for triggering collective agential actions as well as producing co-opted reactions. For more discussion see chapters in John Ascroft, see "Resistances" and "Interpolation" in *Post-Colonial Transformation* (New York: Routledge, 2001), pp. 18–44, 45–56.

[126] Or, as the daughter of Paulo Freire recently pointed to the need for new explorations into the operations of signifiers in her recent book, titled *Pedagogy of the Unfinished* (2007).

[127] Personal communication with Joe Kincheloe who I met for the first time in 2000. He spoke to me of Huebner in these terms. I was directed by my first sponsor, Maxine Greene, to go see Kincheloe upon gaining a two year visiting professorship at Brooklyn College in 2000.

[128] There will a more detailed discussion on how these components of articulation and discourse gets played out in historical contexts later in this chapter.

[129] At the end of this chapter, there will a two-part diagram outlining how in times of crisis or hegemonic struggles, using the Russian Revolution as an example, Laclua (1990, 1993, 2007, pp. 131–133) and Thomassen (2005, pp. 7–15) explain how these processes of subject-position formations and inscriptions on equivalent and differential chains operates, in addition to their corresponding empty and floating signifiers, which act as relays to subject-positions for identity formation and inciting one who is identified and named or who assumes one to be occupying such positions, gets put into actions, agential and co-optive.

[130] Zizek borrows extensively the concept *objet petit a* from its original source, Jacques Lacan (1977), albeit modified to his own perspective in which he uses the concept as a doorway toward seeing how the subject, made in the Other (The Law, The Real, God, or the dominant norm of the group, etc.) and its chains of signifiers, reaches a point in which the subject becomes or crystallizes as a signifier (pp. 214), and in other places in Lacan, how the "signifier represents a subject for another signifier" which circulates in the field of the Other (p. 198, 207). In Lacan's words, these tiny objects circulate in intervals of "intersecting the signifiers, which forms parts of the very structure of the signifier, (and is) in other registers of my exposition, I have called metonymy " Lacan continues to assert (i)t is here that we call desire (which) crawls, slips, escapes, like the ferret (p. 214) .

[131] Still, I argued, these feelings, as immediate as they, are, are nevertheless experienced within words and their chains. As we will discuss, the works of Zizek have been influential to the works of Laclau in the formation of a theory of hegemony and the emergence of socialist and complex forms of democracy. However, as fellow late Lacanians or post-post structuralists maintain, Zizek's emphasis on the Real or immediate experience is often posited as "beyond words" and "resist symbolization." To other late-Lacanians, the Real, however, always manages to "touch" or "brush up" and against the symbolic. See, for example, the works of Harari (2002, 2004), Verhaeghe & Declercq in Harari (2002), Drawers in Harari (2002), Johnston (2008), Daly in Zizek & Daly (2005), Zizek (2006), Nobus (1998), and others.

In these encounters with the Real, there are always fissures and cracks, irruptions, leaking through and into the symbolic, imaginary, and real (SIR) registers or discourses, which become positioned as if in a Borrean knot or located within "quilting points," intertwining into one another, and in moments of *jouissance* or fantasy and pleasures there is a trans-substantiated moment in which the subject enters the object, into a kind of black hole of the object, which produces a "dizzying multitude of associative linkages (condensed). This is also a moment experienced in interconnecting threads (i.e. of a dream condensed or displaced by the analysand for the analyst to view and mirror back to the analysand). That is, how the real offers moments during inhibitions and resistances to see not merely what one wants to say, but what one *really* wants to say. To Johnston (2008) "the real emerges from an impasse ....not (from) a hard external kernel which resists symbolization, but of a deadlock in the process of symbolization (p. 149)" and in those "bordering edges" between subjectivity and the holes within reality, those points of breakdown, in which the Real shines through (p. 161)." To Johnston, this means this analytic can be used to extend Laclau and Mouffe's concept of hegemony in "which particular (demands) strive against each other to establish themselves (in) the enveloping, framing medium ...for 'articulation' of all other particulars (p. 173), as well as a supplement to dialectical materialism in the form of transcedental materialism which Johnston argues, Lacan and Zizek imply and point to.

[132] As we mentioned in the first chapter, quilting points, while similar to the *nodal points* popularized by Lacan, are not the same. To Zizek (1989), in the quilting or *sinthome* experience, the subject undergoes several strands of chains of signifiers simultaneously intertwining themselves like a twisted rope or Borrean knot, thereby producing protrusions, nodes, interstices or protuberances producing experiences which release the subject into passions of pleasure, fantasy, and enjoyment. For additional explanations, see Slavoj Zizek, *The Undergrowth of Enjoyment* (1989), *The Sublime Object of Ideology* (New York: Verso, 1989) and *Enjoy Your Symptom! Jacque Lacan in Hollywood and Out* (New York: Verso,1992).

[133] The notion of journey, using post-structural constructs, I developed in a presentation for qualitative research methodologies, held at *The Eleventh International Conference on Ethnographic and Qualitative Research* at Teachers College, Columbia University, entitled "A Journey into the Post-Structural: A Qualitative Methodology for Examining the Classroom as a Complex of Hegemonic and Counter-Hegemonic Discursive Formations," June 12–13, 1999.

[134] As Pecheux (1982) has pointed out, these spaces are crossed or bridged by various discourses. He refers to as intra-discourses (within consciousness and unconsciousness signifying chains); interactive discourses (which link subjects together as an inter-subjective discursive planes); and trans-discourses (which links subject together over and through various signifying chains as rooted on many discursive formation and institutions). In the latter regard, Pecheux points to how trans-discourse may be linked by metonymic or displaced or floating signifiers which transgress or transfer their meaning contents from one discursive formation to another. A discursive formation may be constituted by meanings of power and their relations, as in class, race, gender, authority, ability, globalization, political economies, etc. and their antitheses: oppositions, resistances, and counter-hegemonic discursive formations. See diagram of metonymic chains of signifiers in a variety of contexts in this chapter, specifically, Figure 54.

[135] For an abbreviated version of my doctoral work, see Lee Fleischer, 'Special Education Students as Counter-Hegemonic Theorizers" in Glenn M. Hudak and Paul Kihn (eds) in *Labeling: Pedagogy and Politics* (New York: Routledge, 2001), pp. 115–125. For my doctoral dissertation, see Lee Fleischer, "Living in Contradiction: Stories of Special Education Students" in *unpublished dissertation*, Teachers College, Columbia University, 1998, 317 pages. wwwcolumbia.edu/cu/web/eresources/ir/dc/diss_browse/tc.html – 543k.

[136] The structure of chains that Randy had drawn was grounded in several diagrams being displayed on an overhead projector. These included diagrams produced by the researcher in variant ways to illustrate Williams's (1977 – Figure 46) theory of hegemony, Pecheux's (1982) concept of discursive formations (Figure 47), and Jefferson and Hall (1975 – see Figures 48-49). These diagrams provided a theoretical base for understanding language as making up discourse as a capillary system of power and how hegemony is fought out in language through its chains and

subject-positions. See below more of Randy's diagrams of chains in which respect is formulated along other chains, aligned and dis-aligned on continuum's from self control to no control, further sutured by cross-over chains which reverse his thinking, assumptions, beliefs, and values in moments of "second-thoughts" which suddenly appear in and through his consciousness. See series of diagrams drawn by Randy and the researcher in Figures 51-54 below.

[137] As Randy and the other students explained, they were (on reflection) manipulated by regular teachers by being given "free passes" to leave and never return to the regular classrooms or get entrance, anytime, into the school cafeteria.

[138] To Pecheux (1982), an inventor of the notion of discursive formations (aside from other versions not applicable to the present study, as found in Foucault's (1972) notions of "statements," or Willemen's (1979) notion of discursive formation as symbolic and imaginary unities, consists of constitutive chains of signifiers, both metonymic and metaphoric, in which discursive formations are linked by various modes of discourse: *intra-discourses* linking subjects via interactions between the consciousness and unconsciousness; *inter-discourses* linking subjects to each other as individual and inter-subjects; and finally, *trans-discourses* linking subjects as crossing themselves in and through multiple memberships in many different discursive formations and institutions.

Or, as it happened with the special education students, how they managed to construct their own discursive formations as well as journeying into other formations constituting their identities in often contradictory and complex meanings; or metonymic understandings of how their memberships are intricate parts to each other and the whole society, as they inscribed their feelings and thoughts on their own and each other's subject-positions surfaces – i.e. a worker may be a feminist, gay, a person of color, religious, and poor and upon meeting another worker, who is atheist, wealthy, and chauvinist, both may have different and novel experiences on contact, and may also find spaces of commonality for grounding coalitions and alliances depending on their intermediate actions and ultimate goals. For detailed explanations, see the recent work of Laclau (2007), Smith (1996), and Thomassen (2005). Also see Figure 54 for how the students imagined how metonymic signifiers or "flying rumors".

[139] As Macedo (2002) critiqued those educators who are presently misusing Freire's work in order to arrive as a dialogical method to have "feel good" or therapeutic group therapy classroom discussion.

[140] Freire's notion of naming is more general without the various "thick and textured" (Geertz, 1973) layers offered by a post-structural paradigm. For example, the constructs as chains of signifiers circulating and crossing on and into the surfaces of subject-positions as speakers and subjects articulate their views of each other seeking to emancipate themselves from oppression and struggle for more say in a democracy.

[141] On the notion of "binary chains," I'm reminded how "we" on the planet too quickly associate on a binary chain the earth with its human race. In this regard, in the remake *The Day the Earth Stood Still* (2008), the alien from out of space, Klaatu, advises a sympathetic scientist on earth, Dr. Helen Benson, that he has come to her planet to "save the earth." He later reminds her that the human race may not be a part of the category of "earth."

[142] In studies critical of progressive schools and their emphasis on "dialogue" it's been noted that not merely having kids converse on a carpet but learn survival skills (Delpit,1986), becomes ignored or obfuscated behind progressive rhetoric. Or, in higher education, Jennifer Gore's study (1993) recognizes how the "circular" arrangements of her students' desks offers to expose vulnerabilities as opposed to the protection they may get from traditional didactic lessons, chairs and desks aligned in vertical, back-to-back positions, and thusly, becoming shielded from teacher surveillances. As Gore also points out, while circular seating makes discussion more facile, there remains, in the design of traditional "rows" of chairs nailed to the floor, spaces for student privacy needed for student freedom and resistance, as passing notes amongst themselves, so that they may be more creative in their thinking and actions. However, cooperative classroom strategies, constructed by Robert Slavin and Jerome Kagan condemn rigid classroom management techniques as no longer necessary in cooperative classes. This is so because students are having so much fun and pursue academic goals

in their small group discussions or dialogues, so there "is nowhere to hide," and thusly, no basis for the need for teacher and administrative surveillances or applications of rigid behaviorist classroom management tools and techniques. See Kagan (1994); Miller, 2000; Robert Slavin (in Callahan, et al. *Strategies of Classroom Teaching*, 1998, 2002).

[143] In the last eight years, by having my education students read Freire and then freely associate their understanding of *Pedagogy of the Oppressed* by their artwork in small groups and presented to the class as a whole afterwards, I have tried to understand why many of my education students (and colleagues) have not penetrated Freire's more deep insights – i.e. as the reversal of roles between students and teachers in which students become teachers, and teachers become students. To my dismay, my students often skip Chapter 1 of *Pedagogy of the Oppression*, and proceed quickly to Chapter 2, because, as they assert, the "language" in Chapter 1 is not clear or confusing. Missed, however, are other reversals, namely how complex coalitions and alliances possible between students and teachers can be constructed in which they may recognize themselves as occupying a more common terrain, coalescing into blocs of differences common enough to re-define themselves and their identifies as occupying roles against administrators and hierarchies as the 'administrated," in which they may have find themselves victimized in and pitted against one another.

[144] I have conducted over fifty such sessions – as many as the courses I taught in education – and have accumulated hundreds of images contributed by my students with their consent to use them in future publications.

[145] See the short discussion introducing Chapter 1 on how we are dichotomized economically and politically as citizens in which media reports position us on the developments of fighting in the Middle East and Iraq yet, we remain, passively, supportive of war; or, how current developments of the marketplace in need of corporate "bailouts," yet at the same time, oppositions persist against "spreading the wealth around" for those of the middle and lower unemployed or partially unemployed classes. Or, after viewing bell hook's film on *Cultural Criticism and Transformation* (1997), why, after the acquittal of O.J. Simpson, so many people of color cheered the verdict, knowing there was very persuasive counter evidence?

[146] In a more literal sense, chains of self-defeating activities can be broken by chains. Upon viewing a recent movie, *Defiance* (2008), and upon attempting to flee their Nazi captors, a group of Jews, after running through a forest, come upon a marsh and lake. They are hesitant to move on, but the leader, exclaims: "If we slip, we will build a *chain* (linking all of us together by our belts and straps)."

[147] This cartoon, dated 1959, and other more recent cartoons like it (but not the above cartoon itself, can be viewed by the artist Herluf Bidstrup in http://geocites.com/Paris/Arc/6990/index.htm?200814.

[148] See Joe Kincheloe, *Critical Pedagogy* (2004a) and *Critical Constructvism* (2004b) as to a clear definition and history of how modernist frameworks of knowledge emerged in the Enlightenment period and through the work of Rene Descartes. Also, for seeking why "post-hegemonic" direction of critical pedagogy is needed, see Joe Kincheloe, "Critical Pedagogy in the Twentieth Century: Evolution for Survival?" in Peter McLaren and Joe Kincheloe, *Critical Pedagogy: Where Are We Now?* (New York: Peter Lang Publishers, 2007), pp. 9-42, and a U-Tube Interview and conversation with Henry Giroux by Joe Kincheloe (2008). See www.Freireeducation.mcgill.ca/content/ henrygrioux interview between joe kincheloe,Canada Research Chair of Critical Pedagogy and Henry Giroux Global Television Network Chair in Communication Studies.

[149] See, for example, an interesting history on such ideas and their powers during the Enlightenment, Peter Watson, *Ideas: A History of Thought and Invention, from Fire to Freud* (New York: Harper perennial, 2006).

[150] As Laclau (1993) and Smith (1996) argues, post-structuralism was preceded by a binary form of structuralism in which the split between signifier and signified were mutually exclusive entities to one another as Saussure intended. However, with the appropriation of Lacan's (1977) insights and analysis to the relations of signifier to signified, there is a constantly sliding (*glissment*) of the signified into and under the signifier, and in these displacements , the former, dictionary-like structure of signifiers no longer has a one-to-one definition to the signified or the word and to its

meaning. Because Lacan's definitions or meanings of words, images, feelings, etc. are always in a state of slippage or contingency, floating, and circulating in which the previous "closed totality" or system of structuralism is transformed into a more open totality or system (Laclau, 1993), albeit a partial system or sets of norms (not rules) already pointed out by Smith (1996) of Bourdieu's notion of "dispositions" or "regulated improvisation." To Laclau, Foucault, a former student of Lacan, sees discourses and discursive formations as "regularity in dispersion," whereas another student of Lacan, Pecheux, understands discourses and discursive formations as comprised by chains of signifiers; specifically, metonymic, floating, and circulating signifiers and their displacements, penetrating each other on at least three levels of discourse: intra-discourses, inter-discourses, and trans-discourses. Pecheux thereupon extends Althusser's work, in terms of identification being more than calling or hailing one into a subject-position of being a "good" subject; but, in terms of counter-identification, in which the "bad" subject assumes or believes what they are doing is beneficial to their interests but, in the process of identification, mis-recognizes their actions; and, in terms of dis-identification, in which people begin to take critical notice of what they assumed was beneficial and now realize it is not. To use Pecheux's example of dis-identification, wars are usually fought by the workers, not the wealthier or bourgeoisie members of the upper classes, the latter who benefit monetarily by the struggles and sacrifices of the former.

[151] Recall my discussion of Berger and Luckmann's seminal work (1966) in which, in moments of " inter-subjective closeness," two or more subjects or speakers begin to know the other better than themselves. They gain further insights of knowing the world around them as they think and talk simultaneously, as opposed to talking then thinking and vice-versa and, after waiting for a moment to pass as they become subsumed into dominant categories by which to identify themselves and others, as being hailed and respond back, and in which they think before or after in accordance with the modernist paradigm of binaries, as thinking versus talking, reflecting versus action, subject versus objects of thought and action. The chance for dominant categories to infiltrate these moments, between subjects, however, is minimized with post-structural constructions of reflection *in* (not before or after) the action and vice-versa, as two or more subjects are linked to each other in discursive (as opposed to dialogical) acts of close inter-subjectivity.

[152] To Lasse Thomassen (2001), a student of Laclau and a member of the Institute of Discourse Analysis at University of Essex in which post-structural theorizing is applied to social, political, and economic issues, the notion of "tendential" spaces inscribed on surfaces of subject-positions means that there are always changing degrees of how one set of inscriptions may have on other sets of inscriptions, imbricated albeit revealing some of their edges on overlapping surfaces in a constant interaction and competition for space, and dependent on the existences of other discursive formations active or not, dominant or not, in the force-fields of discourse.

[153] Freire also maintains critical consciousness experiences may reveal how parts interact with the whole, but these interactions maintain as consistent and unified subjects, as those subjects who are demarcated as antagonistic. Being outside of the equation rather than within, non-antagonistic subjects are perceived by Freire as capable of positing their relations from a more distant position and in which to be able to grasp contradictory and antagonistic relations and images of the oppressed in reflections. Like Freire, N.S. Volosinov (sometimes confused with Bhaktin) refers to these parts of the whole experience as "fleeting" and "adventitious" experiences. As a consequence of not probing deeper in the links and layers of these images to discursive formations and forms, Volosinov assigns little importance to their constructive dimensions (i.e. as metonymic signifiers carving out spaces for articulation to occur between and in relations to parts of the whole and parts to and with each other). To Volosinov (1973), such phenomena are merely parts of the "lower behavioral strata of ideology," a weak force hovering above the economy or dominant modes of production which is capitalism during the historical conjuncture he wrote in the 1920s. Today, however, there is a need for more complex, combined network experiences, as we encounter new conglomerates of international trade and multi-national corporations, government subsidies and bailouts, and the impact of the media's reporting "objectively" but interlocking within these entities in ways everyday people cannot see or understand, let alone critique and act as counter-hegemonic agents (see

Fleischer, 2007). Thus, Volosinov, like Gramsci (1971) and Althusser (1971), give too much importance of economic determinism or notions of classist Marxists in which, "in the last instance," what determines and rules beyond any hybrid combination of consciousness of power relations and discourses, or living in a complex and hybridized society and formation of power relations, determine the outcomes of struggles in capitalist, socialist, and post-colonial countries (See Vijay Prashad, *The Darker Nations: A People's History of the Third World* (New York: New Press, 2007).

[154] I credit this insight with the many readings and discussions I have had with Maxine Greene, my former professor and sponsor at Teachers College, Columbia University in the 1970s.

[155] See, for example, my earlier comments of the seminal work of Berger and Luckmann (1966).

[156] Also, see Apple's (1993) notion of "trans-positonality."

[157] These counter-productive insights I have picked up from my observations of minority and poor groups of people from my work with special education students in New York City to my present work for the last ten years as a teacher educator with urban education students and teachers . Also, I am indebted to the work of Anna Marie Smith (1996) for many more insights illustrating other counter-productive actions and insights.

[158] I have seen this happen amongst my Caribbean students as they vied for higher and lower positions for prestige and importance amongst themselves (i.e. Jamaicans are higher than Trinidadians, who in, turn are higher than Guadeloupians, who are higher than Haitians, and so forth), and then, went on to further articulate their differences as superior to other minority groups, as African-Americans, Hispanics, Moslems and whites (See Figure 43 in Chapter 3) for an illustration accomplished by a few of my education students depicting such oppressive relations.

[159] I credit this insight to my first dissertation sponsor, Professor Dwayne Huebner whose readings in his TY 4200 syllabus included the seminal works of Peter Berger and Thomas Luckmann (1966), and their emphasis on the inter-subjective modes of knowledge construction.

[160] While Freire did read and use Althusser (1971) in the writing of *Pedagogy of the Oppressed*, he chose to ignore what was already inscribed in Athusser's writings. That is, as a former student of Lacan, Althusser was already influenced by Lacan in attempting to find a more complex Marxist problematic which saw the whole of society as a "complex structure of dominance" and in which there existed features of "over-determination" over how less powerful entities got overlaid but not completely absorbed by more powerful entities, i.e. the economy over ideology. This insight of over-determination may have helped Freire understand complex cognitions or how gender, class, race, religion, and authority interact and get (with the use of post-structural constructs) intersected as chains of signifiers, carving out spaces for subject-positions and their surfaces, and further, provide for the links and relays to other discursive formations affecting group and sub-group norms and identities. For example, Freire may have been able to provide more specific maps of how the oppressed could diagram how they become themselves and each other's oppressors.

[161] Unlike the concept of interpellation in which the subject is hailed or called into a subject-position of obedience to the authority of the caller, interpolation provides articulatory spaces for counter-calling or responding back to the caller. See John Ascroft (2001); Paul Gilroy (1987), Stuart Hall (1986) and Edward Said (1978, 1994).

[162] The philosopher and culture critic, Slovenj Zizek (1989) illustrates how there are immediate experiences which shoot through one's consciousness in often unpredictable ways which, to him, cannot be described in language or words because of their *jouissance* nature or the pleasures and fantasies they exude. There is, nevertheless, as we have already pointed to, a growing school of post-post structuralists who argue that such experiences, do "touch" "and "brush" against the symbolic." See Harari (2004), Sherperdson, 2008; Ragland & Milovanovic (2004), and Thurston, (2002) in terms of understanding how every signifier interacts with other signifiers in knots, chains, and overlapping signifying structures whereby intermittent anchoring or quilting points may be metonymically experienced or constructed in *jouissance* between real, symbolic, and imaginary registers, and a fourth ring within a ring or chain (i.e. Borrean Knot), as is outlined and discussed by others, as Harari (2004). Leuopin (2004), Nobus,(1998), and Ragland & Milovanoic (2004). That is, the contents of signifiers may incorporate traces of the economy or class, gender, race, hierarchical

authority, religion, etc. as signifying relays or bridges on which they intermingle and intertwine with one another which serve as intermediate spaces between speakers or subjects as they communicate to each other in acts of articulation. These articulatory acts and their positioning mechanisms in terms of placing subjects into subject-positions as they interact with one another, is further explained in this chapter and the following chapter. For further insights on the subject by Late Lacanians, see Note 30 above.

[163] On this point, in Lacan's last chapter (1977) "In you, I see more than You, I want to annihilate you..." may have been useful in understanding the depths and layers of signifiers and their signifying work as revealing those interlocking ("anchoring" and "quilting points") in which they may have acted as both a base in which actors trigger one another defensively or violently; or, conversely, how actors may use to mirror for conciliation and to analyze and agree on fairness, sensitivity, and justice in their interactions. In any case, anchoring points and quilting points are not permanent. They are subject to the contingent and constantly onslaught of sliding signifiers in which signifieds or meanings are slipped underneath signifiers and their interlocking, intertwining, and overlapping chains in a discursive field of power (Lacan, 1977).

[164] While those familiar with the writings of Edmund Husserl (1960) would argue, there are named structures and processes of thinking and action – bracketing and the *noema-noesis* nexus between thinking and action in constructing meanings. These meanings, however, presuppose intended meanings which exploit and harvest an object in the everyday world, attaching or infusing it with meanings, and derived from its structures of intentionality, or intending constructed objects of meaning. This relationship between the intender and the intended, however, constructed by activity of a consciousness which intends *on* the object, reveals a certain irony in Freire: Freire's use of intentionality and meaning construction (adopted by the writings of Husserl) as originating by meaning constructing individuals, may see parallels to Freire's "banking concept" of education in which meaning construction, in a similar manner, presupposes a top-down flow of construction of objects as "knowledge" in which the intender intends his knowledge onto the intended; or, from another perspective, from teacher to student as the teacher intends to teach his students by depositing his lessons or thought processes into their empty heads as a *tabula rasa*. As Laclau (1985) and Mouffe have insisted, post-structualism does not start with a Descartian-Husserl-like framework in which the subject of the individual is an almighty powerful monarch over their subjects or the object world. As Foucault (1977, 1980) is cited, power circulates and is meant to be seized, not to wait for delegation of the monarch or those above in hierarchical positions giving "power" to its subjects.

[165] Describing her attempts to write about are deceased mother, Kim Chernin (1994) captures a moment in which thought enters in words, as: "...words transcribed missed her, they suffer from her absence. It was hard to believe that they were the same words. That made me aware of how many things, when spoken (and written) are words beside words. The silence that strings them together, that excited rush that carries them out, the brightness of their delivery, the slower measure by which they pause, falter, hesitate, almost stop, (and) suddenly veer off and get going again, with a sharp exhalation of breath, a small dark hand waving the specter away...To get my mother to sound like my mother on a written page, I had to find a voice that was richly textured as her presence, a voice that could, being a paper voice, rely entirely on itself...it had to sound like my mother....it had to have something of me as well, of the way I have listened to her voice throughout our life together.

[166] Linguists and post-structural theorists explain that there are less categories to receive intended meanings than that which is available in language. Hence, there is a need for improvisations, as metonymic and metaphoric constructions must be invented. See Bourdieu (in Smith, 1996; Coward & Ellis, 1977).

[167] This insight was only pointed to by Berger and Luckmann (1965) and Freire (1970) but not expanded as we have done here. For further discussion, see Lee Fleischer, "Approaching a Paradigm for Critical Educational Theorizing: Penetrating the Macro/Micro Divide – Reflections on Teaching a Core Course" in *Taboo: The Journal of Education and Culture*, Vo. 5, Number 1 (Spring-Summer, 2001), pp. 122–137, and Lee Fleischer "Toward a Multicultural, Counter-Hegemonic Grammar" in

Joe Kincheloe, Shirley Steinberg, and Alberto Bursntyn (eds.) *Teaching Teachers: Toward a Quality School of Urban Education* (New York: Peter Lang Publishers, 2004), pp. 209–228.

[168] For more discussion on this point, see the works of Sherry Turkle (2003, 2007). Also, I have approached this context in my work concerned with "counter-hegemonic grammar" in Joe Kincheloe, Shirley Steinberg, and Alberto Bursntyn (eds.) *Teaching Teachers: Toward a Quality School of Urban Education* (New York: Peter Lang Publishers, 2004), pp. 209–228.

[169] One again, the notion of "discursive formations," mainly derived from the pioneering work of Michel Pecheux (1982), who advances Loius Althusser's (1971) attempts of portraying ideology and interpellation; or, how subjects become fixed by being hailed or called into action upon being summoned by authorities. To Pechuex, extending Althusser, one may occupy more than one position in an ideological state apparatus (i.e. schools, family, trade unions, etc.). Taking the traditional Marxist problematic of false consciousness – ideology as a form of one becoming duped by the powers-that-be over the people – to Pechuex – rather than false consciousness, but on another level, *mis-recognition*. Post-structuralists, as Aschoft (2001) and post-colonialists as Spivak (1999) have argued that there are other forces available for resistances to capitalist structures and their administrative and hierarchical counterparts operating in schools; namely, how workers, linked to women, gay, and other insurgent and dissenting parties may bond and form heterogeneous groups in countering the hegemony of today's power elites and their hegemonic discursive formations. Thus, ideology as a false consciousness becomes not a mere epiphenomena reflecting the base (or the economy of capitalism), expressing itself in its superstructures alone. Rather, with a post-structuralist or post-Marxist re-theorization of classical Marxism recasts resistant groups as "interpolating," rather than merely frozen in "hailed" subject-positions to authority as "interpellated" subjects, journeying into and penetrating layers of discourse constituting such subject-positions and ideologies (Baldwin, 1980; Gilroy, 1988; Said, 1978, 1994). In this journey, further, as one penetrates these layers of power, they may also, simultaneously, locate spaces in which to construct bases for new movements and coalitions in which to wage a war and counter-hegemony in order to overturn the old archaic systems of domination and capitalism of modern times.

Thus, post-structualists imagine the subject as a series of overlapping, interacting, and intersecting layers of discourse (i.e. race, class, authority, etc.) in which they may *de-identify* and differentiate and see at what points in the process of signification of dominant discursive formations are "over-determined" and which affect not in simple ways of reflection but more complex and differential ways or how discourse and the subjects attempt articulating resistances of dominant groups which occur in and between dominated discursive formations. For more further explanations on how discursive articulations begin to function as an identifying agent, see Michel Pecheux, *Language, Semantics, and Ideology* (New York: St. Martin's Press, 1982); Paul Smith, *Discerning the Subject* (Minneapolis, MINN: Minnesota Press, 1986); Rosemary Hennessy, *Materialist Feminism and the Politics of Discourse* (New York, Routledge,1993); and George Strickland *English 495: Marxist Cultural Theory: An Online Course from Illinois State University* http://www.english.ilstu.edu/Strickland/495/ideology.html

[170] In this context, subjects become signifiers or – as Lacan cited earlier – positions subjects as signifiers which doesn't necessarily freeze or interpellate them, but further, may offer them spaces for deeper forms of resistances which, as reported by Willis of the Lads, who suffered from counter-availing resistances, may go further in illuminating the structures and processes of hegemony as its enters into one's consciousness by strands of chains and subjection-positions surfaces. As Coward and Ellis (1977) assert: "the signifier cuts out or *articulates* the signified only by relations entered into (and) with other signifiers" (p. 3) and, through connecting to other signifying chains, "that it is never possible to separate the domains of consciousness and unconsciousness (p. 8) in, as Bourdieu (in Smith, 1996) further explains, accounts for "regulated improvisation."

[171] As Anna Marie Smith (1996) explains "dispositions," taken from Pierre Bourdieu's notion of "habitus," means those dispositions, while not as exact or strong as a rule, but is what "produc(es) a "durable disposition" and which "tends to incite regularized practices, but without ever producing

perfect obedience to rules (p. 63)." Smith further explains that such dispositions are part of the articulation process in which subject takes on subject-positions, which act as a mediators in between their structured positions they are "thrown into" (i.e. one's class or gender or race) and which, in between themselves and their structured positions, they are provided with surfaces on subject-positions in which to intercede and negotiate these inner and outer forces. Further, to Smith, these subject-positions and (their surfaces) may also provide student and teacher a basis to interpret and re-interpret their lives in which they may "incite certain practices within specific contexts but never in perfectly predictable conformity" to the norm. Thus, to Smith, " social agents," in an articulatory process which mediates people between themselves and the norms of their group or structured positions (class, gender, authority, race, etc.). "...serve to mediate a process of identification within which subjects may or may not develop a full to partial conscious grasp of the goals that correspond to that subject-position." See Anna Marie Smith, "From Lenin to Gramsci" in Anna Marie Smith, *Laclau and Mouffe" The Radical Democratic Imaginary* (New York: Routledge, 1996), pp. 63–64.

[172] I am indebted to Joe Kincheloe's definition of agency as "in his *Critical Pedagogy: A Primer* (New York:Peter Lang, 2004). Of course the question which remains: What is a *self* or *selves* in the context of oppression and hegemony? Once again, Kincheloe responds by defining hegemony as: "by the process by which dominant groups seek to impose their belief structures in individuals for the purpose of solidifying their power over them. Thus, hegemony seeks to win the consent of the governed without the use of coercion or force" in Joe Kincheloe, *Critical Constructivism* (New York: Peter Lang Publishers, 2005), p. 12.

[173] In this capacity, by allowing students to freely associate via artwork images they interpret which stands for what they think, they read as meanings in their readings within an articulatory process. Stuart Hall has maintained that such a process provides a "a connection or link which is not necessarily given in all cases, as always or a fact of life, but which requires particular conditions of existence (as) ... (being) positively sustained by specific processes (and) constantly renewed and which can be under certain circumstances disappear or be overthrown, leading to old linkages being dissolved and *new connections* – re-articulations – being forged." Continuing, Hall insists that articulation as a practice "does not mean that they (speakers) become identical or that one is dissolved into the (other's articulation or subject-position)." Continuing, Hall cites that "(e)ach (articulatory practice) retains its distinct determinations and conditions of existence. However, once an articulation is made, three practices (identification, inscriptions, and articulation) are needed to construct subject-positions, in which, when they function together, not as an immediate identity ...but as distinctions within a unity." See, Stuart Hall, "Signification, Representation, Ideology: Althusser and the Post-Structuralist Debates" in *Critical Studies in Mass Communication*, Vol. 2, Number 2, June, 1985, pp. 113–114.

As the dictionary defines "articulation" as a practice in which "flexible joints" linking parts to each other and the whole it seeks to represent come about. I am therefore inclined to further refine both Smith and Hall's definitions of articulation in providing a schemata for a counter-hegemonic mode of teaching and theorizing which includes components of subject-positions, identity, and inscription.

[174] As the chair of a student club at Brooklyn College, and an advisor to a student website, called ESO or *Educators Speak Out!*, there were many students who shared the same feelings (although a few wrote against it as well) to support the above diagram and with which they sought to change governing conditions in their schools.

[175] For more detail of this activity of mapping the power lines of administrative hierarchies and their transformations, see Chapter 5.

[176] Interviewing A German-Polish immigrant who was old enough to recount what happened when Poland was occupied by the Nazis during the Second World War, I learned that such fastidious behavior, as perfect tidiness and conformity to the rule assigned to one by the higher-up authorities, in which nothing can dissuade one from their duty and responsibility, in German, *ordnung must zeindt or a mode of behavior,* likened to a bridled horse who has "blinders" installed around the

sides of their head, adjacent to their eyes, thereby causing more focused behaviors as opposed to becoming distracted .

[177] While I have said Volosinov and his Marxist modernist notions of "fleeting" and "adventitious" thoughts as relegated to a "lower behavioral level of ideology," is not to be taken seriously, and considered as mere epiphenomena or "reflections" off the base structures of society, namely the economic modes of production. In taking this position, Volosinov has not furthered or modified modernist frameworks or how signifiers circulate producing second thoughts or glimpses of reality. This is because Volosinov understands such phenomena as mere reflections off the base or macro sources of power (i.e. class, gender, etc.) in society. Volosinov's view is very different from post-structuralists, like Lacan, who see such phenomena as relatively autonomous from the base of society, operating through layers or levels of discourse (like Pecheux, 1982) constituting society. Pecheux, appropriated many concepts from Lacan's revision of Freud as structures of language ("the unconscious is structured like a language") understands such phenomena as if they operate with a life of their own and constitute more complex structures and processes of society – i.e. namely, relatively autonomous discursive apparatuses of society which articulates subjectivity and their expressions (Macdonnel, 1986).

[178] While Laclau admits he is not sure what happens between discursive formations (1993) and their sub-components – i. e. subject-positions, surfaces for inscriptions, and chains of equivalence and differences, as well as accompanying empty and floating signifiers, I would argue, to be consistent using post- Saussurean logic of a de-centered subject and how subjects are formed through reference of representations between signifiers to each other rather than a "founding" or "transcendent" or "underlying" subject or signified (which is an expression of modernist as opposed to post-modernist notions of subjects) – one may infer that these processes are formed by the same lateral actions. Otherwise, as a colleague questioned: "hegemonic and counter-hegemonic theorizing may also be constituents of a dichotomous logic, thereby reproducing itself as an expression modernist as opposed to post-structural thinking." I responded to this colleague by stating that while this may be, intervening between both hegemonic and counter-hegemonic discursive formations, and their signifying chains and subject-positions surfaces intertwining and intersecting each other, on various levels, may also be possible dimensions of cross-signifying materials, processes, and points of connection and entry. These "in-between" discursive forms and formations are themselves, I argued, "floating signifiers" which may bridge or provide a thoroughfare through which flows semiotic meanings and which may point to and refer to points of antagonism. These points, in turn, may trigger very reactive, explosive, and even violent reactions, or, may serve as relays or "points of connection" between two or more discursive formations. I think of how this insight of the structures and processes of discursive formations may serve ESL students. In their instruction to learn a new language in one discursive formation (formal English), they may link this learning to another discursive formation, bridging their own native language, history and culture to formalisms of English (see Fleischer, 2004). In this way, these "in-between" discursive formations, aligned to both discursive formations of linguistic learning experiences, may serve as a linchpin to create new forms of signification or learning a new language without deteriorating one's identity, culture, history, and language nor bastardizing the formal structures of grammar.

[179] In an effort (Fleischer, 2004) to minimize the truncation between learning formal English and, at the same time, making the transition from indigenous to formal structures of grammar, I have advised my ESL teachers-to-be to think of three columns or discursive formations: the first column is the first language is "por favor" (Spanish), the second and transitional column, is sometimes spelled phonetically or another kind of signifier, as "pliz," and finally, the third column is the formal language structure, as in "please." Sometimes, connections are made whereby students may transition from their home to formal languages with the minimum amount of violence done to their identities, histories, cultures, and relationships.

[180] Randy recounted, the special education track in his school has special administrators as distinct from regular school administrators. To Randy, everything in the school is divided between regular and special chains.

[181] The notion of syncretism is mentioned by Freire (p. 163) – though not elaborated to the extent others have appropriated the term to indicate a "a journeying into" the caverns and capillary layers of powers and meanings in which are words transacted between dominant and the dominated, the colonizer and the colonized. See, for example, the works of Gilroy (1987), Bhabha (1989), Said (1978, 1994), Spivak (1999), and Loomba (2008) for further insightful information.

[182] While Freire describes this insight – how the oppressed becomes each other's oppressor, an insight he gained from Erich Fromm (1941) and others, Jacques Lacan (1977) had already gained insight into a similar phenomena, in which "In you, I see and love more than you …I want to annihilate you." In these moments, as if living in a Borrean Knot, or living as if in a rope which intertwines upon itself, producing in some intermittent spaces, protuberances or swellings (Zizek,1989). As further adapted by Slovenj Zizek and his notion of "quilting," adapted from Lacan, may be understood then as a kind of complex link or knot holding many threads brought together in overlapping and complex ways, and which, in an articulating process, as one speaks, they seek to find flexible joints temporarily bringing together disjointed yet intertwining chains of signifiers to form multiple or multifaceted spaces in which they may find new spaces to further articulate and join together in locating the whole or outside of themselves or the Real, its parts – *objets petit a* – or the loss sense of closure and completion.

The same complex arrangements are discussed by Delueze and Guatarri (1972, 1980, 1987) in which hierarchical or "abhorences" or assemblages of chains, consisting of "rhizomes" or unconscious chains of signifiers, desiring machines, or, in Pechuex's (1982) terms, intra-discourses, move in a direction which starts at the middle as a tuber crawling along the surface of the ground (rather than up down like a tree) and then goes off into various fleeting lines of flight, drives, and intensities. To both Delueze and Guatarri, these knots or fleeting directions of signifiers make up a resistance to binary or modernist logic, on one hand, but on the other, at any moment, may also account for "insurgences to fascist concretions and individuals contain(ed) in micro fascisms waiting to crystallize. (1987, pp. 9–10)." These "semiotic flows" and "molecular chains" remain unexplored territory for finding those middle places accounting for hegemonic and counter-hegemonic struggles and how articulation and signification in today's overly digital and media driven society and its emphasis on "number" and linear driven school systems may be "mapped" and exposed and questioning from operating. Finally, one may ask: can these post-structural theories determine also how metonymies (parts in relation to each other and the whole) are fleeting images and messages crossing in and through our minds? In their own way, the writer would argue that this strata of rhizomatic signifiers may also represent a relatively autonomous space in which to pay more serious attention in critical pedagogy and may further disclose how counter-hegemonic teaching and post-structural theorizing may advance critical pedagogy into its "post-hegemonic" phase.

[183] During the Christmas break of 1997, for one week, the students and I occupied a larger classroom in Teachers College, Columbia University, with many chalkboards along the periphery of its walls for as many as four to six hours.

[184] It has long been noted that post-structural constructs and other post-modern or Foucauldean concepts may be very useful for teaching special or disabled students. For an extensive bibliography on how postmodern concepts may be of assistance to disabled students, see http://wwwtripod.com/Fiona Campbell/foucaultdis.htm

[185] This understanding was one of the main findings of my doctoral dissertation (1998) in a follow-up article, "Special Education Students as Counter-Hegemonic Theorizers" in Hudak and Kihn (2001) and a presentation I gave at the *Eleventh International Conference for Ethnographic Education Research*, "A Journey into the Post-Structural," given at Teachers College, Columbia University, June, 1999.

[186] While these "senses" are at best intuitive and affective, unlike the acts of cognition within the framework of modernism, these acts are more complex – combining cognition with affect or, in the case of "close inter-subjective" acts, thinking as one talks or talking as one thinks. (Berger & Luckmann, 1966) The notion of expanding the modernist framework of cognition, from modernism to a postmodern or post-formal framework was first discussed in education by Joe Kincheloe and Shirley Steinberg in "A Tentative Description of Post-Formal Thinking: The Critical Confrontation with Cognitive Theory" in *Harvard Educational Review*, Vol. 63, No. 3, Fall, 1993, pp. 296–320, as well as with Rhonda Hammer and Peter McLaren, in "Re-Thinking the Dialectic: A Social Semiotic Perspective for Educators" in *Educational Theory*, Winter, 1991, Vol. 41, No. 1, pp. 23–45. The incorporation of semiotic forms into cognition, however, has been debated since the late 1970's when Stuart Hall and the Binghamton School or Center of Cultural Studies encountered the Lacanian-based theories in a series of articles written by Rosalind Coward, John Ellis, and others (1978, 1979, 1980) in constituting a new-Athusserian school of thought. The main issue that was discussed then and still needs to be discussed now is how structures and history and culture interact in moments of theorizing. How can the degree of how an act of discourse is mixed with both gradients, cognition and affection, structure and agency (Giroux, 1980, 1981) may be intertwined? Or, how do cultural critics, like Slovenj Zizek, insist that acts of the real by-pass the symbolic and signification or language?

Late-Lacanians and post-post structuralists, insist that whatever the analytical separations of Lacan, Zizek (1989, 1990) and Laclau's adaptations of Lacan, the real experiences which stem from unconscious chains of signifiers – or as Pecheux would argue – from intra-discourses between parts of one's self to the whole – erupting onto and through the surfaces of the consciousness, may be why, as Laclau (2007, pp. 129–133) and Thomassen (2005) explains, surfaces of subject-positions become tendential as they gain a position of emptiness or act as a stand-in, making equivalent, containing or absorbing all other competing subject-positions' signifiers circulating in a chain. However, as Laclau also asserts, when there is an organic crisis, whereby the lines or frontiers separating one camp of force and power from the other is intruded by two or more competing empty signifiers and their equivalent chains, making the lines hitherto no longer separate and clear between two camps, but rather, more blurred, and in which struggles for hegemony are encountered.

To Laclau (see diagram in Chapter 4), in this scenario the "upper" semi-circles, represented in each equivalent subject-position linked to others., becomes transfixed or intersected by the "lower" semi-circles in an equivalent subject-position and chain. Why does one invert over or into the other? What happens to the force of equivalence and difference with these inverted changes? While the upper semi circle is no longer positioned as equivalent to other equivalent subject-position surfaces, what happens when, irrupting through these surfaces, by differential chains of signifiers, making up the composition of the "tendential" surfaces do subject-positions and their interpretive lens get subjects to be incited and act for those others and themselves – for and against — who occupy such positions at the moment or point of irruption? Or, as signifiers break off and become circulating fragments or "floating signifiers" or "flying rumors," to what degree are these signifiers differential and express particularistic positions or express equivalent positions toward building new blocs and alliances in reacting against and fighting hegemony?

Once broken off the main surface of a subject-position, do not other fragments remain on its surfaces, which can be re-activated at a future time? Or, do these "floating signifiers" which have loosened themselves become the nucleus for the formation of new, perhaps, competing equivalent chains, or, in my interpretation, represent new circulating signifiers – perhaps, appearing as metonymies or, as the students of my special education study perceived, as "flying rumors," which acted as a positioning device or force which contained and silenced their voices and made them "put down" each other as "slow," thereby carrying out a hegemonic function of the dominant codes of their "regular" school, maintaining special education students as divided from each other, weakening their chances for solidarity and community. Conversely, these fragments or partial signifiers, *objets petit a*, may also counter-react or form strategies in which student and teacher may "catch a glimpse" of those spaces they may seize or occupy and mount a counter-hegemonic offensive amongst both special and regular school populations and faculty.

[187] To his credit, Henry Giroux called upon the school community of teacher educators and teachers to transform the schools and the world by further examining the dimensions of signification in 1983 (p. 113). Unfortunately, he never pursued this course of action in his subsequent books and publications. Although more recently Ana Maria Araujo Freire (2007), widow of Paulo Freire, is pointing in the direction of the signifier and signifying research as a constituent part making up what she called the "unfinished pedagogy" of Freire.

[188] Thus, as reported recently, President-elect Barack Obama reflected how words and books gave him voice and a critical perspective of his life and the world around him. See, "Michiko Kakatani, "From Books, New President Found Voice" in *New York Times*, January, 19, 2009, pp. A1, A16.

[189] Nagging is the insight produced by Zizek (1989) in which, through experiences of irruption, fantasy, and pleasure subjects by-pass the symbolic (despite objections from late-Lacanians who insist the real always "brushes against the symbolic") and express themselves through the Real, the kernel of human existence and ontology. That is to say, the subject-object is transformed in which the subject engulfs the object or vice-versa in acts of expression, trans-substantiation, and articulation. I felt I observed and experienced these moments when the second year teacher felt pleasure upon seeing her students watched so fastidiously by her school administrators, encouraging them to study for the frequently given standardized tests sanctioned under NCLB; and further, when the other second year teacher derived pleasure for knowing that a fellow teacher was being terminated, as if almost feeling a moment of sadistic pleasure Freire and Fromm refer to in their works by showing how the oppressor regime controls the oppressed to identify with their cause rather than enter into solidarity with fellow oppressed. So deep is this penetration to divide and obfuscate solidarity, Isabel Kershner (New York Times, 2007) reported recently that during the 1960s, Israeli men derived pleasure from a magazine which depicted attractive Nazi women guards beating and torturing male Jewish inmates in concentration camps. Also there's my own experience in dealing with schools as structured by hierarchies which keeps us in states of fear as a somatic feeling like "the chill running up and down my spine." I was recently intrigued by a video at a memorial given to Joe Kincheloe on February 2, 2009, when he said: "We only talk about testing...not about how we became the way we became."

[190] The last time such a problem was addressed, albeit on a more macro level, came with the writings of Bowles and Gintis (1976) and Aronowitz (1973) or how, generally speaking, school hierarchical structures of authority replicate hierarchical structures of authority of the larger society and its institutions. Sorely needed ,then, is a return to these issues from both macro and micro perspectives interlinked with a meso or "in-between" perspectives, or perspectives incorporating semiotics and signifying dimensions of power and hegemony, which this book offers to some extent.

BIBLIOGRAPHY

Adorno, T. (1969, 1980). *The authoritarian personality.* New York: W.W. Norton.

Althusser, L. (1971). *Lenin and philosophy.* New York: Monthly Press.

Appel, S. (1996). *Positioning subjects: Psychoanalysis and critical educational studies.* Westport, CT: Bergin & Garvey.

Apollon, D., & Cantin, L. (2002). *After lacan: Clinical practice and the subject of the unconscious.* Albany, New York: State University of New York.

Appel, A. (2008, December 17). *Where have the bailout billions gone?* Retrieved from http://ipsnews. net/news.asp?idnews=45152

Apple, M. (1979, 2004). Analyzing hegemony. In *Ideology and curriculum* (3rd ed.). New York: Routledge.

Apple, M. (1982, 1995). *Power and education* (2n ed.). New York: Routledge.

Apple, M., & Cameron McCarthy. (1988). Race, class, gender in American educational research toward a nonsynchronous parallelist position. In L. Weiss (Ed.), *Class, race, gender in American education.* Albany, NY: State Univesrity of New York.

Apple, M. (1988, Summer). Standing on the shoulders of bowles and gintis, class formation, and capitalist schools. *History of Education Quarterly, 28*(2), 231–241.

Apple, M. (1999). *Power, meaning, and identity.* New York: Peter Lang Publishers.

Apple, M. (2002). Preface: The freirean legacy. In J. J. Slater, S. M. Fain, & C. Rossatto (Eds.), *The freirean legacy: Educating for social justice* (pp. ix–xii). New York: Peter Lang Publishers.

Aronowitz, S. (1974). *False promises shaping American working class consciousness.* New York: McGraw–Hill.

Ascroft, B., Griffiths, G., & Tiffin, H. (1998). *Key concepts in post–colonial studies.* New York: Routledge.

Ascroft, B. (2001). *Post–colonial transformation.* New York: Routledge.

Ayers, W. (1993). *To teach: The journey of a teacher.* New York: Teachers College Press.

Baker, H., Diawara, M., & Lindeborg, R. (1996). *Black british cultural studies: A reader.* Chicago: University of Chicago Press.

Baldwin, J. (1955). *Notes of a native son.* Boston: Bacon Press.

Berger, P., & T. Luckamm (1966).

Bellack, A. (1966). *The language of the classroom.* New York: Teachers College Press.

Becker, H. (1963). *Outsiders: Studies in the sociology of deviance.* New York: Free Press.

Benton, T. (2007, December 14). Fearing our students. *Chronicle of Higher Education,* pp. C1, C4.

Best, S., & Kellner, D. (1991). *Postmodern heory: Critical interruptions.* New York: Guilford Press.

Bhabha, H. (1989). The third space. In J. Rutherford (Ed.), *Identity: Community, culture, and difference* (pp. 207–221). London: Lawrence and Wishart.

Bodgen, R., & Bilken, D. (1992). *Qualitative research for education* (2nd ed.). Boston: Allyn and Bacon.

Boggs, C. (1979). *Gramsci's marxism.* London: Pluto Press.

Bookchin, M. (2005). *The ecology of freedom: The emergence and dissolution of hierarchy.* Montreal, Canada: Black Rose Books.

Bowers, C. A., & Frederique Apffel–Marglin. (2005). *Re–Thinking freire: Globalization and the environmental crisis.* Mahwah, NJ: Lawrence Erlbaum Associates.

Bowles, S., & Gintis, H. (1976). *Schooling in capitalist America: Educational reforms and the contradictions of economic life.* New York: Basic Books.

Bracher, M. (1993). *Lacan, discourse and social change.* Ithaca, NY: Cornell University Press.

Bredin, H. (1984a). Metonymy In *Poetics today* (Vol. 5, pp. 45–58).

Bredin, H. (1984b, April). Roman Jakobson on metaphor and metonymy. *Philosophy and Literature, 8*(1), 89–103.

Brooks, P. (1984, Summer). Narrative desire. *Style, 18*(3), 313–327.

Callahan, R. (1962). *The cult efficiency*. Boston: Beacon Press.

Campbell, F. (1999). Disability: Using foucaultian tools: A bibliography. See Retrieved from http://members.tripod.com/FionaCampbell/foiucaultis.htm

Carr, S. Where teachers rule. *Milwaukee Journal Sentinel*. Retrieved July 18, 2005, from http://www.jsonline.com/story/index.aspx?id=341727

Carspicken, P. (1996). *Critical ethnography in educational research*. New York: Routledge.

Chew, C. Seattle teacher refuses to administer WASL test to students. *Seattle*. Retrieved April 20, 2008, from Teacherctchew@earthlink.net

Carlson, D. *Leaving children behind: Urban education, class politics, and the machine of transnational capitalism*. Retrieved from www.louisville.edu/jopurnalwaikato/issue6p1/carlso.html

Chen, P. (2008, July 3). On campus, the '60s begin to fade as liberal professors retire. *New York Times*, pp. A1, A20.

Chernin, K. (1994). *In my mother's house: A daughter's story*. New York: Harper/Perennial.

Coward, R. (1976). Lacan and signification: An introduction. *Edinburgh '76 Magazine*, No.1, pp. 6–20.

Coward, R., & Ellis, J. (1977). *Language and materialism: Developments of semiology and the theory of the subject*. London: Routledge, Kegan, and Paul.

Coward, R. (1977, Fall). Class, 'culture' and the social formation. *Screen, 8*(1), 75–105, and Rejoinder, in Marxism and culture. *Screen, 18*(1), Fall, 106–122.

Critchley, S., & Marchart, O. (Eds.). (2004). *Laclau: A critical reader*. New York: Routledge.

Dean, J. (2006). *Zizek's politics*. New York: Routledge.

Deleuze, G., & Guatarri, F. (1972). *Anti–oedipus: Capitalism and schizophrenia* (R. Hurley, M. Seem, & H. Lane, Trans.). New York: Viking Press.

Deleuze, G., & Guattari, F. (1982). Rhizome. *Semiotext(s)*, 1–63.

Deleuze, G. (1987). *Dialogues*. (H. Tomlinson & B. Habberjam, Trans.). New York: Columbia University Press.

Deleuze, G., & Guatarri, F. (1987). *A thousand plateaus: Capitalism and schizophrenia*. Minneapolis, MN: University of Minnesota Press.

Delpit, L. (1986). Skills and other dilemmas of a progressive black educator. *Harvard Educational Review, 56*(4), 379–385.

Delpit, L., & Dowdy, J. (2008). *The skin we speak: Thoughts on language and culture in the classroom*. New York: New Press.

De Pres, T. (1972). *The survivors: An anatomy of life in the death camps*. New York: Oxford University Press.

Denzin, N., & Lincoln, Y. (2003). *The landscape of qualitative research: theories and issues* (2nd ed.). Thousand Oaks, CA: Sage Publications.

Dillon, S. (2006, March 26). Schools cut back subjects to push reading and writing. *The New York Times*, pp. 1A, 120A.

Dillon, S. (2008, February 27). Survey finds teenagers ignorant on basic history and literature questions. *New York Times*.

Dillon, S. (2008, October 13). Under no child's law, even solid schools falter. *New York Times*.

Dillon, S. (2008, November 13). A school chief takes on tenure, stirring a fight. *New York Times*, pp. A1–A25.

Dor, J. (2004). *Introduction to the reading of lacan*. New York: Other Press.

Dunham, M., & Kellner, D. (2006). *Media and cultural studies*. Malden, MA: Blackwell Publishing.

Ebert, T. (1992, Winter). Ludic feminism, the body, performance and labor: Bringing materialism into feminist cultural studies. *Cultural Critique*, 1–35.

Einhorn, E. (2007, June 29). Bad schools getting shut – & principals getting bonuses. *Daily News*.

Everhart, R. (1983). Classroom management, student opposition, and the labor process. In M. Apple & L. Weiss (Eds.), *Ideology and practice in schooling*. Philadelphia: Temple University Press.

Finder, A. (2007, November 20). Decline of the tenure track raises concern at colleges. *New York Times*, pp. A12, A16.

Fleischer, L. (1978). A critique of Ann Lieberman's notion of improving teaching practices. In *Left open: A student newsletter and emancipatory collective*, published by the Teachers College Student Caucus, No. 3, pp. 15–18.

Fleischer, L. (1998). *Living in contradiction: Stories of special education students.* In Unpublished Doctoral Dissertation, Teachers College, Columbia University.

Fleischer, L. (1999, June). *A journey into the post–structural: A qualitative methodology for examining the classroom as a complex of hegemonic and counter–hegemonic discursive formations.* Paper presented at the Eleventh annual ethnographic and qualitative research in education conference, Teachers College, Columbia University.

Fleischer, L. (2001a, Spring). Speaking post–structurally of John Dewey and G. H. Mead: Reflections on teaching social studies in a core course. *Educational Change*, 32–48.

Fleischer, L. (2001b). Approaching a new paradigm for educational critical theorizing penetrating the macro/micro divide. *Taboo: The Journal of Culture and Education, 5*(1), 122–137.

Fleischer, L. (2001c). Special education students as counter–hegemonic theorizers. In G. M. Hudak & P. Kihn (Eds.), *Labeling: Politics and pedagogy* (pp. 115–125). New York: Routledge.

Fleischer, L. (2002). Writing about the fear of power, writing into power. In *Educational change: A journal of role analysis and institutional change.* New York State Foundations of Education Association.

Fleischer, L. (2004). Toward a counter–hegemonic multicultural grammar. In J. Kincheloe, S. Steinberg, & A. Burstyn (Eds.), *Teaching teachers: Building a quality school of urban education* (pp. 209–228). New York: Peter Lang.

Fleischer, L. (2005a, Fall/Winter). Exceptional youth cultures: A framework for instructional strategies of inclusive classrooms. *Taboo: The Journal for Culture and Education, 9*(2), 97–104.

Fleischer, L. (2005, May 5–7). *Counter–hegemonic theorizing through contradictions and discursive formations in teaching social studies.* Presented at the first congress of Qualitative Inquiry, at the University of Illinois at Urbana–Champaign.

Fleischer, L. (2006, Spring). Emphasizing classroom management at the detriment of theory. *Academic Forum, the Academic Affairs Publication, the Official Journal of New Jersey City University, 14*(2), 26–28.

Fleischer, L. (2007). Teaching social studies through post–structural constructs. In D. Macedo & S. Steinberg (Eds), *The media literacy* (pp. 626–639). New York: Peter Lang Publishers.

Forgasc, D. (Ed.). (2000). *Antonio gramsci reader.* New York: New York University Press.

Foucault, M. (1978, Spring). Politics and the study of discourse. *Ideology & consciousness* 3, 7–48.

Foucault, M. (1977a). Nietzsche, genealogy, history. In D. Bouchard (Ed.), *Language, counter–memory, practice: Selected essays and interviews by Michel Foucault* (pp. 139–164). Ithaca, NY: Cornell University Press.

Foucault, M. (1977b). *Discipline and punishment: Birth of the prison.* New York: Vintage Books.

Foucault, M. (1980). *The history of sexuality: An introduction.* New York: Vintage Books.

Foucault, M. (2006). *Psychiatric power: Lectures at the college de france, 1973–1974.* New York: Palgrave Macmillan.

Freire, P. (1970, 2000). *Pedagogy of the oppressed* (30th Anniversary ed.). New York: Continuum Press.

Freire, P., & Macedo, D. (1987). *Literacy: Reading the word and the world.* South Hadley, MA: Bergin and Garvey Publishers.

Freire, P., & Macedo, D. (1995, Fall). A dialogue: Culture, language, and race. *Harvard Educational Review, 65*(3), 377–402.

Freire, P. (2007). *Daring to dream: Toward a pedagogy of the unfinished* (A. M. Araujo Freire, Ed.). Boulder, CO: Paradigm Publishers.

French, H. W. (2004, September 23). Educators try to tame japan's blackboard's jungles. *New York Times.*

Gee, J. P. (1997). *Social linguistics and literacies: Ideology in discourses* (2nd ed.). New York and Philadelphia: Routledge/Falmer, Taylor and Francis.

Geertz, C. (1973). *The Interpretation of culture*. New York: Basic Books.

Giddens, A. (1979). *Studies in political and social theory*. New York: Basic Books.

Gilroy, P. (1987). *There ain't no black in the union jack*. Chicago: University of Chicago Press.

Giroux, H. (1981). Hegemony, resistance, and the paradox of educational reform. *Interchange, 12*(2–3), 3–26.

Giroux, H. (1983). Ideology and agency in the process of schooling. *Boston University Journal of Education, 165*(1), 12–35.

Giroux, H. (1983). *Theory and resistance in education: A pedagogy for the opposition* (p. 113). Westport, CT: Bergin & Garvey Publishers.

Giroux, H. (1992). *Border crossings: Cultural workers and the politics of education*. New York: Routledge.

Giroux, H. (2000). *Impure acts: The practical politics of cultural studies*. New York: Routledge.

Giroux, H. (2007). *The university in chains: Confronting the military–industrial, academic complex*. Boulder, CO: Paradigm Press.

Giroux, H. (2007). Democracy, education, and politics of critical pedagogy. In P. McLaren & J. Kincheloe (Eds.), *Critical pedagogy: Where are we now?* New York: Peter Lang Publishers.

Giroux, H., & Saltzman, K. (2008). Obama's betrayal of public education? Arne duncan and the corporate model of schooling" In *Truthout* Retrieved December 17, 2008, from www.truthout.org/ 121708R.

Good, T., & Brophy, J. *Looking in classrooms* (10th ed.). Boston: Allyn & Bacon.

Gootman, E. (2008, September 12). Low grade for a school of successes. *New York Times*, pp. B1, B5.

Gootman, E. (2008, August 20). Mixed results on paying city students to pass tests. *New York Times*.

Gootman, E. (2008, September 12). In Brooklyn, low grade for a school of successes. *New York Times*.

Gordon, L. (1996). *Fanon and the crisis of european man*. New York: Routledge.

Gore, J. (1993). *The struggle for pedagogies: Critical and feminist discourses as regimes of truth*. New York: Routledge.

Graff, G., & Birkenstein, C. A progressive case for educational standardization. Academe Online. Retrieved May/June 2008, from http://www.aaup.org/AAUP/pubsres/academe/2008/ MJ/Feat/graf. htm

Gramsci, A. (1971). *Selections from the Prison notebooks*. New York: International Publishers.

Green, A., & Sharp, R. (1975). *Education and social control: A study in progressive primary education*. Boston: Routledge & Kegan Paul.

Green, E. (2008, July). Study sought of test gains in N.Y. *The Sun*.

Greene, M. (1976). *Landscape of learning*. New York: Teachers College Press.

Greene, M. (1986, November). In search of a critical pedagogy. *Havard Educational Review, 56*(4), 427–441.

Greene, M. (2008). Wide–awakeness and the moral life. In A. Sadovvnik, P. Cookson, & S. Semel (Eds.), *Exploring education: An introduction to the foundations of education* (3rd ed., pp. 187–192). Boston: Bacon & Allyn.

Griffiths, B. (2008). Stitching the layers of our cultural discourses In B. Griffith (Ed.), *Cultural Narration* (pp. 81–104). Rotterdam, Netherlands: Sense Publishers.

Grossberg, L. (1992). *We gotta get out of this place*. New York: Routledge.

Gutbaum, B. (2002, November 21). *See pushing out at risk students: Discharge figures. A report by the public advocate for the city of New York and advocates for children*. Public Advocate and Commissioner of New York City.

Habermas, J. (1968). *Knowledge and human interests*. Boston: Beacon Press.

Habermas, J. (1972). *Communication and evolution of society* (T. McCarthy, Trans.). Boston: Beacon Press.

Hall, S. (1980). Cultural studies: Two paradigms. In *Media, culture, and society* (Vol. 2, pp. 57–72).

Hall, S. (1985, June). Signification, representation, ideology: Althusser and the post–structuralist debates. *Journal of Critical Studies in Mass Communication, 2*(2), 87–90.

Hall, S., & Jefferson, T. (1975). *Resistance through rituals: Youth subcultures in post–war Britain*. London, UK: Hutchinson University Library in association with Centre for Contemporary Cultural Studies.

Hall, S. (1997). The goldsmith lectures. In *Race: The floating signifier*. Northamption, MA: Media Education Foundation.

Harari, R. (2004). *Lacan's four fundamental concepts of psychoanalysis*. New York: Other Press.

Heath, S. (1977, Winter). Notes on Suture. *Screen, 18*(4), 47–76.

Heidegger, M. (1962). *Being and time*. New York: Harper and Row.

Held, P. (1980). *Introduction to critical theory: Horkheimer to Habermas*. Berkeley,CA: University of California Press.

Heldke, L., & O'Conner, P. (2003). *Oppression, privilege, and resistance: Theoretical perspectives on racism, sexism and heterosexism*. New York: McGraw–Hill.

Henderson, J., & Kesson, K. (1999). *Understanding democratic curriculum leadership*. New York: Teachers College Press.

Hennessey, R. (1993). *Materialist feminism and the politics of discourse*. New York: Routledge.

Hernandez, J. (2008, September 22). A school's grade plummets, and the parents are confused. *New York Times*, pp. B1, B6.

Hernandez, J. (2008, September 23). A school's grade plummets, and parents are confused. *New York Times*.

Hobart, S. (2008, August). One teachers cry: Why I hate no child left behind. *The Progressive*.

Holmberg, D. (2007, July 1). Student evaluations. *New York Times Magazine*, p. 18.

hooks, b. (1984). *From centre to the margins*. Boston: South Bend Publishers.

Horkheimer, M. (1972). *Critical theory: Selected essays*. New York: Seabury Press.

Horowitz, D. (2006). *The professors: The 101 most dangerous academics in America*. Washington, DC: Regnery Press.

Hsu, W. (2008, August 6). Where the race (for Testing) now begins at kindergarten. *New York Times*, .

Huebner, D. (1968). "Curricular language and classroom meanings (1968)" and "toward a remaking of curricular language (1974)" In D. Huebner, W. Pinar, & V. Hillis (Eds.), *The lure of the transcendent: The collected essays by Dwayne E. Huebner*. Mahwah, NJ: Lawrence Erlbaum Publishers.

Huebner, D., Pinar, W., & Hillis, V. (1999). *The lure of the transcendent: The collected essays by Dwayne E. Huebner*. Mahwah, NJ: Lawrence Erlbaum Publishers.

Husserl, E. (1962). *Ideas: General introduction to pure phenomenology*. New York: Collier Books.

Hussey, K. (2008, October 12). More schools miss the mark, raising pressure. *New York Times*, Part 1.

Hussey, K. (2008, October 14). More schools miss the mark, raising pressure. *New York Times*, Part 2.

Johnston, A. *Zizek's ontology: A transcendental materialist theory of subjectivity*. Evanston, IL: Northwestern University Press.

Kagan, J. (1994). *Cooperative learning*. San Clemente, CA: Kagan Cooperative Learning.

Kanpol, B. (1999). *Critical pedagogy* (2nd ed.). Westport, CT: Bergin & Gavey.

Karabel, J., & Halsey, A. H. (1977). *Power and ideology in education*. New York: Oxford University Press.

Karier, C., Spring, J., & Violas, P. (1973). *Roots of crisis: New direction of twentieth century education*. Chicago: McRandy.

Kershner, I. (2007, September 5). Israel's unexpected spinoff from a holocaust trial. *New York Times*.

Kincheloe, J. (1993). *Toward a critical politics of teacher thinking: Mapping the postmodern*. Westport, CT: Bergen & Garvey.

Kincheloe, J., & Steinberg, S. (1993, Fall). A tentative description of post–formal thinking: The critical confrontations with cognitive theory. *Harvard Educational Review, 63*(3), 296–320.

Kincheloe, J., & Steinberg, S. (1998). *Changing multiculturalism*. Philadelphia: Open University Press.

Kincheloe, J. (2003). Values, objectivity, and ideology. In J. L. Kincheloe (Eds.), *Teachers as researchers: Qualitative inquiry as a path to empowerment* (2nd ed., pp. 188–205). New York: Routledge/Falmer.

Kincheloe, J. (2004a). *Critical pedagogy*. New York: Peter Lang Publishers.

Kincheloe, J. (2004b). *Critical constructivism*. New York: Peter Lang Publishers.

Kincheloe, J., & Berry, K. (2004c). *Rigor and complexity in qualitative research: Constructing the bricolage*. London: Open University Press.

Kincheloe, J. (2005). *Classroom teaching: An introduction*. New York: Peter Lang Publishers.

Kincheloe, J., & McLaren, P. (Eds.). (2007). *Critical pedagogy: Where are we now?* New York: Peter Lang Publishers.

Kincheloe, J. (2008). Interview and conversation with Henry Giroux.

Koreta, D. (2008, August 15). Interpreting test scores more complicated than you think. *Chronicle of higher education*, 2008, p. A23.

Kincheloe, J., & Giroux, H. (2008). U–Tube Interview and conversation with Henry Giroux by Joe Kincheloe. See Retrieved from www.Freireeducation.mcgill.ca/content/henrygrioux interview between Joe Kincheloe,Canada Research Chair of Critical Pedagogy and Henry Giroux Global Television Network Chair in Communication Studies.

Kohn, A. (2004). *What does it mean to be well educated? And more essays on standards, grading, and other follies*. Boston: Beacon Press.

Kozol, J. (2005). *Shame of the nation: The apartheid in American schools*. New York: Crown Publishers.

Kozol, J. (2005, September 1). Still separate, still unequal: America's apartheid. *Harper's Magazine*, *311*(1864), 35.

Kovecses, Z. (2005). *Language, mind, and culture*. New York: Oxford University Press.

Lacan, J. (1977). *The four fundamental concepts of psycho–analysis* (A. Sheridan, Trans.). London: Hogath Press.

Laclau, E. (1977). *Politics and ideology in marxist theory*. New York: Verso.

Laclau, E., & Mouffe, C. (1985). *Hegemony and social strategy: Towards a radical democratic politics*. New York: Verso.

Laclau, E. (1990). *New reflections on the revolution of our time*. New York: Verso.

Laclau, E. (1996). *Emancipation(s)*. New York: Verso.

Laclau, E. (1993). *Discourse*. In Robert Goodin & Phillip Pettit (Eds.), *A companion to contemporary political philosophy* (pp. 431–437). Cambridge: Basil Blackwell Publishers.

Laclau, E. (2001). *Philosophical roots of discourse theory*. Retrieved from http://www.essex.ac.uk/centres/TheoStudies

Laclua, E. (2005, 2007). *On populist reason*. New York: Verso.

Lamash, L. (2004). Social history, technology, and the building of inclusive classroom communities. In B. Rainforth & J. Kugelmass (Eds.), *Curriculum instruction for all learners: Blending systematic and constructivist approaches in inclusive elementary schools*. Baltimore: Paul H. Brookes Publishing Co.

Lambert, L. (1995). *The constructivist leader*. New York: Teacher College Press.

Lather, P. (1986, Winter). "Issues of validity in openly ideological research" Between a rock and a soft place." *Interchange*, *17*(4), pp. 63–84.

Lather, P. (1991). *Getting smart: Feminist research and pedagogy with/in the postmodern*. New York: Routledge.

Lee, B., & Malone, J. A. (2007, November 20). The aging professoriate. *The chronicle of high education*, pp. B6–B7.

Leupin, A. (2004). *Lacan today: Psychoanalysis, science, religion*. New York: Other Press.

Lincoln, Y. (1992). Curriculum studies and the tradition of inquiry: The humanist tradition. In P. Jackson (Ed.), *The handbook on teaching*. New York: Macmillan.

Liu, C. (2000). *Coping machines: Taking notes for the automaton*. Minneapolis. MN: University of Minnesota Press.

Loewen, J. (1995). *Lies my teacher told me: Everything your American history textbook got wrong*. New York: Touchstone.

Loomba, A. *Colonialism and post–colonialism*. New York: Routledge.

Lyotard, J. *The postmodern condition*. Minnpapolis, MN: University of Minnesota Press.

Macdonell, D. (1986). *Theories of discourse: An introduction*. London: Blackwell.

McCarney, S. (1993). *Pre–referral intervention manual (PRIM)*. Columbia, MO: Hawthorne Press.

MacLeod, J. (1995). *Ain't not makin' it: Leveled aspirations in low income neighborhoods*. Boulder, CO: Westview Press.

McLaren, P., & Farahmandpur, R. Breaking signifying chains: A marxist position on postmodernism. In D. Hill, P. McLaren, M. Cole, & G. Rikowski (Eds.), *Marxism against postmodernism in educational theory* (pp. 35–66). New York: Lexington Books.

McRobbie, A. (1994). *Post–modernism and popular culture*. New York: Routledge.

Macedo, D. (2002). Introduction to the 30th Anniversary of Paulo Freire's *pedagogy of the oppressed*. In P. Freire's (Eds.), *Pedagogy of the oppressed* (pp. 11–28). New York: Continuum Press.

Medina, J. (2008, October 2). Teachers to be measured on student standardized test scores. *New York Times*, p. B3.

Medina, J., & Gootman, E. (2008, August 27). Plan to give standardized tests to city's youngest pupils stirs criticism. *New York Times*.

Medina, J. (2007, October 15). Making cash a prize for high scores on advanced placement test. *New York Times*.

Medina, J., & Gootman, E. (2007, November 4). New York schools brace to be scored, A to F. *New York Times*.

Meier, D. (2000). *Will standards save public education?* Boston: Beacon Press.

Merton, R. (1949). *Social theory and social structure*. New York: Free Press.

Miller, R. (2000). *Creating learning communities*. Brandon, VT: Foundation for Educational Renewal Publishers.

Mouffe, C. (1988). Hegemony and new political subjects: toward a new concept of democracy. In C. Nelson & L. Grossberg (Eds.), *Marxism and the interpretation of culture* (pp. 89–104). Urbana, IL: University of Illinois Press.

Norbus, D. (1999). *Key concepts of lacanian psychoanalysis*. New York: Other Press.

Perry, T., & Delpit, L. (1998). *The real ebonics debate: Power, language, and the education of African–American children*. Boston: Beacon Press.

Obama, B. H. (2008). Retrieved from www.change.org

Ohanian, S. (1999). *One size fits few: The folly of educational standards*. Portsmouth, NH: Heineman.

Orfield, G. (2001, Fall). Schools more separate: Consequences of a decade of re–segregation. *Re–thinking Schools, 16*(1), 14–18.

Onishi, N. (2004, March 24). Mood sours for Japan's other asian students. *New York Times*, p. A6.

Polkinghorne, D. (1988). *Narrative knowing and human sciences*. Albany, NY: State University of New York Press.

Pecheux, M. (1982). *Semantics, linguistics, and ideology* (H. Nagpal, Trans.). New York: St. Martin's Press.

Pecheux, M., & Fuchs, C. (1982). Language, ideology, and discourse Analysis: An overview *Praxis: Art and Ideology*, Part 2, 3–38.

Perlmutter, D., et al. (2007, November 30). The joyless quest for tenure. *The Chronicle of Higher Education*, pp. C1–C4.

Perry, T., Hilliard, A., & C. Steele. *Young, gifted and black: Promoting high achievement among African–American students*. Boston: Beacon Press.

Peters, M. (1996). *Postructuralism, politics, and education*. Westport, CT: Bergin & Garvey.

Peters, W. (1987). *A class divided: Then and now*. New Haven, CT: Yale University Press.

Popkewitz, T., & Brennan, M. (1998). *Foucault's challenge: Discourse, knowledge, and power in education*. New York: Teachers College Press.

Poster, M. (2001). *The information subject*. Amsterdam, Netherlands: G+B Arts International.

Poster, M. (1975). *Existential marxism in postwar France: From Sartre to Althusser*. Princeton, NJ: Princeton University Press.

Prashad, V. (2007). *The darker nations: A people's history of the third world*. New York: New Press.

Ragland, E., & Milkosevic, D. (2004). *Lacan: Topologically speaking*. New York: Other Press.

BIBLIOGRAPHY

Roman, L., & Apple, M. (1898). Is naturalism a move away from positivism? In E. Eisner & A. Piskin (Eds.), *Qualitative inquiry in education: The continuing debate* (pp. 38–73). New York: Teachers College Press.
Ropers–Huilman, K. (1998). *Feminist teaching in theory and practice: Situating power & knowledge in post–structural classrooms*. New York: Teachers College Press.
Russell, M. (2007). *Husserl: A guide for the perplexed*. New York: Continuum.
Said, E. (1978). *Orientalism*. New York: Routledge.
Said, E. (1994). *Culture and imperialism*. New York: Vintage Books.
Sang–Hun, C. (2008, August 13). A taste of failure fuels an appetite for success at South Korea's cram schools. *New York Times*, p. A6.
Sarason, S. (1996). *Revisiting: The culture of the school and the problem of change*. New York: Teachers College Press.
Sarap, M. (1978). *Marxism and education*. Boston: Routledge, Kegan Paul.
Sarup, M. (1993). *Post–structuralism and postmodernism* (2nd ed.). Athens, GA: University of Georgia Press.
Sartre, J. (1976). *Critique of dialectical reason* (A. Sheridan–Smith, Trans.). NLB Publishers.
Sartre, J. (1963). *Search for a method*. New York: Vintage Books.
Scheikart, L., & Allen, M. (2007). *A patriot history of the United States: From Columbus' great discovery to the war on terrorism*. England, UK: Sentinel Press.
Sengupta, S. (2008, February 6). India's shortage means glut of parental stress. *New York Times*, p. A1, A6.
Sergiovanni, T., & Starrat, R. (1979). *Supervision and human perspectives* (2nd ed.). New York: McGraw–Hill.
Sharp, R., & Green, A. (1975). *Education and social control: A study in progressive primary education*. London: Routledge & Kegan Paul.
Sharp, R. (1980). *Knowledge, ideology, and the politics of schooling: Towards a marxist analysis of education*. Boston: Routledge, Kegan Paul.
Sheperdson, C. (2008). *Lacan and the limits of language*. New York: Fordham University Press.
Shohat, E., & Stam, R. (2003). *Multiculturalism, postcoloniality, and transnational media*. New Brunswick, NJ: Rutgers University Press.
Shor, I. (1986). *Critical teaching and everday life*. Boston: South Bend Press.
Shor, I. (1993). What is critical literacy? Retrieved from http://wqww.Lesley.edu/journals/ppp/4/shor.html
Shor, I., & Pari, C. (Eds.). (1999). *Education is politics*. Portsmith, NH: Heineman.
Shor, I. with P. Freire. (1987). *A pedagogy for liberation: Dialogues on transforming education*. Westport, CT: Bergin & Garvey Press.
Sizer, T. (1997). *Horace's school: Redesigning the American high school*. New York: Houghton & Mifflin Mariner Press.
Slavin, R. (2001). Cooperative learning and the cooperative school. In K. Ryan & J. Cooper (Eds.), *Kaleidoscope readings in education* (9th ed.). New York: Houghton & Mifflin.
Schutz, A. (1970). *On phenomenology and social relations*. Chicago: University of Chicago Press.
Smith, A. M. (1998). *Laclau and mouffe: The radical democratic imaginary*. New York: Routledge.
Smith, P. (1988). *Dscerning subject*. Minneapolis, MN: University of Minnesota Press.
Smitherman, G. (1999). *Talkin' that talk: Language, culture and education in African America*. New York: Routledge.
Sobel, R., & Robb, H. (1966). *From left to right: Teaching controversial issues*. New York: Benziger Publishers.
Spiller, N. (Ed.). (2002). *Cyber–reader: Critical writings for the digital era*. London: Phaidon Press Limited.
Spivak, G. C. (1993). *Outside in the teaching machine*. New York: Roultedge.
Staples, B. (2005, November 22). Why the United States should look to Japan for better schools. *New York Times, and the Editorial Responses*, p. A21.

Steinberg, S. (2007). Where are we now? In P. McLaren & J. Kincheloe (Eds.), *Critical pedagogy: Where are we now?* (pp. ix–x). New York: Peter Lang Publishers.

Storey, J. (2001). *Cultural theory and popular culture* (3rd ed.). Essex, England: Pearson Education Limited.

Strickland, G. (2005). *English 495: Marxist cultural theory: An online course from Illinois State University*. Retrieved from http://www.english.ilstu.edu/Strickland/495/ideology.html

Taubman, P. (2009, in press). *Teaching by numbers: De–constructing the discourse of standards and accountability in education*. New York: Routledge.

Thomassen, L. (2005, April). From antagonism to heterogeneity: Discourse analytical strategies. No 21. Essex papers in Politics and Government, sub–series in Ideology and Discourse Analysis in Retrieved from http://www.essex.ac.uk/goverbment/essex

Thurston, L. (2002). *Re–inventing the symptom*. New York: Other Press.

Trend, D. (Ed.). (2001). *Reading digital culture*. Malden, MA: Blackwell.

Turkle, S. (2004). *From the new reference "How computers change the way we think"*. Retrieved from http://chronicle.com/weekly/v50/i21/21b2601.html

Turkle, S. (2006). *Seeing through computers*. Retrieved from http://prospect.org/print/V8/31/turkle–s.html

Sherry T. (2007). *Evocative objects: Things we think with*. Cambridge: MIT Press.

Veronique, V., & Wolf, B. (2007). *The later lacan*. Albany, NY: State University of New York.

Waller, W. (1932). *The sociology of teaching*. New York: John Wiley & Sons.

Watson, P. (2006). *Ideas: A history of thought and invention, from fire to freud*. New York: Harper perennial.

Weedon, C. (1997). *Feminist practice & post–structural theory* (2nd ed.). Malden, MA: Blackwell.

Whang, P. (2005). Disrupting discipline. In J. Kincheloe (Ed.), *Teaching: Introduction* (pp. 195–206). New York: Peter Lang Publishers.

Willeman, P. (1978). Notes on subjectivity. *Screen, 19*(1), 41–69.

Williams, W., & Ceci, S. J. (2007, March 9). Does tenure really work? *The chronicle of higher education*, p. B16.

Williams, R. (1978). *Marxism and literature*. New York: Oxford University Press.

Willis, P. (1977). *Learning to labor: How working class kids get working class jobs*. New York: Columbia University Press.

Witt, H. (2007, September 25). School discipline tougher on African Americans. *Chicago Tribune*.

Wink, J. (2005). *Critical pedagogy: Notes from the real world* (3rd ed.). New York: Pearson Education.

Wolfe, A. (2005, October 7). The 'authoritarian personality' revisited. *The Chronicle of Higher Education*, pp. B12–B13.

Volosinov, V. N. (1973). *Marxism and the philosophy of language* (Ladislav & I. R. Titunik, Trans.). Cambridge, MA: Harvard University Press.

Woods, G., & Meier, D. (2004). *Many children left behind: How the no child left behind act is damaging our children and our schools*. Boston: Beacon Press.

Young, R. (1980). *Untying the text: A post–structuralist reader*. New York: Routledge.

Zinn, H. (2002). *A people's history of the United States: 1492–present*. New York: Perennial Classics.

Zinn, H. (2006). *Why so many Americans are so easily fooled*. Retrieved from www.progressive.org/mag_zinn0406

Zizek, S. (1989). *The sublime object of ideology*. New York: Verso Publishers.

Zizek, S. (1989, Winter). The undergrowth of enjoyment: How popular culture can serve as an introduction to Lacan. *New Formations, 9*, 7–30.

Zizek, S. (1991). *Looking awry: An introduction to Jacques Lacan through popular culture*. Cambridge, MA: MIT Press.

Zizek, S. (1992). *Enjoy your symptom! Jacques Lacan in hollywood and out*. New York: Verso.

Zizek, S. (1997a, Summer). The supposed subjects of ideology. *Critical Quarterly, 39*(2), 39–59.

Zizek, S. (1997b, September/October). Multiculturalism, or, the cultural logic of multinational capitalism. *New Left Review*, No 225, 28–51.

Zizek, S. (1999). *The ticklish subject: The absent centre of political ontology*. New York: Verso.

BIBLIOGRAPHY

Zizek, S., & Daly, G. (2005). *Conversations with Zizek*. Cambridge, UK: Polity Press.
Zizek, S. (2005). *Iraq: The borrowed kettle*. New York: Verso.
Zizek, S. (2007). *How to read lacan*. New York: W.W. Norton Press.
Zizek, S. (2008). *In defense of lost causes*. New York: Verso.

FILMOGRAPHY

The counterfeiters (2008). Directed by Stefan Ruzowitzky.
Doubt (2008). Directed by John Patrick Shanley.
The reader (2008) Directed by Stephan Daldry.
Kohn, Alfie and Ted Sizer *Standardized testing in our schools*, 1995.
Eye of the storm. Produced by Jane Elliott. ABC Eyewitness News, 1968
Eye on the prize Produced by Blackside and PBS (1976)
Raised voices (1993). Unicef http://www.unicef.orgapublic/vidfinal.htm\
Mardis gras, made in china (2007). Directed by David Redmon
The grey zone (2002). Directed by Tim Blake Nelson
Defiance (2008). Produced and directed by Edward Zwick

INDEX

A
Adorno, Theodore, 168, 184
Agency, ix, 23, 25, 32, 48, 52, 81, 103, 105, 114, 115, 139, 149, 159, 160, 163, 165, 190, 197, 205, 218, 221
Althusser, Louis, 21, 22, 26, 29, 100, 101, 116, 137, 199, 214, 215, 217, 218
anchoring points, 143, 157
Apple, Michael, 11, 20–22, 25, 28, 29, 31, 112, 142, 165, 179, 194, 195, 199, 202, 204, 215
articulation, 22, 26, 35, 45, 50, 96, 99, 107, 108, 111, 113–118, 123, 131, 132, 134, 137, 139, 141, 143, 144, 147–149, 151, 155, 156, 158–160, 169, 171, 177–178, 184, 186, 196, 199, 209–211, 214, 216–218, 220, 222
Ascroft, John, 107, 217
Avdul, David, viii, ix, 12
Ayers, 27

B
Bellack, Arno, 182
Berger, Peter, 10, 30, 31, 37, 38, 53, 96, 153, 199, 214–216, 221
Bhabha, Homi, 27, 159, 176, 220
Borrean Knot, 211, 215, 220
Bourdieu, Pierre, 195

C
Carlson, Dennis, 28, 31, 197–198
Counts, George, 13
Coward, Rosalind, 26, 36, 56, 107, 141, 160, 183, 199, 203, 209, 217

D
Deleuze, Gilles, 116
Delpit, Lisa, 152, 212
Dewey, John, 13, 15, 28
Differential chains, 29, 143–144, 195–196, 209–210, 221
Discourse, 4, 6, 8–9, 14, 21–23, 26–29, 32, 35–37, 40, 43–44, 46, 48–52, 54, 56, 68, 70–71, 73–76, 80, 97, 103–104, 106–109, 111, 113–120, 122–124, 129–134, 136–145, 147–149, 151–152, 154–160, 163, 165, 172, 176–179, 181–183, 185–187, 190, 195–199, 202, 207–212, 214–215, 217, 219–221
Discursive formations, 21–23, 26, 29–30, 32, 39, 44, 49–50, 71, 73, 77, 94, 96–97, 101, 103–104, 107–109, 114–119, 122–124, 126, 128–133, 137, 139, 140, 142–144,

149–152, 154–159, 170, 172, 174–176, 178–184, 186–188, 190, 195–196, 198, 204, 207–208, 211–212, 214, 215, 217, 219

E
Educators speak out!, 218
Empty signifiers, 74, 107, 116, 147, 149, 150, 170, 171, 184, 195, 221
Equivalent chains, 74, 116, 139, 145–146, 148–150, 169–171, 174, 188, 196, 207, 209
Equivalent signifiers, 74, 158
Everhart, Robert, 155

F
floating signifiers, 29, 74, 96, 111, 116, 127, 143–148, 150, 169, 171, 187, 196, 199, 207, 211
Foucault, Michel, 10, 27, 28, 56, 95, 167–168, 216
Freire, Paulo, viii, ix, 10, 23–25, 28, 30–31, 36, 40–42, 52, 53, 71, 73–114, 117, 119, 132–142, 152–155, 157–160, 163, 165–166, 169, 172, 175–177, 179–181, 186–190, 194–197, 200, 205–210, 212–216, 220, 222
Fromm, Erich, 116

G
Gee, James Paul, 37, 156
Geertz, Clifford, 151
Genovese, Eugene, 135
Giles, Sherry, ix
Gilroy, Paul, 144, 152, 209, 215, 217, 220
Giroux, Henry, 21, 25, 28–31, 81, 91, 97, 112, 115, 149, 165, 179–180, 195–197, 207, 213, 221–222
Gore, Jennifer, 185
Gramsci, Antonio, 28, 100, 104, 178, 199, 215, 218
Greene, Maxine, viii, 8, 11–12, 27, 28, 115 165, 189, 210
Griffin, Gary A., viii, ix, 11–12

H
Habermas, Jurgen, 10, 182
Hall, Stuart, 130, 218
Heath, Stephen, 158
Hegemony, 5, 8, 12, 21–23, 26, 35, 37, 40, 42, 43, 47, 52, 70–71, 75, 97–98, 101–102, 104–105, 107–109, 111–112, 114, 116, 128, 130–131, 133, 137–138, 143, 146–148, 150–156, 159, 171, 174–175, 178–179, 188, 190, 193–195, 197–198, 200, 202, 207–208, 210–211, 217–218, 221